CHRISTIAN
COACHING

SECOND EDITION

Helping Others Turn Potential into Reality

CHRISTIAN COACHING

GARY R. COLLINS, PhD

NAVPRESS
Discipleship Inside Out™

NavPress is the publishing ministry of The Navigators, an international Christian organization and leader in personal spiritual development. NavPress is committed to helping people grow spiritually and enjoy lives of meaning and hope through personal and group resources that are biblically rooted, culturally relevant, and highly practical.

For a free catalog go to www.NavPress.com
or call 1.800.366.7788 in the United States or 1.800.839.4769 in Canada.

NAVPRESS and the NAVPRESS logo are registered trademarks of NavPress. Absence of ® in connection with marks of NavPress or other parties does not indicate an absence of registration of those marks.

ISBN: 978-1-60006-361-9

Cover design by Arvid Wallen
Cover image by Shutterstock

Some of the anecdotal illustrations in this book are true to life and are included with the permission of the persons involved. All other illustrations are composites of real situations, and any resemblance to people living or dead is coincidental.

Unless otherwise identified, all Scripture quotations in this publication are taken from the *Holy Bible*, New Living Translation (NLT), copyright © 1996, 2004. Used by permission of Tyndale House Publishers, Inc., Wheaton, Illinois 60189. All rights reserved. Other versions used include the *Holy Bible, New International Version*® (NIV®). Copyright © 1973, 1978, 1984 by International Bible Society. Used by permission of Zondervan. All rights reserved; and *The Holy Bible, New Century Version* (NCV), copyright © 1987, 1988, 1991 by Word Publishing, Dallas, Texas 75039. Used by permission.

Library of Congress Cataloging-in-Publication Data

Collins, Gary R.
  Christian coaching : helping others turn potential into reality / Gary R. Collins. -- Rev., 2nd ed.
    p. cm.
  Includes bibliographical references and index.
  ISBN 978-1-60006-361-9
  1. Mentoring in church work. I. Title.
  BV4408.5.C65 2009
  253.5--dc22
                                        2009009472
Printed in the United States of America

4 5 6 7 8 9 10 / 15 14 13 12 11

CONTENTS

PREFACE

FORTY YEARS AGO, almost to the day, I published my first book. *Search for Reality: Psychology and the Christian* was a 209-page introduction to psychology and how it related to the Bible and to the work of the church. It was priced at $1.95.

All of my life I have been an avid reader, and for most of that time I have been a writer. I never expected to publish anything, so I was surprised when a publisher accepted my first manuscript and then asked for another book. I've been writing books, articles, and newsletters ever since. Most often I write material that is new, but sometimes I have the opportunity to take an earlier book and produce a revised edition. From my perspective, a revision is not a quick tweaking of the previous edition. A revision involves a complete reevaluation of the earlier manuscript, an updating of the endnotes, a rewriting of many of the sentences, usually an adding of new chapters, and a reexamination of the original book's basic ideas. The book that you hold in your hands builds on the first edition and carries over some of the same ideas, but in many ways this is a completely new book — updated, expanded, revised, and more practical than the book that came before.

One thing that has not changed over the years is my appreciation for the encouragement, insights, and prayers of so many people who have come along with me as I have worked on various writing projects. It is risky to list names. The possibility always exists that somebody will be left out by mistake. But I am willing to take the risk and express my appreciation to a number of people who helped make this book better than it would have been without their support.

My wife, Julie, tops the list. For many years she has been my closest friend and my greatest encourager. I am incredibly grateful for her love, patience, and cheerful willingness to do life together and to walk alongside me as I have written year after year.

In addition, my appreciation goes to the following friends. I have thanked them all personally, but for the record, I want everyone who reads these words to know that these people have made major contributions to this book. They know who they are, but they may not know how much they have helped. Thanks to Jean-Christophe Bieselaar, Jan Collins, Jon Ebert, Marcel Henderson, Tina Stoltzfus Horst, Fran LaMattina, Lynn and Robin McAlister, Christopher McCluskey, Josh McGinnis, Linda Miller, Krzysztof Pawlusiów, Mike Ronsisvalle, Judy Santos, Caleb Seeling, Tia Stauffer, Lisa Steiner, Tony Stoltzfus, Christopher Watson, Susan Britton Whitcomb, Jeff Williams, Erik Wolgemuth, and Gary Wood.

Above all others, I am grateful to God, who has given me the health, life, abilities, creativity, and motivation to keep moving forward. To God be the glory.

PART 1

THE
FOUNDATIONS OF
CHRISTIAN COACHING

CHAPTER 1

WHAT IS COACHING?

PLAYA TAMBOR IS a remote resort, a short flight north of San Jose on the Pacific coast of Costa Rica. Only my wife knew why I wanted to go there for my birthday. It was a comfortable vacation spot, but, more important, it was isolated and hundreds of miles away from telephone calls, birthday cards, or friends who might be inclined to throw a party. I was about to turn sixty and didn't want to face this new milestone in my life.

First morning there, I went off to the beach lugging a 670-page book by Betty Friedan, who had written about her own encounters with the later years. I connected with the first words immediately:

> When my friends threw a surprise party on my sixtieth birthday, I could have killed them all. Their toasts seemed hostile, insisting as they did that I publicly acknowledge reaching sixty, pushing me out of life, as it seemed, out of the race. Professionally, politically, personally, sexually. Distancing me from their fifty-, forty-, thirty-year-old selves. Even my own kids, though they loved me, seemed determined to be parts of the torture. I was almost taunting in my response, assuring my friends that they, too, would soon be sixty if they lived long enough. But I was depressed for weeks after that birthday party, felt removed from them all. I could not face being sixty.[1]

I never finished the book, but I mentioned it to a friend when we got home. George Callendine was a former student who had become a consultant to business and church leaders. I accepted eagerly when he offered to take me through the process that he used to help his clients move through transitions and get their lives and careers back on track. This was the birthday present I needed most.

Over a period of months, we looked at my spiritual gifts, abilities, and interests. We sent questionnaires to the people who knew me best and got their perspectives. With my friend's gentle guidance, I looked honestly at my goals, career, place in life, values, passions, style of work, and hopes for the future. I'm sure we discussed my concerns about aging and the irrational fears that my younger friends—the ones who keep me creative and challenged—might turn away from me in my old age. For weeks, I struggled to write a mission statement that could clarify my life purpose and be a filter to guide my decisions and activities in the coming years. In all of this, my friend never made demands, gave advice, or told me what to do. Gently he pushed my thinking in new directions, helped me narrow my goals for the future, and kept my focus on what God might want for the remainder of my life. Sometimes he prodded me to consider issues I wanted to avoid. When I set goals, he kept me accountable for reaching them. If I told him about some vague dream for the future, he asked questions to help me clarify what I meant. Throughout it all, George never stopped giving encouragement. My friend was not counseling me. He was not doing consulting. I can see now that I was being *coached*.

THE MEANING OF COACHING

In the 1500s, the word *coach* described a horse-drawn vehicle that would get people from where they were to where they wanted to be. Many years later, big buses with rows of seats also were called coaches, and their purpose was the same: to get the people to where they wanted to go. Some writers have suggested that the goal was similar in the ancient athletic world, where coaches helped gifted athletes and teams boost their performance and get to the goal of winning in the Olympic Games.[2] Others suggest that it was not until the 1880s that the word *coach* was given an athletic meaning, when it was used to identify the person who tutored university students in their rowing on the Cam River in Cambridge. Whatever its origins, the word stuck and coaches became known as people who help athletes move from one place to another. Over time, the word also became associated with musicians, public speakers, and actors who rely on coaches to improve their skills, overcome obstacles, remain focused, and get to where they want to be. Former Miami Dolphins coach Don Shula writes about the athletes who would come to his team with their skills and talents, ready to submit to the coach whose job was to instruct, discipline, and inspire them to do things better than they thought they could do on their own.[3] The coach leaves each person being coached with increased self-confidence, clearer direction, and greater fulfillment than he or she would have had otherwise.

Coaching might have stayed in the realm of sports and entertainment had it not moved into the corporate world a few decades ago. Faced with the unsettling impact of galloping change, rapid technological advances, and tidal waves of information glut, business leaders began to see that no one person could keep abreast of everything. Micromanaging went out of style. The CEO could no longer manage from the top, keep aware of everything that was going on, and have the ability to tell everyone what to do. Experienced business executives with leadership gifts and management skills were faced with people issues such as communication and relationship breakdowns, high levels of turnover and absenteeism, and low levels of productivity, motivation, and commitment. In companies large and small, people at all levels had to learn how to deal with change, develop new management styles, make wise decisions, and become more effective, all while they coped with their hyperactive lifestyles and increasing stress. Some wanted help with their own life planning and life management issues. There was a need to train workers to think and behave like leaders and decision makers. CEOs and other executives wanted people to guide them into this new world, like my young friend coached me through the transition into my sixties. The coaching principles that athletes and performers had used for years emerged in the business community. Personal coaching moved beyond health clubs to corporate offices and the workplace. According to *Fortune* magazine, coaching became the "hottest thing in management."[4]

A coach is someone trained and devoted to guiding others
into increased competence, commitment, and confidence.

— FREDERIC HUDSON, author of *Handbook of Coaching*

Although the modern coaching movement got its start and had its earliest growth in the management world, today it is hot everywhere except in the church. People are turning to nutritional coaches, fitness coaches, financial coaches, public-speaking coaches, and what have become known as life coaches who help others find focus and direction for their lives and careers. Some people look for marriage coaches, parenting coaches, coaches for their spiritual journeys, time-management coaches, and coaches to help them through life transitions. All of these coaches come alongside to guide people through life's challenges and help them move forward with confidence in the midst of change.

Since the 1990s, the field of coaching has grown significantly. The International Coach Federation (ICF) was founded by a few people in 1992, but with its expansion to thousands of members in approximately ninety countries, ICF is now "the largest worldwide resource for business and personal coaches."[5] Today there are numerous coaching organizations, including the popular Coachville, the Association for Coaching based in Great Britain, the European Mentoring and Coaching Council (EMCC), and Christian organizations, including the Christian Coaches Network. Only a handful of training programs existed in the late 1990s, but one report estimates that more than 300 exist today.[6] Over sixty groups have begun programs to certify coaches, and a number of universities and graduate schools now offer courses and degree programs in coaching. One book has called all of this a "coaching revolution."[7] It is a revolution that shows no signs of slowing down.

Despite this growth and exploding popularity, coaching still draws puzzled stares from people who have never heard of its existence. The coaching books in my library all have definitions, some of which are long and more confusing than enlightening. At its core, coaching equips people to move from where they are toward the greater competence and fulfillment they desire. Stated concisely, *coaching is the art and practice of enabling individuals and groups to move from where they are to where they want to be.* Coaching helps people expand their visions, build their confidence, unlock their potential, increase their skills, and take practical steps toward their goals. Unlike counseling or therapy, coaching is less threatening, less concerned about problem solving, and more inclined to help people reach their potentials.

In the future, people who are not coaches
will not be promoted.

— JACK WELCH, former chairman and CEO of General Electric

Coaching is not for those who need therapy to overcome disruptive painful influences from the past; it is for relatively well-adjusted people to build vision and move forward toward the future. Coaching is not reactive looking back; it is proactive looking ahead. It is not about healing; it's about growing. It focuses less on overcoming weaknesses and more on building skills and strengths. Usually coaching is less formal than the therapist-patient relationship and more of a partnership between two equals, one of whom has skills, experiences, or perspectives that can be useful to the other.

HOW DOES COACHING DIFFER FROM COUNSELING?

Counselors help people deal with problems such as depression, anxiety, inner turmoil, and conflicts with others. Some people come for counseling because of their grief, guilt, insecurities, feelings of failure, or inability to control their anger, addictions, or sexual struggles. Issues such as these imply that something in life is wrong, missing, or needing to be fixed. These are topics that mental health counselors and researchers have studied for many years. They are issues that have dominated the work and writing of pastoral counselors. All of these topics relate to what has come to be known as *negative psychology*. The goal in most cases is to bring counselees from their negative experiences and difficulties into a place in which they are well functioning, better able to cope, and living lives that are more positive and not plagued by problems.

Because these problems differ in their severity and intensity, it can be helpful to put them on an imaginary scale from -1 to -10, with -10 being the worst. For example, a marriage problem might not be very serious or disruptive (-2 or -3), or it might be dominated by intense conflict including violence (-9 or -10). Counselors are skilled in understanding and helping people overcome the issues of negative psychology regardless of the severity. Christian counselors work as servants of Christ, helping others deal with the causes of their distress, get free of the symptoms, find inner peace, and experience mental and spiritual healing. The goal is to bring people to the zero point on the scale. This represents stability.

At the end of the twentieth century, a few secular psychologists and professional counselors began to speak and write about something known as *positive psychology*. These writers argued that traditional psychology has focused too much on the negative issues in life and ignored more positive issues, such as hope, creativity, optimism, courage, responsibility, forgiveness, and other issues that make life worth living. According to the founder of this new movement, positive psychology aims to change the focus of psychology "from preoccupation only with repairing the worst things in life to also building positive qualities."[8] Within only a few years, positive psychology has grown significantly in its influence, popularity, and research support. The founders show no awareness of Galatians 5:22-23 and there is no mention of the Holy Spirit in their writings, but these psychologists appear to be discovering many of the traits that Christians know as the fruit of the Spirit.

Positive qualities also can be put on an imaginary scale in which the characteristics are ranked from +1 to +10, with +10 being the most desirable and positive. Many of us have careers, marriages, spiritual lives, or sexual experiences that we would rate at +1 or +2. There are no major problems and there does not appear to be any need for counseling, but nor is there a sense of deep fulfillment and satisfaction. A person might view his or her work at +2, for example, but long to have meaningful and significant work that could be rated at a +8 or +9.

Whereas counseling deals with negative psychology and helps people move from their problem areas to a point of stability, coaching deals with positive psychology and helps people move to higher levels of fulfillment. Counseling focuses on problems and frequently considers the past. Coaching focuses on possibilities and looks at where people want to go in the future. The Christian coach's work is to meet people on the following scale and move them further along in the direction of the arrow.

-10 -9 -8 -7 -6 -5 -4 -3 -2 -1   0   +1 +2 +3 +4 +5 +6 +7 +8 +9 +10

COUNSELING	COACHING
Negative Psychology	*Positive Psychology*
Focuses on problems, dealing with conflicts, insecurities, spiritual struggles, and emotional issues such as depression, anxiety, and anger	Focuses on finding fulfillment, enhanced performance, team building, vision casting, career growth, and reaching one's goals and dreams
Fixes what is wrong	Enables people to reach their goals
Focuses on the causes of problems that arise from the past and on bringing healing and stability	Focuses on the present and future, possibilities, reaching goals, getting unstuck, and turning dreams into reality
The counselor is the expert who treats patients, provides healing, and directs	The coach and client are coequals who work together to bring change.
Usually done by people with expertise in psychology, psychopathology, and therapeutic skills	The best coaching is done by people with training in such coaching skills as listening, questions, and encouraging

WHAT ABOUT MENTORING, DISCIPLING, AND CONSULTING?

Recently I got an e-mail suggesting that "the term *coaching* is the going word for the personal mentoring movement" and that "one-on-one discipleship [is] not very far apart from Christian coaching, except perhaps the terminology." The writer suggested that we drop the word *coaching* and use the word *discipling* instead. Others have suggested that coaching is a new word for *consulting* and that any of these words might be replaced with such terms as modeling, spiritual guidance, soul care, or brief-strategic therapy.

A young pastor suggested still another term during one of our weekly breakfast meetings. "I don't need a father," my friend said. "I have a good dad. I don't need a counselor, but if I wanted one I would know where to turn. More than anything else, I need somebody to journey with, somebody who has walked the road of life a little longer than I have. I want to be able to come alongside you for an hour or so every week, to talk about life, learn from your experiences, and have you help me avoid some of the potholes on the road." From that point, we called our meetings *journeying* times.

Does it matter what term we use? Certainly coaching overlaps with consulting, mentoring, and discipleship. They all involve a relationship in which at least one person is further along in the journey of life and willing to guide others, often as a trusted role model. All of these terms involve accountability, encouragement, and a commitment to growth. Despite the overlap, however, this book assumes that coaching is a unique process involving skills and assumptions that differ from the other specialties.

Consulting and coaching. In many ways, coaching seems very similar to the consulting that has become popular in business and some church circles in recent years. Usually consultants are paid to analyze a situation and give expert guidance and advice. We once attended a church that had grown beyond its capacity but had no place to expand. A paid consultant was hired to analyze our situation and give suggestions about what we should do. He talked to the church leaders, gave a detailed questionnaire to the congregation, looked carefully at the community, and then gave his analysis and recommendations in return for his consulting fee. Often we need experts like this. If you are sick, you go to a doctor for a consultation about your physical condition and its treatment. In business, a consultant might analyze existing problems and practices, suggest better marketing and business strategies, and help companies improve performance and develop future plans. The consultant is an expert who analyzes and makes recommendations.

In contrast to the emphasis on imparting information through
tutoring and instruction, coaching is unlocking a person's
potential to maximize his or her own performance.

— adapted from SIR JOHN WHITMORE, author of *Coaching for Performance*

In contrast, coaching is much more focused on the individual or group being coached, stimulating these people to make their own judgments and decisions. Coaching does not involve making a diagnosis or giving advice. A coach does not need to be an expert in the areas that concern those being coached. Instead, the coach needs an ability to listen, understand, ask insightful questions, summarize what is being said, and guide as nondirectively as possible while a person looks at his or her own situation, reaches conclusions about what to do, and then takes action. In this process, the coach is an encourager, cheerleader, challenger, and accountability partner, but the coach is not there to give expert advice or direction.

Mentoring and coaching. In his book on mentoring, Ted Engstrom defines a mentor as someone who "provides modeling, close supervision on special projects, and individualized help" that includes encouragement, correction, confrontation, and accountability.[9] According to Engstrom, a mentor is an authority in his or her field as a result of disciplined study and experience. This person is willing to commit time and emotional energy to a relationship that guides an understudy's growth and development.

The idea of mentoring apparently came from Homer's *Odyssey*, in which King Odysseus went to war, leaving his household and young son, Telemachus, in the care of a wise and proven teacher named Mentor. Clearly the king was not in a great hurry to get home, as he was gone for twenty-one years, but when he returned he found that the young prince had become a competent leader and man of integrity, molded by the example, guidance, and wisdom of Mentor. For centuries, the concept of apprenticeship meant something similar: the guidance of an older, more experienced person passing knowledge and teaching skills to one who is less experienced and most often younger.

Although mentoring has become popular among Christians in recent years, its modern popularity arose in the business world, where more established and successful leaders took on the task of guiding protégés in their professional growth. When I began my teaching career as a young professor fresh out of graduate school, a more senior faculty member took me under her wing and gently guided me in the ways of academia. We never used the term, but she was a mentor, helping me become more proficient in my profession and career.

Mentoring still takes place in many work settings, but it is fading in popularity. According to a professor at Northwestern University's Kellogg School of Management, mentoring systems have largely failed. There is no time for this in organizations that are lean and focused on the pressures of change management and strategic planning. People are paid for what they produce, not for the time they spend developing others. As a result, executives and managers are looking for coaches outside their companies and vocations.[10]

A mentor is a more senior individual who imparts what God has given (wisdom, opportunities, and counsel) to a more junior person. In the same situation, the coach is building the client's decision-making ability by asking him to think things through in a structured way. A coach draws out the abilities God has put in someone else. . . . When I'm mentoring, I'm teaching a person, letting him draw from me or learn from my experience. When I'm coaching, I'm pushing a person to draw from his or her own resources and experiences. Coaching is helping people learn instead of teaching them.

— TONY STOLTZFUS, author of *Leadership Coaching*

Coaching certainly deals with career issues, but often the focus tends to be broader. Whereas mentors may exemplify and share expert knowledge about vocational or spiritual issues, coaches do not claim to bring expertise or special knowledge about the client's area of interest. Coaches stand alongside the people who are coached, helping them envision their future directions, guiding as they formulate their goals, and encouraging them to take action steps. Coaches avoid giving advice or specific suggestions. By their example and skilled questioning, coaches encourage, challenge, and motivate others to clarify their own life directions, to gain confidence and commitment, and to move forward to the place where they want to be. Over the years, mentoring has broadened to look more and more like coaching. A major difference, however, is that the mentor works as an expert, while the coach assumes that the client[11] is the one best able and most likely to find direction and move forward.

Counseling or therapy deals mostly with a person's past and
trauma and seeks healing.

Consulting deals mostly with problems and seeks to
provide information, expertise, advice, strategies, and
methodologies to solve them.

Mentoring deals mostly with succession training and seeks to
help someone do what the mentor does.

Coaching deals mostly with a person's present and seeks to
guide him or her into a more desirable future.

— PATRICK WILLIAMS and DIANE S. MENENDEZ,
Institute for Life Coach Training

Discipleship and coaching. Discipleship is more focused than either mentoring or coaching. Discipleship centers on teaching biblical truth and spiritual disciplines to newer or less mature believers. There are different ways of approaching the discipleship task, but often there are set courses of study, a more limited time frame, and a teacher-student type of relationship.

Earlier I mentioned a note that came to me from a Christian leader who argued that *Christian coaching* and *discipleship* are two terms that mean pretty much the same thing. In response I acknowledged that there may be similarities but that unlike discipleship, coaching is not *primarily* about helping people grow spiritually, even though that may be a part of some coaching. In contrast, coaching is about career development, getting unstuck, developing and reaching corporate and personal goals, managing conflict, getting through life transitions, clarifying visions, and building better relationships. I do not see those as the main goals of discipleship.

I doubt there are many (if any) people in the Christian coaching movement who would say that Christian coaching is the same as personal/practical disciplemaking. Coaching represents a set of skills and techniques that can be used effectively to help accomplish the goals of discipleship, but the skills of coaching are used more broadly than the focused goal of building mature disciples of Jesus Christ.

Discipleship deals mostly with spiritual development
and seeks to give instruction and guidance that will
enable individuals to grow in Christlikeness and in
the knowledge and favor of Jesus Christ.

WHAT MAKES COACHING POPULAR?

I have a friend who is an outstanding therapist. His counseling practice is thriving. He teaches doctoral students at a local university, supervises their training, and reads a lot of psychological journals. He has read the first edition of this book, attended some of my lectures on coaching, and even invited me to address his classes. But my friend is very skeptical about coaching. He has an open mind and a gracious attitude, but he wonders if coaching is really a form of counseling being done by people without professional training in therapy. He questions whether coaches are effective, doubts that coaching really is a profession, has concerns about the lack of regulation in the coaching field, and tends to think that coaching is a fad that will fade.

My counseling colleague is not alone in his skepticism. Many coaches recognize that his concerns are legitimate, so each issue is being addressed by academic researchers, analyzed in professional journals, and looked at carefully by businesspeople unlikely to keep putting money into coaching for their employees or executives if there is not a high return on the company investment. Churches and parachurch organizations are putting resources into coaching for pastors, and coach training for small-group leaders, board members, and mission executives. Increasingly sophisticated training and practice is developing in specialty areas such as career coaching, executive coaching, and two areas that will get special attention in the following pages, personal life coaching and leadership coaching. Granted, there are too many certification programs, but the International Coach Federation and other groups are setting rigorous standards that many independent groups are seeking to emulate and surpass. Carefully developed standards of coaching ethics have been formulated, and it seems likely that eventually coaching will be regulated like the established professions. As these trends continue, many coaches are finding that potential clients may have limited interest in a coach's certification but do want to know where the coach has been trained and what evidence exists that the coach has been successful with other clients. *U.S. News & World Report* listed coaching as one of the top ten growing professions and as the second biggest consulting business, second only to management consulting.[12] The coaching revolution that we mentioned earlier clearly is continuing.[13]

WHAT MAKES COACHING CHRISTIAN?

My first introduction to Christian coaching came from a counselor named Christopher McCluskey. In the early part of his career, he worked as a therapist in private practice, but often he saw people in his office who didn't really want or need a counselor. They were not in a state of crisis or struggling with seemingly unsolvable problems, but they had a distinct feeling that something was missing from their lives. They wanted help from someone who was objective, confidential, a skilled listener, and able to give them honest feedback. They wanted a guide to help them find greater peace and joy in their Christian lives. These people were looking for a life coach.[14]

McCluskey took a bold step. After training to be a coach, he closed his counseling practice in Florida, moved his family to a farm in Missouri, wrote a letter to his clients and colleagues explaining his move, and began coaching people using the telephone, fax machine, and e-mail. Today he works as part of the field of Christian coaching, which we will describe later in this book. For Chris McCluskey, coaching is more than his area of work. It's his ministry. It is a way of helping people find God's vision for their lives and learn to live accordingly.

Training programs, books, and professional articles on coaching often mention values and sometimes refer to spirituality. Most often, however, these resources and training materials are for the secular market without reference to anything Christian. It is not unusual to find comments about New Age or Eastern spirituality. In some coaching courses, there is reference to "what the universe has decided" or "what the universe arranges," seemingly in an effort to avoid using the name of God or acknowledging his existence. Despite these trends and the fact that coaching still is new to much of the Christian community, it could be argued that coaching was at the core of how Jesus related to people throughout his ministry.[15]

Jesus came to point people to the Father and show how we could have life everlasting and lives that are more full and abundant.[16] The Christian coach helps people imagine ways in which their lives can be better. The coach walks alongside as people make changes that will improve their careers, their families, their journeys with God, and their world. Like all other coaches, the coach helps people get from where they are to where they want to be.

But Christian coaching has a greater, nobler, and more eternal purpose. At its core, *Christian coaching is the practice of guiding and enabling individuals or groups to move from where they are to where God wants them to be.* Human goals, dreams, aspirations, and gifts are not discounted, as these often come from God. But Christian coaches encourage others to find God's vision for their lives and to move from following their own agendas to pursuing God's purposes.[17]

In his book *The Purpose-Driven Church*, Rick Warren writes about surfers in the ocean near his home. No ever tries to build a wave; instead, "surfing is the art of riding waves that God builds. God makes the waves; surfers just ride them. . . . When surfers see a good wave, they make the most of it, even if that means surfing in the middle of a storm. . . . Our job as church leaders, like experienced surfers, is to recognize a wave of God's Spirit and ride it."[18] This also is the job of Christian coaches. They seek to help people discern what God is doing in the world and in their lives. The coach comes alongside individuals or groups and helps them find their calling as a part of God's divine agenda, riding the waves that he is building.

How do Christian coaches help people see where God is moving or what he is blessing and then catch those waves? By asking thought-provoking and powerful questions, coaches assist their clients to become sensitive to the forces shaping the times in which we live. Coaching enables people to be aware of what God appears to be doing in their communities, churches, and individual lives. Through coaching, individuals or organizations can recognize the gifts and opportunities God has given to them. Christian coaches anchor themselves in basic Christian values and beliefs. They take time to know God better and to listen for his voice. Like the noble people of Berea, Christian coaches listen carefully for messages that might be from God and search the Scriptures to discern what is true.[19] In working with others, coaches help people clarify their calling, discover their visions, and take steps to reach the goals God appears to have put into their lives.

Coaching is the art and practice of enabling individuals and groups to move from where they are to where *they* want to be.

Christian coaching is the art and practice of enabling individuals and groups to move from where they are to where **God** wants them to be.

Christian coaches use many of the methods used by their secular counterparts. Some Christian coaches work only with believers, but others work effectively with clients, groups, and whole corporations where there is no commitment to following Christ. Wherever they work, however, Christian coaches are unique in a number of ways.

First and most important is the biblical worldview the Christian coach brings to the relationship. Even a perusal of the many available books on coaching will show that most authors emphasize the ability of clients to look inside themselves with the guidance of their coaches; to listen for the values, purposes, and visions that are deep within; to focus on inner strengths; and to discover their passions and life purposes. There are no absolutes and few rules in this kind of thinking. And God is nowhere to be seen.

In contrast the Christian believes that humans are created in God's image.

We have fallen into sin, but we are redeemed by the blood of Jesus Christ, who offers forgiveness and salvation as a gift. We can ignore this offer of salvation or we can accept his free gift of abundant life on earth and eternal life that will come after we die.[20] The Christian lives with the awareness that God is sovereign, aware of his people, and willing to guide and empower those who are his children. Like everybody else, we seek to become aware of our passions, life purposes, inner strengths, and visions for the future, but Christians realize that these are God-given and we find ultimate fulfillment only when we are living in accordance with God's plans. For the Christian coach, God—not human ingenuity—is at the core of his or her being, and God is the guide for all coaching work.

What we believe influences who we are and,
in turn, impacts everything we do.

This leads to a second uniqueness of Christian coaching: the person of the coach. If you are a Christian, seeking to walk in the footsteps of Jesus, you will approach every aspect of your life from this perspective. Your commitment to Christ will affect your marriage, parenting, lifestyle, values, spending, time management, vocation, and perspectives that you bring to coaching. What we believe influences who we are and, in turn, affects everything we do. If it does not, there is something lacking in our relationship with Christ, something interfering with our level of commitment, something missing in our spiritual lives. We can maintain a halfhearted devotion to Christ and still work as coaches, but the coaching we do will lack the power and impact that comes when we permit the Holy Spirit to guide our relationships with our clients.

Third, the Christian coach knows that none of us can be completely neutral. One of the goals of a coach is to ask questions that will help others identify and clarify their values but also to avoid imposing his or her own agenda on clients. We rarely advise and never tell people what they should do. Instead, we encourage people to set their own goals and directions, crystallize their own visions, and formulate their own mission statements and plans of action.

Even so, we cannot ignore the clear and final directive of Jesus to his followers: Make disciples. As we have seen, coaching is not discipleship, but we pray for the people we coach and want them, ultimately, to become fully devoted followers of Jesus Christ. The previous sentence will be challenged by many professional coaches who staunchly maintain that coaching is non-directive and that the coach's role is to be neutral. A core concept of coaches, including Christian coaches, is that people adhere to decisions and move forward more effectively when they reach their own conclusions as opposed to when they are given advice or told what to do. Coaches encourage clients to set their own agendas, reach their own conclusions, and set their own plans of action. The coach tries to keep a stance of neutrality.

But no coach can be completely neutral. Even psychologist Carl Rogers, the founder of *nondirective counseling*, replaced this term with *person-centered counseling*, apparently because research was showing that total neutrality and lack of direction is a myth. Even if coaches strive to keep their values and perspectives tightly hidden, they cheer inside when others move in directions that are consistent with the coach's values and there is disappointment when clients move away. Every counselor knows that in time our own values and beliefs slip out despite our best efforts to keep them hidden. Isn't it more honest for coaches to admit that although we genuinely have regard for the independence and decisions of the people we coach, and even though we seek to maintain neutrality, nevertheless we are human beings whose values and views will impact what we say and how we will impact others?

Fourth, although the Christian coach is committed to learning and applying the established techniques of coaching that will be outlined in this book, he or she also prays regularly for clients and is not reluctant to discuss spiritual issues, especially in working with Christians who share worldviews and values similar to those of the coach. Christian values permeate the life of the Christian coach and flow into coaching even as we respect the uniqueness or individualities of clients and fully affirm their right to build lives on values that we might consider non-Christian. Jesus once had a conversion with a rich young ruler who did not want to give up his possessions to follow Christ (see Mark 10:17-23). Jesus did not hide his beliefs, but neither did he force the man to change. The man was given the freedom to build his life as he wanted even though he was settling for something far from the best. At times we must allow clients to have the same freedom.

WHY WOULD ANYBODY WANT CHRISTIAN COACHING?

I have a friend whose work required him to write an important report that needed to be concise and completed by a fast-approaching deadline. When the first draft was completed, he sent it to me and I went over it with a red pen, making a bunch of editorial suggestions before calling him to discuss what he had sent. For more than an hour, we talked on the phone. I did not tell him what changes to make, but I gently pointed out some grammatical errors, inconsistencies, phrases that left me confused, and suggestions for making it better. All of this was in a context of encouragement for the job he had done, enthusiasm about what he had written, and genuine affirmation of him as a person and as a writer. As we talked, I was only vaguely aware that my daughter Jan was in the room using my computer.

She had seen the pile of coaching books on my desk, and when I hung up the phone, she asked if what she overheard had been coaching. That is exactly what I had been doing, even though this had not crossed my mind as my friend and I had talked. He wanted my help in writing a better report, and I responded by raising some questions and sometimes giving him guidance based on my experiences as a writer and editor. He felt some insecurity about the final product, but I encouraged him as we thought of reasons for believing that the report would be well received. He didn't feel criticized or that I had taken the responsibility of rewriting his report and advising him what to do. Instead, he had been coached.

People come for coaching because they want something to be different. The issue may be as simple as reworking an article or as complex as remolding a life, but all coaching is about making changes. Coaches and the people they coach know that for the future to be different, we need to change the way we do things in the present. Sometimes these changes are like my editorial comments regarding my friend's report. More often, changes involve shifts in attitudes, thinking, perceptions, and behavior. There are as many potential changes and goals as there are people who want coaching, but some topics come up repeatedly:

- Developing skills in such areas as athletics, music, money management, public speaking, parenting, and leadership
- Discovering and developing passions
- Finding a life purpose
- Setting and reaching specific goals
- Building a clearer vision for the future
- Developing a mission statement for one's life, business, or ministry
- Learning to manage change effectively
- Learning to relate to people effectively
- Finding clear values
- Building communication skills
- Appraising performance
- Getting unstuck, getting out of ruts, and moving forward
- Learning to think and see things differently
- Expanding the capacity to take action
- Getting free of self-sabotaging behavior and destructive self-talk—the kind of talk, for example, that says, "I can't do it," "Things will never change," "Nobody will listen to me," "I'll never succeed, so why try!"
- Building better teams (in the same way one gets athletes to play for the name on the front of their shirts instead of their own names on the back)
- Building self-confidence
- Finding meaning in what one is doing
- Getting the courage to take risks
- Learning to take responsibility
- Finding the tools, support, and accountability to accomplish more
- Having the ability to focus better, be more efficient, and reach goals more quickly
- Developing a closer walk with God

In all of this, the goal for the coach is to work oneself out of a job so that the person being coached is able to make changes and then move forward without continued assistance.

This is illustrated creatively by the "amoeba theory of management" corporate coach James Flaherty presented in his book on coaching.[21] Back in high school biology, we all learned that amoeba are single-celled protozoa. These amoebas can be moved in at least two ways: They can be poked to respond, or they can be enticed with sugar so that they move in its direction.

This is what behavioristic psychology would see as the most basic stimulus-response methods for bringing change. If the people you coach were amoeba, we could poke them verbally or reward them and watch them go. Sometimes, especially when there is pressure to get things moving, managers, professors, pastors, and even counselors still use this poke and entice approach. Often it works, but only for a while.

As soon as the stimulus ends, the movement stops and it is hard to sustain. When people merely respond to outside stimulation — like the demands of a boss, the advice of a parent, the admonitions of a preacher, or the prod of a teacher — there is little self-motivation to change behavior, rethink values, set personal goals, or discover one's passions. Instead, it is easier to become passive, waiting again until one is pushed. In reality, ambition, goal setting, risk taking, and creativity are all squelched. And because they tend to be smarter than amoeba, humans sometimes even find ways to avoid the poke or get the reward without taking the action. Every day, thousands of workers (and probably a lot of students) sit around in their jobs, trying to look good but doing very little else until they are poked or pulled again.

Certainly this example is unfair to the many research-based, positive aspects of behavioristic psychology, but there is a point in the illustration. To help others grow, coaches need to know their clients, build relationships, take time to assess where others are, and clarify goals. Client and coach need to work together in a partnership that gets things done in the present and clarifies how present learning can be applied in the future. When my friend and I finished going over his written report, he commented that the final document was better than the original and that, in addition, he had learned things about writing that he had never encountered before. He suggested that these would be incorporated next time he wrote a report. That's good coaching: helping another in the present so that he or she is self-motivated and equipped to do better in the future.

The following chapters attempt to give a comprehensive but very practical overview of what coaches do and how they can make a significantly positive impact in the lives and careers of others. Soon we'll move into the goals and methods of coaching, but that's not the place to start.

Have you ever gone to a physician who radiates impatience, always seems to be in a hurry, rarely listens to questions, and lacks sensitivity to his or her patients? Dr. Deme is not like that. When he first became my doctor, I recognized that he was a highly skilled practitioner. Even when he is under pressure — like most in his profession seem to be quite often — he answers my questions, is careful in his work, and shows a sense of humor that jibes with mine. When I have a medical problem, I want a physician who is competent and knowledgeable but also cares about my needs and is able to connect with me on a personal as well as professional level. I want somebody who has the traits of an effective practitioner. Coaching clients want this as well. The place to begin your practical coaching development is to consider what will make you a good coach.

CHAPTER 2

WHAT MAKES
A GOOD COACH?

JON EBERT HAS always been a good athlete. As a kid growing up in the American Midwest, he succeeded in anything he did on the playing field. When he was quarterback on his college football team, he set a host of records. When he was in gym classes and they chose teams, he was always selected first. Most often he was elected team captain, and when he picked kids for his team, he picked the best players first.

One day his dad presented an interesting challenge. "Why don't you start with the worst kids?" he suggested. "Show interest in them. Surprise everybody by picking them first. Give them a chance to play. Teach them to do better. Encourage them so they can build their self-confidence. After all, this is only gym class; it's not a championship game." This was a radical idea, and when my friend tried it, his teams lost a lot of games with very lopsided scores. But the father taught a lesson that his son still remembers: There is nothing more exciting than coming alongside and coaching people who are eager to learn, highly motivated to win, and charged by the fact that somebody finally believes in them. Many of those "loser" players who always had been chosen last in gym class went on to become fairly decent athletes. It all came because of good coaching.[1]

COACHING IS ABOUT BEING

When I went to graduate school, coaching was of no concern to me, but I was eager to learn all the techniques that would let me be a good clinical psychologist. It didn't take long for me to recognize that each therapist was unique but the best ones had something intangible that couldn't be put into my notes or reduced to "how to do it" techniques.

Dr. Baker was one of those therapists. Professor in a course that I took on the Rorschach inkblot test, Dr. Baker had an uncanny ability to make sense of what people saw in those ink blots. In one class, a student started reading the responses of one of his patients from a nearby psychiatric hospital. He didn't get far before Dr. Baker interrupted. "This is a person who has a very high risk for suicide," he said. "Something should be done right away to intervene." The student looked up in amazement and replied that he had given the test shortly after the patient had been brought to the treatment facility because of a serious suicide attempt. Somehow the professor had picked up this suicidal intent immediately. Our class eagerly asked how he had made this interpretation, but he couldn't tell us. He didn't know. He had just done it. Undoubtedly, training and years of experience both contributed to his abilities, but Dr. Baker had a clinical intuition that went way beyond techniques and skills. This inner sensitivity was a part of him.

Most of us know people like this. In the world of sports, there are those who clearly have the innate ability to be effective athletes. It seems to come naturally to them even as it evades others. Some people seem to be natural-born teachers, but that's not true of everyone. Practical experience and training in techniques are always helpful, but a few among us are innately sensitive counselors, powerful public speakers, effective handymen (or handywomen), or gifted musicians. It has something to do with their innate God-given abilities, spiritual gifts, and probably their genes.

Think of yourself. What do you do innately well? If you are inclined to answer, "Nothing," ask somebody who knows you well and that person will have a better answer. When I was in high school, I found myself mentoring the nine-year-olds in my Sunday school class, talking to them about values and coaching them about life. I have been doing something similar ever since. I've lost track of all the kids in that church and today the people I coach are a lot older, but coaching is something I seem to do naturally. It's a part of me. And I was doing it long before anybody had heard of life coaching.

You don't need lots of techniques or years of experience
to be an effective life coach. What contributes to
people most is your level of commitment to them.
That commitment doesn't come from technique or
experience. It comes from the depths of your being.

— DAVE ELLIS, author of *Life Coaching*

Please don't assume, however, that people who want to be good coaches either have the innate ability or they don't. Whereas some people seem to be innately gifted in this area, all of us can learn to be effective. It starts not with techniques but by understanding the characteristics of an effective coach and building these into our lives. Yes, coaching is about what you do, but, probably more important, coaching is about who you are as a person and who you are becoming. If you are a Christian, coaching is also about who you are as a follower of Jesus Christ.

COACHING IS ABOUT CHARACTER

How do companies, organizations, churches, and universities pick new leaders? Often a selection committee is formed to list potential candidates, review applications, hold a lot of meetings, and ultimately recommend the best person for the job. At some time near the beginning of this process, the committee is likely to make a list of the traits, experiences, and abilities the new leader needs to possess. Sometimes these lists are long and include such admirable characteristics as integrity, flexibility, commitment, self-discipline, humility, sensitivity to others, decisiveness, self-confidence, the ability to inspire, high standards, and a commitment to learning and growing.

Nobody would disagree with lists like these. They are life qualities that would be good for anyone to possess, including coaches or new leaders of organizations. But lists like these are of limited value. They are too long to remember and the traits overlap. The lists focus on what leaders can strive to become, but these qualities are hard to measure and it is difficult to know when anyone has succeeded in acquiring them. Sadly, nobody has a surefire effective formula for building these traits into people who want them but don't have them. No doubt some traits are present at birth, part of our genetic makeup, but even these get shaped by what we learn.

Most learning occurs in one of four ways: from instruction, observing others, knowing ourselves, and experience. All of these methods can teach us to be better people and good coaches. We can get instruction and understanding about coaching from lectures, courses, and books. We can learn from other coaches by questioning, imitating, and spending time with them. We learn about ourselves and our own coaching potential by talking with people who know us well, by trying things out, and by taking time for reflection. We learn from experience by doing and practicing. And although all of this is part of becoming a good coach, it also can make us better spouses, parents, leaders, team players or students.

Table 2-1

MARKS OF A GREAT COACH
The Best Coaches Are:
■ Aware of their values
■ Growing in self-awareness
■ Always learning
■ Forward-looking
■ Realistically optimistic
■ Enthusiastic about change
■ Action oriented
■ Flexible
■ Courageous enough to be forthright
■ Sensitive to people
■ Genuinely caring
■ Trustworthy and respected
■ Committed to evaluating and improving their performance as coaches

A search through the Internet or coaching books and articles will reveal numerous list of traits we assume characterize good coaches. Most of these lists reflect the personal observations of the list maker. Few, if any, of the listed characteristics are built on research that compares effective coaches with those who are less effective. Despite this subjectivity, however, some coach traits appear repeatedly on the lists. These include the following plus the marks of a great coach that appear in table 2-1.

Effective coaches know themselves. They are aware of their strengths and weaknesses. They know what they do best. If they are Christians, they probably know and are involved in developing their spiritual gifts. Self-aware people have taken the time to look back on their lives and see what God has blessed. They know what they do well, and often they have clear mission statements. Good coaches are aware of their own core values and beliefs long before they get involved with clients who may have different values. Like counselors, coaches recognize how easily and subconsciously they are prone to move conversations away from client concerns to those of the coach. The good coach is sensitive to these inner tendencies and able to resist them.

Some people learn this self-awareness through counseling. We also learn through being coached. Christians grow in self-awareness through their times with God, prayer, Scripture reading, journaling, quiet reflection, and participation in private or corporate worship. We know too that God teaches us about ourselves through personal experiences and feedback from our closest friends.

Several years ago, I was going through a difficult career transition that I discussed on a regular basis with a good friend. One day he looked me straight in the eye and said, "Gary, why are you so negative about this? Whenever we discuss this issue, you get very critical." I knew that my friend was right and decided on the spot to do something about what he had said. In the weeks that followed, whenever I began to think or say something unkind or critical, I stopped myself. Of course, there is a place for constructive criticism on occasion, but this is different from the ongoing complaining and griping that was becoming a part of me until my friend honestly confronted me with what he was seeing. It helped that he was praying for me regularly and willing to hold me accountable for my critical words. I was more inclined to listen and more motivated to work on being different because it was clear that he cared enough to make me starkly aware of an area that needed change. When we are willing to face our own weaknesses and able to see ourselves more clearly, we are better able to be effective in coaching others.

Effective coaches are sensitive to people. Because coaching is a relationship, it follows that you cannot coach well if you don't relate to people well. You won't relate if you don't care about them and show genuine interest in their lives. People sensitivity involves a natural curiosity about others even as you respect their boundaries and don't pry into areas of their lives in which you have no permission to go.

Good coaches, like good counselors and good friends, have an ability to listen attentively and respectfully. Coaches empathize with the struggles of others even if we can't fully understand. We don't maintain a stony aloofness; we express our feelings naturally and in appropriate ways. We urge people to keep moving, but we aren't pushy. We criticize without being destructive or demoralizing. We share from our own lives without dominating or being self-focused. Those who are sensitive know people rather than just knowing about them.

It's a cardinal principle of good leadership that people will not follow you unless you have their trust. This also is true of good coaching. Trust can never be demanded; it must be earned, and that takes time. Most of us have had experiences of betrayed trust. When this happens more than once or when the betrayal is especially disruptive, any of us would be reluctant to trust again. Trust can be built only when another person is observed over time and in a variety of circumstances but still found to be dependable. Trustworthy people can be counted on to stand by their words and live what they believe. As it becomes clear that they are dependable, they often become respected as well. Sometimes the greatest gift you can give in coaching is the fact that you can be trusted. Betray that trust and relationships are severely damaged, often irreparably.[2]

Effective coaches believe in people. One of my daughters works with inner-city kids who live in a poor neighborhood where most families are dysfunctional and street crime is common. Many of these young people lack social skills or an ability to foresee the consequences of their actions. Often they have no support or encouragement from their families, and most lack any real hope that things will change. Into this environment comes a woman from the suburbs who believes in these kids even though they don't believe in themselves. She shows her beliefs by living in the neighborhood, being present, consistently encouraging, and not being afraid to challenge them because she believes they have potential to do better.

"Believing in people doesn't work at a superficial level," writes Tony Stoltzfus in *Leadership Coaching*. "You can't do this by giving an encouraging word to an acquaintance as you pass each other in the hall. People do not truly feel believed in until they are truly known. The power of belief only flows fully through the channel of open, authentic, personal relationships."[3]

Coaches are convinced that if their clients have needs or concerns, they are capable of finding solutions with the help of another human who believes in them. Christian coaches know that this is how God often guides his children. Clear directions or solutions rarely drop miracle-like into people's lives. Instead, the Holy Spirit guides as people determine what action to take. Sometimes this guidance comes as an inner nudge or sense of direction. Often the Spirit works through the optimistic support that comes from a friend or coach.

Our challenge as coaches is to try looking at people from God's point of view. He knows our sin, our foolishness, our struggles, and our hard-heartedness, but he doesn't give up. Despite our failures, he believes in the potential of the people he created. The coach who has a similar viewpoint can bring incredible transformation to his or her clients.

Effective coaches have synergy with the people they coach. When I was a young professor in a small college, I wanted to have great rapport with all of the students. It didn't take long to learn that this would not happen. There were many with whom I connected immediately, but others had interests and personalities that bonded them with other professors on campus. Those students and professors were different from me.

We all know people with whom we sense a oneness, an awareness that we are like-minded. Call it good chemistry, rapport, harmony, the ability to click or be in sync—this personal synergy is difficult to define, but everybody senses it when they have it. Of course, there can be good communication between people who are not in sync and we can coach such individuals as well. But in general, the better the fit and the sense of unity between the coach and the person being coached, the more likely the coaching will be effective. The good coach aligns with the client to reach some goal. The better the harmony, the better the alignment and the more likely the coaching success.

Effective coaches are flexible. Have you ever heard the story about the frog that was stuck in a deep rut on a country road? A passing bird stopped to ask the frog why he wasn't hopping about at the edge of the nearby pond. "That's an easy question," said the frog. "I can't get out of the rut." A couple of days later, the bird found the frog happily croaking in the sunshine near the water. When he was asked how he escaped from the rut, the frog replied with a wide green grin, "A big truck came along and I had to find a way to get out."

Coaches specialize in working with people who feel stuck and want help in getting out of their ruts. Usually the athletes, performers, parents, or others who seek coaching want fresh approaches for honing their skills and getting free of bad habits. At times, people want more fulfilling lives and help in handling pressure. In executive coaching—the most popular type of coaching at present—the focus is on helping executives improve performance, enhance careers, or work through difficult organizational issues. Some want coaching because they are stuck in frustrating career ruts, looking for creative ways to hop out of their routines or at least make innovative changes.

Coaches have to be flexible because they are change makers. They are also results oriented, optimistic, and willing to give honest feedback. If potential coaches are pessimistic, unwilling to take risks, or more comfortable in their own ruts and set ways, they won't be very effective in assisting others. The best coaches enable others to envision the future, think positively, and imagine brand new ways of doing things. The coach gives encouragement and cheerleading, guiding people to look at things from new perspectives. Because of this innovative mind-set, the coach expects to see failure at times, but when this happens, everybody learns from the mistakes and tries again. And when change for the better comes about, there is rejoicing.

If you are a more cautious person, you may want to stick with coaching in more predictable situations, such as helping people set priorities or learn better speaking skills. The more complex and challenging the situation you and your clients face, the more you need a willingness to be innovative, flexible, and able to think creatively.

Bill Hybels is an author and visionary pastor who has reminded his congregation that sometimes people need to "go for the last 10 percent." We've all had the experience of pointing out weakness in another person but holding back from mentioning those 10 percent issues that we don't want to mention. These are the issues that probably would be most resisted and might harm or even destroy a relationship. These are the issues that pastors almost never mention from the pulpit because they don't want to offend. They are issues that coaches are tempted to avoid because they are uncomfortable to mention. It is interesting that Jesus never had such inhibitions. He had the courage to confront, was not afraid to say things that would be unpopular, and was able to show a fresh kind of honesty. Coaches who follow his example have the license to bring up issues that family, friends, or work subordinates prefer to avoid. In a spirit of sensitivity and compassion, coaches ask for commitments, raise tough questions, and challenge their clients to reach further, think bigger, be flexible, and embrace change.

Effective coaches are driven by firm convictions. Marshall Goldsmith is one of the most famous, successful, and highest-paid coaches in the world. His books and articles have had great success and have led to a host of speaking invitations and consulting opportunities. Goldsmith stays focused on his mission, which is "to help successful leaders achieve a positive change in behavior: for themselves, their people and their teams." He writes that "almost everything I do as a professional is related to my mission."[4] Convinced that his one professional life purpose is to bring about positive change in successful leaders, Goldsmith is able to make decisions about how he lives his life and remains focused on what he does best. Good coaches don't try to coach everybody; they find a niche and work within their area of specialty and conviction.

All good coaches believe a few essential truths, convictions for which they will fight. Leaders with clear convictions find it easier to make decisions. Convictions increase confidence and improve decision-making ability.

— DANIEL HARKAVY, author of *Becoming a Coaching Leader*

But convictions go beyond niches and mission statements. Convictions are based on values, passions, and worldviews. When these are clear, coaches are more willing to talk about uncomfortable issues, challenge others, and live lives that are consistent with their beliefs. Probably most coaches believe in the ability of clients to change. In general, coaches are convinced that lasting change is most likely to occur when clients discover their own visions, set their own goals, establish their own priorities, and determine their own life directions. Christian coaches realize that these decisions are never made alone. There is guidance and empowerment from the Holy Spirit. Sometimes this comes through other people, including coaches, but ultimate progress comes when the client has ownership in the process and is not responding to direction imposed by others.

Effective coaches are psychologically astute. Do people trained in psychology and counseling make the best coaches? The answer will depend on whom you ask. People without psychological training probably would argue that their work has no need for specialized psychological awareness. Often these are coaches who work in the corporate world, where a background in business is valued more than knowledge about counseling issues or psychopathology. In contrast, trained therapists are likely to believe that they have unique skills and training that significantly contribute to coaching effectiveness.

Many people who become coaches (especially life coaches) have backgrounds as therapists or counselors. These coaches bring a number of advantages to the coaching process, including training and experience in listening and responding, the ability to use such clinically based methods as reframing or powerful questioning, and in-depth understanding of human motivation and behavior. Therapists are experienced in helping people communicate and relate to others, knowledgeable about stress management, skilled in the use of assessment tools, and trained in the ability to detect attitudes and behaviors that are signs of inner conflict or other psychological problems.[5] Several years ago, *Harvard Business Review* published an insightful article on "the dark side of coaching" in which the author documented ways coaches can inadvertently harm their clients when there is no awareness of basic psychological dynamics.[6]

How can psychological training be useful in the coaching process? Trained counselors are skilled in active listening, the art of asking powerful questions, and making insightful observations. These are counseling skills, but they can be learned, developed, and brought into coaching. Even without counseling training, many people are psychologically astute and sensitive to others. When they move into coaching, these non-counselors can build on their sensitivity to others and acquire the specialized relational skills seen in all great coaches.

Effective coaches are leaders. Coaches and coaching students sometimes resist this idea. They want to help people move forward, but these coaches claim to have no interest in leadership. It is true that we can coach people without specialized knowledge of the principles of leadership, but it is good to remember that coaching is about using skills that enable people to get from where they are to where they want to be. That's leadership. It's at the core of coaching.

COACHING IS ABOUT LEADERSHIP

It is unlikely that Moses ever heard of coaching, but he learned about it early in his career as leader of the children of Israel. Apparently, his days were typical of the one described in Exodus 18:13. Early in the morning, Moses would take his seat to serve as judge for the people. He sat alone and the people lined up and waited from morning until evening to get his advice. It did not take long for Jethro, Moses' father-in-law, to see that this was poor management and bad leadership. "This is not good!" Jethro said. "You're going to wear yourself out—and the people, too. This job is too heavy a burden for you to handle all by yourself" (verses 17-18).

Then Moses got a little coaching. He explained why he was managing as he was, but Jethro proposed a better way. "Select some new candidates for leadership," he suggested. "Find people with integrity, people who are capable, honest, and God honoring. Then train them carefully. Teach them how to do what you do and let them handle the simpler cases. Permit only the complex issues to be referred to higher levels. That will help you carry the load, making the task easier for you," Jethro concluded. "If you follow this advice, and if God directs you to do so, then you will be able to endure the pressures, and all these people will go home in peace."

Notice that Jethro was not an executive coach or Moses' boss. They were not working for the same company. Jethro did not criticize or condemn the inefficiency of the present system. Instead, he did what modern coaches often do: He observed Moses' performance, made observations, provided options that gave a vision for something better, and helped Moses clear some of the obstacles consuming his life. Perhaps Jethro also stayed long enough to guide and coach Moses on a day-to-day or week-to-week basis as the new policy was put into place.

The men and women who guide . . . will be different leaders
than the ones we've become used to. They will be maestros,
not masters; coaches, not commanders.

— WARREN BENNIS, respected leadership expert, founder of
Leadership Institute, University of Southern California

Coaching is a form of servant leadership that involves encouraging or challenging people to pursue their goals and fulfill their potential. It is not the old style of leadership that involves sitting at the top of some company, organization, or church and passing down orders. When they have to obey orders submissively or submit to dictatorial leaders, people tend to be resentful. Often they do what is minimally involved, but they aren't motivated to develop their own gifts and abilities. When they are coached and led with encouragement, however, they are more enthusiastic, more inclined to grow, and often more able to self-motivate.[7]

Do you think Jesus used coaching with his disciples? He built a trusting relationship with them, was a role model, showed them the way to go, observed their progress, corrected their misunderstandings, and gently encouraged them to go out on their own. Like every good coach, he gave them feedback and reevaluated their performances. He encouraged them but also redirected them when they needed correction.

Notice that Jesus was building a team, but he had a goal of more than team consensus. In some leadership circles today, the main emphasis appears to be getting people together and stimulating discussion until they arrive at mutually acceptable goals and methods. This can be useful if the participants in these discussions are visionary and creative, have ideas about where they want to go, and are open to finding new ways to get there. But the team-consensus approach will not work very well if the group members have no guiding purpose and overarching vision. Groups like this end up committing themselves to mediocrity or everybody agrees to keep doing things in the same old ways that have been used before. Team-consensus groups also have limitations if they are dominated by one very verbal individual who likes to take control. That strong person's agenda is likely to overpower the others and squelch innovation.

Jesus had vision and purpose but was not a dominator and was not trying to build team consensus. He had an incredible awareness of each disciple's personality, potential for impact, and likely points of failure. He guided his team along like a good basketball coach, maximizing their strengths, giving encouragement, exposing them to different experiences, and modifying his guidance as they matured. He coached each of them in slightly different ways because he was sensitive to what made them unique. He knew that they would misunderstand or fail at times. He knew that they would not all win in the end. He had a Judas in the group. But the disciples were coached so that those who remained could continue after Jesus was gone and, in turn, coach others to succeed as leaders. Good coaching is like that. It sets up church or business leaders, spouses, heads of families, teachers, and others to coach others.

COACHING IS ABOUT MOVING FORWARD

When coaching first began to penetrate the business world, it was not always received with enthusiasm. Can you imagine an executive wanting to move ahead in the corporation being told that future promotions would not be forthcoming unless the person saw a coach? Could anybody really trust a coach that was sent by the boss or hired by the company? For many it must have felt like being sent to the principal's office. Later the suspicion moved to the lower echelons of those big companies when supervisors were trained to use coaching instead of giving orders to the employees. The new approach left some of those employees feeling suspicious of the new coaching-based methods and motives.

Today there is a lot less resistance and a lot more enthusiasm, largely because there is greater understanding about what coaches do. Coaches are not there to counsel, offer direct advice, criticize, intimidate, determine who should be promoted, make judgments, or sink anybody's career. The coach's job is not to impose a predetermined agenda on others or force people to change against their wills—although sometimes a little pushing is necessary. Despite the temptation to give direction, talk about oneself, or tell other people's success stories, the effective coach does not dominate the conversation or let it drift aimlessly. What, then, do good coaches do?

Coaching is forward focused. Coaching always focuses on moving the coachee forward.

— FRANK BRESSER and CAROL WILSON,
from *Excellence in Coaching: The Industry Guide*

Sir John Whitmore began his career as a professional racing driver. He won several championships in his younger years but then turned to training others as a business consultant and coach. "Coaching is not merely a technique to be wheeled out and rigidly applied in certain prescribed circumstances," he wrote. "It is a way of managing, a way of treating people, a way of thinking, a way of being." Sir John believes that coaching has two basic purposes: raising awareness and stimulating responsibility.[8]

Raising awareness. Clients usually realize that something is missing from their lives but often don't know what that is. There won't be much progress without an awareness of what is creating the sense of dissatisfaction. One of the coach's first jobs is to help the people they coach become aware. Whenever we know what is controlling or bothering us, we can do something about it, but if we have no awareness, we have no control. That awareness can come as the client reflects on life, often in response to the coach's powerful questions. Carefully designed questionnaires also can be helpful if these are used as tools for getting insight and not as infallible psychological tests. Sometimes coaches will go to the client's workplace and watch what is happening, with the eyes of an outside observer. Still, the most common way to help a client get self-awareness is for the coach to listen in an unhurried manner, giving the gift of his or her presence, asking occasional penetrating questions, and gently giving observations and feedback that can lead to greater insights.

Stimulating responsibility. Individuals or groups can have all the insight and self-awareness in the world, but there will be no change if they do not take responsibility for changing the situation. Every counselor knows that it is easy and much less risky for people to keep talking about their dissatisfactions, blame others for the problems, and do nothing. Clients also can enjoy talking about themselves in the presence of a sensitive coach even as they present creative excuses for inaction. But the effective coach does not let this go on for long. He or she knows that good coaching is concentrated on getting greater awareness and then stimulating focused action. Coaches help people take responsibility for change so they can move forward. This involves clarifying goals, developing a workable plan, and giving encouragement and sometimes guidance as the client assumes responsibility for taking action.

Table 2-2

WHAT GOOD COACHES DO BEST

- Keep aware of their values, beliefs, and biases
- Be trustworthy, available, honest, and committed to integrity
- Be fully present with the client, showing respect, sensitivity, warmth, genuineness, and focus
- Listen carefully without distraction
- Allow the client to set the agenda
- Ask powerful, open-ended questions that clarify issues, stimulate thought, and assess each person's experiences, desires, and goals
- Sensitively guide discussion to consider the person's personal spirituality and walk with God
- Enable people being coached to envision the future, clarify their missions, improve skills, and reach goals
- Resist temptations to dominate the conversation, talk about themselves, and give advice
- Stimulate awareness, responsibility, and change
- Focus on the present and future, not the past
- Periodically restate the agenda, summarize the conversation, and provide feedback when asked
- Encourage and show optimism
- Speak the truth in love, giving reliable feedback and periodic challenges
- Assist clients as they design action, set goals and plan actions, and take steps to move forward
- Provide accountability as needed
- Aim for collaboration and good communication
- Keep confidences
- Follow up after the coaching is completed
- Always remember that coaching depends on personal chemistry between the coach and client, mutual trust and respect, coaching competence, and confidentiality

COACHING IS ABOUT ACTION

Why would anyone want coaching? Consider Hal, an engineer who works for a large company that manufactures computer components. He has a good job with a very comfortable income. Several times he has been promoted and his future looks bright. Now thirty-eight years old, Hal and his family live in a comfortable home in an attractive suburban neighborhood surrounded by others who also are highly successful, upwardly mobile young professionals. The whole family is actively involved in a good church with great programs for the children, lively music, and fine preaching. Recently, Hal was elected as a church deacon, and he continues to teach a children's Sunday school class with his wife.

Hal is also miserable. He has no spare time. His days and evenings are filled to the brim and overflowing with activity. Every morning he gets up early, takes a brief jog, rushes off to work, and goes nonstop all day. Coming home for dinner is only a pause on the treadmill of hyperactivity. There is no time for solitude, no time to relax, no time alone with God. Hal and his wife both feel a depressive weight on their lives and see no way to escape.

I made up this description; Hal does not really exist. And yet he does. Over the years, I have had coaching clients and several close friends who might read these words and think I am describing them. They all fit the picture of Hal. I understand because for most of my life I have been a Hal, and if I am not careful I easily slide back into that old routine again.

Most of the Hals in this world do not need counseling, although many might benefit from an understanding of why they are so driven. Instead, these people—women as well as men—need help in managing their lives and careers. Some of them already use coaches to improve their games of tennis, golf, investing, or money management. Coaches can't tell them how to control their overbearing, time-starved lives. But coaching can help them make decisions, evaluate their lifestyles, build new boundaries into their daily routines, reconnect with God, and feel hope once again. There can hardly be a more needed service in our culture today or a more crucial ministry for the church.

There are a number of reasons why people today use coaches—reasons that help explain why coaching has become so popular.

Coaches guide Christians and others in their spiritual journeys. Many believers are like Hal. They understand the basics of the faith and aren't looking to be discipled. Some may have been longtime churchgoers who are disillusioned with organized religion—people who "like Jesus but not the church."[9] These people want focused time with someone who has been on the spiritual road longer, who has clear beliefs, models Christlikeness, and can coach in our era of empty spirituality, distrust of religion, information glut, and exploding change.

Coaches walk with people through life transitions and other change. Whenever we encounter major changes in our lives—the launch of a new business, a job change or promotion, moving, marriage, divorce, terminal illness, the death of a loved one, or retirement—we usually face uncertainty and the need to readjust. Friends, family, and churches will always give encouragement and guidance in times like these. But transitions take time and often involve important decisions that may go beyond the counsel of a friend. Experienced coaches can guide as people reassess their life goals, find new career options, change lifestyles, get training, reevaluate their finances, or find the information that lets them make wise decisions.

Coaches build skills. This is what the athletic coach does, but the principles go far beyond the world of sports. Good coaching helps people anticipate what they could become, overcome self-sabotaging habits and insecurities, manage relationships, and build effective ways to keep improving. People being coached often need assistance in correcting old ways of doing things and developing new competencies. Spiritual coaches help others build spiritual disciplines into their lives and live in harmony with their core values.

Coaching involves observing your people's performance, praising progress, and redirecting efforts that are off base.

— KEN BLANCHARD, BILL HYBELS, and PHIL HODGES, coauthors of *Leadership by the Book*

Coaches stimulate improved performance. This is of special importance in the business world, where performance is highly related to corporate success. Coaching can enable CEOs and top-level managers to improve their leadership and interpersonal effectiveness, help supervisors at all levels manage more competently, and better equip lower-level workers to function with greater fulfillment and efficiency. Some coaches guide in the development of employee assessment, training, and relationship building. Even as athletic coaching can improve the game of those who play in sports, life coaching and executive coaching can improve the performance of pastors, performers, entrepreneurs, and others whose functioning could be at higher levels of competence and proficiency.[10]

Coaches build teams. I lived in Chicago during the glory days of Michael Jordan's run with the Chicago Bulls. In the beginning, Jordan carried the team with his outstanding abilities and basketball heroics, but as time went on, he appeared to focus more on team building. He never lost his superior abilities and remarkable leadership gifts, but together with team coach Phil Jackson, "MJ" taught his fellow players how to work together as a unit. There are few situations today in which individuals can make things happen all by themselves. Significant accomplishments only come when people work together. Coaches, including pastor-coaches in churches and parent-coaches in families, facilitate that process.

Coaches facilitate communication and better relationships. Sometimes the coach's job is to help people in groups resolve differences, cool tensions, deal with miscommunications and misunderstandings, build trust, or overcome unhealthy competition between members on the same team. Church leadership councils, corporate boards, business partners, or people working together on projects can all benefit from coaching, especially if the group participants have a willingness and ability to enhance their relationships and work together. Relationship coaches are specialists who assist others in creating greater harmony and better communication.

Coaches stimulate vision. I wonder how many churches have no vision. They keep doing what they have done for years, without much change and with little expectation that things will ever be different. Of course, some people are more visionary than others; they think continually and creatively about the future, and they work to make things happen. Most of us are not like that. Our visions are more limited and we are too busy or disinclined to look very far into the future. Coaches can be effective in helping individuals and organizations think beyond the present so they can envision the future and figure out how to get there. Even when visions are clear and concisely stated, however, visions tend to fade when the "urgent and legitimate needs of today quickly erase our commitment to the *what could be* of tomorrow."[11] Coaches can assist individuals, leaders, and team builders to keep cultivating, communicating, and seeking to implement visions.

If you're without a vision, you're without a future.

— LEONARD SWEET, author of *SoulTsunami*

Coaches enable people to set and reach goals. Coaching helps people set short-term and long-range goals. Then coaches help others make innovative plans for getting unstuck, out of ruts, and moving to new levels. Beyond this planning and goal setting, coaches encourage, motivate, challenge, and provide accountability as their clients take steps to move forward.

Coaches improve leadership. This is the role of leadership coaches. They understand principles of leadership, relate well to leaders, and enable people in leadership roles to function more effectively. Coaches equip leaders to guide their followers who, in turn, are better able to see the future, overcome obstacles, build teams, move forward, reach their goals, and become leaders themselves. One of the greatest contributions of leadership coaches is to train leaders so they become coaches themselves, learning to lead by using the principles of leadership.

Coaches speak the truth in love. Good coaches have no desire to harm others or make their lives uncomfortable. But effective coaches know that sometimes the best way to bring positive change is by refusing to ignore harmful behavior patterns or realities that should be faced and addressed. In firm and respectful ways, coaches challenge client attitudes, biases, and detrimental behavior.

Those who solicit a coach are already ascending the mountain; their eyes are focused upward so that they can see the mountaintop. They already glimpse the opportunity to improve. . . . At that point, a coach comes in and helps them to see even more possibilities. A coach helps them make additional changes. . . . The coach will ask the right questions and clarify their convictions. This, in turn, will assist them to change their habits so they can become even more successful and purposeful.

— DANIEL HARKAVY, author of *Becoming a Coaching Leader*

Coaches facilitate improvement. This is a summary of all that has come before. Coaches help people keep from being overrun by change, and coaches help individuals and organizations make things change for the better.

WHAT COMES NEXT?

Coaching is growing within the Christian community. Still unknown in many places or dismissed as a fad, the coaching movement nevertheless shows evidence of gaining momentum and influence. As it continues to grow, coaching is becoming a tool for Christian leaders, mental health professionals, businesspeople, educators, and others who recognize that coaching is a valuable service that can illuminate and mobilize Christian leaders and laypeople alike. Whether they are working with an individual on life issues or in a corporate or church setting, Christian coaches come alongside their clients, listening to their concerns and unveiling dreams, visions, and goals. Coaches support others in getting clarity and perspective while they move forward, guided by the Holy Spirit and supported with prayer. In this way, people are helped to realize their God-given potential and strive to be all God wants them to become. Coaching can bring a fresh approach to the final command that Jesus gave to his followers: "Make disciples." Spiritual coaching is already making inroads into the church, perhaps as a God-given means, used by the Holy Spirit to help revitalize stagnant churches and help Christians in ruts get moving.

In the chapters that follow, we will give a fresh, in-depth, and hopefully interesting look at coaching. We will focus on the practical side of coaching and discuss such questions as: How can you become a good coach? What skills need to be developed? How can we train others to coach? What are the obstacles we need to overcome in effective coaching? Are there dangers in coaching? What are the different types of coaching? Where can coaching be applied?

There isn't a set formula for coaching that everybody follows, but there are principles. What are these? And, specifically, how can you apply them to your life, your ministry, your career?

It's time to get started in finding the answers. We'll begin by looking at how people change and how coaches can be effective change agents, working alongside individuals and teams with the goal of making changes that last.

CHAPTER 3

COACHING:
IT'S ALL ABOUT CHANGE

BEFORE HE BECAME President, Barak Obama spent months building his campaign around one concept: change. All across the country, huge crowds gathered to cheer and wave signs linking Obama's name with change. Soon his political rivals picked up the theme, and debate swirled about which of the candidates could best become an agent of change. On election night, when the outcome was clear, the president-elect and his family appeared before more than a million hometown supporters in Chicago and announced that "change has come."

Politicians are not the only agents of change. The work of coaches is all about change. These are people who encourage, guide, and walk with those who want their lives to be different. Coaching empowers people to find new jobs, work through transitions, improve performance, build better relationships, make wise decisions, transform companies and churches, and reach new spiritual levels. Coaching is about setting vision and reaching goals. When coaching is successful, it's about bringing and maintaining change.

But coaching is more. It also helps people determine what needs to stay the same in these times of constant flux. Coaches encourage others to stake out their core values, established strengths, lasting relationships, basic beliefs, and ethical principles that remain firm and give an anchor to their lives.

———

Coaches are both change agents and constants agents. They help people see what needs to change and what needs to remain constant and unchanging.

—RICHARD J. LEIDER, career development coach, author of *The Power of Purpose*

Let us begin with the obvious: Change is difficult. Walking with people through change can be challenging and often draining. Bringing change that persists is even harder. Most people resist even when they see the need for change and believe that it has to occur. Several years ago, a routine physical examination revealed that I had significant blockage in the arteries surrounding my heart. Overall, I was in great health. I worked out at the fitness club almost every morning and had no noticeable symptoms. I had never been in the hospital, except when I was born, but three or four days after the doctor's diagnosis, I was wheeled into the operating room, where I had a quadruple bypass. Later I learned that in the United States alone, about 600,000 people have bypass surgery every year and 1.3 million have angioplasties. Before leaving the hospital, almost all of these patients are told that they need to make changes in their lifestyles, eating, and health habits. If they make these changes, there is a high probability that they will recover completely and live longer than if they fail to change. These people, me included, have each been faced with a life-or-death choice: Change now or die sooner.

If you were faced with this choice, would you make the changes? Most heart patients begin the change routine enthusiastically, but according to research summarized in Alan Deutschman's book *Change or Die*, only one person in ten actually makes lasting changes.[1] "Some 90% of heart-bypass patients can't change their lifestyles even at the risk of dying. No wonder changing people's behavior is the roughest challenge in business."[2] It also is a difficult challenge in politics. And it's tough in coaching, counseling, ministry, training programs, or the efforts of people to change their own eating habits, spiritual disciplines, addictive behaviors, abusive actions, and perceptions. And it can be difficult to make changes in our minds. If we stop learning, for example, the brain's ability to change slows down. When we don't work at mental rejuvenation, there is a 50-50 chance of senility by the time we reach age eighty-five. "While the issue for the heart patient is 'change or die,' the issue for everyone is 'change or lose your mind.' Mastering the ability to change is a necessity for health."[3]

As a coach, think of yourself as a change assistant and a change initiator. You assist people to accept change, but you also gently encourage them to make changes, even when changing is uncomfortable. Some time ago, one of my friends wrote an article stating that coaches are experts in understanding and bringing change. When I asked what made him a change expert, my friend did not have an answer. He had never studied change or even read a book or article about how we change and why some people resist change. Before we try to facilitate change in our clients or start referring to ourselves as change experts, it can be useful to dip briefly into the huge body of research and publications that enable us to understand what brings and what undermines lasting change.

Some of these research findings are fascinating and very practical. For example, when change is introduced more gradually and set in the context of the familiar, it gets a better reaction and is more easily accepted. When it comes too quickly and when it is too disruptive, change is more likely to be resisted. In his book *Leading Change*, James O'Toole contrasts Franklin Roosevelt with the Communist party leaders of the same era.[4] Roosevelt succeeded in his radical reforms because he set them in the context of traditions, systems, and beliefs with which people were familiar. The Communist leaders, in contrast, tried and ultimately failed to impose a drastically new system that was foreign to the traditions and values of the people.

Many years later, another Communist leader, Mikhail Gorbachev, had a courageous vision for change, but he too was less successful than he might have been. This was not because he ignored the beliefs and concerns of the people but because he failed to develop a cadre of disciples who could champion the need for change and put Gorbachev's creative new ideas into practice.

Under threat people resist, cling to what they have and are,
and become more fixed in their ideas and feelings.

— C. H. PATTERSON, professional counseling pioneer

Christian coaches are best able to help people through change when threat can be reduced, the change process is not rushed, there is respect for traditional values (especially biblical values), the client or protégé feels support in making change, and there are practical guidelines on how to make things happen.

FACING CHANGE

The way people respond to change puts them in one of these four categories:

- *Innovators* are those who value change and try to make change happen.
- *Embracers* thrive on change and accept it enthusiastically, sometimes without much thought.

- *Acceptors* usually resist at first but eventually go along with the change, sometimes because they have no alternative.
- *Resisters* try to protect themselves from the change or prevent it from occurring. These people may not notice the change, deliberately ignore it by pretending that the changes do not exist or are of no importance, or be so overwhelmed by the prospect of change that they push it from their awareness. Some may deny the need for change and stubbornly refuse to budge.

Depending on their personalities and past experiences, most people lean toward one of these four categories. Consider the battles that have taken place in some churches over the topic of music. When a new style of music is introduced into the worship service, this usually is the work of innovators. The embracers jump on board enthusiastically, but the resisters soon appear as well. Their unwillingness to go along with the change may be based on good arguments, but the resistance also can stem from discomfort, feelings of being out of control or threatened, or a desire to maintain the status quo. Acceptors more often take a wait-and-see attitude before going along with the change. Sometimes they do so reluctantly.

Despite the differences in personalities and past experiences, each situation shapes how each person handles change. I like to consider myself an embracer and a change innovator, but there are some changes I accept reluctantly and others that I resist. I discovered this about myself when we moved after more than twenty years living in the same house. I knew we had to do it, but I resisted leaving the old house even though the decision to move made good sense and had been made voluntarily. After we got settled in the new place, I accepted our new home enthusiastically. During that time, a change embracer and innovator (me) temporarily was a resister before becoming an acceptor. Would my responses have been different if we had been forced to move because of a fire or foreclosure?

Often we tend to resist change because we fear the unknown, are unsure of ourselves or our abilities, and cling to the good parts of what we have enjoyed. Sometimes, like Peter stepping off the boat, we doubt God. Dealing with change successfully requires authenticity . . . being honest about how you feel and not stuffing the emotions that accompany change.

— JUDY SANTOS, founder of Christian Coaches Network

If you or a coaching client unexpectedly loses a home, job, or good health, you are more likely to experience or encounter resistance, at least initially. It happens to us all at times. When change smashes into our comfortable worlds, we respond by denying what has happened or trying to ignore or stop the change. If change is dropped into an organization, including the place where you work or worship, some people will use change-resister talk, which is summarized in table 3-1. It is only later that one is able to accept what has happened and respond accordingly, sometimes with the help of a coach.

It should not be assumed that clients can be talked out of their resistance with a few words from the coach. People who resist might even want change to happen, but they might have fear of the unknown, anxiety about letting go of what is old and familiar, or an unwillingness to take risks. At times there is insecurity about the possibility of losing relationships or not being able to cope with the new situation. Resisting change, therefore, may be a means of protecting oneself against the unknown.

Coaches or other change agents must be aware of these insecurities and resistances so clients can go through the process of facing and adapting to change realistically. Without this process, coaching clients are likely to return to their old ways of doing things whenever they reencounter the pressure to think or act in ways that are new.

Table 3-1

CHANGE-RESISTER TALK[5]
How can you tell when a person is resisting change? Listen to their talk. They may use phrases such as the following. Try to respond with words similar to those following each phrase.   ■ "It seems risky." Most change is risky. But if there are no risks, there is no progress. Maybe the risk is worth taking. And what are the implications of not taking a risk?   ■ "We've never done it this way." Sticking with the old way can put us in a rut and squelch some better things that could happen.   ■ "Doing it the old way has worked fine in the past." Relying on past success is a great way to prevent change, encourage complacency, lead to irrelevance, and stifle future success.   ■ "The old way is more biblical." That is a cliché statement that may be hard to defend. And the new way can be biblical as well, maybe even more so.

- "What if we fail or it doesn't work?" That is a risk you have to take if you are to reach goals and move forward. Ask any Olympic athlete. They all train and compete knowing that they might fail. But they move forward anyway.

- "Somebody will criticize." That's true. But in time you may get more criticism if you stay entrenched, and you might even end up condemning yourself if you don't have the courage to step out.

- "I'm too old." That was one excuse that Moses never used. Nobody is too old to learn new things unless they convince themselves that age is a barrier.

- "We don't have the training or competence." In some cases that will be true. So what can you do to get the training? If the answer is "realistically, nothing," then think what you can you do within your current level of competence.

- "I don't feel it is the right thing to do." But we can't base our lives solely on feelings. Often this statement is another way of saying, "I'm scared," "I don't like being out of control," "I'm afraid I won't be able to handle it," "This is threatening and uncomfortable for me." Coaches need to listen to these resistances and discuss them fully before progress can occur.

HOW PEOPLE CHANGE

Most often we don't change until the benefits of going through the change are greater than the benefits of staying where we are. With the recovering heart patients that were described earlier, keeping their old lifestyles was easier and more familiar than making changes at a post-surgery time when everything seemed fine. These men and women were not greatly inclined to make changes in their eating, exercise routines, or lifestyles because their health was good and making changes did not appear to have any immediate benefits.

Most of the people who come voluntarily for coaching are motivated to change. They are not held back by the issues that people bring to counselors: troubling events from the past, inner turmoil, or disabling emotional problems. More often, coaching clients are getting along fine but in some part of life they are stuck. They might want to change, but they don't know what to do or they fail when they try something new. These are people who can benefit from the services of a coach to guide the change process.

In his study of those heart patients and others who seemed unable to change, Alan Deutschman concluded that there are three approaches to change that are often used but rarely work. These might be called the three Fs: facts, fear, and force. Each may bring immediate effects, but permanent change rarely comes solely because people are given *facts* like the heart patients received before leaving the hospital. *Fear* does not work either. There is little value in threatening people in the hope that this will bring about new behaviors. Few drinkers are inclined to avoid alcohol because somebody has tried to scare them into sobriety by showing pictures of people killed as a result of drunken driving. Perhaps least effective is trying to *force* change in people who don't want to change. If you want to coach people through change, don't rely on facts, fear, or force.

What can we do instead? What is most effective in bringing change? Deutschman calls these the three Rs: relate, repeat, reframe. First, good coaches need to *relate* to their clients in ways that build emotional relationships, sustain hope, and inspire. Every dieter knows that losing weight is easier when there is support from a community or an individual who serves as a role model and encourager who believes that the client has the ability to change. Cheerleading can be helpful.

Many executives [and others] stubbornly resist change until they form a new relationship with someone who can inspire and teach them about new ways.

— ALAN DEUTSCHMAN, author of *Change or Die*

Second, for change to occur and stick, there must be something more than words from a teacher or coach. There must be *repetition*. "It takes a lot of repetition over time before new patterns of behavior become automatic and seem natural — until you act the new way without even thinking about it. . . . Change doesn't involve just 'selling': it requires 'training.'"[6] This has implications for coaches as well as for our clients. If you want to change in ways that will make you a good coach, you need to practice, master new habits, learn new skills, and keep coaching. By repeating the basics again and again, new coaching skills are formed and beginning coaches become good coaches.

The third key to change is to *reframe*. Most counselors are familiar with this concept. If you take a photograph and put it in a different frame, everything can look different. In coaching people to change, they need to see their current situations in a fresh way. That's part of what happened to me when I turned sixty and thought I was too old to do anything effective from that point onward. My coach challenged some of my perspectives about my age group and helped me see the potential and possibilities I could have as a person who is over sixty. This was more than positive thinking. It involved looking past the age biases that I was carrying and seeing my stage in life as an era that would be filled with new opportunities and fresh ways to continue my career and mentoring activities. It was not until I started writing this paragraph that it dawned on me that I changed because I reframed my views about my age, all helped by the guidance of a coach.

According to Deutschman, change comes when we "relate, repeat, and reframe. New hope, new skills, and new thinking. . . . That's all the theory you need to get started" as a change agent and as a coach.[7] Undoubtedly, change is more complex than avoiding facts, fear, and force or introducing the three Rs.[8] But the three Fs and Rs can be an easily remembered foundation that coaches can keep in mind as they work with clients.

PHASES OF CHANGE

Of course, many changes occur naturally and without any conscious effort. Consider a ritual that happens every spring. Male frogs sit around ponds and lakes, singing their unique love songs, hoping to attract a mate. The evidence of their success is seen when long strands of jelly-like eggs appear on the water surface and soon change into tadpoles swimming in the pond, feeding on algae and other tadpole delicacies. In the days that follow, a remarkable change takes place. First, tiny legs appear and the tail shrinks and disappears. Before long, the creature becomes a frog that grows in size and strength to await next year's "rite of spring." Similar transformations occur when tiny caterpillars hatch from eggs, grow rapidly, and then form a chrysalis that later splits open so that a beautiful butterfly can emerge.

Every grade-schooler learns about these changes in nature, and most learn the word that describes them: **meta·mor·pho·sis**. The Merriam-Webster online dictionary defines *metamorphosis* as a transformation, a striking change of appearance, form, or structure, "especially by supernatural means."[9] A quick Internet search will show that the word is used in music, architecture, literature, geology, and even therapy to describe significant change for the better. Centuries ago, the writer of the biblical book of Romans used the Greek word *metamorphosis* to describe a transformation that comes from God to those who allow him to change their thinking and character: "Don't copy the behavior and customs of this world," wrote Paul the apostle; instead, "let God transform you into a new person by changing the way you think. Then you will know what God wants you to do and you will know how good and pleasing and perfect his will really is."[10]

Perhaps with these examples in mind, some coaches have built their whole approaches around what they term *transformational coaching*.[11] Sometimes coaching does result in changes that are as radical and transformational as the metamorphosis of a caterpillar into a butterfly or a tadpole into a toad. At other times the process of coaching is less life-changing, especially when the person being coached seeks help to reach specific goals, get unstuck, resolve a conflict, or make a decision. Even when their issues seem to be of minor significance, however, many coaching clients experience a striking transformation—a significant and lasting change for the better. When this coaching is guided by the Holy Spirit and done with a desire to have God lead in the process, coaching truly is metamorphic.

Several years ago, a group of researchers set out to determine how transformational and other changes occur. The researchers were not focused on coaching, but their findings have significant application to anyone who wants to change or help others change. By studying people who sought to free their lives from harmful habits, the research team identified six distinct phases that most people go through as part of the change process.[12] Think how these can apply to you and to your clients.

———————

In my own informal observations of clients over ten years,
all have passed through each of these phases on their
way to long-term change. Knowing the phases has helped me
and other coaches understand where a particular
client is today and where the client needs to go next.
Each phase provides both the learning and the motivation
to propel them into the next phase.

— DANIEL WHITE, author of *Coaching Leaders*

1. Precontemplation. This is the time when people are not considering change and usually have no awareness that change might be desirable or needed. At this stage, few seek coaching on their own, although some may be referred by another person—for example, a supervisor. This is a time when there may be denial that change is needed or fear of facing a situation that needs to be altered. The coach needs to build trust at this point, give reassurance, and help the potential client see the need for change.

I once was asked to coach two executives who had enrolled in a leadership training program. These were competent and creative leaders who were successful in their careers and had no pressing motivation to be coached. One of the executives never made a connection with me. The other agreed to participate as part of the leadership training, but he had nothing in his life that he especially wanted to change. That is where the coaching started. We spent time talking about where he was in his life and his leadership. There would have been no purpose for coaching if he had concluded that he was completely satisfied with where he was. After one or two sessions, however, my new client and I developed a productive coaching relationship that lasted for several months. It began when he completed the simple Graph of Life inventory that appears in appendix A. This triggered thoughts in his mind about how his schedule was out of control and he did not know how to take charge of his overly busy lifestyle. My client recognized that this was preventing him from being a better leader. When he made this realization, he already had moved to the second phase of change.

2. Contemplation. Coaching usually starts at this stage. It occurs when people recognize that change might be needed and beneficial, even though they are not completely committed to doing anything different. Often this is when fear of change begins to surface. The person grapples with whether he or she wants to make the effort to leave the old ways and move to something that is new. Coaches can listen and understand these struggles and this resistance, ask probing questions, and explore the reasons for changing or not changing. Coaches or other change agents can show optimism at this phase. Sometimes it is here when coaches try to stimulate a vision of what can be possible. It is here, as well, when there is an effort to instill hope.

3. Preparation. At this stage, people have decided to take action and make changes, although they might not yet know what action to take. This is a planning stage that involves actively identifying goals, determining what actions can be taken, and getting information. In one of my coaching classes, a student expressed a desire to get into a regular exercise program even though she had little interest in sports and hated going to the gym, especially by herself. Together we explored ways in which she could get exercise that might be enjoyable and sustainable. She mentioned some friends who went hiking for a couple of hours every weekend. In the preparation stage, the student talked about how she could connect with her friends, walk with them on one or two of their hikes, purchase the needed shoes, and get this activity onto her schedule. On paper this may look simple, but it was a huge step forward for a person who had wanted to get into an exercise program for months but had not known how to proceed. The coaching brought a plan to help the student reach the goal, and a coach who could hold her accountable for following up on the strategy.

For major changes to occur, this preparation can be time consuming. Often this also is a time of excitement and enthusiasm mixed with fear and insecurity. Most of us have had the experience of deciding to start something new, getting everything lined up to move forward, but experiencing increasing insecurity and inner doubt or turmoil as we approach the time to start. At this stage, the coach keeps people on target and helps them make decisions for action that are wise, realistic, and consistent with their personalities and values.

4. Action. This is the process of building on the preparation and actually starting something. Often this begins with enthusiasm, but the realities of doing things differently can arouse second thoughts, feelings of uncertainty, anxiety, and tugs to return to the old and familiar behaviors. I see this every January in the fitness club where I work out. New people start the year with determination to lose weight or get in shape. At last they are taking action. Some even hire a fitness trainer to help them develop new exercise routines. As the winter drags on, however, the crowds in the gym begin to thin. Old habits resurface. It becomes easier to miss the daily workout. The pressures of living squeeze out what started so positively. During this action stage, coaches can give support and encouragement, especially near the beginning when the new behaviors are not established. Coaching clients may need repeated reminders of their goals and their reasons for making changes. This reminding and encouraging may be of special importance if there is a relapse and the client reverts to the old behaviors.

5. Maintenance. Eventually, people get into the new behaviors. New habits or ways of thinking get integrated into their lives. But the new ways of doing things are weak in comparison to the old behaviors. Much of this can be explained neurologically. When behavior is repeated over the years, neural circuits form in the brain, and impulses normally travel over these well-developed highways. When we try to change habits, we are introducing new cerebral pathways. The brain knows that something is wrong and tries to go back to the established circuits. Tell the human brain what to do and it automatically pushes back.[13]

Encouragement, persuasion, and incentives can support the new behaviors, but changing a hardwired habit or way of thinking requires a lot of repetition and attention. These changes rarely persist if they come only from the urgings of others. "Behavior change brought about by leaders, managers, therapists, trainers, or coaches is primarily a function of their ability to induce others to focus their attention on specific ideas, closely enough, often enough, and for a long enough time." To change behavior, "focus on identifying and creating new behaviors. Over time these may shape the dominant pathways of the brain. This is achieved through a solution-focused questioning approach that facilitates self-insight, rather than through advice giving."[14] The neural pathway redirections also are more likely to occur if the individual consistently puts his or her attention on making the changes. "Attention continually reshapes the patterns of the brain. . . . People who practice a specialty every day literally think differently, through different sets of [neural] connections, than do people who don't practice the specialty" or keep focused on making the changes.[15]

6. Termination. At this stage, the new behavior or thinking is well established, so coaching is no longer necessary for the change that was desired. In coaching it is helpful to remember that some clients might be involved in making more than one change at a time. As a result, several of these phases may be in operation in the same time period as different goals are being reached.

The coach maintains the patience to allow the client
to move through each stage, knowing that the client's
ultimate success will be better ensured if each stage is
addressed fully according to the client's needs.

—PATRICK WILLIAMS and DIANE MENENDEZ,
coauthors of *Becoming a Professional Life Coach*

BRINGING CHANGE THAT LASTS

Have you ever gone to a conference, been inspired, purchased resources, and left with high expectations for doing things differently when you get home? Perhaps your good intentions have led to some brief temporary changes but then you face the pressures of things that need to be done. Before long your resolutions for change have been buried under a pile of other responsibilities, and soon the conference becomes only a memory. After conferences, only a small percentage of the participants actually make changes. This has led some people to question the lasting value of conferences, sermons, or even coaching, especially when these experiences provide information and inspiration but have no clear follow-up guidelines or goals. It is easy to make decisions to change, and it is easy to make short-term changes, but it is much tougher to make changes that last.

Psychologist Jeffrey Kottler had seen this in his own life, so he decided to get away from his routines for a while and do an in-depth study on what brings change that sticks. As a therapist, he had watched many people in his counseling room who determined to do things differently and failed. Some of these people had not been motivated to change, despite what they said, so there was nothing different. Others encountered obstacles that blocked their movement forward. Sometimes Kottler's counselees did not believe that change was possible. They lacked encouragement from others, concluded that it was better to stay with the status quo, and abandoned their efforts to forsake old behaviors and do things differently.

To research and write about these issues, Kottler temporarily moved to Iceland, where he could have time for uninterrupted study. He did not understand the language and had no friends in his new community, so he had to make changes in his attitudes and lifestyles if he were to adjust and have a productive study time. Kottler learned to make needed changes in his own life, wrote an engaging book about change, and was able to identify a number of guidelines that can bring lasting change in others. Each of these guidelines can be useful for coaches as they work with people who want to make changes that last.[16]

1. Commitment. This is "the single most important ingredient" in bringing lasting change. Commitment is related to how badly the person wants to change and how motivated he or she is to work at maintaining the changes once they occur. Change will last when the person expects to change, is confident that he or she will change, is willing to do whatever is necessary to bring lasting change, and is in this for the long run, not just for the short term.

The possession of the skill of overcoming resistance to change
is what separates the mass of individuals with good ideas from
the few leaders who are able to implement them.

— JAMES O'TOOLE, author of *Leading Change*

2. Attainable goals. Nothing "dooms change efforts more than setting goals that are unrealistic and impossible to reach."[17] Attainable goals are specific rather than vague. They persist longer if there can be consistent and accurate feedback on one's progress.

Every coach has seen clients who decide to make changes but fail to follow through. Resolutions, including New Year's resolutions, can be lofty and inspiring, but they often fail because there is no realistic plan for turning the resolutions into achievable goals. How, then, do we help clients turn mental resolutions into lasting tangible results? Determine precisely what needs to be done and when, where, and how, this will be carried out. "Dozens of studies have shown [that] when people took the time to visualize exactly when and where they would do what they needed to do, they met their goals."[18] It can be helpful, too, if the people who want change are willing to state publicly what they plan to do and indicate who will hold them accountable. Public awareness and peer pressure are great motivators. It helps, as well, if the person who wants to change surrounds himself or herself with people who are encouraging and motivated to be achievers. Indifference in others can be contagious. Enthusiasm in others can be highly motivating, especially when there are specific goals to be achieved.[19]

3. Relapse prevention. In any change, relapse is common. Overall, there are three ways to identify and prevent relapse.[20] First, encourage coaching clients to identify high-risk situations and learn how to deal with the temptations. Second, figure out what coping skills will enable a person to avoid the problems. Third, help each client develop a lifestyle that reduces the possibility of temptation or returning to the old behaviors.

4. Practice. When a new behavior is practiced to the point that it becomes automatic, there is increased probability that it will persist.[21] These practice sessions are most effective when they resemble the actual situations in which the behavior is to be used. Every year in December and January, American football teams play their championship games. Some of these games are played in covered indoor stadiums where the temperature is warm and comfortable, but others are in frigid outdoor stadiums. Practice for these games is most effective when it occurs in settings that resemble the real weather conditions the players will encounter later.

5. Expectations. It should not be surprising that lasting change is most likely to happen when people expect to change and assume that the change will last. Try this as a test sometime. Ask a coaching client to use a scale of 1 to 10 to rate the likelihood that change will persist (1 means that it is largely unlikely there will be lasting differences; 10 means that change is almost absolutely certain). The higher the rating, the larger the likelihood of success. See if this applies in your client. When there is great expectation, there is less relapse.

6. Support systems. The maintenance of change depends, in large part, on whether or not there is a partner or support system to give encouragement and accountability. The most effective support systems are the ones available when needed. They are supporters who identify and celebrate short-term wins on the way to reaching larger goals.

Without sufficient wins that are visible, timely, unambiguous, and meaningful to others, change efforts invariably run into serious problems.

— JEFFREY KOTTLER, author of *Making Change Last*

7. Divine intervention. In addition to Kottler's conclusions, Christian coaches recognize the awesome power of God to bring lasting change that might never come otherwise. The apostle Paul prayed that "from his glorious, unlimited resources [God] will empower you with inner strength through his Holy Spirit."[22] This is the strength that brought radical and lasting change in Paul's own life. He recognized that human effort could be of limited value but that we can do everything with the help of Christ, who continually gave us the strength we need[23] and the wisdom to coach people for lasting change.

CHANGING PETER

Some of the most powerful and instructive examples of lasting change are found in the Bible. Consider Simon Peter, who is one of the most interesting case studies of change in the New Testament. Knowing Peter's future and seeing his potential, Jesus called him a rock, but the disciples might have called him a flake. He was impulsive to the point of jumping out of a boat in a storm in the middle of a lake. In Gethsemane, he was quick to start swinging a sword against the well-trained Roman soldiers. Peter was the one disciple known to challenge Jesus, announcing confidently that he would never deny the Lord regardless of what Jesus predicted. When it came time to wash the disciples' feet, apparently Peter was the only one who said no. In the court-yard, he buckled under the accusation of a lowly servant girl and later, after the Resurrection when Jesus was extending his forgiveness and giving Peter future instructions, the disciple seemed more concerned about what would happen to John. Peter had not learned that making comparisons can be one of the most self-destructive things any of us can do.

But we don't read very far into the New Testament book of Acts to see that something happened to Peter. Following the disruptive events that had shaken his life, Peter the resister had made significant changes. The timid disciple warming himself by a fire in the High Priest's courtyard had become a powerful and courageous orator. The impulsive young fisherman had become the rock that Jesus predicted. The insensitive, seemingly self-centered Christ follower had become the mature, compassionate, Christ-honoring apostle-leader who endured suffering and encouraged the persecuted church with supportive and sensitive letters.

What changed Peter? Second Peter 1 gives us some answers. Peter was changed by a *Person*. He had been changed by his time with Jesus, perhaps without even knowing that the change had taken place. The influence of Jesus is mentioned three times in the opening two verses of this part of the Bible. Peter also was changed because of the divine *power* (see verse 3) that came upon him as he stopped resisting and allowed the Holy Spirit to lead in his life and give the strength and wisdom available to all believers. In addition, Peter became aware of God's *promises* (see verse 4) of divine protection and direction. Surely these sustained him in times of difficulty when he might otherwise have been tempted to return to his old patterns of behavior.

If we read through the book of Acts or through Peter's epistles, we see that Peter also had *passion*. His unswerving determination to spread the good news kept him focused and consistent as he helped lead his fellow believers through the changes that shaped and sometimes threatened to destroy the early church. Peter had a God-given *plan* (see verses 5-9) for strengthening people and preventing them from being ineffective and unproductive despite the change they encountered. And in all of this, Peter had a healthy *perspective* (see verses 12-15). He knew that his life would not go on forever, but he determined to be faithful and productive as long as he had energy and the opportunity to serve. Empowered by the Holy Spirit and looking to his future both on earth and in eternity, Peter overcame his resistance to change.

Coaches help others do the same. We have seen that dealing with resistance may be a common coaching challenge, but you also will encounter embracers and innovators who need coaching as well. These people are eager to make changes, but sometimes they fail to realize the negative impact of their strong opinions and enthusiastic but self-defeating actions. They need to see the importance of introducing their changes with less gusto, more sensitivity, and the expectation that things may take longer to implement than they would like.

Christian coaches are best able to help people through change when threat is reduced, the change process is not rushed, there is respect for traditional values (especially biblical values), the client or protégé feels support, and there are practical guidelines on how to make things happen. This is illustrated in another event in Peter's life.

After Jesus returned to heaven, the Christian message spread and the early church was growing, but only among the Jews. Perhaps there were few of these young believers who thought that the good news from Jesus could be for Gentiles as well as for Jews. So apparently God decided to be the change agent for their thinking. He worked with a Gentile soldier and Peter, who was both a believer in Jesus and a practicing Orthodox Jew. The events recorded in Acts 10 and 11 were more significant than a change in habits or behavior. God was initiating a major paradigm shift that would change the world forever. Consider how God worked a cataclysmic change that came through two humble men. This gives us a model for bringing change especially in groups.[24]

Start where people are and don't be reluctant to start small. An angel came to Cornelius. A vision came to Peter. Both men were receptive. Both were men of prayer. Both were open to new possibilities, although neither was expecting what followed. If you know Bible history, you will remember how God used such individuals as Abraham, Nehemiah, Esther, Mordecai, Jonathan, Joseph, and a host of others. Most rose from obscurity to become leaders God used to bring change.

It is often easier to change something small than to make a big, dramatic change. A bigger change often is not only harder to make but might create severe disruptions in areas other than the ones that need to be changed.

— BILL O'HANLON, author of
Change 101: A Practical Guide to Creating Change in Life or Therapy

Let people ponder and challenge the idea of change. Peter was so perplexed by the vision that he resisted but God repeated the message.[25] Change is more likely to be resisted if objections are ignored or minimized. God dealt directly with Peter's objections.[26] A few days later, Peter was in the role of convincing the people who had gathered in the home of Cornelius.[27] Once again, God showed his approval.

Don't rush the process. It could be argued that the events in the lives of Peter and Cornelius moved quickly, but it took a while for the believers back in Judea to accept the idea that the Gentiles had received the word of God. Peter was criticized for his actions, and he needed time to explain the situation to the skeptical Jewish Christians. As they saw the evidence of what had happened, their objections were answered and they began praising God for the changes.[28]

Every coach, progressive leader, forward-looking pastor, and other change agent knows that change is rarely accepted as quickly and easily as the believers in Jerusalem appeared to agree with Peter and the people who had accompanied him to Joppa.

We return, then, to where we began this chapter: Change is difficult. Walking with people through change can be challenging and often draining. But coaching is all about change, and few things match the fulfillment of seeing another person catch a new vision, be willing to change, and take action to move forward.

Twenty years from now you will be more disappointed by the things you didn't do than by the ones you did do. So . . . sail away from the safe harbor. Catch the trade winds in your sails.

— MARK TWAIN, author

CHAPTER 4

COACHING: IT'S A LOT ABOUT LEADERSHIP

SOMETIMES I THINK I'm a leadership junkie. I like to read about leadership, hang out with leaders, and coach leaders. Sometimes I go to leadership conferences to hear inspiring leader speakers, meet leaders and wannabe leaders, get an update on the latest leadership books, and come home with practical tools and a fresh injection of leadership enthusiasm.

In all of this activity, I have noticed some things about leadership that conference speakers and books rarely mention. For example, I can't remember a speaker ever saying that the people God chooses to lead might not be the people who go to big conferences looking for ways to be leaders. Moses was in his eighties, taking care of sheep and probably not thinking about leadership when God tapped him. When Samuel went to anoint a new king for Israel, apparently nobody thought of David. Even his own father paraded seven sons past the prophet but overlooked their kid brother, the future King David, and left him out in the field with the sheep.[1] When God wanted to impact the city of Nineveh, he chose Jonah to lead this effort even though the first thing the chosen leader did was run away.[2] When a leader was needed to bring the gospel to the Gentiles, God selected Saul of Tarsus, who probably was as unlikely a choice in those days as someone in the Taliban would be in ours. Of course, God never selects leaders who are incapable of leading, but if you look through Scripture and church history, it seems that he often picks people to lead who might not appear to be the best qualified. Many aren't in the best place to lead; others aren't interested. Sometimes he picks leaders who resist the leadership mantle. At other times he chooses people like you, who pick up a book on coaching without expecting to encounter anything about leadership. Even so, all the leaders he chooses are sensitive to his voice and eventually open to his direction.

In the leadership books and conferences, I've also noticed that most messages are geared to people who already have leadership positions — people such as pastors, youth leaders, business executives, and heads of denominations or organizations. It is logical to focus on this group because they comprise the majority of attendees at leadership conferences. But this focus on people who already have leadership positions gives the impression that to be a real leader, one must be at the top of some church or company, leading a team, or holding some other leadership position.

For several years, I had one of those leadership positions: I was president of the American Association of Christian Counselors (AACC). The association began as a group of several hundred counselors, but God built it to almost fifteen thousand members before I left. Assisted by a small team of dedicated employees, I labored with my partner in this venture, working hard and for several years with little or no pay until the organization developed strength, prominence, and impact. At that point, I handed my duties over to a new president and left to pursue other things.

Even though my departure was voluntary, I was surprised at how this decision impacted my life and perspective on leadership. I needed to keep out of the way and let the new administration take over, but it was hard to not be making AACC leadership decisions after this had been my role for almost a decade. I began to think that I was no longer a leader because I did not have a leadership position or a role in any organization.

Then one day I saw these words flashing on the sign in front of a hotel: *Leadership is action, not position.* Had others been with me, they would have seen that I was visibly shaken. I can't describe the impact, but I felt jolted by a charge of hope. It was true: I could still be a leader even apart from the organization I had left. I could be a leader apart from any organization. What now seems so obvious was at that time a powerful insight. It is possible to be a leader even without an office, an assistant, a public platform, a leadership job, or a title.[3] For the first time, I realized that I could lead through writing, speaking, teaching, parenting or one-on-one mentoring. We can lead through the way we live, and certainly we lead through coaching. More than that, if you are a coach, you already are a leader. The two go together.

COACHING AS LEADERSHIP

The tie between coaching and leadership is seen most clearly in the world of sports. Athletes and coaching clients alike seek coaching because they want help in reaching some specific objective or in dealing with a challenge.[4] In sports, the coach is more of an expert, inclined to tell and direct. In executive and life coaching, the coach asks questions and gives feedback that stimulate action. In both settings, coaching involves leading. Both types of coaches are committed to vision casting, goal setting, improving performance, helping others overcome doubts, boosting confidence, building skills, and moving people toward their ideals.

Warren Bennis, founding chairman of The Leadership Institute at the University of Southern California, is a world-renowned expert on leadership. After observing and writing about leaders for half a century, Bennis concluded that they all share one characteristic: They all have a guiding purpose and overarching vision. "Leaders have a clear idea of what they want to do — personally and professionally," Bennis has written. Leaders "have the strength to persist in the face of setbacks, even failures. They know where they are going and why."[5]

Leaders also have integrity. Their word counts. They can be trusted to do what they say they will do. They decide in their minds what is right, and that is how they act consistently. They rarely talk about their morals and standards of conduct because they don't have to. They live what they stand for and everybody sees this, starting with their closest friends and family members. Leaders without integrity are tolerated and sometimes even appreciated for their contributions, but they are never trusted or genuinely respected and they don't have much credibility. "As long as you have credibility you have leadership," according to professional football coach Don Shula. "To me, credibility is your people believing that what you say is something that they can hang their hat on — something they can immediately believe and respect."[6] That's more than credibility–that's integrity.

There are other marks of leadership. Competence, respect, trust, and courage are on most lists. Several mention humility. Great leaders are not puffed up and impressed with their own importance. Speakers at conferences often talk about a leader's commitment, focus, and ability to accomplish goals and engage others in the process. Research studies show that some leaders advance in their careers because they are effective self-promoters. But the best leaders are able to get things done, develop effective teams, and accomplish the goals of their organizations.[7]

These kinds of leaders are not mass-produced. They aren't turned out by reading books or going to conferences, even exceptionally good conferences. They are not leaders because they complete a course in leadership, are elected to leadership positions, or are given leadership responsibilities in their companies, churches, or teams. They are not even good leaders because they have enthusiasm or good character. Good leaders are people who have learned how to think, see situations clearly, and be creative even as they are flexible. And their ultimate success as leaders is marked by both their ability to produce new leaders and the effective performance of these leaders when they are on their own.

A leadership coach is someone who walks with you
for a season, steps into your life and provides feedback,
a different perspective, and when appropriate,
a nudge to move you forward.

— ALAN NELSON, coach, editor of *Rev!* magazine

Good coaching is a key element in producing good leaders. The coach might not be a reader of leadership books or an expert in leadership development, but the best coaches know how to use coaching skills to lead clients so they reach their personal or organizational goals. Coaching is a significant, increasingly emerging form of leadership and leadership training. If you aren't willing to be a leader, then don't be a coach.

DEVELOPING LEADERS THROUGH COACHING

Steve Ogne and Tim Roehl are Christian leadership coaches, committed to developing and empowering leaders, especially younger and postmodern leaders, so they can lead and empower others. Ogne and Roehl have concluded that most coaching is overly focused on performance, productivity, and effectiveness. While these are important, especially in corporate settings, the emphasis on success and achievement tends to squeeze ministry and leadership development out of the picture. Instead, these two coaches focus on the personal transformation of leaders in four key areas: the leader's *calling, character, community* involvement, and connection with the secular *culture.*

A leader who has clarity in his or her call to ministry is better equipped to call others to ministry. A leader of strong character is better equipped to develop character in others. A leader who has experienced authentic community can help others create it. A leader who regularly engages the secular culture through service and authentic relationships with pre-Christian people can lead others to do the same. . . . A coach must focus on the four areas, helping the leader *clarify calling, cultivate character, create community,* and *connect with culture.* As a coach you may focus on only one of these areas in a specific coaching appointment, but you must routinely touch each of these areas in every coaching relationship.[8]

This is one perspective on an area known as *leadership coaching.* The term is widely used but often confusing. Some writers use leadership coaching as a synonym for coaching in general; the emphasis is on coaching, but not much is said about leadership. Many coaches appear to equate leadership coaching with executive or corporate coaching, the general coaching of corporate and business leaders.[9] A few writers view leadership coaching as a way to develop leaders.[10] In this book, leadership coaching refers to the coaching of leaders and potential leaders around two specific issues: enabling leaders to become better leaders and equipping leaders to use coaching as a way to lead others.

Leadership coaching is a twenty-first-century
means to maximizing a leader's potential by helping
him or her to climb further up the hill.

— ALAN NELSON, coach, editor of *Rev!* magazine

A large Christian organization approached me several years ago for help with leadership development among their staff members. I was invited to partner with the organization's leaders to develop a program that would have two purposes. First, we provided coaching for a select group of staff members so they could be better leaders. Second, we agreed to teach these same staff members how they could use coaching principles to lead others. After selecting the program participants, we provided one-on-one coaching for each of them, along with periodic leadership seminars the organization provided. In addition to coaching these staff members about their own personal and career issues, they were coached about ways to lead their staff using coaching methods. Regrettably, we were not able to measure our progress systematically, but the participants were enthusiastic about the experience. Of special interest were the reports that came spontaneously from the people who were being led by these newly trained staff member leaders. "You lead us differently since you got into coaching," one person told her supervisor. "You listen more, show us more respect, and get us more involved in the whole work process." When coaching principles were used to lead, there were clear benefits. The same has been true of other groups in which leaders have been coached and taught to use coaching skills as they lead. Coaching can be used to build leaders, and coaching can be a skill that leaders can learn to use as they lead others.

This brings us back to the work of Steve Ogne and Tim Roehl. These authors recognize that traditional and corporate leadership differs from the leadership perspectives and approaches of those who are younger and postmodern (the terms are not synonymous). We will return to these differences in a later chapter, but the widespread acceptance of postmodern perspectives is changing the way we lead, teach, do ministry, and live. In established corporations and traditional churches, we can equip leaders using older forms of top-down leadership, but emerging generations need, even insist on, a different approach. It is an approach that is more open to coaching as a way to teach and a way to lead.

Coaching paradigms that are overly focused on
performance or productivity are particularly suspect
and resisted by young and postmodern leaders,
who value relationship, authenticity, and community.

— STEVE OGNE and TIM ROEHL, coauthors of *TransforMissional Coaching*

Maybe you've heard about the leadership styles of buffalo and geese. Apparently, buffalo are extremely loyal followers of one leader. They do what the leader directs them to do, follow where the leader goes, and stand around waiting for the leader to show up.[11] Back in the frontier days, the early settlers learned this quickly. If they could kill the lead buffalo, the whole herd would stand around, easily slaughtered because they didn't know what to do when their leader was gone. For many years, human leaders were taught to be like those buffalo leaders. Everyone assumed that the leader's job was to cast a vision, plan, command, coordinate, give directions, and remain firmly in control. The best leaders were thought to be those with the clearest visions, the most brilliant plans, and the most faithful followers. These leaders had power and prominence. They also worked long hours, surrounded by noncreative followers who compliantly did what they were told, no less but certainly no more. Some of those old buffalo-type leaders got pretty stodgy. They didn't change much, and when they reached retirement age, they refused to let go. They didn't want to give up the power, and they didn't have anyone trained and trusted enough to replace them.

Probably you know some buffalo pastors, buffalo professors, and buffalo business leaders who are still around. Most aren't very relevant, innovative, or forward-looking. Most of the people who surround them are aging buffalo and compliant followers who aren't much interested in lifelong learning, creative thinking, or changing the status quo. They may have little interest in coaching.

In contrast, today we have a different approach to leadership. Effective leaders are less like buffalo and more like geese. If you've ever had geese on your property, you're aware that they are dirty, noisy, aggressive animals. But they know how to fly. There's always a leader of the V formation, but that leader changes frequently. Maybe every goose knows how to get where it wants to go, but they fly in formation, changing direction and changing leadership. Goose-inspired leaders equip and encourage everybody in the organization to lead. These leaders are not afraid of change or creativity, not concerned about power and control when they're moving forward; they are more into teaching responsibility, competence, character development, and ownership. When the appointed lead goose in that organization goes on vacation or retires, there are others with the ability and energy to take over. Modern leadership is goose-style leadership.[12]

Leadership is not about what you know or about telling others what you know. Leadership is about building teams, encouraging innovation, thinking strategically, removing obstacles, creating vision, and taking risks. Leadership has little to do with one's title or position. It has everything to do with being trustworthy, supportive, sensitive, aware of trends, willing to try new things—and even cheering when your protégés and followers soar past you to leadership positions of their own. All of this is easy for me to put on to paper and for you to read. It is harder to put into practice. That's where coaching comes in. Coaching empowers leaders to fly like geese and to teach others how to do the same.

LEADING THROUGH COACHING

It is unlikely that anyone really knows how many leadership books, training seminars, and academic courses appear every year. Their content and approaches are different, but their goals are similar. They all exist to equip people to improve in their leadership capabilities.

Of course, there is no formula for leading. A lot depends on the environment where one leads, the personalities and styles of the leaders and followers, the stage where one is in life, and the defining events that shape leaders and their leadership. In a fascinating book on leadership, Warren Bennis contrasted leaders and followers under age thirty (he called them the *geeks*) with those who were over age seventy (the *geezers*). At both ends of the age spectrum, there was one quality that appeared to determine success. That quality was the capacity to adapt. Bennis defines adaptive capacity as "the defining competence of everyone who retains his or her ability to live well despite life's inevitable changes and losses." For example, "people who aged most successfully had great adaptive capacity, continued to learn new things, and looked forward, with eagerness and optimism, rather than dwelling on the past."[13] These adaptive individuals would seem to respond best to coaching, to using coaching methods when they lead, and to being led by leaders who understand and use coaching.

The single best way to develop leaders is to take people out of their safe environments and away from the people they know, and throw them into a new arena they know little about. Way over their head, preferably. In fact, the more demanding their challenges, the more pressure and risk they face, the more likely a dynamic leader will emerge.

— BRUCE WILKINSON, author of *The Dream Giver*

As coaching grows in influence and as more people understand what coaching involves, how will we see coaching and leadership tie together more closely? The following are a few observations.

Coaching and leadership are about experience. In teaching others to coach and to lead, I have learned one core principle: Coaching and leading are skills that are learned through experience and practice. We can learn whenever we experience the coaching and leadership that comes to us from others. Then we practice what we have learned and apply this to others. Occasionally, I have been asked to give a seminar on coaching in which participants would come expecting to hear lectures, take notes, and perhaps watch a demonstration but without participating in any active way. I almost always turn down these invitations. Training seminars need to impart information, but for maximum effectiveness the participants need to see coaching demonstrated, experience coaching themselves, and then practice their coaching skills with others. After taking several leadership courses, one of my friends concluded that the information was helpful but "the best way to become a leader is to lead." The same could be said about coaching. Training can be of inestimable value, being coached by an experienced coach is of great importance, but ultimately the best way to become a coach is to do coaching.

2. Coaching and leadership are about relationships. Coaching is a special kind of relationship. It is a partnership with a purpose — a partnership marked by honesty, respect, trust, and movement toward mutually accepted goals. Good coaches exhibit the servant leadership that Jesus demonstrated in his life and talked about in Matthew 20:20-28. Good leaders do the same. They don't lord it over people, exercise controlling authority, or jockey to get positions of prominence. Great leaders, like great coaches, are great servants.

Coaching is the most important servant leadership element in helping people accomplish their goals.

— KEN BLANCHARD, BILL HYBELS, and PHIL HODGES,
coauthors of *Leadership by the Book*

Coaching is one of the clearest forms of servant leadership. Like a servant, the coach seeks to understand and assist the person being served. That person comes with dissatisfactions about the current state of his or her life, and with uncertainty about how to move forward into the future. The coach meets these desires by being a knowledgeable, vision-sensitive person who comes alongside to provide a consistent guiding relationship. If you want to be a good leader, learn to be a good coach. If you want to be a good coach, learn to be a servant leader who understands and builds relationships.

3. Coaching and leadership are about character and competence. The business world has many stories of highly intelligent, highly skilled executives who are promoted to leadership positions only to fail on the job. In contrast, there are stories of men or women with solid abilities but less-than-outstanding technical skills who are promoted to similar positions in which they soar. One major difference is that effective leaders have a high degree of what we now know as emotional and social intelligence. According to psychologist Daniel Goleman, who has done the seminal work in this area, *emotional intelligence* is the ability to manage ourselves and our relationships effectively. It is based on four fundamental capabilities: self-awareness, self-management, social awareness, and social skills.[14] Somewhat different, but overlapping, is the concept of *social intelligence.* This describes people who consistently show empathy, attunement to the thinking and emotions of others, organizational awareness, the ability to influence groups or individuals, a commitment to developing others, inspiration, and a commitment to supporting and building teams. When highly effective leaders are compared with those who are average, the best leaders have higher degrees of emotional and social intelligence.[15]

Goleman has shown that these characteristics are connected to circuitry in the brain. Drawing on research from neuroscience, we can understand what happens to the brain of another human being when a leader, counselor or coach shows empathy and genuine interest. The neural circuitry in two people becomes attuned so there is an interconnectedness within their brains. People with social intelligence develop cognitive circuitry that connects them with others. This enables leaders and coaches to be more effective and competent in their work.[16]

Of special interest is the finding that emotional and social intelligence are not genetically ingrained, possessed by some people and never possible for others. Instead, leaders and others can learn and grow in social intelligence and develop new social circuitry in their brains. One of the best ways is to spend time with "a living, breathing model of effective social behavior," a person who is at ease in showing genuine people skills. Individuals can grow as effective leaders and sensitive counselors when they "directly experience, internalize and ultimately emulate" what they observe in people who possess the interpersonal skills that reflect their own social intelligence.[17] It will come as no surprise that coaching has become a prime way through which leaders and others can grow in emotional and social intelligence. This, in turn, has potential to increase effectiveness, cultivate character, and contribute to a greater sense of community.

4. Leadership and coaching are about community. It is unlikely that Peter Drucker ever considered himself to be a coach. But this undisputed leadership expert was so forward-looking that he probably anticipated the rapid rise of coaching long before the rest of us even thought about it. Unlike other men who lay aside their creativity and retire to their rocking chairs or golf carts, Drucker didn't quit. In his nineties and going strong, Drucker described the crucial task of leadership: bringing unique people together to define their future objectives so they can move forward in partnership to reach their goals.[18] To me this sounds a lot like coaching.

In his years of research and consulting with businesses, Drucker saw a fundamental problem with society that the business world has been unable to solve. From its beginnings back in the days of the Industrial Revolution, business and industry pulled people out of community. The business and corporate worlds streamlined efficiency, increased productivity, and improved quality control, but in the process they destroyed communities. People today come together to work, produce, market their wares, and make profits, but often they leave their hopes, aspirations, and deepest values at the door. In times of downsizing, outsourcing, shifting values, and postmodernism, they don't find a sense of community at work. Often they don't find it at home, either. There is only one place to find real community, Drucker suggested. That is in the church. Whether big, mid-sized, or small, churches are powerful because they can pull people together, give them opportunites to serve, and connect them with others. What Drucker called "pastoral churches" waste no time regretting a changing world or lamenting the past. Instead, they see change and even hopelessness as opportunities for ministry and a better future. The people in these churches, like the leaders and managers of business, "are consistently people with a vivid sense of the reality of the human world. They rarely have time for theories that don't produce results."[19]

Whatever your opinion of large churches, perhaps you will agree that change often takes place in community. Christian coaches recognize that people commit their lives to Christ as individuals. Each of us experiences individual personal transformation within, guided by the Holy Spirit. But we serve in and through community, and often that is where we are most stretched and challenged. It is in community that we experience our greatest growth. It comes through the relatively few and sometimes declining megachurches but also through thousands of smaller, less visible, people-sensitive congregations. The best of these know exactly what they believe and don't budge on their biblical foundations. But they also are aware of their cultures and gear their approaches to ministry and evangelism accordingly. They know that people today have a host of problems that rarely are solved apart from community, so these churches reach out in compassion. Church growth was a hot topic only a few years ago, but now we know that church health is a better concept. When churches are healthy and helping others to be the same, growth happens.

Coaching will become the model for leaders in the
future. Coaches teach, mentor, and empower. I am certain
that leadership can be learned and that terrific coaches . . .
facilitate that learning.

— WARREN BENNIS, respected leadership expert,
founder of Leadership Institute, University of Southern California

I am a believer in pastoral counseling and Christians being trained as people helpers. Every congregation has people who are innately skilled as sensitive, compassionate, effective caregivers. But this kind of problem-focused caregiving is not for everybody. Some in the church, especially those with a little more experience and maturity, fit better in the role of encouragers, motivators, and guides for others in their life journeys. Someday, "training Christians to coach" could become common parlance and a valuable ministry in the church, even as coaching has become so widely accepted in the larger secular community. Someday, people in the church will recognize that leadership and coaching go together, coaches really are leaders, and the most effective Christian leaders also possess and use coaching skills.

Leadership coaching takes time, commitment, and energy. Coaching does not always work within the corporate world, where everybody is too busy, too intent on producing results, too driven toward career success, or so self-focused that there is little energy or interest in guiding another person to reach his or her potential. Leaders who coach must make the hard decisions that enable them to carve out time to invest in others. It is very difficult to develop this coaching mind-set and put it into practice if you lead a large church or other organization, are busy managing a family, or are consumed with a hectic career. Indeed, there is evidence that successful, high-energy leaders rarely can make the change to become successful coaches.[20] So a whole new mushrooming profession is arising to give coaching—usually for a fee—to those who seek guidance from someone with greater experience and objectivity. These professional coaches are outsiders whom people inside the business world are consulting frequently. Business coaching like this may not happen much in the church, but the broader issue of life coaching has tremendous potential. It can help transform Christian leadership away from top-down managing and into the coaching style of leadership that Jesus demonstrated and that emerging generations appear to prefer.

PART 2

THE SKILLS OF CHRISTIAN COACHING

CHAPTER 5

THE COACHING
RELATIONSHIP

MANY YEARS AGO I started a magazine, and for eight or nine years I was its editor.[1] At the beginning it was an exciting venture with lots of room for creativity, vision, and opportunities to work with innovative people. We knew that start-up magazines often fail, but we were determined to move forward enthusiastically, blazing trails where nobody else had gone. Not many weeks passed before we discovered the difficulty of acquiring quality articles, attracting advertisers, retaining subscribers, getting good design and layout, reaching deadlines, and insuring that each issue would be fresh. One of our biggest challenges came from finding authors who could write without being dull. Around that time I heard that a large magazine publisher used college students to screen incoming articles. Most often the submitted manuscripts were rejected if the first paragraph did not grab the reader's attention. Good articles (and book chapters such as this one) have to connect with people, grab their interest, and keep readers engaged from the first sentence until the end.

The same is true of good coaching. When they approach coaching, some people are not sure what to expect. Some feel intimidated and nervous about meeting the coach for the first time. Like the writer of an article, the coach must take the lead in connecting with the client, building rapport, and establishing a solid relationship. In the following chapters, we will discuss the skills that coaches need to acquire and the process of coaching. Before any of this, however, some rapport-building groundwork needs to be covered.

First, the coach must take the lead in building a *partnership* that will persist and keep the client engaged over time. Second, you need to be clear about the *assumptions* that you and your client bring to the relationship. This includes clarifying what coaching is and what it is not. Coaching is guaranteed to stall if you try to move forward with unclear or different assumptions. Third, near the beginning it can be helpful to *explore the issues* that the client wants to discuss. All of this will enable you to *evaluate the client*, including the pros and cons of working together. Finally, at some time you will need to have an *agreement* about how the coaching will take place. Together these five issues become the core of the coaching relationship.

BUILDING THE PARTNERSHIP

Co-Active Coaching is the title of a respected and widely used coaching textbook.[2] The title and the book both communicate that coaching "involves the active and collaborative participation of both the coach and the client"[3] working together as partners, in conversation, focused on the client's self-discovery, dreams, and goals. Coaching is an alliance between two equals that exists for the purpose of meeting the client's needs and goals. According to the authors of *Co-Active Coaching*, this is not about the coach's expertise, advice, or solutions. The coach does not impart wisdom or give direction. Instead, the coach's job is "to help clients articulate their dreams, desires, and aspirations, help them clarify their mission, purpose, and goals, and help them achieve that outcome."[4] This coequal, coactive focus is what sets coaching apart from counseling, mentoring, consulting, and other more top-down relationships. Coaching begins with the development of a trusting relationship characterized by mutual respect and commitment.

Sometimes relationships like these come naturally and quickly. From the beginning, there is a chemistry between two people. They think alike, have similar perspectives, and quickly develop mutual trust. More often, relationships have to grow over time and partnerships must be cultivated.

Imagine that your life is overstretched, overworked, and overly pressured because of a demanding schedule that you can't seem to control. For you that may be so close to reality that it won't be hard to imagine! You want your career to grow but feel trapped in your current lifestyle and sense that you are close to burning out. Then one day a coworker mentions that he had been helped by a coach and suggests that maybe you should do the same. Your first inclination is to resist. Business magazines describe how personal coaches, some with minimal qualifications, have swarmed the corporate landscape, promising to help people organize their lives, orchestrate their careers, define their dreams, and get on top of their treadmill lives.

You wonder if seeing a coach means admitting that you are in desperate need of help. Perhaps you don't realize that the opposite is more likely to be true in the business world. Frequently, coaching is recommended to people who have obvious potential for growth and promotion but who could use a coach's skills to reclaim control of their time, sharpen their working styles, reexamine values, move through transitions, improve their management skills, grow as leaders, or come to grips with ongoing change.

If you are the coach for a person like this, you have to build trust from the start, especially if your new client is resistant, skeptical, or hesitant. It is easier to work with people who seek coaching voluntarily because they come with positive expectations and a willingness to cooperate. When someone has been sent by an employer or encouraged to come by a pastor or spouse, you must work a little harder to reassure him or her that coaching can be a positive growth experience. Explain that it doesn't involve therapy and isn't about coercion or judgmental evaluations. Your goal is not to become a lifelong mentor. As a coach, you are more like a personal trainer who walks alongside another person and guides until action is taken and goals are reached. Yours is a partnership with a purpose. Usually this message is accepted readily, especially as the relationship grows.

Whatever the reason for coming, the new client needs to sense your respect and commitment to working in a partnership that will make things better. This relationship will grow stronger if you show warmth, understanding, a positive mind-set, and consistent support. According to one early textbook, support constitutes the most distinguishing feature of coaching. No other feature is as important, especially at the beginning. It touches all other parts of the coaching process.[5]

Careful, focused listening is the best way to show support and build the coaching bond. If you have taken courses in counseling, you know that listening involves more than hearing words and understanding what the speaker is saying. When you listen actively, you keep aware of what the person might be communicating with his or her body language, tone of voice, and gestures. Have you noticed how people come alive with enthusiasm when they get to a topic that excites them? They lean forward, gesture more than usual, show more emotion, and speak with a different pitch or speed. Watch for these changes. Watch as well for tears, pauses in the conversation, and expressions of frustration. Ask yourself what they might mean. Resist the temptation to offer your observations or advice, but periodically ask for clarification, gently inquire about inconsistencies, and try giving a summary of what you are hearing. Then ask if your understanding is accurate. In addition to building a stronger relationship bond, the goal of listening is to clarify issues and get an accurate understanding of the client's concerns and perspectives.

In all of this, show curiosity. When you are curious, you move beyond gathering information and encourage the client to be more honest and open. By showing curiosity, you indicate your genuine interest in who the person is, not just in what he or she thinks or wants or says. Curiosity in coaching is more than aimless conversation. Instead, curiosity helps the coach understand the client, who then is enabled to begin thinking about his or her values, perspectives, lifestyle, goals, feelings, and relationships. When coaches express curiosity, they often draw attention to the issues of greatest concern to clients.

For coaching, curiosity may be the quality that starts the process and the energy that keeps it going. The most effective coaches seem to be naturally curious and to have developed their curiosity in a way that opens doors and windows for clients. . . . Authentic curiosity is a powerful builder of relationships.

—LAURA WHITWORTH, KAREN KIMSEY-HOUSE, HENRY KIMSEY-HOUSE, and PHILLIP SANDAHL, coauthors of *Co-Active Coaching*

The best way to show curiosity is to ask questions. You can preface some of these questions with the words "I'm curious about . . ." Other curious questions would be:

- "What's working for you?"
- "What have you tried in the past that has worked?"
- "What hasn't worked?"
- "How would you know if you made a wise decision?"
- "What would it look like if you reached your goal?"
- "What works for you?"
- "What is scary about this?"
- "What fires you up?"
- "What would you like to get out of this relationship?"

These are not questions that ask for information about issues such as the client's job, education, or background experience. Instead, these are thought-provoking inquiries that build the relationship because they make people feel respected, understood, appreciated, and heard. Keep in mind that curiosity questions avoid issues that are only for the coach's personal interest or that are none of his or her business, such as personal questions about sexuality or finances. Be supportive so the person does not feel that you are prying or criticizing.

What do you do if, despite your best efforts, the client remains defensive or resistant? This happens most often at the beginning, when a person who seeks coaching does not know what to expect or a person feels annoyed because he or she has been pushed into coaching. Try not to ignore such resistance or let it distract you. Instead, acknowledge the person's concerns and try to address them. Sometimes people fear that the things they say to the coach will be passed on to others, so they need to be assured of confidentiality. Others expect the coach to criticize or give advice. Explain that coaching is a team effort in which the coach and person being coached work together to clarify issues and come up with solutions.

People don't resist change; they resist being changed.

— DEAN ORNISH, best-selling author of books
on wellness and lifestyle change

Rapport building like this may take time in the beginning, but it lays the foundation for a longer and more beneficial coaching relationship.

CLARIFYING ASSUMPTIONS

Most people seem to appreciate and even enjoy the coaching process. It gives them a chance to pause in their busy schedules and focus on themselves. One of my clients expressed this concisely. "What we are doing is so strange," he said. "I spend my days trying to meet the needs and expectations of other people. I never take time for reflection. For the first time, you are giving me permission to talk about me. What's more, you seem really interested. It's invigorating, but I have to tell you it's also scary."

Might some Christians also think this is wrong? Aren't we supposed to be less self-centered? Isn't our society too "me-oriented," too concerned with our own comforts and successes, too disinterested in the needs of people who are poor or unevangelized? Why should anyone spend time with a coach, talking about himself or herself?

Maybe the best response to these questions is not an answer but a person: Jesus. Think about his walk with the two men on the road to Emmaus. He gave them the gift of his presence and interest. He listened to them as they talked about their confusion and uncertainties. He asked probing questions, gave his support, pointed to the Scriptures, and certainly encouraged and motivated them when he revealed who he was. Their first reaction was to hurry back to Jerusalem to tell others about their experiences, but this only happened because Jesus had coached them through their grief and bewilderment.[6]

These two men had no prior opportunity to wonder what it would be like to spend time with Coach Jesus, but the people you coach might have more curiosity, sometimes mixed with uncertainty. You can deal with this at the beginning as you talk about mutual expectations and assumptions. Table 5-1 gives some commonly accepted assumptions about coaching. You might even want to make a copy of this list and discuss it with the people you coach. In doing this, you deal openly with the questions that many bring to coaching, setting the stage for your ongoing work.

Table 5-1

ASSUMPTIONS ABOUT COACHING
Coaching:
■ Is a collaborative partnership between the coach and person being coached
■ Involves dialogue rather than advice giving, discipling, or therapy
■ Is built on trust, integrity, self-discipline, and accountability
■ Is results-oriented, focused on reaching goals
■ Discusses weaknesses and obstacles but emphasizes strengths and positive change
■ Assumes that people are resourceful and able to set goals and reach them
■ Lets clients define and move toward their goals with God's help and the coach's assistance
■ Helps people reach their peak performance
■ Assumes that life is integrated — we cannot assume that one's work, family life, personal history, spirituality, or lifestyle can be put into neat compartments
■ Embraces change as something that is always occurring, sometimes confusing, often positive, and usually growth producing

Perhaps the key to this list is the reality of the ongoing change that we discussed in chapter 3. Somebody has suggested that there are really only two rules in this life. Rule number one is that God is sovereign. Rule number two is that everything changes except rule number one.

Unlike us, God is always in control, even when we don't understand his ways. And he never changes.[7] This does not mean that he is rigid or uncaring. It means that he is dependable, consistent in his character and promises. His Word is the solid rock on which we can build our lives.[8] He created the world through his Son and he holds it all together.[9]

But ours is a world in which change is always occurring, including the changes that God works within the lives of his followers.[10] Many of the changes are beyond our control; some of these are confusing, disruptive, and upsetting. Other changes come because we make them happen, especially the changes in our attitudes, actions, and ways of living. Of course, permanent damage can result from foolish decisions and unwise changes. But changes also can be positive, leading to growth, life fulfillment, and greater joy. The small changes we make, sometimes with the guidance and encouragement of a coach, can be little steps that lead to bigger change.

At times change is ongoing and not even noticed. Depending on how fast you read, in the time it took to get through the previous page, the earth moved twenty-two hundred miles, ten quarts of blood pumped through your body, sixteen babies were born in the United States, and nine Americans died.[11] The role of coach (and sometimes the role of the counselor) is to help people be aware of change, learn how to cope with change, and make changes that will improve their lives, their careers, their families, and their world.

EXPLORING THE ISSUES

One of my long-term coaching clients is a graduate student in a local university. I first met him in Asia, where he was born and grew up, but we reconnected when he arrived in my neighborhood. Lam (that's not his real name) is bright, articulate, and looking at a promising future. When he arrived to begin his graduate studies, he was determined to get his business degree and then return home to live and work near his parents and other family members.

But then Lam got married and, a year or so later, became a father. After that, he was offered an attractive job that could start now and grow into something larger once he gets his degree. There also are job opportunities back home, so Lam feels guilty about the possibility of forsaking his home-land. But he knows as well that his wife has some hesitations about moving across the Pacific, and they both agree that, all things considered, it would be better for their daughter if they remained where they are. As we have met over the past few weeks, Lam has struggled with the decision about whether or not to go back to his homeland, even as he has debated about whether or not to take the job that has been offered here. During the course of our coaching, he has faced several decision points relating to his doctoral training, including the unexpected retirement of his advisor and the difficulty of finding a new faculty mentor to guide his work.

Lam is a man who has faced several choice points during our coaching time. When we first met, he wanted to get unstuck from the opposing pulls of staying here or going back home. As we have talked, other issues have arisen, some unexpectedly. Coaching is like that. From session to session, different issues might arise. What concerns the client originally may not be a topic that persists all the way through. Even so, there is value at the beginning in getting a sense of the client's concerns. Sometimes I use the following four questions as a mental guideline to help me understand the client's issues. In the process of asking questions like these and listening carefully, it is easier to assess whether or not this is a client that I might be able to walk with in coaching.

How might coaching be useful? This asks about the client's concerns. It lets the coach determine initially what the client wants or hopes to achieve from coaching. The best way to determine this is to ask what the client would like to talk about or achieve.

Where are you now? This is an assessment question. You will remember that coaching helps clients get from where they are to where they want to be. Assessment helps determine where the client is now. This is an effort to determine the client's present status and readiness for coaching.

> If you can't figure out what the person's current situation is,
> don't go ahead and start coaching them.
>
> — EVA WONG and LAWRENCE LEUNG,
> coauthors of *The Power of Ren: China's Coaching Phenomenon*

How would you like things to be different? Here is a quick focus on goals and hopes. This is not always clear at the beginning, but there is value in determining the client's vision or dreams for the future. Ask how the client will know when his or her goals have been reached and what would indicate that the coaching has been successful.

What will get in the way? This is a question about obstacles. Clients often know what will derail their progress, especially if they have been derailed in the past. Sometimes the biggest obstacles are in the clients themselves. Often I ask clients how they might sabotage our work and what I or we might do to get past that. This is an effort to assess the feasibility of entering into a coaching arrangement and uncovering roadblocks that might get in the way of progress.

EVALUATING THE CLIENT

It's a core assumption of coaching that the client sets the agenda and that the coach is nonjudgmental and as nondirective as possible. We will see that coaches challenge their clients at times and sometimes make suggestions. But effective coaches are not in the business of judging, condemning, directing, evangelizing, or preaching to their clients. Many coaches are determined to avoid evaluating anything that the client says or decides to do, so why do we suggest that coaches need to evaluate the suitability of clients for coaching?

The answer lies in the recognition that some people who want coaching are not good candidates for coaching. For example, potential clients who struggle with emotional issues usually are advised to get counseling first and turn to coaching later. This is because coaching is built on the assumption that clients are relatively free of psychological issues that could distract from or undermine coaching. If troubling personal problems do exist, it is best if these can be dealt with before coaching begins. Most coaches are not trained as counselors, and in some countries, including the United States and Canada, it is illegal to counsel without a license except in ministry, academic, and a few other selected settings. For this reason, coaches routinely refer potential clients to counselors and delay the start of coaching to another time.

Even if there are no distracting emotional issues, coaches know that some people are not likely to benefit from the coaching relationship. Coaching is most effective when clients:

- Want to grow and change
- Have made efforts to change within the past year
- Are willing to consider new assumptions, values, behaviors, and ideas
- Are capable of thinking about the future
- Are open to learning
- Are committed to making changes
- Are open to God's leading in the coaching process

- Are willing to learn from others
- Are not afraid to take risks
- Are willing to restructure their lives if necessary
- Are "in sync" and appear to have good chemistry with the coach

Appendix B is a reproducible questionnaire that might help the coach or client determine the likelihood of success for the proposed coaching relationship.[12] Ideally the coach and potential client should decide together about whether or not to move forward with the coaching. Sometimes the coach, the potential client, or both have discomforts about the possibilities of working together. By discussing these concerns, misunderstandings can be removed, potential obstacles can be dealt with, and the path may be cleared for a productive coaching partnership. If there is disagreement or a lack of rapport between the client and coach, usually it is best for the client to find a more compatible coach, hopefully with input from others. When coaching does not seem feasible, it is both respectful and ethical to terminate the relationship before time and money is wasted on coaching that is not likely to be effective or productive.

AGREEING TO WORK TOGETHER

Let us assume that by now you are convinced of several things. You know that coaching can be effective, that coaching is not the same as counseling or therapy, and that coaching is not a new fad name for mentoring or discipleship. You understand that coaching goes beyond corporations, health clubs, or athletic teams. Hopefully you are open to viewing coaching as a powerful way to help people get from where they are to where they would like to be. You value the potential of Christian coaching to help people find God's direction for their lives and get to where God wants them to be. Perhaps you have been coached as a client or you have taken training that equips you to coach others. Maybe you are beginning to believe that you can be a coach.

So you decide to give it a try. When you sit down with your prospective client for the first time or talk on the phone (coaching sessions often take place by phone or the Internet), what do you do besides panic? First, you can raise some questions and listen carefully, putting into practice many of the suggestions that have come in the preceding pages. Second, you can build a more formal coaching agreement or alliance.

Talking together about the coaching. At the beginning, your immediate goal is to get better acquainted with the person who wants coaching and allow that person to know you. Ask your new coaching client to tell his or her story. You can get the process started with questions like these: "What is going on in your life?" "What would you like to be different?" and "What would you like us to talk about?" As you find out where the other person is in life, you may want to ask how he or she got there. There is no cookbook way to do any of this, although later we will give some tools to help you move the process forward. Your big purpose is to listen carefully, respectfully, and with genuine interest. Express curiosity. Try to discover why the client wants coaching. What are the things he or she would like to change? What might be preventing this change? What is working in the person's life and what is not? How would the person being coached like things to be different?

Keep in mind that for many people, this will be a brand-new experience, having somebody listen who is genuinely interested in their life experiences, hopes, and dreams. Like Jesus when he talked with the woman at the well in Samaria or the woman caught in adultery,[13] you might not agree with the client's lifestyle, past decisions, or goals, but at this stage listen with a spirit of love and try to withhold judgment or disapproval. In doing this, you are building trust, often in people who have felt betrayed and unappreciated. You are demonstrating respect and showing that you are real.

Earlier I mentioned that one of our daughters works with kids in some of the poorest and roughest parts of Chicago. One of her jobs is to go into high schools and teach about abstinence. This is not the message many of these love-starved and sexually active young people want to hear. But the kids love her. She attributes this to the grace and power of God, but I wonder if Jan's effectiveness also has to do with her showing these kids acceptance and respect. In public school settings, she is not allowed to mention anything about God, but she shows Christ's love for the kids. They know she is genuine and accepting, even though her skin color and background experiences are different from theirs. At times she has to be tough, especially when some of the people in her classes push the limits, but they all know she cares. Often she challenges them to hope for a brighter future, and they know she believes this is possible. Of course, you are reading the words of a proud dad who, I am sure, has no bias. But it is not surprising to anyone that many of Jan's days are filled with informal coaching.

Your coaching may be more formal, built around a more structured coaching agreement, often termed the *coaching alliance*.

The coaches' work truly depends on the quality and
kind of alliances that are created. We want to create

> alliances that empower clients, support their learning
> and development, clarify . . . and fully embrace the
> partnership between coach and client.
>
> — PATRICK WILLIAMS and DIANE S. MENENDEZ,
> Institute for Life Coach Training

Building the coaching alliance. Early in your first meeting, you should look for an opportunity to explain what coaching is and what it does not involve. You may want to bring a copy of the fact sheet that appears in the back of this book as appendix C. With some people, you may need to say how coaching differs from counseling. It can be helpful to share a little about your background, how you got into coaching, and what qualifies you to be a coach. Discuss the assumptions about coaching that you both bring and try to find some consensus so you have similar expectations. Make it clear that you will keep everything confidential. Decide when you will talk together, how often, and what to do if either person has to cancel an appointment. Talk about boundaries, such as whether or when you can be called at home. If you are charging for your coaching services, discuss billing and payment.[14]

Whether or not you are expecting payment, at some time in the first session, most coaches present their potential clients with a written agreement that describes the services and clarifies the relationship. This prevents misunderstanding and potential conflict. It states what coaching is, what you and your client can expect, and how you will proceed. Appendix D gives an example that you can duplicate or adapt for your own use. Probably you will want to discuss the form with your potential client and sign a couple of copies, one for each of you. At that time, you also may want to give out a copy of the "Getting to Know You" personal information form that appears in appendix E and ask the person to complete it before the next session. Usually I distribute this at the beginning of coaching, sometimes even before the first meeting. After the form has been filled out, we can go through the questionnaire together and use it as a guide for getting to know the new client.

The initial session may be the client's first opportunity to talk with a coach, so the conversation needs to be a model of the kind of coaching demeanor, respect, and openness that is likely to come later. Before or after the first session, many coaches send a welcome packet that clarifies the nature of coaching and gives a written indication of what can be anticipated. There is no formal guideline for developing a welcome packet, but it can be helpful to include the following:

- The previously mentioned fact sheet that describes the nature of coaching and answers commonly asked questions.
- A contract or agreement similar to appendix D that includes a statement about coaching policies and procedures. This might include comments about confidentiality, fees, missed appointments, the coach's background and training, contact information (including the coach's telephone number and e-mail address), and policies about coach-client contact between coaching sessions.
- A client data form, similar to the "Getting to Know You" questionnaire in appendix E.
- One or two assessment measures, such as the "Graph of Life" in appendix A.[15]

COACHING AND THE RACE OF LIFE

Two of my friends once described their adventures running in a big-city marathon. They had trained for weeks and arrived early for the big event. As they waited for the race to begin, they stood in a big crowd of runners with rain and a cold wind cutting into their faces and chilling them through their skins and to the core of their bones. In describing this, their story of self-torture seemed to get more dramatic. I wondered if this were some kind of a macho thing, a type of male bonding, an attempt to prove to themselves that their middle-aged bodies still had plenty of energy and testosterone. Sipping lattes in a comfortable coffee shop months after the race was over, they were reveling in the memories and pleased that they could boast about making it to the finish line — albeit long after the race winners had received their accolades and headed home. My friends almost persuaded me to try it myself next time around, but the more rational half of my brain prevailed and I quickly rejected the idea. To me the whole experience sounded as crazy as hitting yourself in the head with a hammer because it feels so good when you stop. Not everybody agrees. Every year, hundreds of thousands of men and women rise to the marathon challenge. Most know they have no chance of winning, but they are invigorated by the training and motivated by thoughts of making it to the end.

If you are familiar with the Bible, you know how often the writers compare life to running a race. Like the marathon that my friends ran, every life race has periods of extreme discomfort interspersed with excitement and joyful enthusiasm. At times, we all encounter hindrances that impede our progress. Some of these are beyond our control, but many are obstacles we create for ourselves.

In the race of life, for example, we get sidelined when we allow our bodies to get out of shape, our relationships to cool, or our spirituality to be neglected. Sometimes we're distracted from running strong because we look at the crowds, hoping to get applause or wanting to prove something to our critics. Worse is the tendency to keep our eyes on the competition, habitually monitoring the progress of others until we lose our own direction. "Making comparisons is the cardinal sin of modern life," according to business guru Jim Collins. "It traps us in a game [or race] we can't win. Once we define ourselves in terms of others, we lose the freedom to shape our own lives."[16] Think about it: Most of these distractions to the race of life come out of our own insecurities. They show that we need to prove our worth to ourselves.

Strip off every weight that slows us down, especially the sin that so easily trips us up. And let us run with endurance the race God has set before us. We do this by keeping our eyes on Jesus, the champion who initiates and perfects our faith.

— Hebrews 12:1-2

Racers also need objectives. Coaches or their clients can never win the race of life when we have no idea where we are going. If you forget your goals or if you have no life goals, you will lose your motivation and ultimately your direction. It's almost guaranteed! Maybe the writer of Hebrews had this in mind when readers were told to "throw off everything that hinders and the sin that so easily entangles, and let us run with perseverance the race marked out for us" (Hebrews 12:1, NIV). Life runners need to keep their eyes fixed on Jesus. Pleasing him is the Christian's ultimate goal, and when our sights drift elsewhere, we are more likely to grow weary, lose heart, and stumble.[17]

Coaching teaches people how to train for the race of life. It helps clarify their goals and remember where they are going. A sensitive coach can help others avoid the hindrances and entanglements that can slow them down, trip them up, or prevent them from reaching their goals. In a marathon, the runners know the location of the starting line, have the course mapped out, and know where they are going. The location of the finish line is no mystery. This is not so in the race of life. The runners you coach have already started the life race, but often they don't know where they are and have no idea where they are going. Most sense that something is missing from their lives, but they might not know what it is. They might have some awareness of their inner resources and abilities, but they lack clear goals and don't know how to find them. An effective coach can help by developing and using the basic coaching skills discussed in the next chapter.

CHAPTER 6

THE COACHING SKILLS: LISTENING, QUESTIONING, RESPONDING

FOR A NUMBER of years, I have led seminars and taught classes about coaching. The best of these have involved eager students who want to learn and are willing to devote the time and effort needed to develop coaching skills. Recently, I taught a class like this in which the participants were young, creative, businesspeople in a fast-developing country overseas. They had been chosen for the training because of their potential to develop as leaders in the company where they worked. To introduce them to coaching, I had three or four private coaching sessions with each of the participants so they could experience the process as clients. Each of them filled out two or three assessment tools, read an earlier edition of this book, participated in a two-hour introductory session that I led a few months before training, and arrived one Monday morning eager to begin our weeklong intensive training program. Overall, the training went well. Most of the course participants were enthusiastic about coaching when the training was over. The majority continued to use their new coaching skills, and at last report, most are growing in their knowledge and competence as coaches.

As their instructor, however, I made one major mistake. Usually I teach coaching to graduate psychology students or to people trained as counselors. With their therapeutic capabilities and experiences, these counselor-students know about helping skills, such as listening and asking questions. They are ready to jump into the coach training and build on their therapeutic training and capabilities. In contrast, the students in my overseas class lacked these people skills. All had shown significant promise as businesspeople, but they had never heard about effective listening skills. They were overly eager to give directive advice, but they had no training in how to ask powerful questions that would stimulate client thinking and insights. These were people who led by giving directions to subordinates who faithfully followed. When they were asked to do practice coaching sessions, my students were not very good at listening. One young man (who subsequently is becoming a very effective coach) listened to his client briefly and then launched into a lecture about what should be done, ending the monologue by raising his voice and telling the client, "Do what I just said. That's what you need. It will be good for you!"[1]

Before my move into coaching, I taught counseling skills to graduate students, pastors, and other people in different parts of the world. Most of these men and women wanted practical help for learning how to counsel. Some of the students in those classes wanted manuals that would give them recipes for dealing with depression, anxiety, or other psychological problems. They came looking for concise guidelines for dealing with each issue that might surface. Instead, they learned that there are no quick-fix formulas for dealing with real needs in real people. They learned that competent, never-fail, "how to do it" counseling books or seminar tapes do not exist.

Coaching cookbooks don't exist either. Every person is different and so is every coaching situation. Each must be approached in a slightly different way, although coaching at its core reduces to four parts: getting an understanding of where each person is at present, focusing on what he or she wants in the future, finding ways get there, and overcoming obstacles that get in the way. There are many skills coaches can use to enable clients to make this journey, but three are of prime importance: listening, asking powerful questions, and responding. These seem like simple skills, but they can take a lifetime to learn. Even so, beginning coaches can acquire the essence of listening, questioning, and responding. The coach who masters these is the coach who is most likely to be effective and successful.

LISTENING ATTENTIVELY

Here is one of the first lessons of any basic counseling course: Effective counselors listen. The same is true of effective coaches, especially when we are trying to build relationships, clarify issues, and understand the people who have come for coaching. Listening is central to every part of coaching, although it is never more important than at the beginning.

Whenever we ask questions or give advice, we tend to feel in control, as if we are moving the process forward. In contrast, listening demands more patience, concentration, and focus as well as the ability to keep quiet. Listening is a gift to the person being coached. It demonstrates respect, interest, and a willingness to connect and understand.

But listening can be demanding work because the listener's mind has to be active and focused enough to absorb the content and implications of what the client is communicating. In addition to hearing words, effective listeners also try to hear what is below the surface: the person's feelings, insecurities, self-doubt, conflicts, and discouragement. Coaches listen, as well, for things that are positive, such as the client's hopes, strengths, values, passions, competencies, excitements, and dreams. And in listening to what is being said, there is value in listening for what is being left unsaid. The overall goal is to hear the content of what the person is saying and pick up the attitudes, frustrations, and dreams more implied than stated.

Everything in coaching depends on listening — especially listening with the client's agenda in mind. . . . To be listened to is a striking experience — partly because it is so rare. When another person is totally with you, interested in every word, eager to empathize, you feel known and understood. People get bigger when they know they're being listened to. They feel safer and more secure, as well, and can begin to trust. It is why listening is so important to coaching.

— LAURA WHITWORTH, KAREN KIMSEY-HOUSE, HENRY KIMSEY-HOUSE, and PHILLIP SANDAHL, coauthors of *Co-Active Coaching*

Coaches use at least three kinds of listening skills: informal listening, active listening, and intuitive listening.

Informal listening. This is most common. It's the way we listen in our everyday conversations. Often it involves listening for facts or information. If we want to get the weather or the latest football scores, we turn on the radio and listen to what we hear. A friend describes something that has happened or talks about plans for the future and we listen. This kind of communication can be flat and emotionless, like a boring professor giving information to students who dutifully take notes. At other times, we can hear enthusiasm, opinions, sales pitches, or emotions such as anger or sadness.

This most basic kind of listening tends to be passive. The listener may or may not pay attention, show interest in what is being said, respond appropriately, or notice the emotions and attitudes being expressed. In casual conversation, listeners focus on the words but also notice what might be communicated in the speaker's posture, gestures, tone of voice, and pace of speech. In general, it involves listening to what another person wants to communicate. It is listening for what you need to know.

Assume that you are buying shoes in a department store. You ask for the location of the shoe department and listen to the directions. When you get there you ask the salesperson about the type of shoes you want, their cost, whether your size is available. This is listening for facts. It lets you listen for what you need to know, for what applies to you. At the beginning of a coaching relationship, the coach might ask the potential client to give his or her name or to give a telephone number and e-mail address. The focus of this informal kind of listening is to get information.

Active listening. Most of us know the experience of talking to another person who clearly is not listening. Talk to your kids or your spouse, preach a sermon, teach a class, describe your vacation to somebody who didn't take the trip. You might talk enthusiastically with gestures, raise your voice, or even use PowerPoint slides if you are giving a public address, but at times you will be met with blank stares from people who look at you, maybe nod in agreement but have minds that are far away, thinking about other things. At times like this, you are talking but you aren't being heard.

Active listening is different because the listener concentrates on what is being said, pays close attention, shows awareness of the speaker, and sometimes makes brief comments or asks clarifying questions. The speaker knows that the message is being heard. By their posture, attitude, and focus, active listeners show that they want to be in tune with the person speaking. Sometimes known as attentive listening, this involves hearing what is said but also learning from what is communicated through posture, energy level, tone of voice, expressed attitudes, and indications of emotion. Active listening involves more engagement with the communicator, not simply absorbing facts. Unlike informal listening, in which people listen for information that applies to themselves (like hearing the location of a shoe department in some store), active listening has a focus on the speaker. In coaching, the listener is fully engaged in concentrating on what the client is expressing.

The difference between informal and active listening sometimes appears when coaching students are beginning their training. When there is informal listening, the coach pays partial attention but is more concerned about what he or she will say next or how the coaching will progress. In active listening, coaches are not focused on themselves. Instead, they are able to concentrate completely on what the client is communicating. When coaches show this kind of listening, their clients relax and often open up to share more honestly and intimately.[2]

Intuitive listening. This entails a high level of concentration and awareness. The coach listens for inconsistencies that the client may not notice in the conversation, attitudes and emotions that come out with the words, topics that resurface at different times, values and beliefs that can be discerned from what is being expressed, dreams for the future, frustrations, and self-sabotaging behavior that prevents progress. This is the kind of listening that asks, "What am I really hearing, behind the words?" It is listening that is alert to changes in energy and enthusiasm of voice pitch that may either unite or show contradictions between the client's verbal and nonverbal expressions.[3] This is listening that seeks to be aware of the client's agenda, and that often involves intuitively picking up what the client really has in mind.

Rod was a pastor who had seen several churches grow but whose congregations never seemed to get beyond about two hundred people. He had attended enough pastoral conferences to know what steps needed to be taken to get his church growing again, but he never did anything other than talk about his hopes for the future. One of his past congregations had even hired a church consultant who gave suggestions that everybody affirmed but never were implemented. In describing this to a coach, Rod mentioned that he lacked a seminary degree. The coach noticed that whenever it was time to take a step forward, Rod found a reason to back off so there could be more analysis, reflection, and prayer. By listening intuitively, the coach began to see a pattern in Rod that undermined his own stated goals and appeared to come out of his deep-seated belief that pastors without seminary degrees were not good enough to head larger churches. In listening to Rod, the coach heard attitudes and noticed repeated behavior patterns the pastor never mentioned and apparently had never noticed in himself. There would be little likelihood of church growth until Rod could be helped to get beyond his own self-sabotaging beliefs and attitudes.

Good coaches **HEAR** what clients say by listening for their:

H — *hopes* and dreams about how things could be better

E — *energies* and passions that appear to inspire the person,
    but also the energy drainers that pull the person down

A — *attitudes* and *abilities* that impact how one sees potential for the future but that might be squelched or frustrated in the present

R — *routines*, habits, and ways of doing things that might need to be changed

Obstacles to listening. Coaches who are sensitive listeners are able to focus on their clients and avoid obstacles, such as the following, that interfere with listening effectiveness:

- **Thinking about the next question.** We referred to this earlier, but it is worth mentioning again because at times it can be the experience of every counselor and coach, especially at the beginning. The client is talking but the coach is not paying full attention because he or she is trying to think of the next question to ask. Coaching is a conversation between two people. It is not a question-and-answer type of interview, but when a coach is afraid of silence or of not having anything to say in response to a client, the coach starts to focus on creating new questions and fails to listen carefully.
- **Looking for problems, pathology, and past experiences that are creating present difficulties.** This is important for counselors who want to root out problems. In contrast, *coaches* are listening to understand the client's current status, values, strengths, and hopes for the future. When we listen for symptoms, causes of problems, or possible solutions, we are counseling, not coaching people to get from where they are to where they want to be.
- **Distractions.** Sometimes coaches don't listen because they are tired or preoccupied with their own problems or things that need to be done. Early in my career, I had a weekly appointment with a counselee that was scheduled immediately after the mail arrived. Sometimes I would get distracted by the mail on my desk so that I did not give complete focus on listening. For me at that time, my mail was more interesting than the client, and I communicated that by my actions.
- **Biased listening.** All of us have biases and stereotypes that we impose on other people, including our clients. If a client arouses some prejudice in the coach, then the coach listens through the filter of that prejudice. Awareness of these biases and active resistance to them

help get the listening back on track, past the stereotypes, and focused on the client.

- **Interruptions.** This may be more likely when you have a very boring client or somebody who is unusually interesting. The coach may interrupt to stimulate the dull conversation or jump in to be part of an interesting discussion. At times, a coach will make observations or give suggestions, but when coaches start telling stories or giving advice, they have stopped listening and have moved away from coaching.

As a general rule, it is widely assumed that coaches should spend up to 80 percent of their time listening. A minority of the coaching time is spent encouraging clients, giving feedback, making observations, and asking focused questions.

ASKING FOCUSED QUESTIONS

Some of the highest-paid people in the television industry are the men and women who interview well-known personalities. These interviews can be very dull if the questions are vague and the show's guest is allowed to ramble. But superstar interviewers in the media have learned the fine art of getting to core issues through focused questioning. They show that the skillful use of good questions is like the techniques of a brain surgeon: incisive, revealing, and powerful.

I'm not a media interviewer, and probably you aren't either, but we all can learn to focus on issues by making good inquiries. The simplest of these are questions that give information. Here are examples:

- What brought you to coaching?
- What would you like to accomplish in coaching?
- What major things are happening in your life right now?
- How would you like your life to be different one year from now?
- What is getting in the way of these changes or goals?
- What things in life are most important to you?
- What are some ways in which you procrastinate?
- If we worked together, what are some ways in which I could be most beneficial to you?
- What should I avoid because it would not be beneficial?
- If we worked together, in what ways might you undermine or sabotage your coach? How would a coach stop you from doing that?

- Describe some things you have tried in the past to accomplish your goals.
- Tell me some things that really excite you.
- Before we start, it would be helpful if you could describe any insecurity you might have about coaching.

These are discovery questions. They help the coach discover things about the client, but they also do more. They show that questions can stimulate thinking and can enable clients to notice or discover things about themselves. You will notice that none of the questions in the above list starts with the word *Why* (like "Why do you want coaching?") This is because *Why* questions tend to encourage analytical thinking, excuses, defensiveness, or trips to the past. It is better to ask questions that start with *What, When, How, Who, or Where*. Notice as well that some of what appears in the listed examples does not even take the form of a question. The last three are statements rather than questions. But these still have the same impact as questions. They ask for information and clarify issues but in more indirect ways that add variety.

Experienced questioners sometimes use what are known as prompts or probes that may not even be full questions or statements. Sometimes these are brief phrases picked up from what the client has said. They are interjections from the coach that clarify issues further and help the client focus. Here are two examples:

Client: "My wife and I get along pretty well most of the time."
Coach: "Most of the time?"

Client: "Whenever I start working on the novel I'm writing, something gets in the way."
Coach: "Like what?"

Most coaches avoid questions that can be answered by one word or by a simple "yes" or "no." Sometimes those types of questions give useful information, but almost always it is more beneficial to ask what are referred to as open-ended questions. These are questions that can be answered only with longer, more revealing answers. "Were you born and raised in Canada?" is a yes-or-no question that does not give much information; an open-ended question would be something like, "Tell me a little about where you were born and grew up."

What does the coach do? Mostly ask questions. In no
model of coaching does the coach provide the
answers or attempt to solve the problem.

— JOSEPH O'CONNOR and ANDREA LAGES,
coauthors of *How Coaching Works*

Powerful questions. Coaching is not about giving advice or telling people what to do. Coaching is about asking powerful, thought-provoking questions that stimulate fresh thinking, lead to new insights, clarify issues, and challenge clients to explore innovative possibilities. Powerful questions arise out of what the client has said to the coach and what the coach has heard through active and intuitive listening. Powerful questions often catch people off guard and cause them to stop and think. You know you have asked a powerful question when the client pauses, ponders the answer, and maybe says, "That's a good question." It's good because it can lead clients to explore possibilities they may not have considered before or reframe an issue and look at it in new ways. Powerful questions are like prods that stimulate reflection and often keep the person talking. Here are examples:

- What would success look like to you?
- What would make you a better dad?
- What makes this so threatening to you?
- I'm curious—what is the payoff to you for staying in this job that you hate?
- Where is the evidence that you are a bad manager?
- Tell me some things that you could do to improve your situation.
- What gets in the way so that you don't do these things?
- In what specific ways has this impacted you?
- Give me some examples.
- This seems to be something that concerns you and nobody else.
- You say you work all the time because you have a new boss, but you worked all the time when you had a different boss.
- What's going on?
- How would your dad have handled this situation?
- How will you know when you've been successful?
- What you just said sounds inconsistent to me.
- What could you do to align your actions with your values?[4]

As he talked to people, Jesus sometimes used powerful open-ended questions that stimulated reflection and became the basis for his teaching. He asked his disciples who they thought he was (see Luke 9:20). In Luke 18:41, he asked the blind man, "What do you want me to do for you?" When they were in a desolate place facing thousands of hungry people, the disciples asked Jesus how the crowd would be fed. Jesus answered with a statement: "You feed them" (Matthew 14:16). That must have been like a powerful question in that it forced the disciples to think of ways to evaluate and find solutions for the dilemma they faced (see Matthew 14:15-21).

Some powerful questions or question-like statements are inquiries about what goals the client hopes to reach. Other questions focus more on where the client is at present and leave talk about taking action until later. In either case, as clients look into themselves, they get a clearer perspective on their lives and situations, are able to glance into the future, experience glimmers of hope, and recognize that progress is possible.

Don't ask random, aimless questions. Ask questions that have substance to them, questions that help clients get somewhere. Ask questions that challenge the client to think.

— GERARD EGAN, author of *The Skilled Helper*

Less-powerful questions. At times, all coaches ask questions that are not very powerful. These are questions that do not move the action further. They don't help clients think more clearly or talk more freely and constructively. Often these less-powerful questions start with *Why*. They may be long and complicated, or they ask for information that may satisfy the coach's curiosity but do nothing to stretch the mind of the client. The best questions focus on the client; poorer questions draw attention to the coach. Good questions can stimulate a variety of possibilities in the mind of the client; less-powerful questions are manipulative or leading questions intended to shove the client to answer in a way that the coach thinks is best. Good questions deal with specific behaviors or experiences; less-powerful questions are more general. "What one thing could you do now to help you become more successful?" is specific. "What are your thoughts about being successful?" is more general and less powerful.

Good questions pick up on the language, terminology, and metaphors the client uses; poorer questions often miss what the client has said. Recently,

I asked a client to evaluate our first coaching session. He responded that it was good to "get all these issues on the table so we can see them and deal with them." In subsequent sessions, I asked about what was on the table and how we could take some things off the table. In that, we were using the client's imagery.

The miracle question. Steve de Shazer was one of the founders of solution-focused brief therapy, an approach that bears a lot of resemblance to coaching. It might even be argued that contemporary coaching largely grew out of the work of de Shazer and his colleagues.[5] In the 1980s, de Shazer suggested a simple but provocative question that has been used by coaches and many therapists ever since. Here is what now is known as the miracle question: *Assume that tonight you went to bed, and before morning a miracle occurred so that when you woke up, your problem was solved and everything you wished for had taken place. How would things be different?* This powerful question lets the client imagine and visualize how things could be different. It clarifies possibilities and can become the basis for creating specific goals toward which the client can work. The miracle question loses its power if it is asked too often. But it is a question that can jolt people out of their feelings of being stuck and can stimulate creativity, hope, and possibilities for action.

As the coaching progresses, there will be less emphasis on clarifying issues that concern the client and more focus on action steps that can be taken. Even here, the essence of coaching is good questioning, but the focus may shift from where the client is to how he or she can be closer to the stated goals. Here are examples of questions that promote action:

- "What have you tried in the past that was successful and that might be useful to try again?"
- "How could things be different?"
- "What are your options?"
- "What's next?"
- "When do you see signs of progress?"
- "What will you do now and when will you do it?"

Homework questions. Some powerful questions require time for reflection. They may concern issues that could benefit from a longer period of introspection, journaling, contemplation, or in-depth discussion with a close friend. Homework questions are requests for action that the client can ponder and do in such a way that the results can be discussed later. Once more, we can look at examples:

- "Between now and our next session, what could you do to get a clearer perspective on how you could build better rapport with your employees?"
- "You have said that relaxing is hard for you. In the next week, maybe you could take time to make a list of things you could do to relax."
- "You want to be spiritually mature, but you stated that you don't know what that means. How would you respond to the idea that you should take time next week to reflect on what that would look like for you?"

Knowing how to ask questions is the first core
skill of coaching. Questions support clients,
guide their attention, and . . . give the client new
perspectives as they open up possibilities.

— JOSEPH O'CONNOR and ANDREA LAGES,
cofounders of International Coaching Community

Listening and questioning can be discussed separately, like we have done in this chapter, but in practice they are woven together. Sometimes people get new insights when they stop long enough to talk about their lives with somebody who is willing to listen. By listening and questioning, the coach becomes an outside observer who is able to see issues in more objective ways so that people being coached can be helped to do the same.

GIVING RESPONSES

Some time ago, I was invited to do coach training with middle managers of a company in Canada. In preparing for my workshop, I wanted to know as much as I could about the company, their corporate culture, and their expectations for the training we were planning. I learned that the company had prepared for my visit by putting all of the participants through a seminar on "coaching for performance," with an emphasis on two key issues: how to set effective goals, and ways to provide results-based feedback. That seminar leader clearly understood the importance of listening and asking powerful questions, but he knew as well that coaching involves a lot more, including the goal setting and giving feedback that his company had emphasized. Even as they ask questions and listen, effective coaches use a number of responding skills to keep the process moving. Most of these are adapted from the counseling professions, in which skills such as the following, among others, have been used and refined for many years.

Verbal responses. Coaching is a conversation that involves more than a coach's routinely asking one question after another and listening. Like any good relationship, there are brief statements to indicate that the coach is listening. "Uh-huh," "That's great," "Sounds scary," "Wow," "Keep going," "Tell me more," or "What an experience you have had!" are all indicators that the coach is engaged with the client. If the coaching is done face-to-face, the coach also communicates through body language, gestures, eye contact (at least in some societies), and posture. Don't rule out the occasional use of humor, and be alert to metaphors, terms, and figures of speech that the client might use and that you could use as well. For example, if the client talks about getting the big picture or feeling bowled over, try to use that language later because it helps to connect.

Encouragement. Clients often come for coaching because they feel stuck in some difficult situation and not sure how to move forward. Encouragement gives hope, especially when the coach can notice and point to behavior and events that are positive and worth acknowledging, complimenting, or endorsing. Encouragement motivates and stimulates growth but only if it is sincere, non-patronizing, and not used so often that it distracts the client from making difficult decisions or taking needed action steps.

Feedback. This is one form of encouragement, but it involves more. Feedback is most effective when it deals with specific issues, includes affirmation, and points to ways in which there might be further action or improvement.

Self-disclosure. It is wise to be cautious about this because of the ease by which self-disclosing coaches can shift the focus to themselves and away from the clients. Even so, clients can be both encouraged and challenged if they hear brief, specific, not-too-frequent accounts of the coach's own experiences, behaviors, and feelings. Effective self-disclosure is relevant to the client's situation and should not be long-winded or presented as a subtle message that says, "This is how I did it, and this is how you need to do it too."

Focusing on values, strengths, spiritual gifts, passions, attitudes, energy drainers, and past experiences. All of these can have a great bearing on how clients make decisions or get unstuck. They form part of the core of who we are but often are overlooked unless the coach specifically brings them up. One of my clients was stuck in his career and not succeeding like he wanted. When we looked at his values, we found that in the company where he worked, success was not likely to come unless he violated his core values.

He moved to a different line of work when he recognized the conflict between what he valued and what his employer was expecting him to do. By raising issues like these, coaches motivate their clients to look into areas where there can be fruitful discussions and effective decision making.

Immediacy. Sometimes there is value in discussing what is happening at that moment in the coaching or in the coach-client relationship. Usually this is done when the coaching process seems stalled and there can be value in discussing what is getting in the way and what can be done to get the process back on track. Here are examples:

- "I sense that we are bogged down right now. Maybe we should stop briefly and see if we can find out what is getting in the way, what's going right, and what is going wrong."
- "I am wondering, at this point, if we are getting sidetracked onto other things and avoiding the issues you wanted to discuss."

Brainstorming. This has been defined as "a creative collaboration between client and coach with the sole purpose of generating ideas, possibilities, and options."[6] Usually the coach proposes this and makes the first suggestion about what might be done. Both the coach and the client agree that there are no bad ideas in brainstorming and that "out-of-the-box ideas and outrageous possibilities" are completely acceptable. Sometimes one clearly unrealistic or unfeasible idea might give rise to another possibility that is more workable and worth exploring more seriously. The only caution is that the coach should not use this as a way to push his or her ideas or preferences so that the client senses manipulation.

Debriefing. Usually this happens after a client has tried something and returns to give a report. Do you remember when Jesus sent out the disciples two by two and they came back to describe their experiences? They all went off to a place called Bethesda and Jesus listened, encouraged, made an occasional comment, and perhaps asked questions as they reflected on what they had learned. We don't know this for certain, but perhaps the group encouraged one another, talked about what they might have done but failed to do, and discussed how they might take a different approach next time. That is debriefing. It is the kind of discussion that often generates new ways for moving forward.

Requesting. Coaching assumes that the client most often has the ability to come up with the best ideas for dealing with problems and other issues. When we tell another person what to do or give advice, this tends to be ignored or forgotten in contrast to insights and action plans that the individuals come up with on their own. Even so, there are times when the coach has some observations or experiences that could be helpful to the client. Rather than telling clients what to do or making suggestions, coaches more often ask for permission or make requests that go something like this: "I have had some experience about this that might be helpful. Would it be okay if I shared this with you for what it's worth?" Another example might use the "request" terminology: "I would like to request that before our next appointment you take time to think through and write down possible next steps that would enable you to get your promotion." The client can give one of three responses, all of which are acceptable: He or she can say no, say yes, or give a counter offer. If the client agrees to the request, the results can be discussed in a subsequent coaching session.

BEING A COACH IS NOT LIKE BEING A PROFESSOR

I confess that I was intimidated when I took my first practicum as a coaching student and was expected to coach a fellow student in front of the class. I had had the experience of being coached, taken several coaching classes, read a shelf-full of coaching books, taught coaching classes of my own, coached a variety of people, and had even written the first edition of this book. But when I decided to get additional training, I found myself in the practicum class.

From my perspective, the first coaching that I did in that class was a disaster. My classmates were not as hard on me as I was on myself, but even the instructor joked about it as the class progressed and my coaching improved. I clearly remember the biggest observation that came from that initial class experience. Even though I knew about listening, questioning, and responding appropriately, when I got in front of the class, I reverted to being a teacher because that is what I do best and most naturally. In debriefing my coaching, the class instructor said that in my coaching, I talked too much, gave advice, and told too many stories. "You don't sound like a coach. You sound like a professor," she said. It was a reminder that we need to lay aside some old habits when we become coaches. Teachers need to stop acting like professors in their coaching sessions. Counselors need to stop doing therapy or looking for the causes of problems in the past. Pastors need to avoid giving advice and acting like spiritual directors, at least while they are using the principles of coaching.

Coaching is a unique kind of relationship with its own set of skills and ways of relating to others. It even has its own theories and approaches to the coaching process. The next chapter introduces you to a basic four-point model of coaching that can guide your work as you get more involved in coaching.

CHAPTER 7

COACHING MODELS AND ISSUES

NOT LONG AGO, a friend and I were driving a few hundred miles to a conference. Before leaving, he turned on his GPS, hit a couple buttons, and followed the machine's instructions to our destination. A voice alerted us to route changes that were ahead, corrected us when we missed a turn, warned us if there was road construction that might get in the way, kept us informed of the miles we had covered and the miles that were ahead, and got us to the conference site easily and without any hassle. Back in the old days, in the first years of the twenty-first century, we would have called ahead for directions, struggled with a big paper map that was impossible to refold, or perhaps downloaded a printout of our route before leaving home. Road maps still exist, of course, and they can be very useful, but now we have a variety of ways for finding where we are and how we get to where we want to go.

There are no GPS devices for coaching, at least not yet, but there are maps to guide our coaching journeys. Instead of calling them maps, we refer to them as coaching models. Some are more detailed or complex than others, but they all seek to accomplish the same purpose: giving coaches a guideline for their work. Just as we can drive to a destination without using a road map, it is possible to coach our clients without using a model. But both road maps and models can make the journey smoother, prevent unnecessary detours, and help us avoid dead-end streets. Unlike many road journeys in which a group of drivers would all travel the same superhighway to reach the same destination, each coaching trip is unique and takes its own distinctive route. For this reason, coaching models are general more than specific, but they give coaches and their clients useful signposts to guide the journey.[1]

When I go on a trip, I don't spend much time comparing road maps. I find a guide that appears to be helpful and I take off. That probably shows why I've resisted the temptation to summarize a number of coaching models and have decided, instead, to focus on one that works.[2] Doing so lets us pack together what we have considered thus far and get on the road to coaching others.

The coaching road map that we will use in the following chapters has four parts.[3] This makes it easy to remember. Some coaches reproduce this model and share it with their clients near the beginning of the coaching. Doing this lays out the overall purpose of coaching and lets everyone see where the process is going. Other coaches keep the model in their minds, using it to guide their coaching work.

The next six chapters will discuss the model in detail with suggestions about how it can be used. To set the stage for this, we begin by looking at an overview in the next few pages. Please keep in mind that this is a big-picture general guideline for coaching. Most often a coach would not deal with all four parts of the model in one session, and coaching will not always move systematically from one point to the next like the hands on a clock. Sometimes you might skip from one point to another or you might decide to go back to an earlier stage. As you read, ponder how this all could apply to you, even before you start applying it to others.

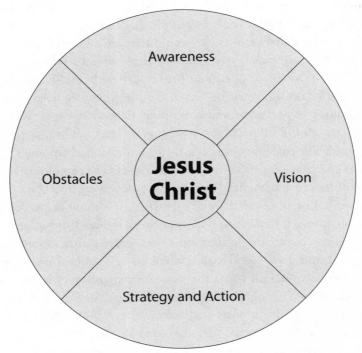

Figure 7-1 The Basic Christian Coaching Model

Before you start around the circle, it is assumed that you will have begun to build a partnership with the person you will coach, clarified what coaching involves, and reached an agreement for how you will work together. Like any relationship, the coaching partnership takes time to build. It needs to be cultivated as the coaching progresses so that coach and client have a congenial ongoing working affiliation.

Most important is that everything revolves around the person of Jesus Christ. He is like the axle at the center, keeping the wheel from spinning off in a variety of directions. In practical terms, what does it mean to have our coaching revolve around Jesus? It means that we commit all of our coaching (and our lives) to his lordship and direction. It means that through Scripture reading, prayer, and worship, we seek to be men and women who know him and are more sensitive to the leading of his Holy Spirit as we coach. It means that we seek to be clear on our values and personal beliefs. We do not reject or condemn those whose values differ from ours, nor do we manipulate clients to accept our convictions or priorities.

Figure 7-2 The Expanded Christian Coaching Model

Even so, we are honest about the values that guide our work. We politely decline to coach anybody who wants our services for the purpose of developing behaviors or lifestyles that appear to be inconsistent with Christian biblical principles and that, as a result, are likely to be self-defeating. We don't judge, but we do maintain our integrity by deciding what is right, as best we can determine this, and by living in ways that are consistent with that decision. Having Jesus Christ at the center means, as well, that we commit to praying for our clients, asking God to change their lives, working in part through our gifts, training, knowledge, and skills as coaches.

AWARENESS: WHERE ARE WE NOW?

As part of my training to become a coach, I took a practicum class in corporate coaching. Each student was assigned to work within a large corporation, doing one-to-one coaching with emerging executives who had been selected for an intensive leadership training experience. Most of us in that course had never heard of the corporation where our clients worked. We knew nothing about the nature of their business, and none of us had any prior contact with the people we would be coaching. In preparation for our work, we were given information about the company, its business, and the high-pressure corporate environment where most of the employees worked. Soon we got to know our clients very well. We learned about their dreams and aspirations. Before long we were walking alongside them as they made decisions and took action to reach their goals. Probably we used different methods and drew on our unique coaching styles, but we all started at the same place. We had to begin by finding out where our clients were at the time our coaching began. It was not until then that we could work with them as they moved from where they were to where they wanted to be.

The first part of the coaching model (awareness) has at least two parts: becoming more aware of the *present* (where the client is now) and becoming aware of the *person* (who the client really is). Later we will discuss tests or other formalized tools that can help us gain greater awareness of where and who the client is, but the coach's best methods are the listening, questioning, and responding that we discussed in the previous chapter.

Becoming aware of the present. This starts with the issues or concerns that have brought your client to coaching. Presumably, he or she is dissatisfied with something in life or at work and wants to make changes. The coach listens with curiosity and tries to discover the nature of these dissatisfactions. What are they? What would the client like to change? What attitudes, behaviors, or people are getting in the way of progress? What about the client's present circumstances? What is the work environment like? Who are the people, the key players, who are having an impact on the client's life at present? What attitudes, frustrations, values, personality issues, and ways of thinking are influencing where the client is right now?

One business owner wanted coaching because his company was stalled. Sales remained about the same, employees never stayed long, morale was low, and there was little change despite periodic initiatives designed to bring growth. Several business consultants had come in to analyze the company and make useful recommendations, but still nothing changed. Then the business owner hired a coach. She asked questions about the company and listened carefully to the answers. She was not a consultant with expertise in company growth. Her focus was more on assisting as the owner looked at his present situation and explored pathways of action that he might initiate. A simple personality test showed that the owner was a task-oriented person, largely insensitive to people. He tended to be a micromanager who was involved in everything and who dominated most of the employees. He squelched creativity, rarely affirmed anybody, and relied on his own ideas and hard work to bring progress in the company. He resisted making changes in himself until coaching helped this man see that his controlling personality and his management style were major factors in the company's lackluster performance. The recommendations of those prior consultants never worked because the business owner tried to initiate them himself but with minimal effect because they were not his own ideas. As he began to change and the employees were invited to get more involved with decision making, the company began to grow and so did morale.

Becoming aware of the person. This true story illustrates the second part of getting awareness. It can be very useful to focus on the clients themselves. This is not in the sense of analyzing their motives, searching the past for the causes of their present behavior, or looking for personal problems that need to be solved. Instead, the coach encourages clients to look at their abilities, strengths, God-given spiritual gifts, weaknesses, passions, and life purposes. The business owner had some understanding of where his business was at present, but he had never thought of his own strengths and weaknesses. Prior to coaching, he had not considered how his own leadership style was driving him to run the company in an autocratic manner. Later, he was surprised to discover that his employees were well aware of the attitudes and controlling leadership behaviors that they experienced every day but that the company owner had never stopped to consider.

The awareness stop on the coaching circle is where your client tends to be at the beginning. In the corporate coaching class that was mentioned earlier, all of the coaches were given information about the company leadership training program in which our clients were enrolled. We were told that each person had taken a group of assessment tests to get an indication of their personality types and leadership styles. Of course, the coaches were not given the results of these confidential tests, but most of the clients voluntarily shared these with their coaches later. In all of this, we were getting to know about the work settings of the people with whom we would be working and were beginning to know about the clients themselves.

VISION: WHERE DO WE WANT TO GO?

A vision is a mental picture of the ideal future. It has to do with what the person wants to accomplish, what he or she would like to have happen, and where the client wants to go. Vision applies to businesses, organizations, churches, families, and people who are building careers.

Having a clear vision is not a problem for some people. They know exactly where they want to go and can articulate their goals easily and often succinctly. A client may want to get a college degree, build a successful business, win an election, lead a church, or become an acclaimed musician. One of my past clients dreamed of writing a book, but he was stuck, not sure how to proceed. He wanted coaching that would enable him to fulfill the vision that was clear in his mind.

This differs from the many people who don't have a vision and don't know how to get one. They may sense that God has some purpose for their lives or ministries, but they have no idea what this is and no clue about how to find their calling. Maybe thousands of books have been written about vision casting and reaching visions, but often we live our busy lives without direction, focusing on the present and giving little thought to where we want to go or where God wants us to go. In contrast, Jesus and many of the biblical writers were focused on the future and guided by the God-given awareness of where they should or could move forward with their lives. They did not ignore the present or discount the past, but they were looking to better things that would come.

Great coaches are visionaries. Great coaches instill, nurture, and encourage vision, then model and motivate surrender to it.

—THOMAS G. BANDY, author of *Coaching Change*

Some people want a coach who will tell them what to do and where to go. Instead, good coaches use focused questions to stimulate the thinking that will let these people discover God's leading for themselves. Coaches call this "stepping into the future." It involves encouraging clients to envision what could be. It's about reflecting, imagining possibilities, and discovering a vision for the days or years ahead.

Sometimes this vision-oriented focus on the future involves major dreams or plans. When one of my friends took over as president of a large Christian ministry, he discovered that the organization was not functioning as well as it appeared to outsiders. Some of the long-term employees were stuck in the past, doing their jobs routinely but without much production and with little awareness of why the ministry even existed. The board of directors knew the original purpose for getting started, but most had given no thought to the changing times in which they lived or to possibilities for the organization's future. With the assistance of a coach, the new president guided the board to formulate and move to reach a fresh and captivating vision. My friend knew that without vision, organizations drift and so do individuals.

This vision-focused part of the model may take a significant amount of time, especially if the concept is new. When I was coached through a career transition, we spent a lot of time clarifying a vision for my future. The coach helped me think about where I was in my life at the time, ponder what I would still like to accomplish, and envision what I wanted my life to look like in the coming years. I never saw a crystal-clear picture of my future. Only God knows the future, so we can only make good estimations of where we are to go. Even so, with an idea of what I envisioned, we were able to move to the next part of the circle and think through strategies and action steps for making my hopes and visions for the future become a reality.

STRATEGY AND ACTION: HOW DO WE GET THERE?

Even when people have a clear idea of where they want to go, they may need help in getting there. This can involve setting goals that are realistic, specific, and measurable. Goals like "losing weight," "being more cooperative," or "paying more attention to my kids" are too vague to be motivating. They tend to be abandoned quickly. Goals that stimulate action involve concise statements such as "Starting after my vacation, I will read a bedtime story to my kids at least four times a week" or "I am going to lose fifteen pounds before my sister's wedding in June." After setting goals and starting to implement them, it soon becomes clear whether those goals are realistic and specific enough to be reachable.

Goal setting may involve something major, such as earning a college degree. But setting and reaching goals also could be a small part of developing a broader overall plan of action. A successful lawyer came to a friend of mine for coaching because he hated his job and found that the long hours kept him from his family. He earned a good salary and was grateful to his wife, who had helped him get through law school, but understandably she was resisting his talk about closing the practice.

The coach listened attentively to these concerns and asked questions about what would make his life better and more fulfilling. She asked why he had entered law in the first place and what he had enjoyed about the field when he started. In those early days, the practice was small. The lawyer was able to be home more often and even took time every week to play golf. This had been a relaxing diversion for him and a complete change of pace that was missing from his currently busy life. Together the lawyer and his coach came up with a plan that would enable him to trim his hours at work so he regularly could have an afternoon off and could go home in time for dinner with his family two nights every week. As part of a larger plan for adding more balance and fulfillment to his life, there were specific and realistic smaller goals that he was able to put into practice immediately with the accountability that came from his coach.

Clients usually come to coaching to do things differently or to do different things. They want to set goals, come up with plans, get into action, and use the accountability of coaching to stay on track. Clients want to be in motion, not standing still, so naturally a great deal of the coach's focus is on moving forward, envisioning the future, and helping clients create the path that will take them there. Coaching that emphasizes moving forward is focused, directed, intentional.

—LAURA WHITWORTH. KAREN KIMSEY-HOUSE, HENRY KIMSEY-HOUSE, and PHILLIP SANDAHL, coauthors of *Co-Active Coaching*

Coaching and business books sometimes describe companies in which the leader has been able to evaluate the current situation and set a clear picture of the future but has failed to turn the vision into reality. Setting a strategy and following through with a plan of action can be difficult even for highly motivated people. Nevertheless, this third part of the coaching model is critical if there is to be success. Let's return to the weight-loss issue that we have mentioned earlier. Maybe millions of people go on diets every year. By stepping on a scale, they become aware of where they are in terms of their weight. They have a vision of where they want to be weight-wise. They even may come up with a dieting plan for reaching their goal. Then they stall.

There is little value in having a long-range strategy for making change if the plan is never put into action. Some people very much want to move forward, but they aren't sure how to do it, their motivation fails, or they lose the courage to take even the first step. This points to several important roles for coaches at the strategy and action stage. First, they stimulate the development of a realistic plan of action. As part of this, clients decide what steps are needed to move forward. Next, coaches ask for commitment, maybe even asking a yes-no question: "Are you willing to commit to this plan?" If the answer is no, there needs to be a new plan. If the answer is yes, the coach and client decide when the next step will take place and perhaps a specific time when it will be done. As movement begins, coaches become encouragers and sometimes cheerleaders. Frequently, coaches become accountability partners, motivating and enabling clients to make the changes they desire and helping them evaluate, change, and restart their action plans if the forward movement stalls. It has been suggested that "without accountability, coaching has not happened, even if coaching skills have been used."[4]

OBSTACLES: WHAT GETS IN THE WAY?

Life is not a smooth journey. Progress is hindered by obstacles, roadblocks, setbacks, and disappointments. Like runners in a marathon, we can be hindered by hurdles that trip us up, slow us down, drain our energy, or force us to give up our goals and abandon the race. These obstacles are not always in the environments where we live or work. Many of our biggest obstacles reside in our minds as self-defeating thoughts and self-talk. We think, *If I go ahead, I will be laughed at or criticized. I'll never make it because it will take too long. Last time I tried something like this, I failed—what if I fail again?* These internal progress stoppers, sometimes called our mental gremlins, can be immobilizing, like huge mountains in the way of progress but mountains that few outsiders see because we hide them in our brains.

Look less at the mountain and more at the mountain-mover.

— BILL HYBELS, leadership expert,
pastor of Willow Creek Community Church

One of your greatest tasks as a coach is to help others uncover, face, and get past the self-defeating behaviors and mental self-talk that hinders progress. Some people come to coaching in the first place because they feel immobilized by barriers they can't surmount. Sometimes people are afraid to take risks. Others are persistent procrastinators. A coaching client may talk about changing but feel so secure in the old ways that he or she keeps making excuses for not taking action. Many coaching clients know the obstacles that hinder their own progress, and they can tell you what these are if you ask.

All of us have blind spots however. We don't always see self-sabotaging attitudes or behaviors in ourselves. If we do see them, we may not want to admit them. Coaches are more objective observers who often see the obstacles more clearly and before their clients recognize what might be getting in the way. As a coach, if you see the barriers, be cautious about pointing them out too quickly, especially if you still are building initial rapport. Instead, when you sense the presence of a blind spot, keep observing to see if your observations are valid. Later you can point out the obstacles in ways that keep your client from being defensive or resistant.

In all of this, remember that obstacles can become a major influence in organizations or groups as well as in individuals. People who live or work together can develop a mind-set that psychologists call *groupthink*. Everybody in the group can think like everybody else. If one group member begins to wonder if the group thinking is correct, he or she dismisses the mental doubt with self-talk like this: *Everybody else seems absolutely convinced that what they believe is valid and that they are making the right decisions. Obviously my doubting thoughts must be wrong. Besides that, I don't want to challenge the group, hinder their progress, or appear disloyal and not a team player. If I do express my hesitations, maybe I could get fired or kicked off the team, so it probably is best to keep quiet.* Sometimes an entire group can think this way. Each person harbors reservations, but nobody mentions doubts. The skilled coach can assist groups or individual clients in considering the possibilities of groupthink, encouraging them to face their external or mental barriers to progress, and getting back on the track of moving to where the client or clients really want to go.

This fourth segment of the coaching model, the obstacle-clearing segment of the coaching circle, may also involve a reevaluation of the progress thus far, sometimes followed by a revisit to the awareness stage and another trip around the circle. This does not mean that coaching goes on forever in circles like a Ferris wheel or merry-go-round. It means, instead, that sometimes after we get past the obstacles, we may want to take a fresh look at where we are now, where we want to go, and the strategies and actions that we have taken or might take in the future. As coaching progresses, new awareness or insights might come to mind, the client may have new experiences, he or she begins to take new actions, and newer, clearer goals may emerge. But unlike the amusement park merry-go-round, the person being coached can stop the action at any time, get off, and go on with life.

After I started work on the first edition of this book, I was presented with an opportunity to be involved in an attractive new coach-training venture. I turned to some close friends for their input, one of whom is a professional coach. These people helped me get a clearer *awareness* of the issues that concerned me about this potential new possibility. They reminded me of what I know about my self, including my strengths, values, passions, and insecurities, all of which were relevant concerns. We looked again at what I had envisioned as the major focus for the next few years of my life, and we discussed how the new venture might or might not fit with my perceived life *vision* from this point forward. We discussed *strategy*, how I might be able to deal with the new opportunity and its impact on other parts of my life. I talked with them about next step *actions* that could be taken, and a couple of them agreed to hold me accountable for what I did next. More than once, I honestly shared fears and other *obstacles* that needed to be dealt with before I could make a decision. These friends were coaching me informally, and their guidance was of immeasurable help. Without thinking much about it, they were helping me get a handle on where I was at present, focus on where I might want to go in the future, and find ways get there. When I reached a conclusion about the new opportunity and then turned it down, I talked with these friends about my decision, and they helped me evaluate what I had decided. Informally, I have done something like this on a number of occasions in my life. Usually in these situations, I have not thought consciously about the coaching model with its four segments, and I have not thought that my wife, close friends, and others have been coaching me when we talked about challenges or new opportunities. But our talks have involved coaching. Many of us coach all the time. Some do it informally. Others develop skills and do it with special competence and expertise.

DOING AND BECOMING

We all know there can be different kinds of change. Some is as radical and long lasting as the metamorphosis of a tadpole into a frog or a caterpillar into a butterfly. Other change is less revolutionary. The same is true of coaching. Sometimes coaches guide people as they undertake down-to-earth efforts for reaching specific goals, getting unstuck, resolving conflicts, or making decisions. This has been the focus of this book thus far. But for many people, coaching can bring about a striking transformation, a significant and lasting change for the better.

I had almost completed this manuscript when I took time to lead a coaching seminar for younger leaders. One of the participants was a pastor who volunteered to be part of a coaching demonstration. He had listened to my discussion of the coaching circle and told me he wanted coaching about his decision to get more education. We started by talking about where he was in his ministry and his vision about where he wanted to go. As he talked and I listened, I wondered if he really was committed to going back to school and starting a doctoral program.

"You've talked about enjoying your ministry and wanting more training," I said, "but I'm not sure I hear much passion. What is your passion?"

Without hesitation, he answered with one word: jazz.

I was surprised because I had not seen this coming. He really wanted to be a jazz musician and admitted that he had always suppressed this desire because he knew it would not be acceptable to his congregation or his family. The more he talked about jazz, however, the more enthusiastic he became. He wanted to keep serving Jesus, doing what he was trained to do, but in coaching he openly expressed his long-hidden urge to be something other than a lead pastor.

I'm keeping in touch with this young leader. I'm not sure he will make a career change, but coaching has stimulated him to give more thought to where he is and to what God might call him to do at the next stage in his life journey.

If you want to help your clients in the short-term, focus on solving problems. If you want to see them radically transformed for life, concentrate on building people.

— TONY STOLTZFUS, author of *Leadership Coaching*

Coaching can focus on helping people *do* things differently, but it also helps clients *be* different. Often coaches focus on behavior change that enables clients to take action to reach measurable goals. It can help young pastors change their job descriptions and follow their passions. At other times, coaches focus on how clients can become different, transformed internally, changed in their ways of thinking as well as in their behavior. That transformation is the ultimate goal of Christian coaching.

PART 3

ASSESSMENT IN CHRISTIAN COACHING: WHERE ARE WE NOW?

CHAPTER 8

GETTING IN TOUCH
WITH THE PRESENT

PROBABLY YOU HAVE never heard about the goldfish named Jonah. He or she — it's hard to tell with a goldfish — spent every day swimming in a little circle in a bowl, not going anywhere because there was no place to go. It is doubtful that Jonah got bored, as goldfish are assumed to have a memory span of three seconds. They can't see the past and apparently give little thought to the future.[1] Jonah won't remember this now, but one day his or her owner decided to clean out the bowl. To keep the fish alive during the process, the owner put a few inches of water into a nearby bathtub and temporarily released Jonah into the larger body of water. An hour or so later, the owner came back and found her pet goldfish in a corner of the tub, swimming in a little circle no bigger than the bowl.[2]

When they come for coaching, a lot of people are like Jonah, going in circles, staying with the familiar routines, oblivious of the opportunities to move away from their secure little comfort zones. Some of the Jonahs we meet really want to explore bigger worlds, but they don't know how to break out of their tedious lifestyles. Some are afraid to try. A few may dream of bigger things and even make plans, but they never get around to leaving the narrow confines of their lives. Others are like the biblical Jonah, who ran the other way when God gave clear direction about moving out in bigger circles.[3]

Without a future-directed orientation everything
becomes hum-drum repetition. Early on, I learned
the importance of hope. So much of life carries

disappointments and jolts. If one loses the perspective
that comes from awareness of God's control of the future,
there isn't much to hold at the end of the day.

—TED WARD, visionary leader, former professor at Michigan State University
and Trinity Evangelical Divinity School

Christian coaches are in the business of helping human Jonahs, both the kind that are going in circles and the kind that are running all the time or running away. Many of the people we coach are swimming in the midst of busy lifestyles, not thinking much about their futures or the possibilities for moving to other things. How do we enter their circles and help them assess where they are? We start by asking what concerns them about their present situations, what frustrates them, and how they would like things to be different. By listening carefully and asking good questions, the coach begins to get a clear perspective on the client's concerns, values, attitudes, circumstances, and ways of looking at life. Together, you and the person you will coach can look for the blocks to progress or the circumstances that are keeping your clients going round and round in tight little circles like Jonah the goldfish. We can focus on the future, asking people about their desires, plans, and dreams, but don't be surprised when some have no idea how to answer. People who have demanding jobs, pressured schedules, or boring life circumstances rarely take time to reflect on such issues as where they are or where they could be going. They give little thought to how things could be different. They keep doing what they have always done because it's easier and not risky.

The coach steps into this circular rut and encourages a time-out. Like the time-outs on a football field, these periods away from the game give the coach and players time to pause so they can evaluate the situation, decide where they want to go, and plot strategy for what to do next. All of this increases awareness of the current situation.

Life coaches start with a survey of the client's whole life,
including health, relationships, career, spirituality, and much
more, and then deal with every aspect of life.

—DAVE ELLIS, author of *Life Coaching*

Many coaches also use a welcome packet to give information to clients about coaching and to acquire information even before coaching starts. This is not something complicated. Along with an information sheet, some coaches send a brief résumé that summarizes their own background and training. Usually the people who want coaching are asked to complete a questionnaire that might request a short autobiography, which includes one's life story, spiritual journey, reasons for wanting coaching, and view of himself or herself. If they have ever taken psychological tests such as Myers Briggs, DISC, or People Map, they are urged to make copies of the results and send these as well. All of this enables the coach to get a mental picture of who the potential new clients are, who God made them to be, and what they might be looking for in the coaching experience.

Coaching books and training programs often include forms that coaches can use to include in their welcome packets. The previously mentioned appendixes C, D, and E contain examples of these forms. These are sample tools that can be adapted to be made unique for each person. For example, if I have business clients who are not Christians, I will change the language in the forms to take out some of the Christian references, even though I leave in the parts about the fact that I coach from a Christian perspective. If you are expecting payment for your coaching services, you would send a slightly different coaching agreement form than if you are coaching people in a church or other setting where they are not expecting to pay a fee.

Another useful tool is the Graph of Life (appendix A), mentioned in chapter 3. This is a variation of the Wheel of Life that often appears in coaching books. Both are designed to give the coach and the persons being coached an awareness of where they are at present as well as where they want to be. Sometimes the Graph of Life is sent with the welcome packet, but it may be better to send it after one or two coaching sessions, especially if the coaching progress seems to have stalled.

Some coaches also use more formal assessment tools. If you have training as a psychologist, you can obtain and use professional psychological tests, but since most coaches are not psychologists, they use other tools that are helpful even though they may not be as sophisticated as standardized psychological assessment measures.[4] If you use any of these tools, it can be useful for you to complete your personal copies of the tests that you will send to clients. This lets you, the coach, experience what others are being asked to do. Later the test results or the questionnaires can be discussed in the coaching sessions.

Be careful not to present too many of these tools at the same time. That could leave the person feeling overwhelmed by the assignments and less motivated to work with you because he or she is afraid that coaching will involve a lot of time-consuming homework. Even more harmful is the danger of creating the impression that you will be able to analyze all of these tests to give a diagnosis of the situation and a prescription for action. That is not the coach's role. You do not want to imply that you are an expert, like a doctor who diagnoses and treats illnesses or a lawyer who evaluates contracts and advises clients what to do next. Present these questionnaires and other tools, one or two at a time, and use them as discussion guides rather than diagnostic techniques. Often these will give you and the people you coach a clearer picture of where they are at present. That awareness is the first part of our coaching circle: helping others see more clearly where they are now, when the coaching begins. This, in turn, can help initiate the process of helping people move toward what they hope to become or want to achieve.

Figure 8-1

There is no secret formula for getting more in touch with the present, but several issues are worth exploring. These are summarized in table 8-1. In addition to learning about the client's present circumstances, it can be helpful to understand his or her beliefs and ways of looking at the world, along with the person's core values. Each of these issues — present circumstances, world-views, and values — will be considered in this chapter. In the next chapter, we will look at passions, personality, strengths, and spiritual gifts. Even as each of these can increase understanding in the people we coach, each can be applied, as well, to coaches. As you read the remainder of this chapter and the next, it may be helpful to apply to yourself what you read. This will give you a better sense of how your clients respond to assessment tools.

Table 8-1

AWARENESS ISSUES IN COACHING
■ Circumstances — What's going on in your life right now?
■ Worldviews — What are your deeply held beliefs and views about the world?
■ Values — What *really* is important to you?
■ Passions — What gets you excited?
■ Personality — What are you really like?
■ Strengths — What do you do well (or best)?
■ Spiritual Gifts — How has God gifted you?

UNDERSTANDING PRESENT CIRCUMSTANCES

Early in their training, a group of nursing school students was given an un-expected quiz. The students did their best to answer the questions, but every-one stopped at the last one: "What is the first name of the person who cleans the school?"

Surely this was some kind of joke. All of the students had seen the clean-ing lady. She was tall, dark-haired, and in her fifties, but why would anyone be expected to know her name? When time was up, the students handed in their papers. They all had left the last question blank. Before the class ended, one student asked if this question would count toward the quiz grade.

"Absolutely," replied the professor. "In your careers you will meet many people. All are significant. All deserve your attention and care, even if the only thing you do is smile and say hello. The next day, everybody in class had learned that the cleaning lady's name was Dorothy. Maybe some of those students also learned a lesson that would stick as they embarked on their careers: It's important to be aware of people.

Jesus had that awareness. One day he was being pressed and jostled by a large crowd when a woman with a chronic illness reached out, touched his clothes, and was healed. Jesus stopped immediately, turned around, and asked, "Who touched my clothes?" The disciples could not believe the question. Everybody was pressing against him, but Jesus was aware that power had gone out of him and that one person in that pushing crowd had a special need that he had been able to meet.[5]

None of us has that ability, but we all can be more aware of our surroundings and our circumstances. For some people, such awareness becomes a fine art. The conductor of a symphony orchestra is aware of every player, every nuance of the music, every note that is played incorrectly. The basketball coach in a hotly contested game knows every team member, every movement, and every strategy that might be used by or against the opponents. The conductor and the coach hear or see what most others miss. In their minds, they envision possibilities that could become reality if everybody played well. There is a determination to build heightened awareness into their players. Life coaches do the same with their clients. They start by asking questions:

- "What would you like to talk about today?"
- "How are things really going in your life right now?"
- "What concerns you?"
- "What matters most to you these days?"
- "Tell me what's working well."
- "Can you describe some things that aren't working very well?"
- "How would you like your life (or your business or your church) to be different?"
- "What is getting in the way of these changes?"
- "Please tell me about some areas in which you might be stuck right now."
- "What have you been doing to get unstuck?"

All of these questions help to clarify the present circumstances of the person who has come for coaching. They are questions that can be asked of individuals or discussed by groups. These are the awareness-building questions that help to answer the question "Where are you now?"

Many people come for coaching because they are stuck. One of my clients was a middle-aged pastor who had been trained as a therapist but had left his counseling practice because he disliked handling all the details and paperwork of running a counseling business. Sensing that he should enter the ministry, he completed a seminary degree and became pastor of a small church where the congregation was not growing and the people were set in their ways. The therapist-turned-pastor felt stuck in a dead-end, energy-draining career. He wanted coaching that would get the stalled church moving, but the more we talked, the clearer it became that he felt stuck in his own life and career, frustrated and immobilized about what to do next. It emerged that he had no passion for trying to revitalize stalled churches and that he really preferred to be a therapist but without the busywork that had driven him from his profession. Eventually, he joined the staff of a large Christian counseling center where he could draw on both his counseling and theological training, working with motivated counselees in an environment where a competent office manager took care of the details involved in running the counseling business.

Several years ago, I read about a bright and energetic business consultant named Keith Yamashita, who works with individuals but more often with companies that are stuck and want to get moving again. Yamashita writes that most of us get stuck for at least one of the seven causes summarized in table 8-2.

Table 8-2

WHY INDIVIDUALS AND ORGANIZATIONS GET STUCK[6]
People feel stuck for a number of reasons, including at least one of the following. Individuals, organizations, and teams stall when they feel:
■ **Overwhelmed.** This involves a feeling that there is too much work, too much scrutiny, or too little time, energy, or people to get everything done. When the tasks ahead feel huge, there is procrastination and uncertainty about where to begin.
■ **Exhausted.** Tired people lack energy. They tend to lose vision, purpose, and enthusiasm. Team camaraderie fades. Patience is in short supply. Conflicts and criticism are more in evidence. Everything stalls.
■ **Directionless.** Everyone may be busy and working through to-do lists, but sometimes there is no vision or big picture of the future. Team members have no common goal, so each works independently and progress is limited.
■ **Hopeless.** When there is no sense of achievement (often because there is no clear purpose), the motivation to keep working dries up, successes become fewer and the effort does not seem worthwhile.

- **Surrounded by conflict.** It is difficult to keep moving forward in the midst of disagreements, communication breakdowns, misunderstandings, and gossip. This is like a dysfunctional family trying to plan a wedding or family reunion.
- **Worthless.** Motivation and progress stall when individuals or team members feel unappreciated, overlooked, unrewarded, or unacknowledged.
- **Alone.** This is a feeling of isolation that may come to a whole team, company, or church. Each individual works independently with no sense of belonging, identity, team spirit, or camaraderie. Often this comes because there is no visionary leader who unites people into a common purpose.

Each of these is a topic that could be dealt with in coaching. For example, people who feel overwhelmed can benefit from backing away from the pressures, discussing them with a coach, and finding ways to take charge of their out-of-control lives. Recently, I was feeling pressured by writing deadlines, meetings that I needed to attend, and commitments that I had accepted but had no time to fulfill. For several hours, I met with a coach at a Starbucks. We considered what was making me feel pressured, exhausted, and stuck. With the coach's sensitive listening and effective questioning, I came up with a plan in which I would cancel some things, set up a realistic schedule, not take on anything new for a period of several months, and set up an accountability program whereby the coach and a couple of friends would pray for me and hold me accountable to stick with the program. Most of the planning came from me. The coach provided an environment in which I could devise a strategy for getting out from under my self-created load and start moving productively again. All of this started with a clearer picture of my life circumstances at the time.

Many times the understanding and the answers to getting unstuck are found in other parts of the coaching circle. When we feel directionless, for example, there is value in focusing on vision and setting realistic goals. When team camaraderie fails, it is good to revisit the vision, maybe recast it, look again at the strategy, or focus on obstacles that may be hindering progress. Then we take action to make changes.[7]

Coaching like this most often takes place in telephone or face-to-face conversations, but at times it occurs in the midst of people's lives. For example, some executive coaches go to their clients' places of work, follow them around for a day or two, sit in on their meetings, and interview their associates. Of course, this can be an invasion of privacy unless the coach has permission, but these kinds of observations can be very revealing. The outside observer often sees things that the insider misses. Even if you don't make a site visit, you still can learn by observation. If a person talks about the importance of exercise but never makes time for working out, you have heard words not backed by actions. If someone agrees to do things differently but never gets beyond making promises, you suspect that there is limited commitment to making change. Often this shows an unspoken, sometimes unrecognized, fear or resistance.

UNDERSTANDING WORLDVIEWS

Prior to 1954, most people believed that a human being was incapable of running a mile in less than four minutes. Then an English runner named Roger Bannister proved them wrong. "Doctors and scientists said that breaking the four-minute mile was impossible, that one would die in the attempt," Bannister said later. "When I got up from the track after collapsing at the finish line, I figured I was dead." In describing this achievement, one executive coach concluded that "in sports, as in business, the main obstacle to achieving 'the impossible' may be a self-limiting mind-set."[8]

Every coach and everyone who comes for coaching has a mind-set. Some call this a life perspective, a mental model, or a worldview. This is an inner set of beliefs and assumptions about how the world works. Worldviews influence how we make sense of life, decide what is right and wrong, choose values, view other people, make decisions, evaluate circumstances or events, settle on a lifestyle, and plan for the future. Even though worldviews can shape so much of our lives, it seems that most people drift into their worldviews without giving them much thought. They pick up perspectives from their past experiences and from other people, subconsciously piecing together a way of viewing the world that might be fuzzy and filled with inconsistencies. Even so, this is what we really believe about the universe and the way it operates. Worldviews are life perspectives that we rarely question, almost never mention to friends, and usually ignore unless somebody or something disrupts what we believe by showing a different point of view.

Worldviews or mental models are deeply held internal images
of how the world works. All of our actions, thoughts, and
feelings arise from our mental models of the world around us.

— DANIEL WHITE, author of *Coaching Leaders*

The most useful worldviews are held with conviction, but they are not so rigid that they never change. Less-adequate worldviews, like faulty eyeglasses, can cloud our vision and hinder our efforts to see things clearly. When there are conflicts or other differences of opinion, often the differences reflect the underlying worldviews of the people involved. A prominent example is the ongoing conflict over abortion. Pro-choice and pro-life advocates have different, deeply held worldviews, which leads to conclusions that clash.[9]

Christ followers do not have identical worldviews, but from a Christian perspective, the most well-rounded and useful worldviews deal with at least five major topics. First is what we believe about God including whether or not he exists, what he is like, and the extent to which he influences our world and our lives. Second, each worldview includes one's perspectives on the universe. How did it come into existence? Is it orderly or more chaotic? Do supernatural interventions ever occur, including what might be viewed as an answer to prayer? Third, how do we know anything with certainty? Can we trust our senses? Will logic get us to the truth? To what extent should we look to a sacred text or to the wisdom of others? How do we even know what is truth? A fourth issue concerns morality, how we determine what is right and wrong, whether absolute standards exist, and how we live and coach ethically. Finally, there are beliefs about human nature. In what ways are we different from animals? What is our destiny? Do individuals have a preordained calling or an eternal future?

These philosophical and theological issues rarely are discussed in coaching,[10] but they shape the ways our clients think and the ways in which coaches do their work. As they listen, sensitive coaches begin to detect the worldview perspectives of their clients and sometimes need to gently challenge worldviews that might be hindering progress. Good coaches also give thought to their own worldviews and how these may be impacting clients or the coaching process. By his determination and training, Roger Bannister challenged the worldview that no human could run a mile in one minute.

FOCUSING ON VALUES

Values are difficult to define and hard to identify. They are the foundational beliefs that anchor our lives, the things that matter to us, the nonnegotiable characteristics that most clearly define our identities. List the five or six traits that describe you, your company, or your church and you are getting close to your values. The people who know you best can state your values because they have seen what motivates and most characterizes you. Our true values tend to be reflected in our daily lives, but they emerge with special clarity in times of stress, crises, or important decision making. When we are under the gun, we immediately respond with actions guided automatically by our values.

People who have not thought about their values are more easily swayed by circumstances, fads, and the opinions of others. In contrast, people who live in harmony with their basic life-governing values sense greater inner peace and usually feel that their lives are on target, more fulfilled, and less out of control. Leaders who know and abide by their values are more decisive and effective. Companies, churches, and organizations guided by clear values are more likely to move forward with less floundering and vacillation.

Values are not characteristics that you pick at random and drop into your life. They often come into your life as you are growing up. They are like an umbrella under which everything else in your life fits. Values are the basis of your character, actions, attitudes, ethics, and personal beliefs. They define who you are. Often they remain hidden and sometimes they are even denied or squelched. But until they are identified and articulated, it is unlikely that an individual or a church can move forward with confidence or with God's leading and blessing.

Values generally remain consistent, but they can be changed. When Christ comes into a life, for example, the person becomes transformed into a new creature.[11] The Holy Spirit takes up residence within, and if we don't squelch or quench the process, there is an emergence of Spirit-produced values and Spirit-molded fruit. Love, peace, patience, kindness, goodness, faithfulness, gentleness, and self-control form the core of who we are.[12] For the Christian, values like these are at the foundation of one's character; they are the basis of all decision making.

Clear values motivate us. By their very nature, values give us energy. We are drawn to them because we find such fulfillment when we live and work in accordance with them. By knowing our values, we have a better ability to answer tough questions such as *Who am I? Why am I here? How do I want to live? What kind of person do I want to become? What legacy do I want to leave?* When these issues begin to get clarified, we are freed to move ahead with greater confidence.

Think of the person who lives with Christian values and recognizes that he or she is a child of the King, with divinely given gifts that empower believers to serve God and others more effectively. Making money or being successful may be on that person's list of values, but there are others of greater importance, such as being truthful, growing spiritually, and impacting people. These higher values can motivate and stimulate us to move forward.

When individuals or groups are stuck, they often lack an inner sense of where to go. Getting them in touch with their values clarifies where they should not go and often motivates them to move in the value-fulfilling directions where they should go. When values are taken seriously, they bring people together and keep them focused. When difficult decisions are demanded, clear values tend to shunt us in the right directions.

Values have the power to guide and motivate workers just as well or better than any army of supervisors.

— NOEL M. TICHY, author of *The Cycle of Leadership* and
The Leadership Engine

When football coach Bill Parcells wrote *Finding a Way to Win*, a book on leadership, he built the whole manuscript around values.[13] The most effective leaders are those who know their values and live accordingly, Parcells argues. The chief difference between winners and losers is that winning individuals and companies have thought about their values and apply them more rigorously.[14] When crises or crucial decision times arise, values-driven people are able to respond quickly and appropriately. They have thought about their values. They live in accordance with their values. They make decisions and respond in line with their values.

The same is true for effective coaches. You will never reach your maximum effectiveness as a coach until you are aware of your values. People being coached will never move forward until they deal with the issue of values. And no church, college, organization, or business will survive with strength and soar with success until the people involved have committed to a common set of values.

The problem with most leaders today is they don't stand for anything. If you don't stand for something, you'll fall for anything.

— DON SHULA, highly successful NFL coach,
coauthor of *The Little Book of Coaching*

The ServiceMaster Company is a large international conglomerate that began in 1929 as a small moth-proofing business. The founder and his immediate successors were deeply religious men who wanted to serve other people and serve the Master, which accounts for the company name. From the beginning, the business was built on a firm and clear set of values. Today, if you visit the ServiceMaster headquarters near Chicago, you will see these company values prominently engraved on a marble slab. They also are prominent on the company website. The company exists to: honor God in all they do, help people develop, pursue excellence, and grow profitably.

Clear values help us make decisions. Some values are more important to us than others. I value efficiency, but I value excellence even more. If I am faced with the choice of producing something quickly or taking the time to produce something of quality, I try to opt for the latter even if the delay has a financial or other cost. ServiceMaster could have chosen other values, but it lives in accordance with their four key guidelines, which determine company policy and direction. It is not easy to arrange values in order of priority, but when coaching clients can do this, it sets guidelines for making good decisions later.

Clear values are the foundation for growth. Coaches help others envision the future, develop goals, make major decisions, and plan ways for moving forward. Christian coaches guide in spiritual and personal development, helping others to mature into greater Christlikeness. All of these activities are built on values. It is inconceivable that there can be significant progress in coaching if the people being coached have never thought though their values. It is unlikely, too, that coaches can be maximally effective in stimulating growth if they don't have a clear perspective on their own values.

Clear values bring inner peace. It is hard to hold on to values when everybody around thinks differently. Consider the person who values being successful and values spending time with the kids but whose boss values employees who work late and rewards those who comply by giving promotions and raises. That is when people are tempted to tone down their values or push them aside. When that happens and values are squelched, we often make decisions based on the probable short-term benefits. We might even be rewarded and applauded. Nobody will question the decision because compromise is common and many agree that few people always live in accordance with their inner values. But decisions that ignore values often are regretted later. No person will be fulfilled, satisfied, or at peace if he or she neglects the things that matter most. In contrast, when people live and act in accordance with their values, they experience an ongoing sense of fulfillment and inner joy.

When your daily activities reflect your governing
values, you experience inner peace.

— HYRUM W. SMITH, author of
What Matters Most: The Power of Living Your Values

This discussion of values has strong practical implications for Christian coaches and leaders. To a large extent, the Bible is a book about values. We are called to love God with all of our being and to love others. We are called to be faithful to our spouses and diligent in raising our children. We are instructed to forsake selfish ambition, envy, the love for money, and dishonest gain. The Bible values forgiveness, purity, faithfulness, obedience to God's Word, humility, servanthood, diligence, and compassion. Ignore these and the other biblical values and you will experience disharmony and a lack of inner peace. The people we coach often know this, but often no sooner do they ask for our help than they begin to compromise, lower their standards, conclude that they are trapped under the power of nonbiblical values. Our task is to stay with them, encourage, and at times gently prod.

But for the Christian who leads and who coaches, nothing is more important than to live in accordance with his or her own values and let others see this. There will be times when the personal costs of living our values will be high. You will wonder if you are doing the right thing. You may question whether this really brings lasting peace and fulfillment. Even so, the leaders and coaches who ultimately win, those who gain respect from the people they lead, are those whose lives are based on values. In time, people begin to see your character and they are attracted. Your example may be the greatest encouragement you can give the people you lead and coach.

COACHING AND VALUES

Focusing on values can be a significant part of evaluating where clients are at the beginning of the coaching process. A clear awareness of values can help in determining one's vision for the future and can guide the process for achieving goals. Sometimes people stall in their lives and careers because they are uncertain about their values, not living in accordance with their values, or facing value conflicts. All of these are areas in which coaching can be beneficial.

Uncovering values. How does a coach help people identify their values?

Start with the simplest and most direct way. Ask, "What are the key values at the core of your life?" This will take a while to answer, especially for people who have never given their values much thought. Encourage them to take time to reflect on their lives and to think of times when their values rose to the surface and guided a decision, appeared in times of crisis, or came out in behavior.

Once clients are conscious of values, they act as the true north point of a compass, guiding coaching clients in a direction that makes their life journey less haphazard and more purposeful.

— adapted from PATRICK WILLIAMS and DIANE S. MENENDEZ, coauthors of *Becoming a Professional Life Coach*

The discovery and clarification of values can be more valuable if clients ask close family members or friends to identify the values they see. Sometimes the people who know us best can most clearly identify values we don't see in ourselves.

One creative coach asks people to imagine that they are at the top of a tower, high above the ground, with a steel beam connected to another tower.[15] "Would you cross the beam for a thousand dollars?" he asks. "Would you cross for a million? What if one of your children was in danger of falling from the other tower and could be rescued only by you. Would you go?" Another coach asks, "What would be so important to you that you would hold to it even if nobody else knew, even if you never got paid or acknowledged for it?" Exercises like these reveal a lot about what people really value most.

Sometimes it is helpful to give a list similar to the one shown in appendix F and ask the person to select the ten or twelve values that best apply. Whatever list or lists you select — make up one of your own if you wish — suggest that the list of values be ranked from the most important to the least. Then ask clients to think about examples to show how the list plays out in real life. What is the evidence in daily life that these really are the values that make a difference? Which appear most often? Which almost never appear at all?

Other values-discovery exercises can include the following questions:

- "If you can take only ten values with you into a strange and possibly dangerous territory, which are the ones you absolutely must have?"[16]

- "What values would you fight for? Are there any you would die for?"
- "What values are so important that you would quit a job if they were violated by your employer?"
- "How would the people who know you best describe what you are like?"

Clearly, all of this is more than a ten-minute exercise. Likely, it will take several hours, but it can be valuable as the person being coached sets goals and strategies that are in accordance with one's core values. Recognize that the list is likely to be refined with new values added and others deleted in the light of further reflection.

Living one's values. I have a few friends whose lives revolve around getting ahead, making money, being successful, pleasing the boss, and getting promoted. Some are committed to building a church or improving their skill in some hobby. Ask about their values and they would say that building their marriages and families are important values. They genuinely want this. They also want to be growing spiritually. But look at their lives and their habits and you see something different. Their lived-out values and their stated values are not the same. Some of these people genuinely want to live according to their desired values but have no idea how this can be done.

A values-based life is a fulfilled life. When coaching
clients live their lives in line with their values, it engenders
a sense of well-being, self-respect, and self-esteem. When
they live a life that violates their values, it can lead
to confusion, frustration, and depression.

— PATRICK WILLIAMS and DIANE S. MENENDEZ,
Institute for Life Coach Training

This is where coaching can be of great value. Coaches or the people we coach can talk enthusiastically about their values. They might be able to state their values, cite the values and mission statements of their churches, or point to the listing of values in their companies. But if nobody lives out their values, the statements are meaningless. When value statements are ignored or when values are not even identified clearly, then frustrations will continue, progress will stall, and it will always feel as if something is missing. The good news is that change is possible. And among the first steps, none is more important than identifying values. Then when we live our values, there is greater cohesion in our lives.

Resolving value conflicts. These conflicts can be of two types. First, two people or the members of a team may have conflicting ideas about what is important or right. When people are divided in their core commitments, it is impossible to work together smoothly. Coaches can assist as team members discuss their value differences and try to reach some common ground.

In addition to the conflicts between people, there can be value conflicts within. Consider, for example, the person who wants to serve Christ but also wants to engage in pleasure-seeking behaviors that violate biblical principles. Or think of a young husband and wife who both are committed to building their marriage and to building their careers. These sometimes conflicting values may create dissonance within each of them and between them. A coach can help clients prioritize their values and restructure their lifestyles.

Changing values. Have you ever noticed how some people change when they get behind the wheel of a car? In the office or at home they might be gentle, friendly, and likable, but on the road they become aggressive and highly competitive, weaving in and out of traffic, determined to get ahead of the other drivers who are sharing the road. When it comes to patience, courtesy, and caution, a lot of drivers run on empty. Psychological researchers have begun to study this road rage with the goal of helping aggressive drivers change.

We know that people can change their behavior, but can they change their values? Values tend to be tenacious, but they are not inborn, implanted in our genes. They form early in life as children watch their parents and later as they are influenced by their peers. Sometimes values are shaped by early experiences, such as the deep distrust of men that may develop in a young woman who has been abused. The media also molds values, as do teachers, personal heroes, spiritual leaders, and members of a gang. Churches influence values. So do coaches who realize that some people will never make progress until they change their deepest values and inner convictions.

Values never change overnight, but they can change over time. Sometimes change occurs as people honestly think about the implications of the things they stand for. Assume that you know a person who values making money and having power above all else. What are the implications of this in terms of the person's marriage, family, health, stress level, and reputation? A money-driven, power-hungry individual is unlikely to stop long enough to think about this until another person, maybe a coach, questions the deeply held, life-shaping values. Sometimes even that doesn't work. It takes a wake-up call, such as a heart attack or the arrest of a son, to be the jolt that stimulates change.

When people see the wisdom of changing their values, often they begin to take action. The leaders of churches that are losing both members and impact should insist on keeping their biblical foundations, but they may be motivated to change some deeply entrenched values about music styles, the way they worship, or how they reach out to others. Companies that have value clashes between departments must be willing to face these and make changes. Coaches may help this process, but lasting change will never come unless there is at least a willingness of the people involved to consider change. And the Christian coach knows that ultimate value change is always a Spirit-led inner transformation. When we coach Christians, we can challenge values inconsistent with biblical teaching, encourage change, and guide as the change process occurs.

Most coaching is not about changing values; it is more about clarifying values and helping people recognize values, live with them, and then build on their values as they move toward their goals. It can be tempting to skim the issue of values so we can move quickly to the sometimes more exciting topics of setting goals and planning strategies. Try to resist this temptation and don't rush the process. When the people we coach take the time and make the effort to focus on their values — the things that matter most to them — they will be more aware of where they are starting in the change process and in a better position to work on their coaching goals and issues. And they'll be more motivated to keep moving forward.

CHAPTER 9

GETTING IN TOUCH WITH THE PERSON

CHRISTIAN BOOKS ON leadership focus on outstanding biblical leaders like Moses, Joshua, or Nehemiah. The apostle Paul gets less attention in the leadership books, perhaps because he never led armies and nations or orchestrated projects such as building a city. Instead, God used him to lead a movement, and very often, it seems, Paul led by coaching. For long periods he was in prison, where he had no prominent public platform, but he moved individuals and small groups by his letters. When he realized that his life was nearing an end, Paul wrote epistles to Timothy and Titus. These were very personal and show that the writer knew his young protégés well.

Would you agree that Paul also knew himself well? Romans 7:21–8:4, for example, is an intensely revealing account of his own struggles. Much of 2 Corinthians gives a glimpse into Paul's responses to unjust criticism. He was aware of his own strengths, weaknesses, and spiritual gifts. In turn, he had the credibility to help others make similar God-directed self-evaluations.

Students who enroll in counselor training programs almost always are required to get counseling for themselves before they can be considered qualified to help others. This counseling helps students build self-awareness and deal with issues in their own lives. Coaching is similar. One study suggested that while coach training and knowledge is helpful for beginning coaches, there are even greater benefits when the trainees received personal coaching in addition to their training. These students showed "reduced anxiety, increased goal attainment, enhanced cognitive hardiness and higher levels of personal insight."[1] When coaches-in-training were coached personally, they developed greater understanding of the coaching process. "Being a coach was harder than I imagined," wrote one student. Being coached greatly clarified the process and helped build coaching skills. These beginning coaches, like the people we coach, were less encumbered by their own issues when they got a better awareness of who they really were. For both coaches and clients, getting in touch with ourselves is a foundation for effective coaching. That includes awareness of the present circumstances, worldviews, and values that we considered in the previous chapter. Awareness also includes familiarity with one's passions, personality, strengths, and spiritual gifts.

PURSUING PASSION

At a meeting to discuss a possible business venture several years ago, I took my seat at a big conference table, was introduced to everybody in the room, and then was asked a significant question: "Gary, tell us your passion." It didn't take long for me to respond, but later I wondered what the people at that meeting might have thought if I had stumbled my way through those first few minutes. Worse, I wonder how they would have reacted if I had said, "My passion? I have no idea!"

Passion is a powerful underlying emotion that energizes and drives us. It may show itself in ravenous sexual lust or vehement anger, so strong that all caution or rational thinking is thrown out with abandon. This negative view sees passion as self-centered, obsessive, and out of control. But the word has a broader and much more positive meaning. Passion can be seen in ardent love, deep compassion, or boundless enthusiasm that energizes people and moves them to greater heights. In his book *The Passion Plan*, psychologist Richard Chang describes passion as *personal intensity*. "If you have passion for something, it strikes a chord in you. It heightens your awareness, engages your attention, and kindles excitement"[2]

Your passion is what fires you up. It is a driving force that can give your life its greatest energy and fulfillment. If you get in touch with your passion (or passions) and let it motivate you in healthy directions, passion can be a powerful influence for good. It can invigorate your life and raise you to higher levels of achievement and self-satisfaction. If you ignore your passion or let it fade, your life becomes duller, emotionally flatter, less fulfilled, and sometimes tinged with apathy. Like a speech or sermon without passion, life without passion can be boring, colorless, and uninspiring.

Passion is empowering. You may bludgeon it, suppress it,
squash it, or lose sight of it, but it is a given, a constant.

Your passion is ready and willing to provide all
the stamina and inspiration you need.

— RICHARD CHANG, coauthor of *The Passion Plan*

But when passion is recognized and allowed to work, it empowers ordinary people to make great things happen. In attracting visitors to a resort area, one travel advertisement proclaimed this about skiing: "Ability is not necessary. Passion is." You don't have to be among the best skiers in the world to enjoy skiing, the advertisement stated. "You need a fondness for adrenaline, a rapid heartbeat, a yearning to feel the same way about winter as you did when you were twelve years old." That's the kind of passion that drives avid skiers. It also drives determined golfers, dedicated musicians, and hobby enthusiasts of all kinds. No professional athlete reaches the top without passion. In business, leadership, ministry, teaching, and public speaking, passion is the spark that ignites people and motivates them to action. Without inner passion, no coach will ignite a fire in others. And the people you coach will not reach their goals until they discover and are moved by passion within themselves.

Most people dream big dreams, especially when they are young. But the dreams are abandoned when obstacles appear or when we realize that dream fulfillment takes a lot of work. This can happen to any of us. The initial excitement calms down and we admit to ourselves that failure is a possibility, so we slide back to less challenging pursuits and more routine activities. Years later we sense the emptiness and feel the loss of dreams that we never fulfilled. A major task of effective life coaching is to help people keep their dreams alive or rekindle passions that have faded.

God has put a driving passion in you to do something
special. Why wouldn't he? You are created in his image —
the only person exactly like you in the universe. No
one else can do your dream.

— BRUCE WILKINSON, author of *The Dream Giver*

Passion is a lot like ambition. Both motivate, goad, and inspire. Both can be used for personal gain. This especially is true of the selfish ambition that the Bible so strongly condemns.[3] But the Scriptures are filled as well with examples of men and women whose ambition and passion were directed by God. Caleb, Joshua, Nehemiah, Jeremiah, Peter, and John are among those who were passionate about fulfilling God's will for their lives. Paul once wrote that he was compelled to preach the gospel. It was a passion that he could not dismiss or resist.[4] A God-ordained passion begins to feel more and more like something we cannot ignore unless we decide to be deliberately disobedient.

Some Christians distinguish between passion and calling. A passion is something that arises from our life experiences and personalities. It brings fulfillment, joy, and productivity. It can come into the life of anyone or characterize any highly motivated group. A calling is more God focused. A call is consistent with one's strengths, abilities, and passions, but a call involves an inner conviction that this is a unique commission from God. Usually, perhaps always, it is about serving somebody else, not about the person who is called. It may involve sacrifice, giving, and determination that invariably flow from deep love for Christ and a willingness to obey without reservation. For the committed Christian who senses a call from God, it is something that cannot be ignored or rejected.[5]

Lead a life worthy of your calling, for you
have been called by God.

— Ephesians 4:1

Who do you know that is excited and driven by a passion or calling? The question might be hard to answer because so many people have let passion drain from their hectic lives. Their schedules have grown busier and busier, filled with pressing things that need to be done and a never-ending lack of time. Ask what excites them and most won't have an answer. Invite them to tell you their passions and you might get a blank stare. Helping them identify their passions can be one of the coach's biggest challenges.

It also can be one of the most fulfilling. When there is passion, life is fuller and more fun. That does not mean that life is easier. Passion implies emotional intensity that is neither healthy nor practical to sustain 24/7. Athletes passionate about winning also tend to be fervently committed to the discipline, determination, stamina, expenditure of energy, periods of rest, and boring hard work that turns passion into productivity.[6] Passion keeps the drive alive and fuels the fire within our souls. Working with people to find, develop, and pursue their passions has a quality of explosive excitement for everybody involved. This can extend to you as you look at your passions and use similar methods to help others find their passions as well.

FINDING YOUR PASSION

Chariots of Fire was an Oscar-winning movie about two runners, a Jewish Englishman (Harold Abrahams) and a Scottish Evangelical (Eric Liddle), who competed together in the 1924 Olympics in Paris. Everybody expected Liddle to win the hundred-meter race. He was assumed to be the fastest in the world. He also was a strict observer of the Sabbath who refused to run because the race was scheduled for a Sunday. Even pleas from the British royal family fell on deaf ears, but Liddle agreed to run later in the four-hundred-meter race. He ran with passion, breaking the world record, winning by a comfortable margin, and earning a gold medal.

Liddle was born of missionary parents in China, and his goal was to return there as a missionary following the Olympics. In a now-famous statement, he once said, "God has made me to be a missionary, but he also has made me fast, and when I run, I feel God's pleasure." Sometimes I tell clients about Liddle or remind audiences about his story and the movie. I ask them to fill in the blank in this sentence: "When I _____, I feel God's pleasure." This is a difficult assignment, but what people put in that blank often is the core of their passion.[7]

I have a friend who claims that I wear my emotions like a badge on my sleeve. It is easy for him to tell what I'm thinking because he can see it in my eyes, my posture, my speech. You'll see this in the people you coach and they may see it in you. Talk about something that interests you minimally and you're not very animated. Get to a topic that is close to your passion and you come alive, your speech is a little faster, perhaps you are leaning forward and gesturing more. If you think to look for this in the next few days, you will see it in others and in yourself.

The giants of the faith all had one thing in common:

neither victory nor success, but passion.

— PHILIP YANCEY, author, *Christianity Today* columnist

This leads to a very effective way to get in touch with passions. Suggest the following to the people you coach, but start first with yourself. Think of some people who know you well, who have talked with you often and spent time with you. Ask these people what they see as your passions. Once when I was being coached, my wife walked down the hall and my coach called out, "Julie, what is Gary's passion?" She answered without hesitation and she was right. Have the people you coach ask this of their close family members or coworkers and there is likely to be a consensus, at least if the person being coached still shows glimmers of passion that others can recognize.

It also can be helpful to think back to times in your life when you were excited to be alive. This might take a little mind stretching, but it's worth the effort. Start with your childhood and work forward. Try to think of specific situations in which you were bursting with enthusiasm and so fulfilled or focused on what you were doing that you lost all awareness of the clock. These might have been times when you were working on a project, involved in a mission trip, caught in a challenging sport, or spending time with somebody who was creative or fun to be with. Write down these examples. Do you see any patterns—similar types of experiences that typically fire you up with enthusiasm?

While you are looking back, reflect on this question: When you were a kid and your parents couldn't find you, what did they assume you were doing? Were you doing creative things, exploring your environment, planning plays, or engaging in imaginary games with your friends? I hated going to bed as a kid, so on many nights I tried to smuggle a book under the covers. I remember hiding a flashlight under the pillow, pulling the covers over my head after my mother left the room, and reading when my parents thought I was fast asleep. I've been a voracious reader all my life. It's a passion.

Here's another thought. If money were no problem, you had all the time you needed, and there were no health limitations or other obstacles, what would you do? An interviewer asked some kids in a very poor country what they *would like to be* when they grew up. Each child was interviewed privately, but their eyes all sparkled as they enthusiastically described their dreams of becoming doctors, teachers, missionaries, and leaders. Then the researcher asked what they *expected to be* when they grew up. Their faces grew sad and they talked despairingly about being poor farmers, hardworking laborers, or caretakers for their own unhealthy kids. Even as children, their youthful passions were tempered by the reality of their impoverished environments.

Most of us live in much better circumstances and are further along in life, but many of us are like these children. We also have buried our passions under a load of reality. We have forgotten what we wanted to do when we grew up. Now, it is unrealistic to think of going back, of becoming professional athletes or pursuing careers that take years of schooling. But by pondering what we would like to do if we had no hindrances, we get a flicker of insight into our long-buried passions.

Table 9-1

FINDING YOUR PASSION
■ Ask somebody who knows you well to identify your passions.
■ Think of times in your life when you felt exuberant and excited to be alive. What might this say about your passion?
■ When you were young and your parents could not find you, what did they assume you were doing? What does this say about your passion?
■ If you had no limitations in terms of money or time, what would you like to do?
■ Look at your environment. Does this reveal what really interests and excites you?
■ Search the Scriptures, wait, and pray that God will reveal his passion for your life.

While you are doing some of this, look around the rooms in your home, maybe the room where you are reading these words. Look at your office, your bookshelf, the pictures on your walls. What do you see? How is the place decorated? Then ponder what kinds of movies you like. What music do you prefer? Who are the people with whom you really like to spend time? Are there passionate people whom you would like to meet and get to know? Maybe the answers to these questions reveal passion that you have been expressing even without your awareness.

PUTTING PASSION INTO YOUR COACHING PRACTICE

If passion is an emotional force that invigorates our lives, where does it come from? A lot comes from our past experiences and the people with whom we have associated. A few years ago, the front page of the *Chicago Tribune* showed a color picture of a very old lady wearing a woolen hat and a well-worn sweater, both bearing the Chicago Cubs insignia. Apparently, she had been attending Cubs games since she was four years old and still had hopes that her perennially unsuccessful team would win a championship someday before she died. You have people with similar devotion in your community. They are passionate about the local sports team—dyed-in-the-wool fans. This passion may have come from their families or their friends, but it was not carried in their genes. It probably didn't come from God. They learned it as children and it isn't likely to budge just because they support a team that keeps losing.

In contrast, passion in the lives of committed followers of Jesus Christ often arises from the indwelling influence of the Holy Spirit. At one time, we were far away from God, but because of his grace and the shed blood of his Son, we have been brought near to him.[8] Now we are God's works of art, created in Christ Jesus to do the good things that God has prepared in advance for us to do.[9] Our goal is to find out what pleases the Lord and do everything for the glory of God.[10] It is inconceivable that he would impassion us about anything that would not bring him honor.

I doubt that God is in the business of playing hide-and-seek with his followers. He does not call us to do the works that he has prepared for us to do and then keep his divinely created passion hidden so that only the lucky ones discover what it is. We may need a coach to help bring it out. We may tap into the passion-finding tools we have been discussing. But, ultimately, people who pray for God's leading and submit to his sovereignty will know the passion or the calling that is his plan for their lives.

> We are God's masterpiece. He has created us anew
> in Christ Jesus, so we can do the good things
> he planned for us long ago.
>
> —Ephesians 2:10

Once you or a person being coached is in touch with this inner passion, what happens next? How do you channel that passion into action? We all know people who talk about their passion or passions (there can be more than one) but don't do anything about it. Sometimes they want to move forward but don't know what to do. That is why some people want coaching.

Passion can be like a raging river, filled with energy, driving through the valley, creating whirlpools, currents, and rapids. If the water is not controlled by a levee or channeled through a dam, it can spread in unexpected directions, battering, flooding, destroying. Uncontrolled and unchanneled, even God-given passion can be like that water. Its energy is wasted rather than focused and directed. The dam or the conduit that directs the passion into worthwhile directions is what we might call purpose. If you are like me, you have known passion-driven people who never discovered how to purposely direct and focus their passion into positive outcomes.

Passion without purpose is meaningless.

— RICHARD CHANG, author of *The Passion Plan*

This has implications for Christian coaching as we come alongside those people who know their passions but are frustrated because they are not successfully living their passions. It is easy for these people to be frustrated. They may have jobs that earn good incomes and sometimes bring acclaim and success. But the work is exhausting, uninspiring, and ultimately unfulfilling. They know it would be irresponsible to quit, give up the income, and risk taking on something new. It also can be scary. I know because I have done it three times in my life. It worked successfully for me, but it might not work well for others. For most people, it is better to start with small short steps for putting passion into practice.

Make a commitment. To start, think about whether you really want to live guided by your passion or your calling. Do you remember the Old Testament account of Nehemiah? He is often seen as an outstanding leader who had a God-given passion to rebuild the walls around Jerusalem. We know that he accomplished what he set out to do, but it must have been difficult to get started. Privately, he wept over the state of his hometown. He prayed diligently. He planned for what he would do if the opportunity ever came. And he waited for God's timing.

All of this inner struggle impacted Nehemiah so much that everybody noticed, including his employer, King Artaxerxes. When the time came to tell the king about his passion, Nehemiah was "very much afraid" (Nehemiah 2:2, NIV) to say what he felt impassioned to do. But during his long waiting period, Nehemiah had set aside his doubts, if he had any, and firmly concluded that he was fully committed to going ahead with his passion.

It's tough making a commitment to live out your passion and then sticking with what you've decided. There is no questionnaire or formula for deciding if you really want to do this. You can and should discuss it with others. You can write down the pros and cons. I frequently ask God to keep stirring up the passion in me, to not let it fade, to bring reminders of what needs to be done. We all know that it's easier to get busy with other things and let the passion fade. But some people can't ignore the inner passion force because it never goes away. They have to say yes. It is only then that they can start taking action without being dissuaded. Coaches help people through this commitment process.

Table 9-2

PUTTING PASSION INTO PRACTICE
■ Settle this tough question: Do I really want to be guided by my passion? Seek divine guidance. Discuss this with others. Write down the pros and cons. You won't go anyplace until you settle this. ■ Pray diligently and plan carefully. ■ Find supportive passion-boosting people. ■ Face and rise above the obstacles.

Pray and plan. After he learned about the needs in Jerusalem, Nehemiah mourned and wept, but he didn't retreat into long crying spells. Instead, he fasted and prayed.[11] Apparently, this was more than a casual prayer; Nehemiah prayed day and night. He praised God for his attributes, confessed the sins of the people, and claimed the promises of God. In all of this, Nehemiah poured out his passion to God and asked for divine intervention. Later, in the royal court, Nehemiah prayed a short prayer for strength and wisdom before answering the king's question about the passion.

We aren't told specifically that Nehemiah was making plans while he was waiting, fasting, and praying, but clearly he had thought through what was needed. He had a plan in mind that enabled him to respond in detail and without hesitation when the king asked what was needed.[12] Later chapters in the book of Nehemiah show that his plan was flexible. He learned that God often changes our plans and gives a better way, but this does not rule out the importance of thinking ahead in practical ways.

Have you ever noticed how easy it is to plan first and pray later? Often we don't pray at all until we get stuck and need to be rescued. Without prayer, passions often fade, plans falter, and we go off on dead-end pathways. Persistent prayer and Spirit-guided planning keep passions alive and focused in the right directions.

Get information. Mike McGill was a student in his mid-twenties when he first learned about the sexual exploitation of children in underdeveloped Asian countries. Perhaps I was one of the first people he told about his growing passion to mobilize the groups that were working to stem the tide of sexual abuse throughout Asia. One semester he used his tuition money to buy a plane ticket that would take him to some of those abusive countries. For those of his friends who were more cautious and less inclined to take risks, Mike's decision to fly to Asia may have seemed foolish and impulsive. When he boarded the plane, he could not see his final goal, but he knew that the first step was to go on a fact-finding trip to see for himself. He got a clearer picture of the current situation, talked to people who had passions similar to his own, built relationships with future partners, and has had a significant impact even as he has worked to fulfill his passion. In the process, he allowed God to fuel the flames of his passion further.[13]

Find supportive people. Over the years, I have been amazed to see how God has brought encouraging supportive people into my life when I needed them most. The group is not large, but they believe in me and fuel my passion, often with telephone calls or e-mail messages that come just when I sense that the passion is fading. There are many skeptics in this world. They can point out dangers that we need to see, but skeptics often kill passion. Their skepticism shows how much we need friendships and frequent contact with inspiring people who share the goals, urge us on, and help us keep the passion alive.

Answer this question for yourself or ask your coaching clients: "Who are the trusted people that fuel my passion and keep me from losing sight of what I want to accomplish?" Cultivate contacts with these people. Share your enthusiasm and be encouraged. Expect that these conversations will clarify and solidify your passion. The passion promoters who enter our lives, seemingly by divine appointment, can make the difference between movement forward or passion that fizzles.

Life and work decisions based on both gifts and
passion produce energy, flow, and aliveness.

— RICHARD J. LEIDER, author of *The Power of Purpose*

Face the obstacles. While some people can be passion boosters, others can be your passion busters. They may not even realize the devastating impact of their criticisms, negative comments, or lack of support. They distract us from our passions or discount their value. They may believe that passionate people are unrealistic, impractical dreamers. They can give frequent reminders that what we want to do cannot be done. Slowly they chisel away at our dreams. If you read through the book of Nehemiah, you will meet a lot of these people. They ridiculed, criticized, distracted, intimidated, sabotaged, and tried to build doubt into the minds of the workers who were building the walls with Nehemiah. Consistently, he responded in the same way. He prayed, dealt with the resistance in practical ways, but kept moving forward in accordance with his passion.[14]

Almost everybody who accomplishes something in this life has passion and a sense of direction. These people aren't dissuaded by obstacles or swept along by circumstances. Few expect to head big corporations or lead armies, but they are leaders, nevertheless, who know where they are going. They attract the attention and get the cooperation of others who want to go in the same direction.[15] Like all of us, they have setbacks and frustrations, but overall they perform creatively and energetically because they are pushed by passion, convinced they are contributing to a purpose larger than themselves.

Apparently, the original Greek word for *enthusiasm* meant "filled with God."[16] Christians who have passion are people filled with God. They radiate enthusiasm about their lives and their activities. If they are leaders and coaches, they inspire and motivate others by their Spirit-led passion and sense of purpose. And they help others catch the passion and get a sense of purpose as well.

PERSONALITIES AND CULTURES

Kevin is one of my neighbors, a young man who works in a computer software company where his superior knowledge and technical skills have brought affirmation from his employer and respect from his coworkers. In spite of his capabilities, Kevin's career seems to be stalled. The problem has nothing to do with his work. According to his supervisor, Kevin has missed promotions because he lacks the ability to relate comfortably to people. As we talked about this in a grocery story parking lot, he asked if I thought he could change or if this social awkwardness was an indelible part of his personality.

Centuries before the word *personality* was ever used, the ancient philosophers and sages discussed innate characteristics that differentiated one person from another. Some of these traits appear inborn, but most are developed or shaped by the experiences of life. If we are to understand the people we coach, it can be helpful to be aware of their personalities in addition to the values and passions that we have considered thus far. Personality characteristics can be measured by a variety of inventories, some more valid than others, but personality traits also appear as we talk and interact with others. The good news is that many of these traits can be changed, including the shyness and lack of social skills that characterize Kevin.

The work of psychologists Howard Gardner and Daniel Goleman, among others, has shown that intelligence is not limited to the ability to think logically. In addition, there can be linguistic, creative, musical, and other types of intelligence, including what Goleman has termed social intelligence.[17] This involves empathy, social awareness, interest in individuals, the ability to build relationships, and a talent for inspiring and fostering positive feelings and inspiration in others. In chapter 4, we referred to Goleman's research showing that people with social intelligence are most effective as leaders, viewed more positively by others, better able to work in teams, and more inclined to get promotions.[18]

You may remember our discussion of what happens to the brain of another human being when a leader, counselor, or coach shows empathy and genuine interest. The neural circuitry in two people becomes attuned so that there is interconnectedness within their brains. My neighbor Kevin, and those who are like him, can grow in social intelligence and develop new social circuitry in their brains when they spend time with people who possess effective interpersonal skills.[19] Kevin can be taught to change, especially if he has a socially intelligent coach. The change that can come to his brain is nothing mysterious, esoteric, or New Age. It is explained by emerging brain science that helps us understand how one individual can influence another and how people who are stalled in their lives or their careers "can be trained in specific areas where developing better social skills will have the greatest payoff."[20] Can other personality traits change as well, in part through changing brain circuitry? Probably so, but before the desired goals can be reached, there must be an understanding of where an individual is (first stage of the coaching model), including his or her personality.

This discussion should note that individuals are not the only ones with personalities. Teams, groups, and even large organizations have personalities too. Have you ever gone into a store or church and been able to pick up the feel of the place? Some churches are warm and friendly. Others are highly intellectual, seemingly humorless and stodgy. You might agree that many churches reflect the personality of the leader. Perhaps the brain circuitry of the pastor affects the brain circuitry of the church members. Something similar may happen when a company president or store owner unconsciously shapes the personalities of their businesses. Maybe it is simpler to assume that every team or group has a personality or pervasive atmosphere that others learn to pick up. Often this atmosphere is termed *group culture*. It is the personality that can characterize everything from a marriage all the way to a large corporation, denomination, or political party. Even as they facilitate changes in individuals, corporate coaches sometimes are involved in helping dysfunctional group cultures make changes as well.

FINDING STRENGTHS

Before reading further, you might want to pause for a few minutes to answer these two questions: What are your major weaknesses? What are your strengths?

For many of us, the list of weaknesses is longer and easier to compile. Depending on where you grew up, your parents and teachers may have de-emphasized your strengths and focused on how you could overcome your weaknesses. In the home where I grew up, there was love and support, but I never got much affirmation. Instead, my parents focused on the lower grades on my report cards. The message was "It is wonderful that you got an A, but you need to focus on those subjects in which you did not do as well. You need to be better at math." The motives of my parents and teachers were admirable. They wanted me to do well in everything, so they focused on the areas I should have been improving. But they ignored my strengths.

Your strengths — your love of problem solving, your intuition,
your assertiveness, your altruism, your analytical mind — are
your natural appetites, and are irrepressible. Your strengths
are not only activities for which you have some natural talent;
they also are activities that strengthen you.

— MARCUS BUCKINGHAM, author of *Go Put Your Strengths to Work*

Sometimes this is supported by the American (and Canadian) admiration of people who rise above their weaknesses and achieve great success. Everybody applauded when cyclist Lance Armstrong overcame cancer and went on to win the Tour de France several times — without the steroids that disqualified others who sought to follow. Faults and failings are worth our attention. It is important to improve, or help others improve, in our areas of weakness. This can be a major emphasis in coaching. But a more recent, strength-focused way of thinking has emerged. After thirty years of research and interviews with more than two million people, the Gallup organization reached this startling conclusion: "The evidence is overwhelming. You will be more successful in whatever you do by building your life around your greatest natural abilities rather than your weaknesses."[21]

Is it surprising that strength-based coaching has emerged as a new direction for many coaches and their clients? This approach does not ignore weaknesses or the need to make improvements in our lives. But the emphasis on strengths is becoming more prominent, doubtless because the research evidence for a focus on strengths is impressive.[22] People who work primarily in their areas of strength are more engaged in their work, more fulfilled personally, and less inclined to leave their present employment or locations. Entire companies and churches have sought to discover the strengths of their people and build their communities in such a way that each person works in his or her area of competence.

How do we discover our own strengths or find the strengths in the people we coach? Several strength-finding inventories exist,[23] but it may be simpler to ask clients to list their strengths. Suggest that they ask the same from people who know them best. My family and my closest friends know my strengths better than I can recognize them in myself. This clarification of strengths is an exercise in serious contemplation of what the individual does well. The strength-finding process is better when it builds around answers to questions like these:

- What do I do best?
- Are there things I do better than most anybody else?
- What would the people who know me best say are my strengths?
- Looking over my life, when did I do something that was especially successful?
- What in my life does God seem to have blessed?

Companies and churches can ask similar questions.

As you seek to walk in the center of God's will, it's important
to establish the spiritual markers in your life that have led
you up to the place you now stand. Looking back on what
God has done in your life may bring great clarity toward
what he wants to do in your life in the days to come.

— HENRY and MEL BLACKABY,
coauthors of *What's So Spiritual About Your Gifts?*

With some coaching clients, there may be a need to get past the belief that focusing on strengths is a waste of time. Some Christians assume that this is an exercise in building pride because we are dwelling on our own capabilities and accomplishments. Instead, it might be better so see this as a way to discover and acknowledge the talents and capabilities God has given each of us. This can be a cause for thanksgiving and then for conscientiously developing and building on the strengths and capabilities God has given.

UNDERSTANDING SPIRITUAL GIFTS

This brings us to an aspect of coaching that is uniquely Christian. The Bible does not say much about strengths, but spiritual gifts are mentioned in several places, especially in Romans 12:4-8, 1 Corinthians 12, and Ephesians 4:4-16. According to these passages, the Holy Spirit gives special gifts—abilities and responsibilities—to believers who want to be obedient and be led by God. There is nothing wrong with wanting the more desirable of these gifts,[24] but these gifts from the Holy Spirit have nothing to do with the advancement of one's career or the accomplishment of personal goals. The gifts are distributed by God, only to believers, according to his discretion and for the sole purpose of equipping his people to do his work and to build and strengthen the church.[25]

Several inventories exist to help coaches and their clients discover their spiritual gifts (see appendix G). These can be helpful in understanding each person with whom we work and in assessing where our clients are, both at the start of coaching and later. We should add, however, that some writers are critical of these inventories, concluding that they uncover natural talents and strengths that have nothing to do with spiritual gifts.

Christians are seeking the gifts of the Holy Spirit and not the Holy Spirit Himself. If we seek the gifts of the Spirit and not the Holy Spirit Himself, we'll always focus on self. . . . There are no gifts apart from an intimate relationship with the Spirit.

—HENRY and MEL BLACKABY,
coauthors of *What's So Spiritual About Your Gifts?*

In their book *What's So Spiritual About Your Gifts?* Henry and Mel Blackaby argue that many Christians are seeking the gifts of the Holy Spirit but not the Holy Spirit himself.[26] The Blackabys acknowledge that spiritual gifts often are similar to strengths but there are differences. Both strengths and gifts come from God, but whereas we all have strengths, the only people who receive spiritual gifts are those who walk in intimate relationship with the Holy Spirit. Strengths enable us to build careers and accomplish goals. For believers, there also may be a desire to use God-given strengths to bring him honor. Spiritual gifts are more restricted in that they come only to people committed to building the church and honoring God. Strengths involve activities that are invigorating and easy to do. Gifts may be special endowments from God that are inconsistent with our natural talents but able to empower us to fulfill a God-given assignment that is not always easy. Paul the apostle was gifted by God to speak powerfully, but public speaking was not one of his natural strengths. Gideon was unimportant and probably uninspiring although, like everyone else, he had strengths. Then God gifted him to be a leader, described him as a mighty warrior, possessed him with the Spirit of God, and enabled him to defeat an army that outnumbered Gideon's little band of soldiers by a ratio of four hundred to one.[27] Don't spend a lot of time trying to identify spiritual gifts, the Blackabys suggest. Instead spend time getting to know the Holy Spirit intimately. Then, at his discretion, he will clarify his vision for your life and give you the gifts you need when you need them, whether or not you take a spiritual gifts inventory.

The Blackabys argue their case persuasively, but many would be reluctant to embrace their thought-provoking analysis wholeheartedly. Clearly, God's gifts are given to accomplish his purposes, but it seems that God does not always wait to reveal his gifts until a special need arises. Many Christians and their coaches have found great value in looking at spiritual gifts. Knowledge of these can be a helpful indication of how God has prepared us for service and life direction even before unique situations arise.

LOOKING FORWARD

We have seen that coaching involves four overlapping steps: becoming aware of the present and the person, focusing on the vision for the future, planning and taking action to reach the goals, and dealing with the obstacles that get in the way. We improve awareness of the present when we get in touch with ourselves and focus on such issues as values, passion, and strengths. All of this involves building awareness of the present. In the following two chapters, we turn to the next part of the coaching model: clarifying the vision of where we want to go or where God seems to be leading.

PART 4

VISION IN CHRISTIAN COACHING: WHERE DO WE WANT TO GO?

CHAPTER 10

CLARIFYING THE VISION

I CAN STILL remember the arrival of the circus when I was growing up. Early in the morning, my grandfather would take me to a field near our house to watch the excitement. It's a faded memory now, but I know there was activity everywhere. The circus train had arrived during the night, and by the time of our arrival at dawn, the animals had been unloaded and there had been great progress in getting the tent ready to be raised. Even my childish mind wondered what it must have been like on rainy mornings when the cold, drenched workers were wallowing in the mud.

After World War II, the circus went indoors, into arenas and coliseums, where tents were unnecessary. When television made its appearance, interest in the circus began to lag and crowds got smaller. Then in the 1970s, aware that the two-thousand-year-old circus tradition was fading, Monaco's Prince Rainier III established an annual festival where the best circus acts in the world would compete for awards and prize money. This helped to rekindle enthusiasm. But then came something else: Around the world, the circus began to reinvent itself for the new millennium.

Last time the circus was in our town, once again the performances were taking place in a tent. But this was no ordinary tent. Set in the middle of a football stadium, the tent was an eighteen-hundred-seat luxury facility with hardwood floors and red velvet seats. It was climate controlled for maximum comfort, according to the upbeat advertising, with tickets available online through the Internet. Sensitive to animal rights activists, some circuses, like the fabulous and successful Cirque du Soleil, have eliminated animal acts all together. The performers combine dance, theater, mime, music, and computer technology with acts of human daring and aerobatic agility that rival anything else in the entertainment world. Every year, a symphony orchestra near our home presents a highly acclaimed Christmas concert that combines impressive circus acts with classical and seasonal music.

What changed the circus? Most likely a few men and women with vision began to imagine a future that few others could see. Without that vision, the circus today might be dead or like too many contemporary churches, academic institutions, and government agencies: doing what they have always done in the same old ways but wondering why they are declining, lifeless, or stagnant in an era of vibrant change.

Almost without exception, the books on leadership that line the shelves of my office cite vision as the one indispensable ingredient of effective leaders. "There is no more powerful engine driving an organization toward excellence and long-range success than an attractive, worthwhile, and achievable vision of the future, widely shared," Burt Nanus wrote years ago in *Visionary Leadership*.[1] The same is true of the individuals we coach. People with vision have a clearer direction of where they want to go. Without vision, people flounder, deadlocked by tradition, drifting and stumbling while the world soars forward.

Vision leads the leader. It paints the target. It sparks and fuels the fire within. Show me a leader without vision, and I'll show you someone who isn't going anywhere.

— JOHN C. MAXWELL, leadership expert, author

Despite the importance of vision, visionary leaders are in short supply. The church hungers for leaders with vision and so does the government. If you can help people to find clear vision and move in the direction of their goals, then you are well on your way to success as a coach. If you take the time to apply the vision-finding principles to yourself, you can benefit personally and have a greater understanding of what your clients are being urged to do.

GETTING THE BROADER PICTURE

Moses and Joshua were among the most successful leaders in the Bible. They led a group of people on a wilderness journey that lasted forty years. When they reached their goal, only three of the thousands who started the journey had made it to the borders of the Promised Land: Moses, Joshua, and Caleb. All of their followers were under forty years of age. None had lived in permanent communities or experienced the revolutionary events that God had used to bring their nation out of bondage almost half a century before. These were restless people inclined to be critical. But three men kept confronting them with a God-given vision for the future. As a result, the people moved forward.

Martin Luther King Jr. inspired people from the steps of the Lincoln Memorial because he painted a picture of what the future could be like. Big visions bring big commitments and lift people out of the monotony of their everyday lives to put them into a new world filled with opportunity, challenge, and hope.[2] Visions can involve millions of people. An example is Dr. King's dream of a fully integrated America. But visions also can be very personal, such as the vision you may have for one of your kids or the vision a coaching client may have about his or her future career.

Coaching is an effective form of leadership that stimulates vision and moves people forward. As we have seen, it involves clarifying the present, focusing on the future, and reaching goals by taking action and overcoming obstacles. To clarify the present, we help people get in touch with their circumstances and themselves, including the driving passion that keeps them moving forward. As he led his nation, Moses was passionate about reaching the Promised Land, and this kept him going despite opposition and obstacles. As a personal inner force, passion *drives* us forward. But most people also need a mental picture of where they are going. They need a vision of what can be possible. Vision *pulls* us forward. Once that vision clearly is in mind, we can deal with the practical strategy steps of getting where we want to go.

A vision is not a dream but a reality that
has yet to come into existence.

—NEIL SNYDER, JAMES DOWD, and DIANE MORSE HOUGHTON,
coauthors of *Vision, Values and Courage*

A vision is a clear picture of something we want to have exist in the future. It is a target we intend to reach. It encourages people to think beyond what is and visualize what can be or will be. Visions inspire and visionary leaders attract followers because both capture the imagination and excite people to anticipate dreams that are possible to achieve. To accomplish this, visions must be about potential for the future but anchored in the realities of the present. Visions, like coaching itself, provide an image of how we can get from where we are now to where we can and believe we should be.

Once it is clear, a vision can be described in a few words. The ideal vision statement is short, concise, and easily remembered. Here's mine: *I envision a worldwide army of competent, Christ-honoring caregiver leaders equipping others to impact the world.* There are others building the caregiving army I envision. I'm not the only one. But everything I do is geared to building this army around the world.

Notice that my envisioned army will be *competent.* The people who serve will have training and be skilled. For me this means they will be culturally sensitive, Spirit-empowered, and both biblically and psychologically astute. This army is also *Christ-honoring.* I am a Christian, commissioned like all Christians to make disciples.[3] I see great value in non-Christian relief efforts, social work, and counseling, but my focus is on building a competent army of believers devoted to honoring Christ. This will be an army of *caregivers* who are Christian coaches and counselors. I am not focused on building caregivers who are relief workers, social activists, teachers, or providers of food and medical services. These are all very important and I can support most of their activities with enthusiasm, but I have decided to keep my emphasis on Christian counselors and coaches. My emphasis is also on building *leaders* who, in turn, can recruit, train, and send forth others to be competent, Christ-honoring caregivers. I'm not focused on building business leaders, pastoral leaders, athletic leaders, or any other kind except when these people are becoming Christian caregiver leaders. Because my focus is on leaders (including emerging leaders), I rarely speak to congregations in churches or teach groups that do not consist of leaders. The emphasis on leaders keeps me focused and helps me make wise decisions about my work and my priorities. My vision statement ends with words about *equipping others to impact the world.* I have many friends who are training future counselors and coaches who will find jobs in their communities or open private practices and do very well. That's too narrow for me. I want to build leaders who have a passion for impacting the world for Christ through their caregiving, their coaching, and their commitment to equipping others to do the same.

My vision is big, but it is focused. It did not appear after ten minutes of thought. It emerged over many months as I prayed, discussed it with others, reflected, and revised the statement often. I can't guarantee that it will never change. Visions don't fluctuate from day to day, but they do evolve. Even so, I suspect that the essence of my vision will stick with me for the rest of my life. Here are some other visions, each of which is held by somebody I know or have known:

- A church of fully devoted followers of Jesus Christ reaching and growing others
- A football championship
- A successful published novel
- An institute that teaches people from other countries to be leaders
- A business that honors God, helps people develop, pursues excellence, and makes a profit
- A treatment center for troubled adolescents
- A youth center for inner-city kids
- A retreat center for burned-out pastors and their spouses
- A church of people who are stirred by God's Word, struggling well with life together, and serving others wholeheartedly

---

Vision defines what you stand for, why you exist,
and who your team [or you] will become.

— DANIEL HARKAVY, author of *Becoming a Coaching Leader*

Notice that these visions are all something that will be. They are end products, often tangible and observable, more like nouns than like verbs.

Mission statements, in contrast, are more declarations of action. They may involve build*ing* a church, work*ing* to win a championship, develop*ing* a company or grow*ing* an organization. These are action words (building, working, developing, and growing), describing something that is being done. We will discuss mission statements more fully in the next chapter.

FINDING THE VISION

Our discussion thus far may be familiar territory. You know the importance of having a vision, that people without vision drift or die. You are aware that the same is true of churches, companies, and organizations that have no vision. You may realize, as well, that finding a vision can be difficult. Most people don't see the need for this or they never take the time or energy to think about visions for their own lives. Helping people focus on a concise and enduring vision can be a big challenge for coaches. Some of our clients will come with a vision. They want coaching so they can better accomplish their goals and hopes for the future. Others are stuck or dissatisfied, lacking direction, and needing to develop a clear and compelling vision for their lives and organizations. The remainder of this chapter and the next will focus on the second major piece of the coaching model: enabling people in coaching to clarify their visions and think about where they want to go or where God wants them to go.

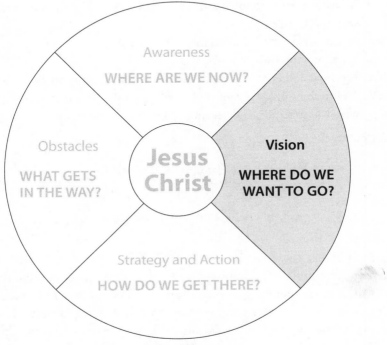

Figure 10-1

With some frequency—in sermons, seminars, and the media—we are reminded about more recent visionary people who, in different ways, changed their worlds or the course of history. Mahatma Gandhi, Nelson Mandela, Martin Luther King Jr., Mother Teresa, Billy Graham, Walt Disney, or Bill Gates might come to mind immediately. We admire the unusual ability of these and other well-known visionaries to see what others can't see about their times or the future. We applaud their tenacity, their refusal to be deterred by even the greatest obstacles, their willingness to abandon everything else so their visions can become reality. As we look in awe at the few people who lead movements, revolutions, or nations, we conclude that visionaries are rare and not like us. They must be a special breed of individuals who wouldn't understand how most of us are locked into routine daily activities. We're busy getting through today and have little time or energy to think about the future except, maybe, in vague and general ways.

I agree that some people, maybe a select few, have an unusual ability to anticipate future trends and the courage to lead others forward. In our own ways, however, all of us can be visionaries. If you think you can be a leader without being a visionary, forget it. Nobody will follow your lead if you don't know where you are going. If you want to be successful in your work, raise your kids effectively, be a good teacher, grow a church, or build a business, you need to have a vision.

That's the tough news. Here is the good news: God gives vision to his people. Each of us is unique, and he has a unique vision and purpose for each individual.[4] Some visions might be big and all-embracing; most will be smaller in scope but equally a part of God's plan. Some people are in touch with the vision God has for their lives. For others, the vision is fuzzier. But it can get clearer for you or your coaching clients.

Visions come from two sometimes overlapping sources. Visions can be created or discovered. *Created visions* come from the innovative thinking of individuals or groups. The best of these are clear, specific, compelling images of the future that arise from the careful thinking of perceptive, insightful people. Most often these reflect the values, passions, and dreams of the vision casters. These visions are not necessarily bad, wrong, or selfish simply because they are human inventions. In his wisdom, God may guide the shaping of visions that come to people who give little thought to the possibilities of divine intervention. Surely, he also leads when we seek his guidance in the vision-casting process.

Discovered visions are pictures of the future that come from God. There were times in the Bible when God supernaturally gave somebody a vision. It happened to Moses when he heard a voice from the burning bush. It happened to Mary when an angel told her about the coming Messiah and to Saul of Tarsus on the road to Damascus. On rare occasions, something like this may happen today, but usually God reveals his vision in less dramatic ways, through the guidance of the Holy Spirit. Rick Warren notes that "it isn't our job to create the purposes of the church but to discover them."[5] How is this done? How do we discover a personal vision or vision for a group, church, or organization?

Pray. Do you or the people you coach really want God's vision? If a vision begins to emerge, are you and your client willing to work toward making the vision a reality? I remember having lunch with a young pastor talking about vision. He expressed a desire to have a clear vision for his life and church but admitted that his ministerial duties were so consuming that he rarely took time to think about vision and spent even less time praying. I've never been to his church, but apparently it is floundering, not going anywhere. You can guess why.

Don't rush the process. I was impatient when I was being coached about my vision. I like to make decisions quickly and move forward enthusiastically. I wanted to get the vision on paper as soon as I could, but my coach kept saying the same words: "Don't rush it. Try to get it close to a dozen words or less. When you have it, you will know." The last sentence bothered me most. It sounded vague and mystical. Even so, there were times when I thought I had the vision encapsulated but it didn't feel right. When I got it right, I knew.

Sometimes leaders and others need to make quick decisions. There is no time to wait and think. Clarifying a vision is not one of those rush times. The sense of greatest clarity comes when we wait on God, seek to discern his guidance, and trust that the Holy Spirit will make the way clear. That is likely to take time, and perhaps the process does seem vague. But very often when we get it, we will know.

Look inside. Think again about your gifts, your values, and your passion. These will be at the core of your vision. Ponder these questions: *What really moves you? What makes you cry? What brings a glow of joy into your life? What arouses enthusiasm?* Think about these things for a while and you are likely to get closer to your vision.

> Discerning a vision is neither straightforward nor predictable. Sometimes it takes a few weeks of diligent effort; sometimes it takes years. The process is perhaps more important to God than the outcome because the effort we go through draws us closer to him.
>
> — GEORGE BARNA, researcher, author of *The Power of Vision*

Get information. A vision is about the future, but it comes from the present. Look at your world. What could change? What should change? Visions almost always come from dissatisfaction with the way things are and a desire to make it better. "A God-ordained vision will be in line with what God is up to in the world," writes Andy Stanley.[6] If you don't know what's happening in the world at large or in the smaller world where you live every day, you aren't likely to get a clear vision.

Let's go back to that pastor with the struggling church. To get his church moving, he probably doesn't need to know a lot about world politics or big business, but he does need to look at what is going on in his community and in the lives of the people in his congregation. Periodically, I look at Acts 17, where Paul was waiting in Athens but not wasting time. He looked around at the community, talked with the people, saw what they were worshipping, and learned about their culture and poetry. In doing this, he earned the right to be heard, got a clearer vision on how to speak to the Athenians, and was used by God to make an impact.

Finding a vision is not like crystal ball gazing, trying to predict the future. Visions come to those who notice current trends, see what is going on, and trust God to show how their gifts, strengths, values, and passions can be directed in ways that challenge the status quo and make a difference for the future.

Learn from visionary people. Try to find somebody who will meet with you and talk informally about vision. That can be the role of a good coach. When you feel as though your life has no vision, there are few things more inspiring than a sensitive, encouraging friend or coach whose very enthusiasm gets you moving. But be careful. Some people are so bubbly with enthusiasm and revolutionary ideas that they scare anybody who doesn't share their energy. Some of these people see themselves as motivators when they really are intimidators. Don't limit your learning to people you know. You can learn from the lives of visionary people whose examples may inspire you even though you'll never meet. Listen to tapes that can help you think through your vision. Read books.[7]

Get a vision check. Every vision is different, but all good visions share similar characteristics. Yours might not meet all of the guidelines of table 10-1, but if too many of these are missing, you may need to go back to the drawing board. Look over these characteristics yourself and then discuss them with a friend who can help clarify your vision further. If you are a coach, discuss this table's information with a client.

Table 10-1

EVALUATING YOUR VISION
Each vision is unique, but clear God-given visions will have similar characteristics. God-given visions are: ■ **Consistent with Scripture.** No vision from God will violate any biblical teaching. Every vision for an individual or organization is consistent with God's plans as recorded in God's Word.

- **Consistent with your strengths, spiritual gifts, values, and passions.** Visions that persist and inspire will align with who you are.
- **Worthwhile.** God-given visions are worth living for, sacrificing for, committing to, and maybe even dying for.
- **Clear and concise.** They are easy to understand, remember, and communicate.
- **Characterized by high ideals.** Every good vision must include commitment to excellence, integrity, respect for people, and similar values.
- **Ambitious.** The best visions will guide, often amaze, and move people forward toward something much better than the status quo.
- **Scary.** God-given visions can be life-changing, pulling us out of our comfort zones, instilling awe, and stretching us beyond what we might see as our limits.
- **Unique.** Does your vision really reflect who you are? If people who know you well are surprised by your vision, then you probably don't have the right vision. And if your vision is the same as everybody else's vision, something is wrong.
- **Compelling.** Visions feel right. They excite, motivate, and generate enthusiasm. The more you reflect on the vision, the more you are convinced that this is what you have to do. If your vision brings a ho-hum response from others, something is wrong. If it doesn't inspire you, forget it. Visions that don't inspire aren't God-given visions.

KEEPING VISION ALIVE

The best coaches are those who can encourage and energize their coaching clients as they go through the vision-finding process. But that is not the whole process. If you are like me, you have met a number of visionary people. They think creatively, anticipate how things could be better, talk enthusiastically about their expectations for the future, and sometimes devote many hours to making elaborate plans. But like fireworks on a dark summer night, their visions explode on the scene, create a big impression, and then fizzle. Visions are exciting and motivating, but it is hard to keep them alive and self-sustaining after the initial brightness begins to fade.

*Vision doesn't stick without constant care and attention.
The urgent and legitimate needs of today quickly erase our
commitment to the* what could be *of tomorrow.*

— ANDY STANLEY, pastor, author of *Visioneering* and *Making Vision Stick*

The following paragraphs describe some of the most obvious vision-eroding influences, but you may think of others. This could be used as a checklist for determining what needs to be changed so visions can be kept alive in you or in the people you coach.

Why might a vision die?

The vision might not come from God. Do you remember Simon the sorcerer, who amazed everybody with his magic and liked to boast about how great he was? Then he saw the awesome power of the Holy Spirit and offered to pay Paul by the same kind of power. Immediately, he was castigated for his motives. Simon's vision was to be more powerful, gaining benefits that would be to his own advantage. This self-centered vision was not from God, so it could not be sustained.[8]

George Barna has written that "God communicates His vision only to those who have persisted in knowing Him intimately, for His vision is a sacred part of unfolding His eternal plan. This means that your motives for seeking a vision are crucial. . . . Your motives must be pure and your heart willing not only to receive the vision, but also to commit yourself to seeing it come to pass."[9]

The vision may be too complex and difficult to understand or remember. Have you ever heard a student describe a professor with words like the following? "He is brilliant, but when he teaches he is dull because he can't communicate clearly." Maybe the same could be said of some pastors, politicians, or authors. Certainly it is true of visionary people who come up with long, multi-paragraph vision statements and then wonder why nobody understands, remembers, or buys into the vision. In his insightful book *Making Vision Stick*, Andy Stanley gives several principles to increase the adhesiveness of a vision.[10] The first is to state the vision simply. Good visions are short visions. Rarely, if ever, did God give a commission or vision that was unclear or too complex. Coaching can enable people to formulate visions that are concise and easily remembered.

There may be no deep commitment to the vision. It is easier to create a vision than to keep it alive. Vision maintenance takes commitment, but most visions are not worth the dedication, sacrifice, determination, and persistence needed for the vision to be cultivated and realized. One focus of coaching is to join with the client to determine his or her level of commitment to the vision. Compelling visions stick. Others get lost in the complexities of daily living.

There may be no clear underlying values. It is widely accepted that big companies that last and thrive are businesses built on firmly held beliefs and values. When nobody knows the company's core values or when these are ignored, problems arise sooner or later. There will be compromises, integrity lapses, and questionable decisions that begin to crumble the company foundations. The same is true with vision. When there are no clear underlying values, vision will be hard to sustain.

There may be no encouragement. It is possible to sustain a vision all by yourself. Over the centuries, many missionaries have clung to their visions alone and in remote places. More often, however, visions fade when they are held by only one or two people who have little or no encouragement, support, or people who come alongside to help and pray. Many years ago, I learned that if a person has a vision from God, most likely God has given that same vision to others. And he has a way of putting those visionary people together. If they encounter each other and then compete, everybody loses and the vision erodes. If they cooperate in a team effort and encourage each other, the vision moves forward. Almost nobody fulfills a God-given vision alone.

All God-ordained visions are shared visions. Nobody goes
it alone. But God generally raises up a point person
to paint a compelling verbal picture.

— ANDY STANLEY, pastor, author of *Visioneering* and *Making Vision Stick*

There may be no fresh reminders of the need. Sometimes visions fade because we get used to things the way they are. We've all lived in houses where something needs be fixed but we don't get around to getting it done. The longer we go without making the improvement, the more we adjust to the way things are and the less we think about the need to make the change. Visions are like that. Even visions from God can be pushed aside by procrastination until we don't see their need any longer.

Stanley argues that every vision is a solution to a problem. Vision is more likely to last and have impact when it is linked to a need and presented or viewed as a solution to that need.

There may be no progress. It is hard to maintain a vision when nothing seems to be happening. Most Christians are aware that God's timing is not the same as ours. Even when progress appears to be stalled, there are times when God is active behind the scenes, working to bring about what he has planned. Enthusiasm is motivating, but enthusiasm fades when there is little evidence to sustain the hope. Often the coach's role is to be a hope-giver and encourager even when there seems to be slow progress or none at all.

The vision may be allowed to fade. For many years, my wife and I sat under the ministry of pastor Bill Hybels, who often remarked that visions leak. Like air that seeps out of a balloon or water that drains from a damaged cup, visions fade away if they are not replenished regularly. It can be useful to print visions in the church bulletin or hang them in a frame on the wall, but soon they become part of the environment and cease to be noticed. Leaders, including coaches, must find ways to repeat the vision in different ways so that the message keeps being reinforced. Both coaching and forward progress can stall when visions are allowed to fade.

The vision gets buried. In leadership or in coaching, visions often are formed and promoted with enthusiasm. A group of people or a coaching client may jump enthusiastically into the process of implementing a vision but then something gets in the way. Over time, the vision is buried under the distractions of daily living, pressing needs, or the emergence of newer and seemingly more exciting projects. Dreaming dreams can be invigorating. Implementing a plan to turn those dreams into reality can be tedious. As a result, the visions get pushed aside and hidden under other ideas or activities. Periodically, the vision needs to be revisited to determine if the vision casters want to maintain and continue to pursue their original goals.

There will be obstacles. Almost always, visions disrupt our lives and shake us out of our apathy. Share your vision and somebody is certain to say it can't be done. Try to make it happen and you'll get criticism and maybe outright resistance. Ask Nehemiah. He had a God-given vision for rebuilding the walls around Jerusalem, but he had opposition from the start. Some came from the local leaders who were threatened by Nehemiah's vision and determination. Other opposition came in the form of fatigue and disagreements between the people who were working on the wall-building exercise. Nehemiah prayed and then intervened to deal with the obstacles and make changes in his action plans.[11]

What does all of this mean for coaching? In addition to helping others clarify their visions, the coach watches for influences and obstacles that can suck out the enthusiasm, kill the vision, and discourage the visionaries. Coaches are cheerleaders for their clients and their visions, stimulating forward movement so the goals are reached and dreams realized.

KEEPING VISION IN PERSPECTIVE

One of my younger friends is a recent college graduate who works as a trainer in a fitness club. I don't know him well, but I suspect he would not resonate with the message of this chapter. Larry (that's not his real name) is still "trying to find direction." He is intelligent and socially engaging, is an interesting conversationalist, and is seemingly enthusiastic about his work, but he has no vision for his life and sees no reason to have one. "I just go with the flow," he says. "I don't have any plans for the future. Maybe that will come sometime, but for now I'll do whatever."

Recently, Larry ran in a marathon. He trained for months, getting his body ready for the morning when he joined thousands of others on a twenty-six-mile run. Clearly, he had a vision, a goal, and a plan of action that he rigorously followed in preparation for the race. Will he find visions and goals for his life and career as he gets older and more focused? Would marriage or parenthood make a difference? Would things change if he got a promotion at work or found a job with leadership responsibilities? More important might be the question of whether he needs to find and develop life visions.

There are many people like Larry, people of all ages, who are content to "go with the flow" and avoid the careful development of visions and agendas. Probably millions of people never think about vision. They are content to go on with their lives, not giving much thought to the future, largely impacted by circumstances and sometimes by the latest trend or fad. If I were coaching Larry, I would not criticize his lack of vision casting, but I might remind him about the focus of his marathon run and encourage him to be open to the value of goal setting and planning for other parts of his life.

In my mind, I also would remember a poignant message that Rick Warren sent to his congregation and the people on his mailing list when his daughter-in-law was gravely ill following surgery to remove a brain tumor. Warren wrote:

> There is no such thing as long-range planning! When life throws you a curve-ball, like our sudden discovery of Jaime's brain tumor, we realize once again that much of our schedule is often beyond our control. Unforeseen crises prove the futility of long-range planning. No one but God knows the future. While the Bible tells us that we ought to prepare for the future, no one can predict the future. No one. As Jeremiah said, *"Lord, I know that a person's life doesn't really belong to him. No one can control his own life." (Jeremiah 10:23, NCV)*

The Living Bible translation says it this way: "O Lord, I know it is not within the power of man to map his life and plan his course." The godly way to plan is scenario planning—having the attitude of, "We'll do this . . . IF such and such happens . . ." This is the kind of planning that the Bible recommends: *"Instead, you ought to say, 'IF it is the Lord's will, we will live and do this or that.'" James 4:15 (NIV)*.[12]

Pastor Warren was writing about long-range planning, but his words could apply equally to vision casting, goal setting, and taking action steps. None of these is wrong or unbiblical. They are at the basis of coaching. But all of our work as coaches, including all of our work with the Larrys of this world, needs to be kept within the perspective of God's greater plans and sovereign control over our lives and circumstances.

TIME FOR A QUIZ

Somebody once sent me an e-mail message that began with a series of difficult questions like these:

- Name the five richest people in the world.
- Name five people who have won a Nobel or Pulitzer Prize.
- Name the last half-dozen Academy Award winners for best actor and actress.
- Name the last decade's World Series or World Cup winners.

I couldn't answer any of these questions, but then I read some that I could answer:

- List a few teachers who aided your journey through school.
- Name three friends who have helped you through a difficult time.
- Name five people who have taught you something worthwhile.
- Think of a few people who have taken the time to make you feel appreciated and special.
- Name several heroes whose stories have inspired you.

It is easy to understand what this illustrates. We rarely remember the famous people who rose to stardom, but we rarely forget the people who impacted us personally. That is the essence of coaching. We make a profound impact on the lives of our clients when we can help them in their journeys, guide them through difficult times, teach them things that are worthwhile, or make them feel appreciated. And when we help the people we coach find vision and enable them to sustain that vision, we are doing an important — no, a noble — work.

Does a coach ever set the vision for another person? People can be inspired and motivated when an orator or inspirational leader sets a vision for others to follow. Visionary pastors have been used by God to set direction for their churches. These clearly stated visions motivate others to sign on and get involved. We all like to be a part of something that is on the move, led by somebody with vision. Some Christian leaders have urged parents to set visions for their children, teachers to set visions for their students, husbands and wives to set visions for each other. When we set visions for others, we show our confidence in their abilities and potential. Many people long for someone who believes in them and is convinced that they have potential.

For people to be part of the dream,
they need to be part of the process.

— DAVE COLLINS, author of *Vision That Works*

But we must be careful about setting visions for others. What happens if your vision for another person is not God's vision? What happens if your vision really reflects your desires and insecurities? I saw this repeatedly when I was a professor. Students would confide in me that they really did not want to become pastors, businessmen, or doctors but were being pushed by their families, especially by parents who paid the tuition and believed that they had the best visions for their children. Some of these parents were disappointed in their own lives or careers, apparently trying to find fulfillment by goading their children where the parents never were able to go. This can create tremendous pressure, not only in children but in others who respect and want to please a mentor or hero. By going in a different direction, these people can feel a great weight of guilt, sometimes self-imposed. They don't want to disappoint or appear ungrateful, but they struggle with the knowledge that their hearts and passions are not where some other respected person wants them to go.

Coaching and parenting are both better if you present options casually, helping people build visions consistent with their gifts, talents, passions, and interests. All of us who coach others, including parents, need to be careful that our enthusiasm for another's potential does not push him or her in the wrong direction.

When others are given encouragement, even as they are helped to find their own God-given visions, they can begin to move where God is leading. The next three chapters describe how this is done.

I'll make a prediction. If you and your team will set aside time to define the problem, state your vision as a solution, and discover a compelling reason why now is the time to act, you will walk away from that meeting, or series of meetings, with more passion for what you are about than you thought possible. Something will come alive in you. And when you talk about your vision, you will be more convincing than you've ever been before.

— ANDY STANLEY, pastor, author of *Next Generation Leader*

CHAPTER 11

MOVING WITH A MISSION

GUSTAVE WAS AN exceptionally gifted engineer who gained fame as the builder of several impressive structures throughout Europe. Near the end of the nineteenth century, he won a contest for the design of a structure that would mark the Universal Exhibition in Paris, a world's fair marking the centennial of the French Revolution. For two years, more than three hundred workers labored to build what emerged as the tallest structure in the world. They began their work in January of 1897 and spent the first months using shovels to dig out the foundation. The dirt was taken away in carts pulled by horses and steam locomotives. After that, construction moved quickly and on March 31, 1889, the engineer led a group of officials up 1710 steps to plant the French flag on the tower that was named after its designer, Gustave Eiffel. The officials in Paris were hoping that the tower would stand for twenty years. Now, more than a century later, it still stands firm, one of the most recognized structures in the world.

I love Paris. I try to get there as often as I can, and with every visit I pause frequently, especially at night, to look at Gustave Eiffel's creation and twenty thousand flashing lights that make their impressive display every hour on the hour. Unlike the nearby Cathedral of Notre Dame, which took almost two centuries to complete, the Eiffel Tower went up quickly and its creators saw the results of their labors. But these and many other impressive structures would not be here today if their designers had not begun with a vision, a picture in their minds that could see the final result long before construction ever started. I read someplace that Walt Disney "saw" Disneyland before anybody dreamed of its possibility. John F. Kennedy saw men walking on the moon long before there was technology for putting them there. In 1945, a scientist named

Vannevar Bush published an article in the *Atlantic Monthly* about a machine "in which an individual stores his books, records, and communications, and which is mechanized so that it may be consulted with exceeding speed and flexibility." Bush called it a memex.[1] We call it the personal computer.

Most visionaries are like these innovative people. They see the vision first. Then they go about making it happen, most often working together with others in teams. This works fine for building towers and cathedrals or creating something as complex as the personal computer, but can it be relevant for ordinary people like you and me or the people we coach? Our personal visions usually are much smaller, but the principles for creating them are similar, regardless of size. We start with something that is big and broad, maybe something that looks impossible. Then we begin to think of the small and doable steps we could take to get to our goal. This becomes the blueprint for action. That blueprint is what we will call a mission or purpose.

THE PURPOSE-DRIVEN LIFE

I have never met Rick Warren, but like millions of others I have heard him speak, read some of his books, and heard a lot about his ministry in Southern California and around the world. Warren's book *The Purpose-Driven Church* had a profound influence on me when it first appeared.[2] Rick Warren and his wife had a vision for building a local church, but to do this they needed to have a clear purpose of why that church would exist. "A church without a purpose and mission eventually becomes a museum piece of yesterday's traditions,"[3] Warren wrote, perhaps thinking of some of those massive, magnificent, and most often empty cathedrals in Europe. He and his wife didn't want a church built on tradition, programs, big buildings, or a pastor's personality. Instead, they wanted to discover what God's unique purpose was for their church so they could build accordingly. They studied the Scriptures and concluded that their church had to be defined by what we know as the Great Commandment and the Great Commission. The Great Commandment is to love God and to love our neighbors as ourselves.[4] The Great Commission instructs us to make disciples.[5] Warren turned this into Saddleback Church's slogan: "A Great Commitment to the Great Commandment and the Great Commission will grow a Great Church."[6] From this the church members focused on discovering God's specific purposes for their church. They settled on five: evangelism (winning people to Christ), worship (experiencing God), fellowship (family building), edification (Bible teaching), and ministry to the needy (serving and sharing). Unless there was an intentional mission to balance all five,

Warren knew that his church would be like most others that focus on only one or two and neglect the rest.[7]

A mission statement is, in essence, a written-down reason for being — whether for a person or for a company. It is the key to finding your path in life and identifying the mission you choose to follow. Having a clearly articulated mission statement gives one a template of purpose that can be used to initiate, evaluate, and refine all of one's activities.

— LAURIE BETH JONES, author of *Jesus, Life Coach*

What the people at Saddleback have found to be true with a church applies equally well to businesses and individual lives. Having a purpose has been described as "the starting point for great companies."[8] Workers perform better and find more fulfillment when their employers have a clear mission or purpose that makes the workforce feel important and part of something worthwhile.[9] No one wants to reach the later years and conclude that his or her life has been meaningless and without purpose. "Finding one's mission, and then fulfilling it, is perhaps the most vital activity in which a person can engage," according to Laurie Beth Jones, who wrote a best-selling book on how to create a mission statement for one's work and life.[10]

Mission statements or life purpose statements (we use them interchangeably in these pages) give us direction. They provide a way to organize our lives and set us on course to bring our visions to reality. When we know and can state our purposes for living, we're most likely to be fulfilled, especially if our mission statements reflect our best understanding of God's plans for our lives. Mission statements can take a long time to become clear. At their core, they reflect our values, worldviews, and visions, but they also are succinct. Jones gives three elements to a good mission statement: They should be no more than a single sentence long; they should be easily understood even by a twelve-year-old; and they should be able to be easily remembered, able to be recited by memory even if someone is holding a gun to your head.[11]

A life purpose statement . . . some call it a mission statement . . . is the answer to the questions: What will I

> leave behind? What difference will I make in the lives of
> those I touch? Finding and claiming a life purpose gives
> [coaching] clients a powerful direction for their lives.
>
> — LAURA WHITWORTH, coauthor of *Co-Active Coaching*

Several years ago, sixty students who had attempted suicide were asked why they had wanted to end their lives. The majority, 85 percent, said they had tried to kill themselves because their lives seemed meaningless and without purpose. More important, perhaps, was the finding that 93 percent of these students who reported no reason for living were socially active, achieving academically, and on good terms with their families. But their lives were empty because they had no direction.[12]

Without purpose we lose motivation and sometimes lose health and even lose life. Consider people who retire and lose the will to live because they no longer have a purpose for living. A major value of coaching is to walk alongside people who want to find and maintain a worthwhile life purpose.

FINDING A PURPOSE

Nobody sits down and dreams up a life purpose within a few minutes. It takes time to envision and build what Rich Warren has called "the purpose-driven life."[13] It also takes time and a lot of reflection to develop a statement that captures the essence of where one wants to go in life or with one's company or church. God guides in various ways, but most of us don't find our life missions until we are aware of our values, passions, strengths, and visions.

As you or your coaching client begins this process, start by trying to complete this sentence: "My life purpose is . . ." If you are focusing less on a whole life purpose and more on something specific like winning a tournament trophy or getting promoted to a better job, you can try something like this: "My purpose in reaching this goal is to . . ." Then ask if this gives a clue to your wider life, company, or church mission. Remember that purpose or mission statements are action statements. Try completing your sentence with words that end in *ing*, like "My mission is working to . . ." "studying for . . ." "building . . ." The wording of my mission statement changes slightly from time to time, but it involves variations of the same words and ideas. My life purpose involves *encouraging, equipping, and empowering emerging leaders to reach their potential and make an impact.* Appendix H gives guidelines for helping to clarify a life purpose. Table 11-1 summarizes characteristics of effective mission or life purpose statements.

Table 11-1

MARKS OF AN EFFECTIVE MISSION STATEMENT
Effective mission statements are:

Effective mission statements are:

- **Consistent with Scripture.** God gives us the purpose in our lives, and this will always be compatible with biblical teaching.

- **Consistent with your values, passion, vision, strengths, and spiritual gifts.** A life purpose will also be compatible with who God made us to be.

- **Short.** Long mission statements are easily forgotten and can lead to confusion rather than clarification.

- **Specific.** Whereas a vision can be more general, a mission statement needs to be specific because it is a blueprint for action.

- **Statements of action.** Mission/purpose statements indicate what you will do. Many of the words in the statement are verbs, ending in *ing*.

- **Clear and easy to remember.** If your vision statement is vague, it will not be very motivating and it will be difficult to remember what you are setting out to do.

- **Measurable.** You might not have this in the statement itself, but the mission statement must point to what can be seen and measured. The statement should be able to answer this question: "How will anyone know when the mission is being accomplished?" For example, if your mission is to teach English to immigrant people, how will you know when you have succeeded? If you can never demonstrate what you set out to do, your mission statement won't be very helpful.

- **Motivating.** The words have to ability to inspire and imply a compelling reason for moving forward.

The first time I worked on a mission statement, my coach urged me to do a SWOT analysis. It was a time-consuming and difficult exercise, but it turned out to be very helpful in clarifying my mission and setting the course for my future. SWOT is an abbreviation of four categories: strengths, weaknesses, opportunities, and threats. I began by listing my *strengths*. My wife and a couple of close friends looked over my list and made additional suggestions. Then I tried to write some practical and concrete ways in which each of these could be developed in practice. For example, public speaking is one of my strengths. I listed this and then wrote that I could put this into practice by speaking at conferences, leading seminars, and teaching in colleges and churches. I also can improve as a speaker by listening to other speakers and trying to discern what makes them effective.

Don't ask yourself what the world needs; ask yourself what makes you come alive. Then go do that because the world needs people who have come alive.

— HAROLD WHITMAN

Next I listed my *weaknesses* and wrote some practical ways or places I could face my weaknesses and rise above them without being over-powered by them. Many people find it easier to list their weaknesses than their strengths. All of us experience failures as we grow up. Parents, teachers, and peers remind us of our inadequacies. We learn about the things we do not do well, and eventually the list of our perceived weaknesses gets imbedded in the circuitry of our brains. Satan may play a role here too. He is well aware of our weaknesses, likes to remind us about them, and has a way of discouraging us from thinking we ever will rise above them and become all that God wants us to be. One item on my weakness list is a too-busy lifestyle. I also tend to be a people pleaser who has difficulty setting limits or saying no. As I was doing my SWOT, I decided to ask my accountability partner to hold me responsible for getting more balance into my life.

The next assignment was to list the *opportunities* I have and decide what I should respond to in light of my strengths, gifts, values, passion, and overall vision. Sometimes I get opportunities to speak at conferences. I put this on my SWOT list and wrote that I should cultivate these opportunities. To avoid the too-busy lifestyle, I decided to restrict my speaking in two ways: limit the number of speaking engagements so that I am not overwhelmed, and accept only those opportunities that are consistent with my interests, mission, and areas of competence.

For some people, this may be the hardest part of the SWOT analysis because they don't have many opportunities. Sometimes opportunities really are there but are not noticed until we look more carefully. At other times there can be value in finding ways to create opportunities.

Finally I listed the things that are *threats* to me. I knew in my heart what these were but struggled to put them on paper, where even my coach might see them. I know that everybody is threatened by some things or people, but most of us don't like to admit our threats. Eventually I wrote the names of some people who threaten me because they always appear so much more successful or competent than I am. I wrote, too, that I was threatened by the thought that none of my books in the future would get published, that they wouldn't sell, and that my writing might be dismissed as being lightweight. My coach urged me to write some sentences about what I would do to avoid being squelched by these threats, so I wrote that I would get an agent who would help me craft better books and find ways to get them published and marketed. And that's what I did.

All of this came alive when I met with a little team of people who periodically got together to help me keep my life on target. They went over the SWOT list with me. They added some things to the lists, encouraged me to delete others, and helped me make action decisions for the future. As they coached me, my mission became clearer. It didn't pop out and hit me, but I had a better idea of where I was and what I needed to do if I were to move forward. Not everybody will have a team of close friends to go over their SWOT summaries. But this is an exercise that a coach and coaching client can do together to get a clearer picture of what might become reality in the future.

TWO DEAD ENDS

My first permanent full-time job was at a little college in Minnesota where I taught psychology. At the time, I had never heard of a mission statement but I knew what I wanted to accomplish in this new position: I wanted to be an outstanding teacher. I was young, enthusiastic, creative, and determined to be more interesting than some of the professors whose classes I had suffered through during my years as a student. In a course on learning theory, for example, I required all the students to get away from their textbooks and study the learning behavior of real-live white rats. Quickly I discovered that this was a wonderful way to reduce the size of my classes and encourage students to change their majors to something rat-less like music or mathematics. The brave souls who stayed put their rats through all kinds of intricate learning exercises, including learning to run through mazes. Eventually all the rats learned because they didn't eat unless they were able to find the food at the end of the maze. I should add that the students learned as well. They didn't get food at the end of a maze, but they were conditioned to get grades at the end of my course based on how they had run through the class assignments.

When the rats first entered the mazes, they all hit one or more dead ends before they found the right route to the food. The little white animals we used in that course would have been pretty stupid (and hungry) if they had kept going along the same dead-end route every time they were put in the maze.

I sense, however, that some otherwise intelligent people—like some businesses, churches, and professional organizations—keep going along the same old routes and wonder why they make no progress toward reaching their visions. Of course, many of these have never developed visions, so they don't even know where they are going. But why would people or groups who do have a vision nevertheless go down dead-end routes? The answer may lie in two common and major mistakes that appear again and again: Some people have vision but never move; other people have vision and never stop. You will see both mistakes in your coaching, or maybe in yourself.

Too many people, when they make a mistake, just keep stubbornly plowing ahead and end up repeating the same mistakes. I believe in the motto, "Try and try again." But the way I read it, it says, "Try, then stop and think, then try again."

—WILLIAM DEAN SINGLETON, newspaper owner, publisher

There are many reasons people never move. Some have failed in earlier efforts, so they are reluctant to try again. Other people are not risk takers; they only move forward when the outcome is certain. A lack of resources may dissuade others and so can the belief that a vision is unrealistic or a project too big to accomplish. Then there are those who have been intimidated into inactivity by unsupportive and critical relatives, bosses, and other influential people who keep saying, "It can't be done." It is hard to move forward when you have no support. For others the problem is procrastination. Churches and organizations may never move because they have no leadership or because they spend all their efforts trying to get a consensus from everybody who might be involved. In all of these situations, a coach can give encouragement and help clarify ways to get moving.

In contrast, people who are going all the time have no problem with a lack of movement. They rush from project to project, a whirlwind of activity, enthusiastically embracing new ideas, always pushing forward. But sometimes these people have few priorities, no focus to their activities, and an inability or reluctance to say no. Often these dynamo people are fans of the latest fad. Every new idea is seen as an adrenaline-driven call to action. In their enthusiasm they may enlist others to give support and get involved, but these supporters are forgotten when a fresh idea or new project appears. If a church or organization has such a leader, failure is almost inevitable. The people who sign on to one of the visions eventually lose interest. They feel left behind and disappointed because they realize that the creative visions and inspiring mission statements so powerfully advocated by a leader aren't being supported by someone who persists, so the dreams never become solid reality.

Someone has said that a hunter who chases two rabbits misses both. It's worse for a person who chases a variety of visions and tries to enlist others in the hunt. Sometimes these people need counseling to uncover the reasons for their hyperactivity and to get help in recognizing that God never calls any one person to do everything. More often they need a coach who can help them set priorities and clarify options that will enable them to reach their most important goals. Hyperactive visionaries also need to realize that dreams die when they aren't cultivated and nurtured.

PURPOSE-DRIVEN COACHING

Several years ago, I was at a pastors' conference where I had been invited to give a talk. Before my speech, the leader of the denomination excitedly outlined his vision for the future. He talked about his goals for the churches and described what each of the pastors would be doing to implement his plan. Seated next to me was a business consultant who leaned over and whispered confidently that the plan we were hearing would never work. After the meeting, he explained why. Can you think of the reason?

"The vision belongs to the speaker," my friend said. "It doesn't belong to the pastors. They have been informed of the plan but were not consulted. They have no ownership in the project and, despite what they might say at the meeting, it is almost certain they won't get involved once they get back to their congregations."

He was right, of course. Even the best-crafted visions and most motivating mission statements will fall flat if there is no ownership or little commitment. Purpose and mission statements are meant to clarify direction, guide decision making, mobilize, and motivate individuals or groups of people as they move forward. But these statements need to be tools that stimulate action rather than words that hang in a frame on the wall. Coaches can assist in the clarification of visions and the development of purpose statements, but they also can play a significant role in assisting others to move forward in line with the mission. In what ways can this be done?

People with clearly defined missions have always led
those who haven't any. You are either living your
mission, or you are living someone else's.

— LAURIE BETH JONES, author of *Jesus, Life Coach*

Get a clearer picture of where the client wants to go. The vision part of our coaching model (see figure on page 174) seeks to clarify the question of where the people being coached want to go. A mission statement gives a generalized action plan for bringing the vision into reality. But sometimes there needs to be a clearer picture of what the end result will look like. Clients need to answer this question: "If you reach your goals and fulfill your mission, what will it look like specifically?" At one time I coached a middle-aged woman who wanted to change careers so she could "serve the Lord through teaching." I urged her to give me a picture of what that would look like. I asked what I would see if I could watch her serving the Lord through teaching five years from now. Ideally, where would she be teaching? Who would she be teaching? In what context?

As a part of my coach training, I took a class in which all of the students were asked to give their vision and mission statements, along with their plans for bringing change. I was amazed at the vague language that some of my classmates used as they talked about their visions of "growing in depth," "getting in touch with myself," "discovering my inner self," or "maturing spiritually." All of these are worthy aspirations, but how will anyone know when these goals have been reached? What does it mean to have grown in depth or discovered one's inner self? Specifically, what will it look like to have matured spiritually?

In coaching, encourage your clients to look periodically at their vision and mission statements. Is what they originally wrote clear and understandable, or is the language vague and nonspecific? Suppose, for example, that I want to learn to play the guitar as a way to relax. Better than saying I intend to become a guitar player, it is more realistic to say that in the next month, I plan to find a guitar teacher who will help me purchase an instrument and that I'll be able to play basic chords and simple tunes by this time next year. My guitar coach will be able to tell me if my goal is attainable and realistic. If not, I will need to revise the commitment, make it more doable, and start again.

Setting a clear picture of the future is not always easy. Learning to play the guitar at an elementary level is a specific and attainable goal. Building a church to reach a whole neighborhood is much larger and harder to describe in detail. Circumstances change and so do we. The specific goals that we set now may be altered as we start to implement a plan of action. In addition, Christians know that many of the God-given biblical goals were general and not very detailed. Consider the instructions to build an ark, defeat an army, or "leave your native country . . . and go to the land that I will show you."[14] Without a vision and purpose, there is less likelihood of movement forward. And if we cannot get a concise picture of where we want to go, a somewhat cloudy and tentatively held vision can guide our actions better than if we had no vision or mission at all.

Mission statements are like campaign promises:
easy to make, hard to live up to.

— MARCUS BUCKINGHAM, motivational speaker,
author of *Go Put Your Strengths to Work*

Evaluate the coaching client's commitment level. Assuming we all are busy, what will the person being coached have to give up in order to make the changes? Has he or she thought what might happen if change is not as fast or effective as hoped? Remember that commitment is a choice. Even telling others about a commitment makes it a little more serious. Sometimes a coach will emphasize the importance of commitment by drawing an imaginary line on the floor and asking the client to step across the line but only when he or she is ready to move.

One morning following his resurrection, Jesus had an after-breakfast conversation with Simon Peter. Sitting on the beach, Jesus asked the same question three times, and after each response he gave the apostle a similar message.[15] "Simon, do you really love me?" Jesus asked. "Then feed my lambs . . . take care of my sheep . . . feed my sheep." Peter was hurt because he was asked the same question three times, but maybe Jesus was testing his commitment level. That morning, Peter learned that the remainder of his life would not be easy, but surely the seaside conversation cemented his commitment to Christ in the years that followed.

Look at your own commitments. Perhaps this is obvious, but coaches also need to look at their commitments on occasion. Sometimes we agree to be involved in the coaching process but find ourselves overbooked and overextended. The person you are coaching must work to make the changes, but his or her motivation will lag if the coach makes a commitment to come alongside to give encouragement and guidance and then doesn't follow through with enthusiasm and encouragement. Don't commit unless you can follow through.

Ultimately, all great visions degenerate into hard work.

— Anonymous

Be a consistent encourager. Imagine a football coach who pulls his players together in camp before the season begins. The coach gives several impassioned motivational speeches, seeks out the different players, and individually gives them both guidance and encouragement. At the end of the training camp, he inspires the whole team with his rhetoric so they go forth fired up and determined to win a championship. Then suppose that for the regular season, the coach sits in the stands and watches the games without giving any additional input or encouragement. We all know what would happen, and you can see the point of my example. You are the chief cheerleader for your clients. When things are not moving ahead smoothly or when the person being coached seems stuck and discouraged, you may be the only one who can say by your words and actions, "I believe in you. Keep going!"

A DIFFERENT PERSPECTIVE

It is time now to move away from the assessment of where we are and the envisioning of where we want to go so we can concentrate on the challenging process of making it all happen. Before we take that step into the next section of the book, it is worth looking briefly at a perspective on coaching that is different from the one we have been proposing.

In his book *Coaching for Performance*, John Whitmore proposes what he calls the GROW approach.[16] It assumes that coaching involves:

- *GOAL setting* to help people determine what issues they want to work on and where they want to go
- *REALITY checking* to explore where people are now, including the frustrations, obstacles, and resistances that they need to overcome
- *OPTION strategies* or courses of action that could be taken to reach the goals

- **WILL-*based actions*** that help people do what needs to be done and when

When I first read this, it seemed that the four steps were out of sequence. Don't we assess reality first and then set our goals? That is the way most of us think, but it is superficial logic according to Whitmore. When we identify issues and then start with assessments, as we have been proposing in these pages, we are liable to set goals that are too negative, too much in reaction to a problem, limited by past performance, smaller than they should be, and lacking in creativity. In leading groups, Whitmore likes to encourage team members to start by dreaming about what could be and coming up with ideal long-term solutions and possibilities. Only then can there be a healthy assessment of the present and an outline of the practical steps needed to get to the goals.

Whitmore's perspective is worth considering, especially if you coach groups. Vision casting and planning ahead can be stimulating and exciting for a team. This can carry the group along until they are motivated to begin the harder work of assessing the present and developing a plan of action. Whitmore might agree with the coaching circle model that forms the core of this book, but he shows that there is no rigid or preferred order of priority for assessment, vision casting, strategy, action, and dealing with obstacles. All coaching starts wherever the clients find themselves. Eventually all four parts of our circle may need to be considered, but there is no set starting place, finish line, or established steps from getting from where a client starts to where that client wants to be.

Whatever approach, however, it is likely that taking action will be a major part of the coaching. It is to this that we now turn.

PART 5

STRATEGY, ACTION, AND OBSTACLES IN CHRISTIAN COACHING: HOW DO WE REACH OUR GOALS?

CHAPTER 12

COACHING FOR ACTION: GOAL SETTING AND STRATEGIES

SEVERAL YEARS AGO, I spent time with an executive coach who specializes in life planning. Early one morning, we drove to a retreat center, checked into a couple of rooms, and spent the next two days working on my life plan. As part of our coaching agreement, I had selected three people who would pray for us during this intensive experience, and we sought God's leading as we began our work. To get started, my coach asked what I was hoping to accomplish during our time together. Then he asked me to tell my life story while he listened and took notes. Next we related all of this to five life domains: personal life, family life, spiritual life, vocation, and community involvements. The coach asked me to share what seemed good in my life at that time and what was lacking. He wanted to know what was confusing about my life, what I really cared about, what I wanted to change, and what dreams I had for the future. Later we spent time discussing my talents, strengths, passions, and hopes. We talked about my relationship with God and with my family.

None of this was rushed. We were meeting in a rural retreat center where the environment was conducive to contemplation. For most of this time I was with the coach, but he also made time in the schedule for me to be alone with God and with all of the data we had discussed. The coach and I agreed that human planning will always be limited because we can't predict unexpected events or know how God may intervene in our lives.[1] But planning can be useful, especially if others are involved,[2] so we moved forward. As a result of our discussion, reflection, and prayer, I came up with a list of goals for the next stage of my life. Then we developed action steps and devised a basic strategy that I agreed to implement.[3]

Parts of this two-day process were easy for me. It can be refreshing to tell your life story to somebody who really wants to listen. It is good to look at one's passions, values, and strengths. I tend to be a visionary, so thinking about the future was easy and invigorating. The hard part was setting specific goals for the future and taking the action to turn my visions into reality.

The LORD will work out his plans for my life.

— Psalm 138:8

I am not alone. Abundant evidence shows that individuals and organizations can develop inspiring visions and mission statements but then fail to move these dreams into tangible action.[4] In a recent year, forty CEOs of the top two hundred *Fortune 500* companies were forced to resign because they failed to turn their company visions and big plans into successful outcomes.[5] In earlier chapters, we have seen how this stalling applies to dieting. When they want to lose weight, most people know how much they weigh and may have a vision for the ideal weight and body build they would like to possess. Some might even have a plan for trimming pounds, so they start on a diet. Then the weight-loss plan comes to a standstill because sticking with the diet is hard and many dieters have unrealistic expectations about how quickly and effectively the diets will work.

There can be many reasons for our failures to reach goals, but sometimes the problem centers around our too-busy lifestyles. We may talk about making changes and having vision, but how can anyone find the time and energy to follow through? Coaches and experienced leaders see this often. Visions fade and projects fail because of interruptions, overcrowded schedules, fading commitments, and the lack of realistic action plans. They also fail because we try to make things happen on our own.

Centuries ago, King Solomon wrote about issues like these in the Old Testament book of Proverbs:

- Plans succeed through good counsel; don't go to war without wise advice. (20:18)
- Plans go wrong for lack of advice; many advisers bring success. (15:22)

- We can make our plans, but the LORD determines our steps. (16:9)
- Commit your actions to the LORD, and your plans will succeed. (16:3)
- You can make many plans, but the LORD's purpose will prevail. (19:21)
- Trust in the LORD with all your heart; do not depend on your own understanding. Seek his will in all you do, and he will show you which path to take. (3:5-6)

The message is clear and still relevant in the twenty-first century. For lasting change, we need the help and guidance of others. Even more, we need to submit our plans to God, asking him to refine them, trusting him to direct them, and expecting him to guide them through godly advisors. This is a foundation for Christian coaching. It is not an option. For coaching to succeed, God must be at the core.

Joshua was not a coach, but he knew this principle. When he took over as leader of the Israelites, he had passion, vision, and a clear mission: to lead hundreds of thousands of wilderness wanderers across the fast-flowing Jordan River and into the Promised Land. When they arrived at the river, it was at flood stage. There was no bridge and there were no boats, but none of this seemed to bother Joshua. He expected that God would show the way, even though they had never traveled there before.[6] On the night before they were to move, Joshua told the people to consecrate and purify themselves, "for tomorrow the Lord will do great wonders among you."[7]

Idea generation and implementation are very different activities. Impressive are those who can really do both, but also those who know they can't.

— Source Unknown

At this time, Joshua announced the strategy for crossing the river. The plan involved getting packed and ready to follow the priests who would be carrying the Ark of the Covenant.[8] Then there was action. The priests picked up the ark, hoisted it to their shoulders, and stepped into the river. It is challenging to think that the water did not stop flowing *until* the priests took action and stepped off the dry land. As soon as they got their feet wet, the water piled in a heap upstream and the people walked across on dry ground.[9]

Look again at the coaching circle and you will see that Joshua's leadership illustrated the next segment: deciding on a strategy and then taking action to help us get to where we want to go.

Figure 12-1

GETTING A STRATEGY AND SETTING GOALS

Some of the people we coach can state their end goal or final objective within the first few minutes of coaching. If someone wants help in finding a new job, controlling finances, setting limits on a thirteen-year-old, or losing fifteen pounds, the coaching may be focused and short-term. More often, coaching is broader, often set within the context of one's entire life. One of my current clients would like coaching to guide her through a career reevaluation. We have spent time evaluating who she is and what she does well. In our conversations around vision and mission, my client has been clarifying where she would like to go in the rest of her life. Hopefully this has been helpful, but our coaching will not be successful until she can set specific goals that will enable her to make the career change she so strongly desires.

The change process starts with an agreement that something needs to be changed. Then the coach and client may go through a goal-setting process similar to the outline in table 12-1. It should come as no surprise that the coach does not set these goals. He or she comes alongside the person being coached and together they think through and clarify the goal-setting process. Sometimes brainstorming is a good place to start, coming up with as many options as possible. Ask what has worked in the past and what has not worked. Consider what might be tried in the future. As the list of possibilities evolves, some will be rejected. Others can be recast into SMART goals: goals that are specific, measurable, attainable, realistic, and within a time frame that the coaching client can accept. You may discover later that the time frame may not be realistic in practice—things usually take more time than we expect—but by setting a time to get things done, there is more motivation to get moving. "I will prepare a résumé soon" is not nearly as motivating as "I will have the résumé done by noon next Monday."

Table 12-1

SETTING GOALS
The goal-setting process may differ from client to client but usually goes through similar steps:

Step one:	Clarify and agree on the end result or results (the desired outcome).
Step two:	Put this on paper. What you write can be revised later.
Step three:	Start with the desired outcomes and then, working backward, mutually brainstorm about some possible interim goals.
Step four:	Agree about which of these alternative interim goals you will pursue. Recast each of these as SMART goals: specific, measurable, attainable, realistic, and with a time frame.
Step five:	Arrange the agreed-upon goals in order of priority from the first and most realistic to the end result.
Step six:	Write down indicators that will show clearly when each goal has been reached. Do this with at least the immediate goals. The others can come as you get closer to the end goal.
Step seven:	Put this list on paper.

Movement like this is smoother when people realize that they are not alone in the journey. The coach is a constant guide and encourager, but other resources are available, including spiritual resources. Christian coaches must never underestimate the power of prayer or the ways in which Christians are buoyed by the promises of Scripture. God has promised to instruct and teach us in the ways we go.[10] Trust in him and he guides our paths.[11] When Jesus' followers were facing a major change, he told them that he would be with them always.[12] He promised to send the Holy Spirit, who now lives within each believer as a guide and comforter.[13] And as members of the church, Christians can find individuals or large numbers of people to give support, encouragement, and accountability during times of change.

In all of this planning, remember that goals are not set in cement. They are always open for review and modification. Often the first goals in a sequence will be clearer than the ones that come later, but as progress is made, any goal can be revised, skipped, or even abandoned. The idea is to come up with a plan for moving forward.

Christians must never forget that God's plans often evolve. We don't always see the whole picture at the beginning. We might not be able to fill out the entire seven-step program in detail from the start. When Moses stood in front of the burning bush, he got a partial picture of what was coming, but God did not reveal the entire strategy in detail. He said, "Now go, for I am sending you to Pharaoh. You must lead my people Israel out of Egypt" (Exodus 3:10). Moses was told to assemble the elders and he was given words to say. He was instructed to go to the king of Egypt and to relay what God had commanded. Moses was clear that the end result was to settle in the Promised Land, but initially he saw only the immediate goals. The overall plan unfolded in greater detail as he went.[14]

STRETCHING

If we took a survey of athletic coaches, many would agree that their job is to instruct, inspire, and even push people with talent to do more than they could ever imagine or do on their own. Business coaches do something similar and so do the coaches of actors, speakers, and members of health clubs. This is stretching. It involves stimulating the imagination to dream of possibilities that seem way out of reach. It is nudging people from their familiar and comfortable routines of doing the same things in the same ways while they expect different results. Stretching lets people see that their current knowledge, skills, and actions aren't likely to take them much further than where they are already. Stretching is more than asking what someone would like for the future. It encourages uninhibited, creative, imaginative dreaming about what could be if there were no financial or other restrictions. This kind of thinking is stimulated by questions or statements that begin with words such as "What if . . . ?" "Why couldn't you . . . ?" "Let's think what would happen if . . ." and "We need to . . ."

The goal of stretching is to get people thinking in new ways, coming up with new options. Sometimes coaches can stimulate clients with questions and prompts like these:

- Imagine that you have achieved your goal. What does this look like?
- Imagine yourself in the future and tell me how you got there.
- If money or time were not limits, what would you do now to move forward?
- Be creative and tell me what resources you could draw on to help you move ahead.
- What might change around you in the future that you need to prepare for now?
- What might you do that is outside your comfort zone but that might get you closer to your goals?

In a classic book about visionary companies, James Collins and Jerry Porras introduced the concept of BHAGs—big, hairy, audacious goals.[15] All companies have goals, according to these writers, but most of these are safe, nearsighted, not very challenging, and well within everybody's comfort zone. Such goals do little to move the company forward. In contrast, BHAGs seem impractical and impossible at first, but they stretch everybody. John Kennedy had such a similar goal when he summoned Lyndon Johnson to the oval office for a no-nonsense talk on the day when Russian cosmonaut Yuri Gagarin was launched into space. Kennedy's BHAG was to land a man on the moon. Maybe Lance Armstrong had a BHAG when he decided that a cancer survivor could win the Tour de France. Did a largely unknown black U.S. senator named Barak Obama have such a goal when he faced a small crowd of supporters on a freezing winter day in Illinois and announce that he was going to run for the presidency?

The people we coach may not be building space programs, cycling records, or presidential campaigns, but they are building lives and often they benefit from stretching. Sometimes the people we coach are building careers, companies, projects, or organizations. When a friend and I took over leadership of the fledgling American Association of Christian Counselors in 1991, we had only a few hundred members. "Someday we can have thousands," my partner said, expressing a BHAG even before we had heard the term. Then we went to work to make it happen as God led and empowered our efforts. Several years ago, I heard Jim Collins speak to church leaders, urging them to hold firmly to their theological foundations but then to think big, to dream about ecclesiastical BHAGs. If the coach does not help another person reach beyond what he or she can grasp easily, then maybe the coach isn't needed.

TAKING ACTION

Discussing BHAGs and setting goals can be stimulating, but to make progress we must stop talking and start taking action. This is where managers often fail in coaching employees. It's where CEOs fail in building strategies and leading their companies to meet corporate goals. Political leaders can be the same. They can be soaring visionaries on the campaign trail, inspiring their audiences with promises that are vague and wrapped in rhetoric. After the election, some of these newly elected officials have limited ability to think strategically and get everyone moving in the same direction, toward the same goals. A team may agree on what needs to be done and have good intentions about following through, but if there is no clear plan of action and no encouragement from the leader, there is no progress.

Here is where athletic coaches can be our teachers. Teams that win championships are coached by men and women who can articulate their goals, be aware of player strengths and weaknesses, push for improvement, give encouragement, and show the team members how to play strategically. If a coach doesn't inspire confidence and check progress, the athletes may never take action to better themselves or work to win. As a result, nothing changes.

Anyone can dabble, but once you've made that
commitment, your blood has that particular thing in it,
and it's very hard for people to stop you.

— BILL COSBY, entertainer

Once our coaching clients have clear goals and a plan for action, there must be commitment to making everything work. The coach commits to sticking with the client, giving encouragement, and guiding the process; the person being coached agrees to take action to move ahead. Commitment implies that there is no turning back, so the coach may need to get specific answers to questions like these:

- "How willing are you to commit now to this plan?"
- "If you don't feel ready to commit, how does the plan need to change so you will make a commitment?"
- "What are you going to do first?"
- "When will you start?"
- "When will you have it done?"
- "Who will you tell?" (Commitment is stronger when somebody else knows.)
- "Who will give you support and keep you accountable?"
- "On a scale of one to ten, what is the likelihood you will do what you have agreed to do?"

Regarding this last question, coach John Whitmore has discovered that people who give themselves a score of less than eight seldom follow through.[16] Because of this, whenever a rating is seven or less, he encourages the client to look again at the goal and think of what needs to be done to raise the rating. This may include lengthening the time or reducing the size of the task.

In taking action, some people may push themselves into unfamiliar territory, attempting things they never thought possible. These people need encouragement and help to keep the process moving. Without sounding demanding, the coach might make suggestions like, "Why don't you send me an e-mail when you get this done?" or "How would you feel if I called you on Tuesday about eight to see how it's going?" Some coaches use requests. "I'd like to request that you make the phone call in the morning." If the client does not agree, then ask for a counterproposal that he or she feels able to follow. Often the degree to which a person takes action is an indicator of his or her intent and commitment.

Once the process gets started, review progress often. If something is working, congratulate the person and encourage him or her to keep going. If a goal is not reached, discuss possible reasons for this and find ways to revise the plan so success will come on the next try. Coaches do not blame, scold, or judge; instead, they help in ways that are mentioned in the New Testament. They encourage, build up, confess, strengthen, show kindness, and care for one another. At times the coach will offer a gentle challenge: "I notice that you did not follow through on what you promised, so I'm wondering what it would take for you to get there now?" Life coaching has no place for the tirades we sometimes see in athletic coaches who stomp on the sidelines, scream, swear, intimidate, and shout names at their players on the assumption that this will motivate them to do better. At best the impact is temporary.

In all of this discussion about setting goals, stretching, and taking action, there is one missing piece. Many times goals do not get reached and plans fail because the expectations are beyond the capabilities of an individual client, company, or athletic team. When I was a teenager, I wanted to be an athlete but I had no athletic skills and couldn't catch a ball or throw with any accuracy. This left me feeling inadequate and sometimes inclined to question my own masculinity. I moved beyond all of this when I reached adulthood and exceeded in other areas, but suppose one day I decide to become a professional football player. Even if I could develop a clear vision for my new athletic career, set concise goals, stretch my thinking, and develop a strategic plan for taking action, I would fail because my body is too old and my athletic abilities are still lacking. Ridiculous as it may seem, this example is similar to the thinking of some company executives who are hired because of their vision casting but who fail in getting things accomplished. These leaders may take pride in dreaming big and expressing ambitious plans for expansion, but failure is likely if the organization lacks the money, staff, expertise, and production capabilities to reach their big hairy audacious goals.

"No matter how well you execute, the risk of failure increases markedly when the ideas you develop don't fit with your existing capabilities or force you to acquire those capabilities at too high a cost," write strategy experts Larry Bossidy and Ram Charan.[17] What is true of corporations can also apply to churches, community organizations, and individuals who come for coaching. Even as a coach encourages clients to stretch and have big dreams, sometimes his or her greatest contribution is to raise questions about whether the stated goals and action plans are beyond the client's capabilities.

> While stretch goals can be useful in forcing people to break old rules and do things better, they're worse than useless if they're totally unrealistic.
>
> — LARRY BOSSIDY and RAM CHARAN,
> coauthors of *Execution: The Discipline of Getting Things Done*

Good coaches tend to be risk takers. We guide people into new ventures and encourage them to take on fresh challenges that they might have neither the courage nor the insight to embrace otherwise. Such risk taking is always threatening. It moves us away from our places of comfort and into unfamiliar territory. Some people, the more adventurous, do this better than most. Other clients are more cautious. They can benefit from challenges to make big plans, but they also need a coach who raises cautions if clients are moving completely out of the range of reality. Most of us reach goals best when we have a friend, guide, or coach to stretch our visions, encourage us along the way, help us anticipate obstacles in the road, assure us that ultimate success is possible, and help us find goals and strategies that are likely to be reachable.

MOVING THE PROCESS FORWARD

Coaching is well suited for the times in which we live. Few people are content to listen passively to boring speeches or college lectures, stay working for autocratic employers with top-down leadership styles, or dutifully follow the guidance of advice givers who rarely allow for feedback or discussion. Except for some of the oldest or those who most fear change, the people we coach do not want how-to-do-it lectures from aloof advice givers. Most contemporary clients prefer to be involved in every stage of the coaching. They want to participate in the process of clarifying the issues, determining where they are, getting a vision and mission, coming up with a strategy, and taking action to make the plan work. They want ownership in any plan, and they value connectedness with others.

For these reasons, they value the partnership that characterizes coaching. How, then, can coaches connect with their clients, helping them make plans, take risks, and increase the likelihood of reaching their goals? In ways that are sensitive and nonintrusive, coaches can help move the action forward in several practical ways.

Clients usually come to coaching to do things differently or to do different things. They want to set goals, come up with plans, get into action, and use the accountability of coaching to stay on track. Clients want to be in motion, not standing still.

— LAURA WHITWORTH, coauthor of *Co-Active Coaching*

Stimulating confidence. Picture a toddler standing at the edge of a swimming pool, looking at the outstretched arms of her father who is standing waist deep in the water encouraging her to jump. She wants to make the leap, but she's scared. At times we are all like that. We need self-confidence, the belief that we can do it, the assurance that we won't get hurt. Those beliefs are hard to hold if we have jumped in the past and failed or if we have been told repeatedly—maybe by a parent or teacher—that we can't do it and will never succeed. Coaches stimulate confidence by teaching skills, encouraging reachable small steps, modeling what they want to teach, and showing their belief in the client. Maybe nothing motivates us more than the realization that somebody significant believes in us and won't be dissuaded from that belief.

Standing for. My friend Al is twenty-one, an aspiring musician with plenty of talent and potential. Most evenings after work, he practices with his band. Most weekends, if they find gigs, they give concerts, even if they aren't paid, and don't sell many of their CDs. Al has dreams for his future. He works hard to reach his goals. But there must be times when he wonders why he is doing what he does. Does he lose perspective at times and forget the vision, passions, goals, and hopes that got him going in the first place? I'm not Al's coach or mentor, but periodically I drop in to the restaurant where he works to see how he is doing and cheer him on. In our casual conversations, I remind him of his values, his potential, and what he is working for. Mentors, professors, and classmates do this with students who easily get caught in the pressures and distractions of life and lose sight of what they want to accomplish. I hope I do something like this when I talk with Al.

Coaches sometimes refer to this as standing for what the client believes and wants. Someone has suggested that coaches serve as containers for each client's dreams, visions, and goals. When these fade from memory or are lost in the busyness, coaches are there, standing for what clients consider to be important, bringing reminders of what is possible and what can transpire. The world is filled with stories of people who succeeded in reaching their goals because somebody believed in them, encouraged them, gave inspiration, and stood for what they were seeking even when others thought the goals were foolish and unattainable. One of the most rewarding and fulfilling parts of coaching is this standing with others and standing for what they want to achieve.

Giving feedback. As part of his training program, Jesus sent out seventy-two people in little groups of two, telling them to preach, heal, and spread the word about the kingdom of God. Earlier we noted that when they returned, they all got together for feedback. Maybe Jesus listened to their stories, cheered their efforts, and gave both instruction and coaching about how they could do better next time. There was a time of rejoicing because of what had been done and praise to God because of how he was at work.[18] This feedback must have built confidence in the seventy-two, so they were encouraged to go out again.

Feedback can be of two types: positive and corrective. Positive feedback points to what has been done well and often is accompanied by affirmation and praise. This maintains motivation and encourages an employee or client to keep moving in the same or a similar direction. Corrective feedback points to what may have gone wrong and involves coaching about ways in which things could be done differently in the future. Corrective feedback is not intended to blame or criticize. It is given in a respectful manner that focuses on the problem and not on the individual or his or her perceived faults. Often there can be affirmation for what did go well, along with encouragement about what can be improved. In both cases, feedback should be empathic, specific, focused on behavior, and constructive. In coaching, feedback should be presented tentatively since the coach is not an expert. There always should be opportunity for discussion, and sometimes a new action plan will evolve.

Most people are motivated to keep going when they get consistent, specific, honest, loving feedback, even if it is not all positive. Good feedback stretches, encourages, corrects, and builds self-confidence. Without it, clients can miss seeing the effects of what they do. When there is no positive feedback, many clients, employees, or team members lose inspiration and stop moving forward. After teaching a corporate seminar about the value of feedback, one of my friends ended with these words on his last slide: "The absolute worst kind of feedback is none at all."[19]

Empowering. In one of his last statements on earth, Jesus stated that all power ultimately belonged to him.[20] He noted that the power possessed by humans comes from the Holy Spirit and not from some inner force or other external source. Christian coaches keep this perspective in mind as they encourage clients to draw on the power they have been given to accomplish what they seek to achieve.

People cannot take risks unless they feel safe, unless they feel secure that they will not be unfairly treated, embarrassed, harassed, or harmed by taking action. When we feel safe we become more open to outside influences and learning.

— JAMES KOUZES and BARRY POSNER,
coauthors of *The Leadership Challenge*

At times, most coaches meet clients who are afraid to take risks or try something new. How do we empower these people to step forward confidently? We can start by reminding clients of their God-given strengths and capabilities and encouraging them to think of times when some similar situation has been successful. I often ask clients to tell me about activities in their lives that God has blessed, and then we apply this to the present. Sometimes encouragement alone is helpful, especially when coaches agree to stand with clients, emotionally and in prayer, as they take action. Some coaches encourage clients to act as if the things they wanted or imagined have already occurred.[21] This gives people confidence to act in less-tentative ways. One other suggestion is to be a model for our clients. The danger in this is that coaches might draw too much attention to themselves, but if we can share from our own experiences, on occasion and with the client's permission, this adds to our authenticity, encourages our clients, and empowers them to follow in our footsteps.

Providing accountability. It can be difficult to make changes on our own. This is especially true when we seek to change long-established habits. Accountability is a core element of recovery programs and groups like Alcoholics Anonymous. It is a core feature of coaching as well.

Accountability in coaching can focus on eliminating undesired behavior or developing something new. Sometimes clients are urged to keep a diary of their behavior and report weekly or daily on their progress. At other times the accountability takes place on the phone or Internet. One of my friends asked if I would hold him accountable for what he watched on television when he was away on business trips. Alone in his room at night, he had begun watching pornography and he wanted to quit. We agreed that he would call and give a report after every trip but that I also could call him, even when he was at his hotel. The knowledge that he would be giving a report curtailed his porn watching significantly, and eventually the problem disappeared, especially when he changed jobs.

More often, coaching involves holding clients accountable for positive changes that they want to make. One of my clients is a manager who did not see any need to compliment his employees when they performed well. He agreed that this lack of affirmation might be contributing to the low morale in his department, so he started giving one compliment a day and telling me when he did it. This kind of accountability can work with people who want to start and maintain an exercise program, do better time management, or spend more quality time with family. The process works best when there are clearly defined commitments and each person knows what is to be done and how this is to be reported. When the client fails, the coach's goal is to help find out what happened and discuss with the client what changes need to be made to increase the prospects of success in the future.

If you want to make a difference . . .

you've got to make time for strategy.

— MICHAEL E. PORTER, professor at Harvard Business School

Keeping hope alive. Leaders specialize in keeping hope alive, and so do coaches. When the disciples began to realize that Jesus was serious about dying and leaving, they got anxious, so the Lord started his final instructions with words of hope. "Don't . . . be troubled," he said. "Trust in God, and trust also in me. . . . I will ask the Father, and he will give you another Advocate who will never leave you. . . . I have told you all this so you may have peace in me. Here on earth you will have many trials and sorrows. But take heart, because I have overcome the world."[22]

When hope is missing, coaching rarely is effective. Like parents who stay at the side of their small children as they start to walk, good coaches stay with their clients to give hope and encouragement, especially when they make those first action steps. We are more inspired to move toward our goals when a leader or coach recognizes our efforts and shares the conviction that we can do even better.

There are many ways to help clients set strategy and take action to get from where they are to where they want to be. But sometimes progress is blocked by obstacles—the experiences, circumstances, people, attitudes, inner self-talk, or emotions that get in the way of progress. These obstacles might emerge in the first session or they might remain hidden, undermining the coaching until they emerge and are handled later. We turn now to discuss these obstacles. When they are faced and defeated, coaching is freed to move forward to success.

CHAPTER 13

COACHING THROUGH OBSTACLES

PROBABLY YOU HAVE heard people joke about having only two seasons of the year: winter and road construction. Where I live, as soon as summer arrives, the construction crews go to work, improving the roads but tying up traffic for months and for miles. Everybody knows that travel times and frustration levels are likely to go up along with the signs announcing, "Construction ahead."

Coaches work with people who are like those delayed drivers. We come alongside people who are hindered in their progress because of obstacles in the road. At times these obstacles are the reason clients come for coaching in the first place. These may be people who are aware of their uniquenesses. They know their values, possess driving passions, and are clear about their visions. Some of these people may even have mission statements and carefully devised goals. But there is little or no progress because of their inability to identify or get past psychological and other obstacles that get in the way. Instead, they face frustrations and delays like drivers experience in those construction zones. Coaches become like those men or women with flags who stand at the roadside guiding each driver around the barriers.

Like all of life's roadblocks, the barriers that arise in coaching are of all types and sizes. They occupy an entire section of the coaching wheel because they need to be faced and overcome; they cannot be ignored. But obstacles make their appearance at any time in coaching and at every part of the coaching circle. Some are common and easily identified. Others are unique and so well hidden that they don't appear until later in the coaching process. Some of the obstacles come from outside the person being coached. Perhaps he or she wants to move on a career path but a difficult boss or discriminating company policy stands in the way. Less visible are the internal obstacles. These are the more subtle fears, attitudes, habits, insecurities, and distractions that drain away energy and threaten to scuttle the coaching.

Figure 13-1

Ferdinand Fournies is an internationally known management consultant and business coach who helps employers manage their employees. In an ambitious project to discover why people don't do what they are supposed to do, Fournies surveyed twenty-five thousand managers and supervisors from around the world. The goal was to help business leaders discover the roadblocks that were preventing employees from being more productive, but the survey findings can apply to coaches as well. What obstacles were preventing people from doing what they had agreed to do? Here are the first nine from the list:[1]

1. The employees don't know what they are expected to do specifically.
2. They don't know how to do it.
3. They don't know why they should do it.
4. They think they are doing it but they are not getting feedback.

5. There are obstacles in the way, beyond their control.
6. They don't think it will work.
7. They think their ways are better.
8. They think something else is more important so they set different priorities.
9. There is no benefit (positive consequence) if they do it.

The researchers concluded that most of these reasons fall into two broad categories: lack of direction and lack of feedback. People are not clear about the direction to go, and when they start moving they aren't able to evaluate how they are progressing. Notice that only one item on this list deals with obstacles beyond the person's control, but even this kind of barrier can be surmounted.

Notice too that some of these obstacles might be considered external, whereas others are internal. The external barriers come because an outside supervisor has not given feedback or clear directions on what needs to be done. Other obstacles may be internal. They don't arise from the workplace or the behavior of a manager. These internal barriers often remain hidden except to the worker, who might not know how to do the work but maybe feels insecure or too embarrassed to ask for clarification. Both external and internal barriers get in the way of coaching effectiveness.

EXTERNAL BARRIERS

How many people have too much to do? Almost everybody I know fits that category, including me. We complain about our hectic lifestyles but sometimes wear busyness as a badge of honor as if hyperactivity is a mark of importance. Certainly, a lot of this busyness comes because of demands from other people. If you or a client works for a demanding boss or if you are a mother caring for preschoolers, you don't have a lot of control over your schedule. In situations like these, the demands that come from others keep us hopping. There is limited time to do all we have to do, let alone work on the suggestions of a coach.

Table 13-1

EXTERNAL BARRIERS TO COACHING (A Partial List)		
Barrier	**Impact**	**Coaching Suggestions**
Distracting life events	Diverts attention from coaching, consumes energy	Deal with the life event (such as the illness, family death, or move), then return to coaching later
Too many demands	Feelings of pressure, distraction	Reevaluate priorities, learn time/schedule management, find a helper
Difficult people	Drains energy, consumes time	Set boundaries, avoid power struggles, say no, confront if possible, reevaluate priorities
Criticism from others	Fear of rejection, self-doubt	Evaluate the criticism and the critic (some criticism is worth ignoring), refine goals if needed, don't get distracted with self-defense, keep going
No clear boundaries	Circumstances and people disrupt our time, set our agendas, prevent work on coaching and other issues	Be clear about limits, learn to say no graciously and firmly, try to get rid of whatever is making you a people pleaser who lets others set your agenda
No accountability	Fading of vision, motivation, determination, commitment, and willingness to persist	Find someone to hold you accountable
No evaluation from others	Discouragement, loss of motivation, stalling, confusion	Find a way to get honest feedback
Energy drainers	Distractions, interruptions, depletion of energy, loss of time, loss of patience	Identify drainers, take action to remove them or to reduce their influence

Table 13-1 lists some of the common barriers to coaching that appear to be rooted in people and circumstances we can't control. If you look at this list closely, however, you will see that many of the external barriers we blame on others could have roots within ourselves. For example, demanding schedules that we attribute to other people may come because we have allowed our schedules to be too full, because we're people pleasers who haven't learned to say no, or because we like the invigorating adrenaline rush that pumps us up while we scurry from activity to activity. Some coaches have suggested that many of us experience what they call OOPS: Overly Optimistic Planning Syndrome.[2] Coaches even encourage this in their clients, urging them to take on too much in their efforts to reach their goals. We can blame others and call ourselves victims of outside pressures, but in reality we have more control over our lives than we admit.

Be always unhappy where you are if you want to reach where you are not. If you are pleased with what you are, you have stopped already. If you say, "It is enough," you are lost. Keep on walking, moving forward, trying for the goal.

— AUGUSTINE, early church father

But consider the never-ending needs of chronically ill relatives or the pressing work deadlines that consume our time. In situations like these, there are only two alternatives: do nothing and give up, assuming that things will not change; or determine to make whatever immediate changes we can and then take initial steps in the direction of removing, altering, or learning to live with the barrier. Guiding people in decisions like these is an important part of coaching. We use the same principles we have been discussing in previous chapters, but we focus on the short-term goal of dealing with the impeding barrier. As the coach guides in this process, he or she is careful to encourage clients to consider and evaluate the costs of each action. Quitting a demanding job will be too radical in most cases, but can there be ways to make the situation more tolerable, such as getting an assistant, reorganizing priorities, dropping some things from a schedule, or changing a mind-set?

ENERGY DRAINERS

One theme runs through all of our discussions about obstacles: the idea that life is filled with energy drainers. These can be difficult people, work pressures, emotions such as anxiety or depression, unmet needs, or even what have been called the gnats of life—those small hassles that we endure and try to brush off like flies at a picnic. For many people, clutter is an energy drainer—like the piles of papers that accumulate on our desks and silently cry out for the attention we never have time to give. To-do lists can drain energy by reminding us of all the things that need to be done. The lists rarely get shorter. Some items get crossed off, but additional tasks are always being added to the list. Computers and other electronic devices provide more contemporary energy drainers. For many of us, e-mail messages and text messages never go away. They come at all hours of the day and night, go with us if we take laptops or cell phones on vacation, and often demand immediate attention. Someplace I read that whenever we are interrupted in the midst of concentrated work, it takes twenty-five minutes to get back on task. This leads to one other kind of energy drainer: distractions. If you have a bell on your computer announcing the arrival of each new e-mail message or if you are the parent of small children, you completely understand the energy-draining power of distractions.

Energy drainers appear at different times as we go around the coaching circle. They divert us from our goals, undermine effective leadership, drain away motivation, and create both frustration and discouragement. They need to be identified, discussed, and handled or they will continue to do their vitality-depleting work. Appendix J is a tool that you may want to revise or duplicate and use with the people you coach.

Master coach Diane Menendez taught me many of the basics of coaching, including ways to deal with energy drainers.[3] Once they are identified, she suggests that we ask a few questions about each one:

- **What is this energy drainer costing me in terms of time, energy, money, and peace of mind?** Focus attention on energy drainers that are costly. Live with the others or put them aside until later.
- **Is this something that is likely to disappear in time, such as a winter cold?** If so, it can be tolerated for a while until it's gone.
- **If it is costly and likely to persist, what action can I take to eliminate the energy drainer or reduce its impact?** Sometimes this means applying principles of time management or dropping things from your schedule. It may mean having a garage sale, taking a vacation, or blocking out time to complete the most needling item on your list of things to do.
- **What is positive about those energy drainers and what can I learn from them?** When we know what drains our energy, we can take steps to prevent a reoccurrence in the future.

Look straight ahead, and fix your eyes on what lies before you.
Mark out a straight path for your feet; stay on the safe path.
Don't get sidetracked.

— Proverbs 4:25-27

If a demanding person is draining your energy, for example, ask how God would want you to respond. Probably setting boundaries is appropriate, but is attending to that person a ministry that God has given you? This process of reevaluation is an example of the reframing that we mentioned in a couple of other chapters. Take your energy-draining frustration and frame it differently so that you can see it in a different perspective. Maybe some of our most disruptive energy drainers can be turned into something beautiful and fulfilling. Reframing is a technique that can be very useful in coaching. It is a technique you can teach your clients.

In one of her coaching classes, Menendez told the story of a young entrepreneur named Jerry who had an unusually high need for achievement. He poured himself into his work, but the need to succeed spilled over and impacted his family, his church, and the rest of his life. Jerry began bossing around his relatives, trying to organize the lives of people around him, and complaining about a church committee that was not doing enough. All of this was alienating people, frustrating Jerry, draining his energy, and doing nothing to meet his achievement need. A coach helped him set priorities in his work, back off on his criticisms of the family and church committee, and focus on less-alienating ways to meet his needs. Jerry learned from his coach what many of our clients will learn from us: When we have strong unmet needs, these will dominate our lives and drain our energy. Sometimes the best way to deal with energy-drainer obstacles is to focus on needs and how they can be met more effectively.

Another technique is to focus on energy gainers. These are people, habits, activities, and anything else that gives us energy. Exercise, a walk in the park or a mall, being alone, time with a hobby, meeting with a friend in a coffee shop, or involvement with good friends can all give energy, providing they do not distract us so we lose focus. Ask your clients to think of people in their lives who are natural energy givers. These individuals are rare but tend to be encouragers, optimistic, enthusiastic about life, and interested in others. Their presence invigorates others and provides energy to replace what is sucked out of us by the energy drainers. If you can find them, spending time with upbeat people like this can be inspiring and energizing.

INTERNAL BARRIERS

Timothy Gallwey must have been surprised when his book *The Inner Game of Tennis* became a best seller over three decades ago.[4] Some of the old pros and tennis instructors were not enthused about his approach, but players devoured it eagerly. Gallwey argued that most good players know all about techniques, but many fail to realize that "the opponent within one's head is more formidable than the one on the other side of the net." The new approach involved helping players recognize, and then remove or reduce, the internal obstacles that get in the way of performance. Only then will the game flow more smoothly and performance improve.

In the years that followed his first book, Gallwey applied the principles to golf, music, and more recently to work.[5] He argues that to thrive in the world of work, as in life, we need to deal with the inner obstacles of resistance to change, fear of failure, procrastination, stagnation, doubt, and boredom. These self-distracting thoughts undermine our confidence and need to be replaced by mental visions of our goals and a determination to pursue these unremittingly. He adds that having a coach to deal with the obstacles and help people refocus attention can be as important in life and in the board-room as it is on the tennis or basketball court.

Table 13-2

INTERNAL BARRIERS TO COACHING (A Partial List)		
Barriers	**Impact**	**Coaching Suggestions**
Habits	Get in the way of taking action	Admit habits can be changed by repetition of new behaviors, find ways to give reminders whenever the habit appears, reward success
Fear, insecurity	Stops you from taking action	Pray, read Philippians 4:6-7, talk openly to a friend, challenge defeating self-talk, build a positive attitude, take small steps and notice what happens, stop imagining worst-case possibilities

Negative mind-set	Convinces you it can't be done	Challenge harmful self-talk, replace negative beliefs with positive ones
No commitment or ownership	Motivation drops, goals are forgotten or abandoned, there is no lasting movement forward	Rework plans to achieve more ownership, ask for a commitment, urge accountability
Resistance to change	Cooperation drops even though you have superficial agreement	Look for "gremlins" (self-defeating talk), review value of change, get a new commitment
Impatience	The process is rushed, making failure, disappointment, and loss of interest more likely	Demonstrate patience and show small evidences of progress
Boredom	Loss of interest and motivation	Reclarify the focus, link growth to passion, find ways to instill or renew interest
Changed goals	Realization that the initial goals or vision no longer fit, loss of motivation	Look again at the earlier parts of the coaching circle, especially passion, vision, mission, strengths, and strategy; redefine the goals and seek a fresh commitment
No place for God	Vision and goals are limited without divine guidance and power	Pray, ask God to direct every step of the way, trust him to lead, seek to align coaching and goals with Scripture, seek Christian accountability

There may be hundreds of internal obstacles to coaching success, some of which are summarized in table 13-2. Most can fit into four categories.

First there are *habits*. We learn to do things in certain ways so that they happen automatically. When I make a turn in my car, I put on the turn signal. I do it without thinking; it's a habit, easy to do automatically because of the way my brain has become wired. If I try signaling in some other way, such as putting my arm out the window like they did in the days before turn signals, this is disrupting. It goes against the neural circuits of the brain, so change would be possible but slower in coming.[6] Many of us work in the same habitual ways, respond to frustrations with the same reactions, or use similar approaches when we tackle new projects. If these old patterns stop working efficiently, we use them nevertheless because they are familiar and usually we aren't even aware of their influence.

A second category of external obstacles is *fear*. Moving out of our comfort zones and doing things differently is scary. A sport's columnist in our local newspaper once described a well-known college coach who was rigid and abusive in treating his players. He remained "in his university bunker, re-assured by those who blindly worship him, blaming it all on the idiot media, refusing to surrender," apparently seeing no reason to change. Eventually he was fired, but even if he had agreed to change, it is unlikely he would have known how. Change for him would have shaken his whole coaching style and caused him to risk the failure he so strongly feared. Some of our coaching clients may have similar fears. When the need for change becomes clear, coaches must move slowly through the process of helping others see this need and then build the courage and skills to take action.

Third, a whole group of obstacles relates to *mind-set* and worldviews. Earlier we noted that most of our perspectives on the world and on life are subconscious, influential, and well entrenched. Often they are accepted without question as attitudes that come from our parents or from other significant people.

We don't see things as they are; we see things as we are.

— The Talmud

I have a friend who grew up hearing repeatedly that he'd never amount to anything, so he developed a defeatist, I'll-never-be-able-to-do-it mind-set that he has spent years trying to shake. When he went for coaching, he could spend hours talking about passion, visions, and goals, but whenever he started moving forward, the old attitudes would raise their objections. Some coaches refer to these entrenched attitudes as our inner gremlins.[7] These are the running narratives that go on in our brains—the in-grained, self-talk ideas that shape our attitudes and impact our actions. Gremlins are internal saboteurs that object to change, point out our weaknesses or inadequacies, and cite reasons we can't move forward. These imaginative gremlins say things like, "This is stupid, too risky, not worth doing, or probably going to fail." Most often the gremlin self-talk says, "I can't do it," "Everybody will think I'm crazy," "There can never be change around here," "It's not good to risk making mistakes," "I don't have the training to do this," "It's too impractical," "There will never be enough money," "People will laugh," and other variations of self-sabotaging thinking.

These attitudes exist from the beginning of coaching but usually stay hidden until one starts talking about change. The coach and the person being coached need to look for them, challenge them, and replace them with different mind-sets, such as, "I'm capable especially if I have support," "The world is really an okay place," "If I try and I flub, people will still accept me," and "It doesn't matter what the people in my neighborhood think, I'm going to do it anyhow." By drawing on the Bible, Christians can add a few others. "I can do all things through Christ who strengthens me,"[8] "When I am weak that is when I am strong,"[9] "Because of his divine power, I have everything I need for life and godliness,"[10] and "If I trust in the Lord and acknowledge him, I know he will direct my steps so I can step out confidently."[11] Coaches quickly discover that their efforts will not succeed until self-sabotaging mind-sets are recognized, challenged repeatedly, and replaced with healthier perspectives.

This leads to a fourth set of obstacles that relate to what we might call personal *identity*. For years I saw myself as a single graduate student. Shortly after I got my degree, I also got a wife and went to teach at a little college where I was a married professor. It was hard for me to shift my identity. I kept forgetting about the change, and it took a while for me to fit into the new roles. The same thing happens when people retire or change jobs.

What would happen if a bully boss or an insensitive parent decided to make changes and become more supportive and understanding? Everybody would be confused. Nobody would know how to respond. Some people might resist because they don't like the change. As a result, that employer, parent, or other person who had decided to change might decide to revert back to the same old ways of doing things. It would be easy to conclude, "I'll never change. What I've been doing for all these years is just the way I am!" Changes like this that involve one's self-identity are especially hard without another person, maybe a coach, who walks alongside giving encouragement and guidance.

As you become aware of these obstacles, you will recognize that they impact coaching in two ways. First they keep people stuck in old, often inefficient ways of doing things. That is what initially leads many people to sense that something is missing or wrong so they seek the help of a coach. Second, the obstacles get in the way of the coaching process just as they already are scuttling other parts of the person's life. If they are not dealt with, they will pop up repeatedly and the coaching will stall.

GETTING PAST THE BARRIERS

How do we respond when we encounter construction zones on the roads? In most cases we slow down and sometimes we are forced to stop, at least temporarily. Sooner or later we find our way past the obstacles and continue on our journey. This is what happens in coaching. The coach and client slow down and then work together to get past the hurdles that have appeared on the road.

All of this begins by recognizing that obstacles exist and by trying to size up the situation as best we can.

What specifically are the fears, inner gremlins, attitudes, pressures, and events that slow progress?

- When are these barriers most likely to appear?
- What triggers their emergence?
- How might clients be sabotaging themselves so progress stalls?
- What might be done to stop this?
- What has worked in the past when similar situations arose?
- What did not work and how does that relate to the present?
- What additional information might be valuable and how might one get this?
- What are the resources and who are the people who might help?
- What are ways to move forward even though money or time is limited?
- What things might need to be accepted because they cannot change?
- How can the client work within these realities?

Notice that these are all questions that can stimulate discussion and action possibilities.

At some time during this process, there will be resistance, even by clients who want to be coached, who want to get over the hurdles. At the beginning of the goal-setting process, most people are enthusiastic about pondering how they can map out a plan that will make things better. Similar enthusiasm can also arise when the coach and client begin discussion about how to overcome obstacles. Once again, however, insecurities might make their appearance. Fear of change or reluctance to take action can grind progress to a halt.

Resistance appears most strongly in the middle phase of a coaching process, after clients have fairly clear pictures of how they want to evolve but are finding all kinds of reasons why they can't do it. The secret to doing resistance work is to cooperate with it. It is not your job to remove it.

— FREDERIC M. HUDSON, author of *The Handbook of Coaching*

Dealing with obstacles can be threatening because we don't know what to expect if we change. Clients can think of many reasons for not going forward, and they resist even more if they feel pressure from a coach or someone else. It is best to acknowledge the resistance, talking about it to show that you understand it. Then focus again on future hopes, goals, and purposes. This keeps the emphasis on growth and often helps people see that there are small, doable, less-threatening steps that might be taken to get past the hurdles even if the client does not see a need for larger changes. As the process gets moving, with support and encouragement from the coach, trust continues to build, people begin to move, and often the value of changing and surmounting the obstacles becomes more apparent.

A DIFFERENT SET OF OBSTACLES

Maybe the least recognized of all obstacles are those that don't even exist in the people we coach. These are hurdles that lurk in coaches themselves. They are obstacles that sidetrack us or cause us to get stuck so we are less effective in guiding others. When I was taking my first coaching course, one of the students stated that she was not coaching anybody because she wanted to avoid the "imposter syndrome." Her own insecurities and fear of change were getting in the way and holding her back. Maybe she had convinced herself that there was truth in the self-talk that said, "I don't know enough to coach,"

"I'm not capable of doing this," "Nobody will respond to my coaching, especially since I am a novice," "What if people see my insecurities?" "What if they learn that I'm inexperienced?"

She is not alone. Some evidence has shown that most of us feel like imposters, especially at the beginning of our careers.[12] More surprising, perhaps, is the finding that even people with stellar credentials and accomplished careers can feel like imposters. Many capable people downplay their achievements. Some have a gnawing fear that they are less capable than their successes suggest. When a coach lacks confidence or is sabotaged by his or her own insecurities and inner gremlins, coaching is less effective and clients are given less valuable guidance. If the insecurities are too strong, the coach's attention is diverted and the person being coached feels alone, causing the process to stop moving forward.

How can we stop feeling like fakes and coach with greater confidence? It helps to be patient, recognizing that with more experience, there are fewer tendencies to feel under-qualified. Listen for positive feedback. Self-defined imposters don't absorb compliments well. They are more likely to discount or ignore affirmation and cling to their self-debasing beliefs.

In addition, we should fight compulsive work habits. Feelings of incompetence often push people to work harder, hoping to accomplish more, but there is little evidence that more work produces more confidence. It also helps to discuss insecurities with a friend, counselor, or coach. Like their clients, coaches also benefit from partnerships and accountability relationships with others.

If two people are in a boat and one stops rowing,

you both go in circles.

— Anonymous

A different set of hurdles for coaches comes with their fears of making mistakes or their realizations that they continue to make mistakes. One common error is being too directive, deciding what is best for clients and then steering them by giving advice.[13] This probably reflects our own insecurities and need to be in control. Other mistakes include judging people instead of affirming them, making suggestions that you regret later, letting your mind drift during coaching sessions, and spending too little time with the people you coach so they don't feel the support and guidance they need. The best response when we make mistakes is to admit them, apologize, correct them, and move forward. People are willing to forgive brief lapses in concentration or coaches who are too directive, especially if the mistakes are acknowledged and infrequent. A bigger problem for many coaches is an inability or unwillingness to forgive themselves.

Very different are the obstacles that come to coaches when they reflect on the coaching process itself and see its weaknesses. One of my clients was a coach whose biggest inner barrier concerned his doubts about the assumptions of coaching. "I agree that vision setting is important," he said. "I see the value of making plans, setting goals, and taking action steps. I have seen people grow through coaching. But I wonder if coaching largely is a human-centered process that leaves out God." My client commented how God sometimes gives us new visions and directions we may not have anticipated and may not have been able to discover in coaching. Sometimes he directs our steps in his own ways and his own timing, regardless of our coaching models and procedures.

This young man was wondering if his coaching was less focused and potentially less effective because of his own struggles about the secular underpinnings of his work. Together we discussed several biblical endorsements of planning, especially in Proverbs. We agreed that the coaching circle and other models are useful guides. But we also agreed that Christian coaches must never forget that God is in control and that sometimes he intervenes in ways that violate the methods we have learned in coach training. These are important issues for Christian coaches to consider and discuss. It is true that coaching tends to be a human enterprise, often done without acknowledging even the possibility of divine intervention. But coaching also could be seen as a human tool that God has permitted us to discover. It's a tool that he uses often, even though it never replaces unexpected divine intervention. My client continued building his coaching career when he was able to see that God appears to use coaching to accomplish his sovereign purposes.

Sometimes the obstacles coaches face are completely apart from the coaching process. When a friend lost her mother unexpectedly and suddenly was responsible for her aging father's care, she realized that her coaching effectiveness was beginning to suffer. The events in her family were taking her time and draining her energy even though they had nothing to do with her coaching skills. For the good of her clients, her father, and herself, she took a short break, stepping away from coaching until she could reorganize her life and be less distracted by the events in her family.

Taking a coaching break is not always necessary, but one step you can take is to find a coach for yourself. We can be very effective in talking with others about their lives, passions, visions, plans, and goals, but it is harder to focus on our own. Often another coach can help us keep direction in our own lives, become aware of obstacles, and take action so we can move forward. Everybody benefits as a result.

INTERMISSION

Like an intermission in a concert or a time-out in a football game, we come now to a pause in our journey through the emerging world of coaching. We have looked at the growth of coaching, defined its meaning, and shown how it ties to leadership and change. We've discussed coaching skills and spent several chapters describing a practical model of coaching that describes how it is done. This becomes a road map for anybody who wants to move forward on the coaching journey.

Now we make a turn to look at more specialized aspects of coaching. We'll begin by tapping into the experience of several successful Christian coaches who work in different settings and apply their coaching skills to specialized groups of people. Then we'll shift to professional issues, such as how you can get more training if you want it, what certification is all about, and how you can apply coaching to people with cultural backgrounds other than your own. We'll look at the present status and future direction of coaching and then help you determine where you might fit into the coaching revolution. We've gone through the basics. Now we can explore the exciting ways in which coaching can be applied.

Our short intermission is over. It is time to go back to our seats and move into the concluding acts of our story.

PART 6

SPECIALTIES IN CHRISTIAN COACHING

CHAPTER 14

TRANSITIONS AND LIFE COACHING

I HAVE A FRIEND, we'll call him Stan, who lives in my neighborhood and attends a nearby church. After going through a divorce, Stan accepted a job in our area and moved from his home in the South. He doesn't have a lot of friends here, but he is active at church and successful in his profession. Even so, Stan is not fulfilled in his job. He is bored with his work, despite a couple of promotions, and really wants to go into ministry. He can't afford to attend seminary full-time, however, and his degree in chemistry has not given him the best preparation for taking courses in theology. Stan is in a long period of transition that started with his divorce and relocation. He knows his values and his passion. He has a vision, and he even has a plan for getting to where he wants to go. But he needs encouragement, somebody who can help him make periodic adjustments to his strategy, a coach who can help him reach realistic subgoals and help him keep focused on his final objective.

We don't all go through divorces, career changes, or moves across the country, but we all go through transitions. Some of these are predictable and likely to happen to everybody: moving from high school or college into the job market, from being single to being married, from having teenagers in your home to being empty nesters, from employment to retirement. Many of these changes come with the different seasons of life. In their twenties and thirties, most people are getting established on their own and moving into careers. In their forties and fifties, many continue to build their lives and families, but some shift into new directions before it is too late to change. The sixties and seventies bring retirement and new challenges as people move into old age. The later years are times for reflection, leisure, and sometimes disappointment over missed goals or opportunities. Moving through these seasons brings commonly experienced changes in our careers, marriages, families, and perspectives on life.

Other transitions are more traumatic and unpredictable. We all know people who have been laid off unexpectedly, forsaken by a spouse, brought low by an illness, or abruptly disrupted by an accident, family crisis, or natural disaster. Some people need counseling to help them through these times of stress; others look for coaches to help them readjust their lives and bring back some semblance of order and fulfillment.

There were times when mentors, relatives, neighbors, and friends were freely available to walk with people going through transitions. These informal caregivers gave encouragement, support, and suggestions. They were there when life got too busy or stressed. They were listening ears when people needed to deal with a crisis, make a decision, dream about the future, or just talk.

All of this is changing, at least in the parts of the world where most of us live. The pace of life has become faster and everybody is busier. Most of us have no less of a desire to care, but we have a lot less time. Pastors have continued to fill the caregiving role, like they have for centuries, and the world is filled with people who still take the time to listen. But coaches have emerged to fill a void left by former mentors and wise elders. In his textbook on life coaching, Dave Ellis has written that life coaching is a process in which a coach provides a partnership to help others improve their quality of life, discover their passions, find their purpose for living, and get free from their limitations, fears, and other obstacles so they can achieve their goals and life dreams.[1] As the name suggests, life coaching is about improving life. Many topics are discussed in these life coaching sessions, but this chapter will focus on two of the most common issues that these particular coaches encounter: coaching people through transitions and enabling clients to find more balance in their lives.

WALKING THROUGH TRANSITIONS

Judy Santos has coached a lot of people through transitions. Professional life coach, founder of the Christian Coaches Network,[2] and experienced coach trainer, Judy got into transitional coaching after she went through seven major life changes within a period of nine months. In preparing to write the next few chapters, I looked for experienced coach leaders who worked in each of the specialty areas we will discuss and who would agree to an interview. Judy was one of the first people I wanted to contact.

"I've worked with myriads of people in transitions, including career transitions, moves, and losses," Judy told me over lunch in a Seattle café. "Transitions represent a time of major change. Often we resist change because we fear the unknown, are unsure of ourselves or our abilities, and cling to the good parts of what we have enjoyed. Sometimes, like Peter after stepping off the boat, we doubt God. Dealing with change successfully requires authenticity: being honest about how you feel and not stuffing the emotions that accompany change.

"The kinds of transitions people bring to me in a coaching situation are not those you get broadsided with, like a sudden death in the family, losing a child suddenly, or having your house blown away by a tornado. Usually I see transitions that are anticipated, although people don't generally recognize them as being times of transition. And therein lies a lot of the challenge. People aren't aware that they are in a time when there's going to be different emotions, and so there tends to be a lot of confusion. If people realize that this is, in fact, a time of major change and they're working through it with a coach, this makes it much easier, more complete, faster, and better. The more authentic the person is willing to be, recognizing the emotions, the easier the transition will be."

It is easy to assume that all transitions impact us negatively, but Judy was quick to point out that some transitions are positive and welcome. It also should be remembered that while some of these changes are involuntary, others are voluntary "and reflect a conscious decision based on the belief that moving forward can lead to something better. In any case, choices abound. Exploring them fully is beneficial to the person being coached."

As Judy shared these insights, it occurred to me that transitions might be put into one of four boxes that look like this:

	Voluntary Transition	Involuntary Transition
Positive (desirable) Transition	Example: Buying a better house	Example: Unexpected promotion
Negative (undesirable) Transition	Example: Moving away from friends	Example: Family death

In times of transitions, clients sometimes question whether they made a wise choice and perhaps even consider going back to what they left behind. Real estate agents call this "buyer's remorse," when purchasers wonder if buying the new house really was a good idea. In transitions like these, the coach's job is not to give advice. The coach "supports clients in hearing themselves; reviewing their vision, purpose, and values; allowing them to reach a conclusion that they can live with long term.

"Turn the telescope backward and help the client see the big picture," Judy suggests. "Ask powerful questions that will bring clarity to the client:

- Don't over-dramatize or over-sympathize.
- Don't assume your client sees all facets of the process. Keep track of the progress.
- Don't overlook the importance of a support system. You may be one of the ballasts in your client's life.
- Don't patronize your client by minimizing adjustments or making false assurances.
- Don't hesitate to ask your client where he or she has a sense of peace.
- Don't assume (or say) you know exactly what the client is going through. You don't.
- Don't assume you know everything about your client. Sometimes clients don't think to tell you everything.

"I once worked with a client for several years and never knew that there was a key person in her life who helped her out with everything from hosting dinner parties to child care to assistance with her business. It never came up because it was never an issue, until this person suddenly died. Her absence created a huge hole in the life of my client, both emotionally and physically. She shared the information about her death with me and how this had impacted her. Had I not known that, I might have put forward an inappropriate challenge for that time in her life or been insensitive to her raw emotions.

"Even as life is a series of changes, it also is a series of choices. They only become more complex as we get older. We choose whether to accept or reject Jesus. We choose a life mate. We choose education. We choose a career. We choose whether or not to have children. We choose how we want to live. We choose the people who are in our lives."

As we continued with our conversation, I was reminded of some guidance that Judy gave in one of the online newsletters she produces for the Christian Coaches Network. Her suggested ways to make transitions easier are listed in table 14-1.

Table 14-1

WAYS TO MAKE TRANSITIONS EASIER[3]
Major life transitions can catch us off guard, even when we expect these changes or think of them in positive terms. Coaches can help others:

- Remember that life is a series of changes
- Know that with every major change, there is both a gain and a loss
- Allow themselves to honor and acknowledge their feelings of both anticipation and sadness
- Write in a journal and give themselves permission to be honest in acknowledging and expressing their feelings
- Walk the bridge between what they are leaving behind and what lies ahead
- Get closure on the part of life being left behind, by saying what needs to be said, reflecting on that part of life, and possibly writing letters to others who are involved
- Deliberately keep some constants so that life will not be over-whelmed by the change
- Begin to anticipate the new chapter in life with excitement, even writing down the good things the person looks forward to experiencing or doing
- Reach out to others in the new situation and develop a sense of community
- Be prayerful, remembering that God's path never leads us to where his grace will not keep us

"Coaching people through transitions often involves sharing information such as this with an individual. It involves helping people move from assessing their life situations and dealing with the grief that accompanies their losses. Ultimately, the coach encourages people to see a vision for the future and find ways to move on." Coach Judy described some of the ways in which she does this:

"I start by finding out what they would like to create, what they feel God's will might be. A lot of people are really foggy on that, because searching for God's will can be a very frustrating experience. I try to draw out of people what it is that they really feel passionate about, what they're excited about, listening for indicators. Sometimes it's difficult for people to identify those things, and it's fun as a coach to help people discover what may be inside. Sometimes they enjoyed something in the past but maybe haven't done it for a long time because they've been in a situation that's either been really unhappy or hasn't allowed them the time and space to do the things that they enjoy. Sometimes this leads to a career change. Sometimes it means retraining, going back to school. I ask questions such as, 'If you could design your life exactly as you want it, what would it look like?' 'What do you think God wants you to do?' 'How are you including the Lord in your plans?' 'What are you doing to seek his direction?' Those kinds of questions often challenge people to new ways of looking at their situations.

"I see coaching a person through a transition as something like walking across a bridge. You are very aware of your present surroundings, you know that the bridge is there and maybe you know that the other side really is better than this side. But halfway across, you wonder if this was really one of your better ideas. The side behind looks so warm and welcoming, while the distant shore ahead can appear to be cold and foreboding."

In coaching her clients through their life transitions, Judy Santos does what coaches do best. She listens, challenges, asks questions, tries to enlarge the perspectives of the people she coaches, encourages them to envision the future, helps keep them focused, allows them to make choices, and rejoices with them when they get to the other side of the bridge.

TRANSITIONAL CHANGE

Coaching people through transitions may be of more importance than many of us realize. There is a large cost to society and to individuals if transitions fail, according to accumulating research.[4] When groups of people are unemployed, unable to transition to new jobs, "the very social structure of a community disintegrates. Violence increases, families fall apart, crime and drug abuse escalate, and individual mental and physical health deteriorate. . . . Those who have poor career adaptability skills are more likely to be unemployed. Number of arrests, low academic achievements, low aspirations, and formation of deviant friendships are strongly related to unemployment in young adults."[5] These words were written by psychologists, but the conclusions apply equally to coaches. When transitions are successful and "individuals go back to work their mental and physical health improves. . . . If we want individuals to be mentally healthy and to contribute to society as a whole, we need to find ways to support them in voluntary transitions and to bolster their resources during involuntary transitions."[6] What could be a more significant role for competent coaches?

Table 14-2

HUDSON'S FOUR PHASES OF CHANGE[7]

Phase 1 — The *Go For It* Phase: Dreaming, Planning, Plateauing

This is a period of success, stability, creativity, and energy. This is when people dream, launch projects, and work to win. People feel invigorated, challenged, fulfilled, euphoric, optimistic. Many also feel fatigued, short on time, overwhelmed, competitive.

This phase ends when people succeed and have no more challenge. It is then that they plateau, lose their momentum, feel trapped, have a "been-there-done-that" feeling, or hit a wall.

Phase 2 — The *Doldrums* Phase: Being Out of Sync

In this period, people feel bored, stuck, disappointed, without purpose. Often they feel trapped, sensing decline, restless but resisting change.

This phase ends when people either reevaluate their dreams and return to phase 1 with new enthusiasm and commitment or end the earlier chapter of their lives, say good-bye, and move on.

Phase 3 — The *Cocooning* Phase: Finding New Passion and Purpose

This is a time of withdrawal for reflection, strategic planning, and life evaluation. People feel sad, empty, lonely, angry, grieving, disillusioned, sometimes betrayed. Frederic M. Hudson writes, "People who cocoon come to terms with who they are without their previous roles dominating them. They work through an identify crisis and take time out, psychologically speaking, for soul searching. Little by little, out of solitude grows a resilient self, anchored in core values and inner peace and challenged by new purpose and passion. Life is transformed."[8]

The phase ends when people set new directions and decide to get more involved with others and move forward. Many pick up new hobbies, move, change jobs, become more spiritual, take courses. Often there is a shift from doing to being.

Phase 4 — The *Getting Ready* Phase: Starting a New Chapter

People feel hopeful, trusting, creative, a "lightness of being," excitement. Reengaging involves *creating* new ideas and possibilities, *experimenting* with new ideas and projects, *networking* with new types of people, and *prioritizing* by setting new goals and values.

The phase ends as people return to the Go For It phase. Often they feel fulfilled, confident, self-motivated, focused, and unstoppable.

Frederic M. Hudson was an early leader in the coaching movement who worked with hundreds of corporations, not-for-profit organizations, government agencies, universities, and individual coaching clients. Much of his work involved helping people grow and make transitions. Drawing from these experiences, Hudson proposed that life transitions—some expected, some not—involve the four phases summarized in table 14-2.[9] Perhaps you can think of times when you moved through these phases yourself or when you saw something similar in the lives of the people you coach. Hudson believes that in addition to individuals, families, communities, churches, businesses, colleges, and other "human systems" also go through these phases. If so, then the essence of transition coaching is helping people through these changes. Table 14-3 gives Hudson's suggestions about how this coaching can be done.

Table 14-3

COACHING AND THE FOUR PHASES OF CHANGE[10]	
Phase 1 — The *Go For It* Phase	
Goals for Person Being Coached	*Coaching Activities Include:*
■ Dream (or dream again) ■ Make plans ■ Take action ■ Reach goals ■ Sustain and enjoy success ■ Reevaluate with new goals and dreams	■ Career training ■ Improving time management ■ Stress management ■ Building networks ■ Learning life balance ■ Accepting and enjoying success
Phase 2 — The *Doldrums* Phase	
Goals for Person Being Coached	*Coaching Activities Include:*
■ Keep hope alive ■ Cope with negative emotions ■ Sort things out ■ Accept change ■ Create an exit plan ■ Let go ■ Ponder new possibilities	■ Encouraging change ■ Discussing disappointments ■ Evaluating what might come next ■ Challenging people to avoid destructive behavior, such as self-talk ■ Planning how to say good-bye
Phase 3 — The *Cocooning* Phase	
Goals for Person Being Coached	*Coaching Activities*
■ Turn inward to take stock ■ Rethink values and goals ■ Consider spiritual renewal	■ Encouraging journaling ■ Taking a sabbatical ■ Spiritual and personal stock taking

- Plan new goals
- Renew trust and self-esteem
- Find new passion and purpose

- Encouraging change
- Stimulating hobbies, training, and travel
- Strategic planning

Phase 4 — The *Getting Ready* Phase

Goals for Person Being Coached
- Move in new directions
- Create new ideas and possibilities
- Take new risks
- Become more creative
- Reassess values

Coaching Activities
- Encouraging experimenting
- Trying new ideas and projects
- Encouraging networking/new friendships
- Choosing new priorities and strategies
- Simplifying lifestyles

Where is God in all of this? Hudson doesn't say, but Christian coaches realize that God is always present when changes take place. He understands the enthusiasm of the *Go For It* stage even when we often forget him in the midst of all of the activity. He understands the doldrums and helps us through, enabling us to deal with the anger, sense of betrayal, and disappointment. When we lack the motivation to move on, he sustains, often through the ministry of a coach. When we get to the cocooning stage and eventually become ready to move forward, he helps us pause while we find a new sense of God-given purpose, passion, and direction. Then, if we let him, he guides the self-renewal process and the move into a new *Go For It* stage. If you haven't seen these phases in the people you coach, eventually you probably will.

FINDING LIFE BALANCE

In their popular textbook on life coaching, Laura Whitworth and her coauthors have written that in our "chaotic, high-speed world of schedules, commitments, stress, and demands on time and energy, there is a yearning for something called balance."[11] The writers add that many clients come to coaching because they can no longer handle the continual change and stresses of life. These coaching clients rarely ask specifically for help in bringing balance. Instead, they come focusing on some area of life that is out of alignment or lacking stability. But the topic of "balance is always part of the coaching backdrop whether it shows up in every coaching call or not."[12]

Balance is not a static state of equilibrium; it is a skill that can be developed, a skill that enables us to say no as well as yes, a skill that enables us to maintain equilibrium in a world that pulls us in different directions and takes away our freedom to choose. "When it comes to balance, clients want the ability to juggle the precious priorities of their lives so that [they are] more empowered and less at the mercy of circumstances and other people's expectations and demands."

Christopher McCluskey is a life coach who struggled to find balance in his own life and family and who coaches others in balancing their lives today. When Christopher left his Christian counseling practice in Tampa Bay and moved to a tiny farm community in the foothills of the Ozark Mountains, he and his family wanted a lifestyle that was less cluttered than the busyness of a bustling metropolitan area. They now live in rural tranquility, surrounded by horses, cattle, rolling hills, and open fields. It is from there that Christopher teaches telephone classes and serves as director of the Professional Christian Coaching Program at the Institute for Life Coach Training.[13] He is also president of Coaching for Christian Living, one of the most successful Christian coaching practices that I know of. More than any other person, Christopher McCluskey introduced me to coaching and has been a prime encourager as I have taken formal training, grown as a coach trainer, and written this book. I called his farm in Missouri and we talked about life coaching and balancing lifestyles.

"Coaching for balance begins with helping people figure out what they value most in life and then ordering their lives around it," Christopher began. "A person will never feel balanced if he or she doesn't have a personal vision of what a balanced life looks like. So we begin by identifying a person's most deeply held values and then clarifying the vision that arises from them.

"What is balanced at one season of our lives may be entirely out of balance at another. Sometimes, for a while, certain activities may have to be moved higher on our priority list, which means other things must be moved down, but we can still find balance if we are consciously making those choices based upon our values and vision.

"In contrast, imbalance occurs when we don't examine our most deeply held values, when we have no clear vision for our lives, and when we become driven by circumstances. We pursue someone else's vision for us or chase after what the world says we should value. We deal with the urgent rather than the important. We are not purpose-driven.

"People who are purpose-driven know that some seasons of life will require huge amounts of energy in one area, so they change their lifestyle to accommodate that area and then close out that season when it is ended. They don't try to do several different major things in the same season, continually adding more and more onto the pile of their lives. There is balance in knowing why you are doing something—doing it—and then being done with it. Know when to say no so you can say yes to the things that matter most."

In our long conversation, we talked about the pressure many people feel trying to get everything done when time is so limited. Christopher responded with the suggestion that balance is not simply a matter of keeping all the balls in the air; it is taking time and having the discipline to set down some of the balls and not keep picking up additional things to do. This requires familiarity with values again and often benefits from the accountability that a coach can provide.

When the McCluskeys moved, Christopher hired a private coach to work at making the transition easier. "Part of that was trying to figure out how to get into the field of coaching, but a lot of it was for developing a plan to live out our vision. The plan is very important. If a coach does not help his or her clients develop a concrete plan and hold them accountable for it, he or she has failed them as a coach. Plans may change over time, but the coach ensures that there *is* a plan and encourages the client to work toward it. Coaches hold clients to their plans. When the clients become distracted, coaches remind them of their values and why they're doing what they are doing."

In this process, "obstacles are going to arise; they are inevitable, and they must be dealt with in a forthright manner so they don't come back to haunt you later. Using the analogy of a sailboat on a chartered course, the captain has a vision of where he wants to go and an ideal path to get there. He also has reality, which dictates that while he is following that path, he may have to alter his course several times to compensate for the obstacles that arise. Many coaches are fond of the phrase 'I can't change the wind, but I can adjust the sails.' Deal with obstacles directly as they arise and oftentimes you will find that they add excitement to the journey and are rich opportunities for growth."

LIFE COACHING FOR LIFE BALANCE

Christopher McCluskey has a fascinating theory that can assist coaches as we help our clients handle transitions and navigate their lives. Here is how he describes the process.

"Imagine a triangle with three words at the corners: worship, work, and play. If you take out the time we spend sleeping or handling utilitarian things such as taking a shower or driving places, most of what we do each day can fall into one of these three broadly defined activities: worship, work, and play.

Part 6 | Specialties in Christian Coaching

"Worship is, of course, your time at church, doing your morning devotions, spending time in prayer, meditation, silence, and solitude. Worship is also your acts of service, such as ministering to your family, visiting shut-ins, serving on church committees, volunteering at your children's school, and being active in your community. God can be greatly glorified through all of these. But worship also includes those times when you unexpectedly experience a taste of God. You stop and drink in a sunset, watch a squirrel bury a nut, consciously feel the summer breeze on your face, gaze into the flowers of a busy florist's shop, or bask in the laughter of your grandchildren playing. As you do these things, you acknowledge the Lord, thank him for what you are experiencing, and praise him for his goodness.

"The key in all of these acts of worship is that they require something of you. They don't happen without you making concentrated time for them. And when you do, not only is God glorified but you are also refreshed. True worship fulfills our highest calling, which, as the Westminster catechism puts it, is 'to glorify God and to enjoy him forever.'

"Work is the vast majority of what we do during our daily lives. It includes our jobs, homemaking, paying the bills, mowing the lawn, buying the groceries, and the other labor-intensive things we do. We spend a lot of our time at work. And like worship, it should require something from us as well as something that we get back. We are tired after a job well done, but we feel invigorated by it. It is very satisfying to put in a good day's work, to know that the bills are done, to see the freshly mowed lawn, and to have the pantry stocked.

"Play is the final ingredient in a well-balanced life. Play will be different for different people, but play is definitely not 'vegging out' and doing nothing. As with worship and work, true play requires concentrated time and effort. Whether it's playing on the church ball team, exercising, horseback riding, doing a hobby, playing an instrument, reading a book, going on a date, or engaging in a game with your kids, play requires something of you and it puts something back.

"That's the litmus test for each of these activities: Each requires some kind of investment on your part—some degree of planning or conscious attention, some form of active participation—and each of them will pour something back into you. When you have a genuine worship time, it feeds the reciprocal relationship of God being glorified and your spirit being blessed. A good day's work is tiring, but it leaves you feeling good about what you've accomplished. And true play may cause you to work up a sweat, invest in lessons, spend money others might consider 'wasteful,' or spend time others consider 'unproductive.' But true play will always feed your soul.

"Most people don't live that way. Look now at the triangle with the arrows. In many of our lives, especially in Western culture, we "worship" our work. That's what we sacrifice to and make the focus our lives. It's where we derive our sense of security and our sense of worth. Work becomes our object of worship instead of God. Christians are supposed to get their sense of security and worth from him. We're supposed to sacrifice to him. And as we do so, he pours into our spirits what we really need. But instead, too often, we worship our work."

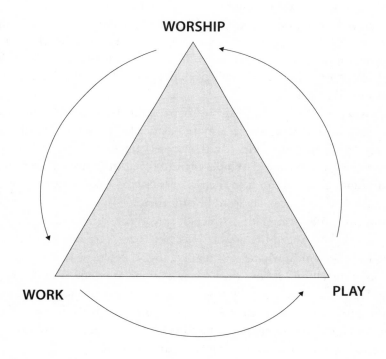

Figure 14-1

"Not only do we worship our work but we then 'work' at playing. It's hard work for many of us to play because we don't value it highly enough, so there's no time or money for it. When I bought my horse, I really had no business doing so from a financial standpoint, but I valued the playtime that riding gives me. My mother often recited the quote, 'If I had but twopence, with one I would buy bread and with the other I would buy hyacinths, for they would feed my soul.' Play feeds our soul. I named my horse Hyacinth because she feeds my soul.

"If we do allow ourselves to play, we often turn it into a competition: Our ball team has to win, we have to be the best at our instrument, we turn our hobby into a side business. We set goals, keep track of our performance, and end up wringing every bit of fun out of play. It's just like work, except we don't get paid!

"And look at the model again. We 'play' at our worship. We don't take it seriously and give it precedence. It's an afterthought. We lack discipline because, again, we don't value it highly enough. Consequently, our worship doesn't allow God to fill us. Our spirits are starved because we are not feeding on the Bread of Life and drinking his Living Water.

"When we worship our work, work at our play, and play at our worship, we are completely out of balance. Nothing is able to nourish us. Work reaches the point of diminishing returns, where we're still putting in but getting nothing back. Play and worship aren't given the priority they need in order to feed us as only they can.

"This is where life coaches can be so tremendously helpful. They can help a person think through what a more balanced life would look like for them. They can help people identify their core values, find the vision that arises from these values, and develop a plan to bring their lives more in line with that vision. Coaches can help their clients clarify what vibrant worship, meaningful work, and true play would be for them.

"It's so easy to be scattered, distracted, spread too thin, with too many balls in the air. A balanced life doesn't look like that. A balanced life allows you to be fully present in whatever you are doing. If you're working, you can totally pour yourself into it, and then when it's done, it's done. You can wipe your hands, go off and play — fully play — without being distracted by things at the office. And when you're in worship, your mind can be fully focused on the things of God. You can enjoy just basking in his presence because you are not distracted by other things fighting for your attention.

"The passionate pursuit of a balanced life calls us to a challenge I have posted on the bulletin board above my desk: "I want to be where I am when I'm there." Balance allows us to be at worship without thinking about work. It allows us to be at work without dreaming about our next vacation. It allows us to be free at play. A balanced life, based on our values and vision, allows us to be where we are when we're there."

This is a model that assists coaches, but it does more. It can be explained to your clients and used as a guide to help them find greater life balance, deal more effectively with transitions, and face other life coaching issues.

CHAPTER 15

RELATIONSHIP AND MARRIAGE COACHING

ALMOST TEN YEARS have passed since I first read the story of Coach Ricky Byrdsong, but his story continues to be an inspiration long after the tragedy that ended his life. In his book *Coaching Your Kids in the Game of Life*, Ricky described the day when he was a tenth grader, nonchalantly sauntering through the hall at Frederick Douglass High School in Atlanta, when he heard a call that changed his life forever. It sounded like a loud thunderclap rolling down the hallway, but every male in the school could recognize its source. Coach Lester was a 6-foot-four-inch barrel-chested man whose very presence commanded respect. And that day, his booming voice was calling Ricky.

"Hey, son!" he said, staring up and down at Ricky's six-foot-five-inch frame. "You're too big to be walking these halls and not playing basketball!" He paused and then added, "I'll see you in the gym at 3:30 . . . *today*."

Ricky didn't know a thing about basketball. He didn't even have any basketball shoes, and his single-parent mom didn't have any spare money. But he was afraid of not making an appearance, so he went to the gym and began a journey that led to an outstanding career that took Ricky to the top. He coached college basketball for eighteen years and eventually became head coach of the Northwestern University Wildcats. But he never forgot what Coach Lester taught, beginning on that day in the high school hallway. He made Ricky and the other players understand the importance of being part of a team with a purpose. He gave Ricky a vision of what he was capable of doing and then helped his young protégés reach their goals.

Then it all ended, as suddenly and unexpectedly as it began. Walking in his neighborhood on a warm summer night, Ricky was gunned down by a white supremacist on a killing rampage. A few months later, Ricky Byrdsong's book on coaching appeared, but it went far beyond basketball. "My responsibilities as a coach were to inspire and equip my players to achieve their dreams," he wrote. "The game of basketball was only a means for preparing my players for a bigger and more important game — the game of life."[1]

Ricky described how Coach Lester had done this many years earlier. "If only every kid had a Coach Lester to call him out, to believe in him, give him a goal, work with him to help him reach his potential — what a difference it would make. When I drive around now and see kids hanging out on the street corner, I pick one out of the crowd and think, 'Man! If someone could just do for you what Coach Lester did for me.' That kid doesn't have to end up hanging around the street corner . . . or in prison . . . or in the morgue. What if, at a critical point in his life, someone would say, 'Hey, son! Come here! You can do . . . whatever! I'll see you today at 3:30.' That kid would be there and it would change his life.

"But there aren't enough coaches to go around."[2]

COACHING AND RELATIONSHIPS

Relationships are at the core of almost all coaching. Ricky Byrdsong was a Christian who apparently felt called to coach young people in the game of life, even more than in the game of basketball. His book coached parents on how to coach their children so they would have vision for the future, lasting values, the ability to hurdle obstacles, and an awareness of parental support and presence as they make decisions. This type of coaching can happen in reverse as children learn how to coach their parents. Pastors are learning to coach parishioners, many managers coach their employees, professors coach their students, and friends coach friends. All of these involve relationships; many involve coaching people who want to build new relationships or improve relations that already exist. All of this has led to a growing specialty known as relationship coaching.

Over the years, I have come to know several coaches who specialize in relationships, but most of my learning has come from long conversations with a former student named Jeff Williams. After graduation, he built a successful career as a marriage and family therapist, then moved into a couple of administrative positions in national marriage ministries designed to strengthen and heal marriage and family relationships. Now Jeff has settled into what clearly seems to invigorate him the most: coaching individuals and couples to improve their relationships. He and his wife, Jill, feel especially called to encourage and equip couples, particularly Christian couples, to strengthen and heal their marriages to be all that they can be for God's purposes. They provide some direct service and give training for couples to do the same ministry they do.[3] Because Jeff has training and considerable experience as a coach, I asked how relationship coaching differs from other types of coaching. I was not surprised when he gave this concise and thoughtful answer:

"I find more strong emotions in relationship coaching than in other types of coaching. The life coaching I do is often about purpose, schedule, and values. Business coaching is often about personal and organizational performance goals, and career coaching is often focused on strengths, gifts, and temperament. Relationship coaching is often about pleasure, pain, or confusion. The impetus to seek relationship coaching is often something painful— a disappointment, betrayal, or simply an area of dissatisfaction in a relationship. Relationship coaching helps people to believe in their capacity to skillfully and successfully engage relationships."

From there, we talked about the uniqueness of relationship coaching and how it is done. "I define relationship coaching as the discipline of believing in my client's ability to engage in and sustain a healthy, pleasurable, and productive relationship," Jeff began. "Relationship coaching begins with my client's agenda, so any goal they have that aligns with and is not contradictory to biblical principles for relationship is fair game as a goal for growth or change. Relationship coaching, as I see it, can be about a person's relationship with God, spouse, child, friendship, business or ministry partnership, or any other any relationship that is of major concern. I believe that anyone interested in strengthening or healing an important relationship and willing to take responsibility for their own growth and change can benefit from relationship coaching.

"I try to do relationship coaching with all participants present in order to facilitate their communication and explore the goals of their relationship. When I can coach only one person, I spend a lot of time asking questions about the ideal future that my client would like to experience in the relationship."

MARRIAGE COACHING

I knew that Jeff's greatest interest was in coaching couples. It's a specialized form of relationship coaching, and I was sure that Jeff Williams could answer some questions I have not found in any of the coaching books that line my shelves.

First question: What is marriage coaching?

Jeff gave me a somewhat formal written answer: "Christian marriage coaching is the application of Christian coaching concepts and skills to facilitate growth, healing, and change for couples. Everything that applies to coaching individuals applies to coaching couples. The objective of marriage coaching is to facilitate identification of growth goals that both partners are motivated to pursue and the action steps to accomplish these goals. Once goals are determined, coaches collaborate with the couple to develop and choose action steps. This process is obviously more challenging than coaching individuals because each partner's perspective must be drawn out, clarified, and understood before goals are negotiated and decided and action steps chosen.[4]

I knew that Jeff and his wife, Jill, do marriage coaching together, so I asked my second question: What were his observations about doing coaching together as a couple?

"It is great for our relationship because it provides something meaningful for us to do together," he responded. "A couple can make a great team if they understand their differences. But coaching together requires a lot of communication: before, during, and after sessions. That is how we stay clear on our goals, methods, and rationale for asking certain questions or focusing on different facets of the couple's conversation.

"Couples love talking to us as a couple. They feel more understood since both a male and female perspective is represented. In addition, couples are helped when we model conflict resolution, courtesies in communication, and specific relationship skills, such as active listening, or a dialogue exercise to help them see how we talk about a sensitive issue."

In response to my request, Jeff gave a brief case history that is especially useful in showing how a coaching session can be set up, even if the problem is not related to marriage. "Bob and Renee agreed that their marriage was stagnant. They didn't have huge problems and they didn't want counseling, but like most couples they did have some issues, and they wanted to be proactive to solve them instead of waiting for things to get worse. Both noticed some patterns they wanted to break, and they were both agreeable to setting some goals. Their communication became strained during Bob's busy season at work, and those were the times that Renee didn't feel heard or cared about. This resulted in her being less willing to be intimate with Bob. That was a problem for Bob, as it would be for most men. He agreed that communication could be improved, and, yes, he wanted more sex. 'We're not sure we need counseling or that we want to go to counseling, but we are stuck, and coaching sounds interesting. What is it?'"

The coach explained that marriage coaching is a conversation about how a couple can grow and change in their marriage. As coaches, Jeff and Jill will ask questions to understand what the couple wants to be different in their relationship. They might say, "We will begin by helping you explore areas for growth or change and then narrow those down to one or two very specific and measurable goals. All along you will be the ones to choose and set goals and specific action steps to achieve those goals. We facilitate your conversations and provide support, encouragement, and accountability to accomplish the goals you set. Coaching lasts as long as you want it to, and you'll tell us when you're done according to when you've accomplished what you want to. It's your process, and we are your servants to facilitate your growth and change. You are free to adjust any variable in the process according to what you want, including duration of sessions, frequency of sessions, and the content you present to us. It's all in your control. We assume that we're having this conversation because God has initiated some growth and change in you and you want to respond to his prompts to make your marriage more like he wants it to be. So you listen to God, to each other, and to us. We too listen to him, and to you, and facilitate the process of communicating about your honest thoughts and feelings. We are like gardeners that facilitate the growing process, but we don't make anything grow. That's up to him and you to respond to what he is doing."

Jeff went on to set some guidelines for this couple. First, he said, "We are your servants in this process. To us this is a sacred privilege to come alongside you to assist in your growth. Second, we will always be seeking to work ourselves out of a job. We want to help you as efficiently as possible. We have no desire to keep you as clients indefinitely, but that doesn't mean we'll kick you out too quickly. We can make the decision together about when to end our coaching. Third, if something isn't working for you, say so. We are in process too, and we want to grow and change. Teach us to be more helpful, or fire us if we aren't. In that event, we will be professional and help you locate and connect with other coaches or other resources. Our heart is for you to be successful. Fourth, expect that you will internalize some of the values, principles, and processes that we share with you and use with you."

This "couple" coaching relationship brings us to my third question. It could be a little more controversial. Every relationship coach and marriage coach that I know has been trained as a therapist, and most have practiced as marriage counselors before shifting to coaching. Marriage coaching sounds a lot like counseling. How, then, can non-therapist coaches do relationship coaching if they are not counselors or if they have not had special training as relationship or marriage coaches? Jeff's answer reflects his caution about coaches crossing the boundary into counseling when they are not trained or licensed to do this: "All coaches should refrain from telling their clients what to do. Non-therapist coaches, such as lay coaches employed in church or community marriage ministry settings, need to be especially careful to do nothing that can be construed as the coach's taking responsibility for the couple's relationship or telling them what decision they need to make about their relationship. Non-therapist coaches should be trained in a model that teaches how to facilitate couple's conversations, encourage sharing, and handle emotional or difficult conversations. They should be equipped with tools (at a minimum) to assist in building closeness, resolving conflict, speaking and hearing strong emotions, and negotiating requests for change in the relationship. In addition, non-therapist marriage coaches should have their work monitored by a more experienced marriage coach, and they should have ongoing consulting and supervision relationships in which they are accountable for their coaching."

BACK TO THE BASICS

This chapter began with Ricky Byrdsong coaching his young basketball players to play together in teams. Jeff Williams has taken us through the maze of relationship coaching and opened our eyes to the potential, complexity, and crucial importance of this coaching specialty. We have not yet looked at the work of corporate coaches who intervene when there are tensions in the workplace or coaches who work with church boards and try to bring harmony when there is dissention. We have not discussed family tensions that come with the oft-noted pull between one's job and one's family. All of these, too, are relationship coaching issues.

Could it be that this chapter points to some of the core reasons for the persisting tension between counselors and coaches? Certainly, the methods of coaching can be applied to individuals, couples, and groups to improve relationships in healthy people. But the line between marriage counseling and marriage coaching seems very thin, and the potential for crossing boundaries seems high, especially in coaches who do not have a high level of training in marriage therapy, conflict resolution, or relationship issues.

I am reminded of an old friend who has a successful and visible, highly demanding, time-consuming career. He also has a wife and five children. Several years ago, the oldest made a sobering comment that had a big impact on his father. "Dad, when I ask you to do something with me, you always say, 'Later,' but I know that this means, 'Never.'" The father did not like that. He wanted to change. I don't know if he ever hired a coach, but he needed some help to get control of his work-dominated lifestyle and his frustrated family relationships.

When he told me this story, I thought of our model for coaching. My friend was aware of the issues he faced at work and home. He knew the obstacles in himself and in his work environment. He even has an idea of where he wanted to go, but he didn't know how to get there. His son's comment brought the abrupt realization of something many parents never consider: There needs to be a clear picture of the values and visions that parents want for their marriages and their kids. If you or the person you coach does not have these, then there will be no clear direction for parenting. The culture—including peers, television, the Internet, and other media—will instill the values and set non-Christian directions for your family. But it's never too late for a family to catch a vision and live in accordance with the values that count. For my friend and his wife, their challenge was to set a direction for their family and rekindle relationships within the home. Relationship coaching can help with that. But when potentially debilitating problems creep into relationships, the work of the relationship coach needs to give way to a more psychologically astute counselor.

CHAPTER 16

CAREER COACHING

MARSHA HATES HER job. Every morning she gets out of bed and into her car, where she drives for half an hour on congested roads to reach her office. Once there she spends each day doing work that is not very challenging, sitting in a chair that is not very comfortable, working with people who are not very interesting, listing to the criticisms of a boss who is not very sensitive. Marsha may sound like a figment of somebody's imagination, but she is not a fictional character. She is very real. We have talked several times about her frustrating work situation. When she was younger, her parents discouraged her from going to college, so she applied for a job in a company near her home and has been there ever since. Marsha has the ability to do better, but she lacks the motivation, or maybe the courage, to make a change. It is easier to stay where she is—miserable but secure in her job—than to find another line of work or place of employment.

Work has a central place in the lives of most adults. It defines who we are, shapes our self-concepts, and determines our standards of living. Abundant research shows that work has a bearing on our physical and mental health.[1] People who are unemployed or underemployed have more physical problems and are more prone to depression than workers who like their jobs. Work will not be mentioned in all of our coaching sessions, but it has a bearing on almost every issue our clients raise.

For example, consider how the world of work is changing. There are fewer jobs for unskilled workers or for people like Marsha who never went to college. Compared to a few years ago, many occupations require more education, more specialized training, and higher levels of certification and competence. Shifting from one job or career to another requires adaptability and self-awareness, according to a research-based article on work transitions.[2] That's a problem for people who are dependable workers but don't like change and don't have a lot of self-awareness. If a job or career change becomes necessary, the smoothness and success of the transition will depend on the individual's emotional, mental, and social abilities along with his or her energy level and courage to make the move. The subsequent shifting and readjusting to something new can have implications for the job-changer's family relationships, spirituality, lifestyles, and personal finances. Is it surprising that Marsha sticks with her unfulfilling job even though she hates it?

CAREER COACHING BASICS

Keith Webb is a coach and coach trainer who lives in Singapore and helps nonprofit organizations, Christian ministries, teams, and individuals multiply their cross-cultural impact. He writes that "career coaching focuses on aligning a client's passions, skills, and values with their work. In a lifetime we typically change careers ten times and 90 percent of American workers don't like their jobs. Often this is because our jobs don't tap into our core passions and strengths. Career coaching offers clients the opportunity to discover their calling, strengths, values, and desired contribution, then helps them align work or manage retirement for a more fulfilling life."[3]

To better understand career coaching, I enrolled in the certified career management course at Career Coach Academy,[4] a virtual coach-training school headed by its founder, Susan Britton Whitcomb. Warm, vivacious, and highly skilled as a coach, Susan taught our basic career coaching class, guided by her detailed and fact-filled class syllabus. The course was not taught from an explicitly Christian perspective,[5] but it was clear from the beginning that Susan Whitcomb is a believer. Partway through the class, she called one day and asked if I would review and consider endorsing her new book, *The Christian's Career Journey: Finding the Job God Designed for You*.[6] This is not a coaching book, but it presents a very practical Christian perspective that coaches can apply to themselves and to clients dealing with career issues.

From God's perspective, work appears to have four key purposes, the Whitcomb book suggests. Work is a setting where we write our life story, an incubator in which we grow our faith, a training ground to increase our capacity and influence, and a stage on which we reflect God's image and love. In career planning and development, it is helpful to know our values, strengths, spiritual gifts, personality traits, interests, and passions, but none of this matches the importance of being available to respond to God's three callings on our lives.

First, we are called to *be his follower*. This is the priority call. Second is the career call to *do his work*. Third is the ongoing, faithful call to *persevere* and become like Christ. These are not once-in-a-lifetime calls. They come repeatedly from the Sovereign God who wants us to hear and to take action.

Incorrect beliefs, unconfessed sin, and a lack of faith can make it difficult to hear God. Even so, any of us can discern his will when we want to hear it, listen with an attitude of humility and praise, be willing to accept what he communicates, and obediently respond with action. All of this is important background that applies to any of the types of coaching clients Susan identifies. She describes them as career explorers, career hunters, and career conquerors.

Career explorers are looking for a job or career. If we went to a career counselor in high school, we most likely took a group of tests, talked to the counselor, and explored career possibilities. We were teenagers in that explorer stage. But explorers can be of any age. These coaching clients may know what they can do best and often have some idea of what they might like to do, but the future is fuzzy and stepping out may be overwhelming. Career coaches ask questions to help these clients identify their strengths, talents, and interests. Sometimes assessment tests are used to clarify possible directions. The coach helps explorers make a wise career choice, discover a better place to work, or move to a potentially more satisfying career.

Career hunters are clearer about direction. Often they know their strengths and have a clear idea of the work they want to do. They may be ready to move, but they don't know how or where to go. They want a partner who will work with them actively to develop a résumé, find job opportunities, prepare for interviews, and learn how to negotiate salary.

Career conquerors have found their careers and may be happy in their jobs. They are not looking to change vocations, but some might need help balancing their work with their personal relationships, better controlling their schedules, or communicating better in the office. These people could benefit from assistance in preparing for a promotion or developing skills that will advance their careers. This is a huge coaching market, not focused on career selection but more geared to career growth and advancement.

Notice how these career issues cut across some of the other specialties we have been considering. Career issues can be part of life coaching, relationship coaching, coaching people through transitions, and coaching around spiritual formation and growth. Career issues can also rise to the top of importance when job seekers cannot find employment, when there is loss of a job, or when someone's long career comes to an abrupt end.

In writing this chapter, I determined to go through the Career Coach

Academy course training manual and summarize the most relevant conclusions from this fact-filled notebook. It did not take long for me to abandon this massive information-gathering mission. Instead, I had a long discussion with Susan Whitcomb herself. I asked why she got involved in career coaching and what led her into training career coaches.

ONE CAREER COACH'S JOURNEY

Clearly, Susan sees her career track as God directed. "He graciously overruled my lack of vision," she stated. "He used people and events to draw me toward work that would be incredibly fulfilling." Fresh out of college with a degree in music therapy, Susan found a therapy job and settled into her new position, committed to "healing the world." Like many young graduates, she later decided to look for something else, returned to her home community in California, and took a series of secretarial jobs. One day she met somebody who wanted to develop a résumé-writing service. Susan joined the project and later took over as the business owner.

"I enjoyed résumé writing," Susan continued, "but some people would come back later and say 'I got the job but I hate it.'" Before long the business expanded to helping people search for jobs. At about the same time, Susan attended a career coaching workshop at a conference on career management and felt drawn in like a magnet. Then she immersed herself in coach training and soon founded Career Coach Academy. She and her colleague Nancy Branton later developed Leadership Coach Academy.[7] Currently, Whitcomb operates a variety of training programs, including one that develops certified job-search strategists.

How would Susan define career coaching? "From a Christian perspective, it involves supporting people as they clarify what God has called them to do. The coaching relationship is the incubator that gives people courage to move forward, to align their work with their calling and values, and to be of use to God whether in the marketplace, the mission field, or a local ministry."

It is clear that Susan sees career coaching as a special calling. It goes beyond tapping into human uniquenesses. It opens the door that will allow God to play a bigger role in people's lives. It concerns more than fulfilling our dreams. It helps people see that they could be "a transformation force," employed by God, able to have a significant ministry regardless of their career choice. I was reminded of the biblical admonition to "work willingly at whatever you do, as though you were working for the Lord rather than for people."[8] Career coaching can better equip people to work within God's workforce.

As we talked, I raised a question about differences between career coaching and career counseling. Susan agreed that the lines are becoming more blurred between these two areas. They use many of the same skills, but counselors have a more clinical perspective. They are more inclined to look at the past and how that impacts a career decision. They analyze, explain, and tell. In contrast, career coaches focus more on the present and the future, using powerful questions to draw out what their clients want to create in their work life. Both coaches and counselors use assessments that can expedite career selection and development. Tests sometimes confirm what the client suspects, but they are tools that help to bring clarity rather than devices that tell us what to do.

Because Susan is a career coach trainer, we discussed why education in this area is important. "It helps to have expertise and knowledge of resources that cover the career continuum," Susan responded. For example, in the midst of job changes, many people need to know how to find a new job, write a résumé, and network into the hidden job market. It can be helpful to know about the hiring process, what to expect in an interview, and how to prepare. There is value in knowing about personal branding and how to position oneself in the marketplace. It helps for clients to know that "most employers don't care about your dreams. They care about what a potential employee can contribute to the bottom line." All of this can come through coaches who have expertise in career issues and are able to share more resources than they might if they were working as life or relationship coaches.

In all of this, the Holy Spirit is the career coach's ally. He guides the process and enables us to work with the belief that one's relationship to God is at the core of career work. God is in control of who we are and gives us the wisdom to know what we do with our careers.

CAREER COACHING, COUNSELING, AND LEADERS

When the first edition of this book was being written, I discovered the work of a former career counselor who had spent twenty years counseling and developing programs to help people build their careers. After that she shifted to coaching, and today Marjorie Wall Hofer works with leaders and corporate executives, coaching them in career-related issues.[9] Earlier I had asked for her comments about how career coaching differs from career counseling.

"Career counseling, especially at the college level, is heavily focused on testing and on specified steps to reach a decision," Marjorie explained. "It tends to be a more formal walking through a process. This differs from career coaching, which tends to be more tailored to the individual's whole needs.

Coaching focuses on what a person needs to learn in order to design a career or develop a life plan that fits for that person's current stage in life.

"In *career discovery* coaching, individuals do not know what career they want. The coaching approach is not a matter of giving a formula but of finding what is keeping them from making that discovery. In *career development* coaching, individuals typically have a direction within a career field, but they want to build upon their career foundation or find a niche within it. Coaching takes the approach of finding out what's missing and what's keeping them from moving to the next level.

"For example, I had a client who was very much a futurist. He easily saw and lived in the future. While that was one of his assets, it was also a detriment. He was stuck living in 'what might be.' Unfortunately, when something didn't lead quickly to that vision, he became despondent and sought some other goal. Living in the future kept him from becoming successful. He was missing the idea of focusing on the present steps that might eventually lead to the future he hoped for. While he still needed to ask what he really loved doing and hoped to be doing, he needed to get involved with that work at some level. Then, day after day, he could take action steps that would move him toward his ideal."

I asked Marjorie if she ever had worked with people whose careers had come to a stop, perhaps through an unexpected job termination or the collapse of a company. She talked about a client "who sold his business but stayed on for a year or so to make the transition to the new ownership. When he stepped out of his role, the new owner didn't manage properly, so the business was forced into bankruptcy and this affected my client's present-day income. He had had success. He had risen to the top, but it had slipped away through circumstances outside of his control. Like most adults, it was some unsatisfactory situation in life that forced him to reexamine his career path and his work life. He was asking what happened, what was really important, and what he should do next.

"Unlike many young adults who are starting their careers, older workers need to give greater consideration to their financial situations, personal values, and life circumstances. They consider their abilities and what they lack, their personal working styles and career interests, their societal and family influences, and how these balance against what they love and value. Almost always, those who come to me are faced with a dilemma — a dilemma that pits a strongly held value against a financial reality, for example — and see no easy solution for it. It is at this point that coaching helps the most. Why? Because the coach asks the questions that sift through all the trash talk and second-guessing we adults tend to do. It has helped many people just like this client arrive at the solution to their career dilemmas most quickly.

"I work in the secular business world, but my Christian perspective pervades everything I do. It pervades the concepts I know about and the concepts I introduce to my clients, yet I do not necessarily introduce them as Christian concepts. I have to be able to say them in a way the client will hear.

"Recently, I spoke to a client about forgiveness. I guess my Christian paradigm is so much a part of me that I never realized that some people might not understand forgiveness. This particular client had been very turned off to anything Christian, and I've had to educate him about forgiveness in a way that he could hear so as to benefit him. I needed to teach him what it looked like in action and why it was a necessary part of moving forward in his career as a leader."

PROTEAN CAREERS

Career coaching tends to be built on the assumption that most clients will work for a business, organization, or individual employer. This is the idea that we build our careers by staying with one company, like Marsha is doing, or by moving from one job or career to another but all within the confines of the different employers for whom we work.

This is changing, at least in some parts of the world. Several years ago, a book titled *Free Agent Nation* documented how a vast number of American workers are free agents, "job-hopping, tech-savvy, fulfillment-seeking, self-reliant, independent" workers.[10] Many are self-employed people who work at home and on their own. They have been described as having *protean careers*, presumably after the mythical Greek god Proteus, who could change forms, like an amoeba, in order to adapt to an oncoming threat.[11]

The protean career is one in which the person, not an organization, is in charge. Freedom, growth, self-fulfillment, and mobility are valued more than job security, salary, title, or position. These values appear across the career spectrum, from undergraduates and graduate students to professionals and individuals in all types of work or phases of business. Invariably, these people possess self-awareness and adaptability. Most are constant learners, open to new experiences, resilient in the face of transitions, future oriented, and not afraid to initiate new challenges. They are people who notice how the world of work is changing and constantly reevaluate their capabilities. In times of career difficulty, the protean careerists can see potential in less-than-optimal conditions. Although many work on their own, others work for companies even while they retain their free-spirit attitudes.[12] Might it be possible that some readers will see themselves in this paragraph?

This discussion suggests at least two coaching implications. First, coaching for protean careerists may differ from coaching with clients who lack protean traits. Free agents and protean careerists can present challenges to coaches, but often these people are lively and fun to work with, especially if the coaches are a little free-spirited and protean themselves. Second, maybe successful independent coaches must also be protean careerists. Without these characteristics, a career coach or client might work best in more structured settings.

Career coaches work with people at all stages of career choice and growth. Some coaches are more specialized, however. They work with leaders in companies and organizations. They are known as executive coaches. These are the people who pioneered coaching as we know it. They are the specialists who work in the business and corporate worlds but whose skills extend far beyond large companies. In the next chapter, we meet some of these leadership-oriented coaches.

CHAPTER 17

EXECUTIVE AND BUSINESS COACHING

HAVE YOU EVER gone to a conference or seminar, heard a great lineup of challenging speakers, exchanged ideas with a variety of interesting people, taken notes and picked up a few books, gone home inspired to apply what you have learned, and then forgotten it all? It's a common experience. A convincing body of anecdotal and research evidence shows that conferences, especially lectures, don't make much lasting impact.[1] Once we return to our normal routines and workplaces, we get swept up in the realities and pressures of the things that need to be done. We put aside our conference notebooks and new learning, slip back into our old schedules, and never get around to applying what we learned. The same result could come from taking a course in coaching or even from reading this book. This is sobering when we ponder how much money, energy, and time is wasted when training programs fail to make a difference.

It will come as no surprise that cost-sensitive companies, educational researchers, and even a few churches have looked carefully at transfer of training from conference to workplace and how this could be better. Research shows, for example, that conference participants are more likely to apply their learning when they have been included in the conference planning, when the conference design includes guidelines for applying the learning, and when conferees return to a workplace where there are opportunities to use what has been learned.[2] The effectiveness of the training is even better when the participants get one-on-one executive coaching after the conference or seminar.

In one defining study, a group of thirty-one managers attended a training program and then went back to their jobs. The training must have been effective because the managers' productivity increased 22.4 percent, which is relatively high. In addition, some of the trainees got one-on-one coaching for eight weeks. This included goal setting, collaborative problem solving, getting feedback, enhancing self-awareness, having input from supervisors, and receiving evaluation of the end results. Compared to the group that got training alone, the training-plus-coaching group had an 88 percent increase in production. Researchers concluded that executive coaching provided a safe, personalized environment in which practice and feedback could take place. The training provided a period of abstract learning, but the coaching took this further because it stimulated concrete involvement in activities and projects that were specific to each participant's work responsibilities.[3]

This is only one example of ways in which coaching can apply to the business world and to business leaders. Executive coaches assist companies in their vision casting and long-term planning, enabling them to overcome obstacles and reach their goals. Coaches guide in the career development of executives and team members, assist those who are transitioning into new work roles, coach younger leaders as they move to higher levels of responsibility, and help companies become more focused, efficient, and productive. Many busy CEOs and other executives like coaching because it helps them address corporate and personal issues that often go unattended in the rush of everyday business life. This coaching is most effective when it is a practical, goal-focused form of personal, one-on-one learning. It can be used to improve the executive's performance, help him or her work through organizational issues, and prevent career or company derailment.[4] The best executive coaching gives honest, reliable feedback that leads to practical ideas for moving forward, all without pushing or taking too much time. All of this is summarized in the title of one textbook that describes executive coaching as a process of "developing managerial wisdom in a world of chaos."[5]

Executives often want coaches who understand the corporate environment and know about managing people and resolving conflict. When you coach at this level, you have to demonstrate competence, self-assurance, and enough courage to ask the insightful tough questions that most executives never hear. The higher businesspeople rise in the organization, the less honest feedback they get, the more isolated they feel, and the fewer opportunities they have to discuss issues openly with people who can be trusted and who aren't trying to get something in return. Many businesspeople, especially executives, live with constant pressure but have few peers and fewer still who understand. Often these leaders want coaching about their work but need guidance as well in dealing with their families, insecurities, self-awareness, and careers.

EXECUTIVE COACHES AT WORK

Executive coaching usually refers to work with leaders who are at the top or upper levels of their organizations: CEOs, vice presidents, and managers. In practice, coaching can occur at any level of an organization, and the coach's role depends on where he or she works. In this chapter, we will use the term *executive coaching* to include organizational, business, and corporate coaching, all of which involve helping people in business work through work-related and sometimes personal challenges so they can transform their learning into results that benefit the organization.[6]

To give us a glimpse into coaching in the corporate world, I turned to three highly competent Christian executive coaches, beginning with Linda Miller. A Master Certified Coach and a leading corporate coach, she splits her time between two organizations. She does ministry work with pastors and denominational leaders, working through Coach Approach Ministries,[7] and is employed by the Ken Blanchard Companies, where she serves as global liaison for coaching.[8] *Coaching in Organizations: Best Coaching Practices from the Ken Blanchard Companies*,[9] an excellent book that she coauthored, is one of the best available introductions to coaching in the corporate world. If you go to her website,[10] you will find serious material, but the home page also shows Linda's warmth and sense of humor. The page opens with the croak of a frog and a little riddle. When five frogs are on a log and four decide to jump off, how many do you have left? The answer is five because there's a difference between deciding and doing. Linda helps corporate leaders do both.

Early in her executive coaching career, Linda met with a company vice president who wanted to hire a coach for one of his senior staff members. The executive wondered if Linda could do the job. She told me about the meeting.

"The first thing he asked was, 'What makes you credible?' He knew I had never worked in his particular industry, so I burst out laughing and said, 'I have no idea. I don't think my degrees or my background or anything like that is going to make me credible. Let's continue this meeting and at the end you tell me if I'm credible.' So this guy grilled me and I just responded. At the end of the meeting, he said, 'Yes. You're credible.' The next day, he called me and said with a laugh, 'You handled that really well.'

"There was no way I could prove my credibility. The person he wanted me to work with had more degrees than I have, and the man who was interviewing me had degrees from some of the top schools in the nation, so I knew that talking about myself wouldn't convince him that I was credible. Instead, he needed to know me. We needed to look at the challenges for that particular corporation or the individual I would coach to see if and how they could be addressed.

"There's a huge hurdle to get over if you don't have corporate experience but want to be considered credible within a corporate arena. I don't have this background. When I first got into the corporate arena, I wasn't sure it was going to work for me, but everybody said, 'Don't worry about it—you have a presence to carry yourself into it. It's going to be okay.' I have come to understand that presence means having congruence inside and out, having confidence without being arrogant, speaking the truth in love and with integrity, realizing that value comes from creating an environment of trust rather than working hard to create value.

"I was at a coaching conference when I introduced myself to a woman I had never seen before. I said, 'I've very rarely seen the kind of presence that you have.' I found out that this woman was looking for a coaching position and eventually she got it. I had spent only ten minutes with her, but I knew she could do it because of the way she carried herself. It was that presence about her."

Because Linda coaches both ministry and business leaders, I asked if this kind of work is possible for coaches who aren't perceived as leaders and who don't think of themselves as leaders. Linda pointed to the coach's competence.

"The leader being coached needs to know that the coach has something to offer. There's got to be depth or substance in the coach, along with an awareness of leader characteristics and the challenges a leader faces. I'm not sure how a leader would respond to a coach who had not been in leadership at all. There has to be something that allows that coach to be credible, and often that credibility needs to appear in the first two minutes of the conversation. It has to be established very fast. Most times this is unspoken because you have only a few minutes. For example, I think people who coach leaders need to be really congruent. Their words, their behavior, the way they carry themselves—all areas need to be congruent, and this shows up quickly."

At this point, the conversation shifted to the challenges of coaching potential leaders. Linda was enthusiastic.

"I think coaching is most valuable with the up-and-coming, the fast-trackers in an organization, because whatever they have been doing to get to the level they are has been absolutely right on. But a lot of times, for them to take the next step in their leadership role, they need a whole different set of competencies. They need to know how to network in a different role. They may need to know how to lead rather than manage. With emerging pastors and leaders, coaching can be very valuable, but this raises an important point: Coaching is not just for people who are in trouble or having difficulties, although sometimes that's how it's thought of. Coaching is really for people who are doing well and are ready for their next level of development or are ready to think about what's ahead for them. These people are invaluable to a ministry or company, and coaching can be a huge benefit in their development and retention.

"Let me give you an example. One of the emerging leaders I coached was in a very large professional-services firm. This person had done very well and was being promoted to the next level. When the company hired me, I was informed that there might be some relationship issues holding him back from moving up in the organization, so he and I started talking about that. There were several relationships that had been broken or damaged because of his style, including the way he communicated with people. We came up with a game plan for how he could go back to those people, each one, and clear the air so that he could get their endorsement and support as he moved forward. His willingness and their responses turned out to be really powerful. We also started talking about the fact that he was not giving credit where credit was due. He thought that in order to advance, he needed to take credit rather than give it, so we started to work on changing his interpretation about giving credit. This person was not a Christian, but I shared the principle of 'Give and it shall be given to you,' and he actually started doing it."

This led to a discussion about being a Christian coach in a secular company. "When I'm coaching pastors or other Christian leaders, I use Scripture as much as I can and we pray together," Linda said. "With corporate leaders, I am always listening for any kind of faith language that indicates an opening for a conversation about the Lord, and if I hear one, I ask for permission to talk about spiritual issues. With nonbelieving corporate leaders, when there is a Scripture that I believe fits the circumstance, I will ask permission to share it. They always say yes. I don't think I've ever had anybody say no, even some very adamant nonbelievers. In fact, they frequently express appreciation! I'm not sure that leaders have many people in their lives who speak and share truth, so those with whom I've worked have been very open. Coaches who focus on leadership need to be sensitive and bold enough to speak truth to leaders, for we know that the truth is what sets us free.

"I'm always praying and asking the Lord to help me see the person from the perspective that God sees, not from my perspective. I want to see the person through the Lord's eyes, seeing his perspective even if it's different from the person's or from mine. As Christian coaches, we can rely heavily on the Holy Spirit, and I often get a hunch about something that I believe the Lord is quickening. I've come to rely on these 'quickenings,' knowing that they are from the Lord, and often, in speaking from this different perspective, it's exactly the truth the Lord is using to get the person's attention."

FROM QUICKENINGS TO ONBOARDING

I turned next to a long conversation with Marcel Henderson, who oversees executive coaching within one of the country's largest financial institutions.[11] Despite her significant role as vice president for executive development, Marcel is warm, gracious, and down-to-earth. She carries an array of responsibilities, including: giving oversight to about 150 executive coaches, establishing guidelines and criteria for coaching in her company, ensuring quality, evaluating effectiveness, and staying abreast of what is happening in other organizations to establish best practices for the greater good of coaching. She also consults with senior leaders "regarding alignment of coaching with talent identification and human capital initiatives and oversees the development of the coaches."

I asked Marcel to give her definition of an executive coach. She answered that an executive coach is "a seasoned professional who can effectively partner with individual leaders to help them identify and develop a set of goals to improve or enhance their professional performance. Some of the coaches' work includes but is not limited to collecting and analyzing issues about the leader's performance, fostering greater self-awareness (including diversity and cross-cultural capabilities), assisting in action planning development, and providing ongoing support as the leader works toward behavioral change. The best of these coaches has the ability to show measurable outcomes for the coaching they've provided."

We discussed coaching that identifies and assists emerging leaders as they develop their talents and prepare for greater leadership roles. As an executive coach, Marcel works almost exclusively with top-level leaders in her organization, including the work of her company regarding "onboarding." This is the process of helping new employees adjust to their companies and assisting newly appointed or promoted leaders to adapt to their work roles. Marcel mentioned research indicating that 40 percent of executives fail to make the transition to a new position and leave within eighteen months.[12] Of those who fail, 70 percent leave because they are not able to understand and connect with the company culture, people, politics, or ways of getting things done. Most make the decision to leave within the first few months. In contrast, when there is coaching for people transitioning into new roles, they are much more likely to survive and thrive. This could have staggering implications for coaching new pastors, employees, CEOs, and leaders outside as well as inside corporations.

As we discussed the diversity of executive coaching, I asked Marcel how she got into this work and how others might become executive coaches themselves. She replied that she "had the unique opportunity to be in the right place at the right time when coaching came on the scene in corporate America. At the time, our company happened to be implementing leader core competencies. We wanted to provide leaders with formal feedback and coaching with regard to how they were performing against those competencies. Based on my prior leadership and management training experience, I was selected and trained in a formal feedback and coaching process, which was my introduction into the coaching field. That was more than ten years ago. Since then I have attended many training sessions for coaching (both internal and external) that my company has fully supported and funded to ensure we have highly seasoned coaches in the organization to support our senior leaders."

From our conversation, it became clear that coaches often move into work that fits their prior experience and background. Marcel agrees that one does not need business experience to be an executive coach, but she noted that "some leaders would never work with a coach who does not have business experience."

And how does Marcel work in a large corporation and still see herself as a Christian coach when the name of Jesus is rarely mentioned? She responded, "Because I work in a corporate setting, many people think that spirituality is off-limits, but I beg to differ. There are many ways that my coaching is Christian.

"For one, I pray for my clients before and after I meet with them. I realize that the Holy Spirit can do amazing things if I have properly prepared myself, and I use skills and natural talents, such as my intuition, when I'm with a client. I pray for the Holy Spirit's discernment and guidance before I meet a client. After a session, I pray that my clients will have the fortitude to move ahead with what they want to do to be a more effective leader. My philosophy is that good leadership is Christlike and by coaching leaders to be more effective, they are taking on Christlike behavior, even if we never speak about it.

"Second, as an executive coach, I use a holistic view with my coaching. This means that I encourage clients to bring their whole self to the coaching engagement. Through years of coaching, I have learned that we can't compartmentalize our lives. We are spiritual beings both in and outside the corporate setting. If clients bring up the topic of spiritual practices or beliefs, I will ask them how they want to integrate that into their coaching just like I would if they brought up the topic of health, wellness, education, or relationships. All of these areas of our lives make up who we are and how effective we are in our professions. If they don't bring it up, then my hope and prayer is that what we accomplish in coaching will bring light on what they may be missing in their spiritual practices and may surface later as they explore greater purpose or vision for their lives."

FROM BIG CORPORATIONS TO SMALL-BUSINESS OWNERS

Most mornings I drive by a modest home on a busy street a few blocks from where I live. Two or three years ago, I noticed that the home owners had taken out the garage door and replaced it with a large glass window. Shortly thereafter, a sign went up advertising a new dress shop that specialized in selling prom dresses and wedding gowns. Week after week, the same dresses were in the window, so I was not surprised when the business closed and the garage was returned to its original purpose. I have often wondered what went wrong. More than that, I have felt sad for the people who had sunk their money into a venture that failed and must have been very disappointing.

The failure of small businesses is relatively common, and so are the struggles of owners who try to keep their businesses alive. That's where another business-related coaching specialty appears. Probably it should not be termed executive coaching, but its focus is on issues that can be similar to those faced by the bigger corporations. Small-business coaching has unique challenges in addition to the production deadlines, financial concerns, management dilemmas, marketing issues, and employee problems larger companies face. Unlike the big corporations, a small-business owner often runs a company in which family members are key employees, major investors, or both. "In small business coaching, business and personal issues are intertwined," writes small-business coach Bill Zipp.[13] "Coaching the business" involves working with company leaders to build a strong, self-sustaining company. Personal coaching builds healthy relationships and balanced lifestyles with individuals in the business.[14] I know several people who specialize in small-business coaching, but to get more information I decided to reconnect with Gary Wood, who has a coaching practice in Canada, north of Toronto.

Gary is a committed follower of Jesus Christ and a multitalented coach who has long had a coach of his own to help him keep perspective. After he became a Christian, Gary and his wife became involved in ministry, including ten years full-time as administrators of a Christian nonprofit organization. He has served on several boards of directors and been able to see how they function, what works, and what does not work. Since becoming a certified corporate business coach, he has provided personal and executive coaching to clients ranging from executives in *Fortune 100* companies to pastors, directors of community organizations, and owners of small businesses who want to "move forward with greater effectiveness, less stress, and more satisfaction."

I asked about Gary's company that offers executive and personal coaching,[15] and here is his reply:

"I work primarily with executives and leaders. This includes people who are either developing their businesses or who've reached a point in their businesses where it's almost become too big for them to handle, so they're feeling pressure. Over the years, 80 to 95 percent of my business has been working with Christian owners, professionals, executives, leaders, and pastors. They come for coaching because they want something to be different. They want to break through their often self-imposed thinking and limits. These people reveal everything to me. I know their numbers; I know their competitors; I know their clients. And my purpose in being there, 110 per cent, is to see them be successful.

"One example is a Christian consultant who traveled around the world. He worked by himself most of the time, so he wanted someone to partner with, someone with whom he could think out loud. That's the way I assisted him, helping him develop personally and professionally. Our synergy allowed him to think bigger than he might normally have thought while he was constantly on his own."

Gary told me previously that he had built several businesses and had spent most of his working life as a small-business owner. I asked if a person without business experience could coach in this area. "It's not impossible," Gary answered. "When you're working with small-business people, they have certain interests concerning their businesses that they want someone to talk to about. For instance, with many of my Christian clients, we talk about them underselling themselves, and therefore we look at their fee structure. If you don't have a sense of business, you may not feel very comfortable working with those areas; you'll stick simply to the people end of it and avoid the business issues. I can float back and forth between both. I don't mind talking about money, policies, employees, or anything else. Because of my business experience, all of those things combine. I feel quite at ease talking about them and equally at ease making the switch to speak about personal or spiritual concerns."

I asked Gary if he read books and magazines about leadership and business in order to keep up with trends in those areas. I was not surprised at his yes answer. "I regularly go to one of the big chain bookstores and learn about the latest trends in anything to do with contemporary living, working, and leadership. I want to know the terms my clients are using. I want to understand. My passion is to be of the greatest assistance I can be. When somebody like the client I just mentioned comes to me, I head to the literature or the

Internet to find out what I can about his or her business.

"I once had a client in Korea who told me what business he was in. He had a very specific title within the company and asked if we could work together the following week, so I went on the Internet to find more about his company and what he did. On the company's website, I found an ad for a position that had the same title he had. It listed all the qualifications and duties. I was pleased because this was helpful background material. But when I mentioned this to the client, he said, "That's impossible. There is only one job in this company that has that title, and that's mine." The following week, we shifted our coaching emphasis to finding a new job.

"I try to know something about my client's business. I can know some of the terms and issues so when I come alongside him, he can sense that I'm a guy who understands. The key point of this for any of our clients is knowledge, integration, application. What I'm doing as a business coach is assisting them in taking knowledge that they already have, both personally and professionally, and integrating that into their own lives so they can go out and apply it. The problem is that we attend seminars, get knowledge, and learn the facts, but often we can't integrate this and apply it. That's where coaching rises and shines, helping people integrate and apply their knowledge not only professionally but personally."

While I had Gary on the phone, I wanted to ask about his work coaching church boards. The principles seem similar to coaching teams of coworkers or coaching boards of companies. We began by considering the coach's qualifications for this kind of work.

"I think there is a distinct advantage in having had board experience. I've been on boards for a number of years now, and when you are there, you get to know the nuances of a board. It doesn't take long to pick them up.

"Board dynamics often are about people issues. You have people who are quiet; you have others who take the lead and do the talking. Then the quiet people start to think they don't have anything to offer. We need to coach these people to speak up, to believe that they do have something to offer. We need to coach those people who talk nonstop to slow down, to listen to the others. Some quieter members need to speak up and realize the value of their contributions, and some more vocal people need to be more restrained, actively listening and collaborative. And some need to get off the board altogether and make way for fresh energy, vision, and leadership.

"In addition to people issues, we need to look at the process. Often boards stop asking questions because they become dependent on the leader or on a very few people. They assume the leader must be on top of things. Then it's easy for a board to lose momentum. A week can easily stretch out into two weeks or two months, or worse still, it's just days before the next meeting and agreed-to assignments still haven't been completed.

"That's where discipline and technology can help. Sometimes I put a board together on the phone with a bridge call, every week. Then they're talking with one another; they are getting together enough that they're understanding one another; they're hearing each other. Also, they are working together in between calls, because they have a coach, they have me, to hold them accountable. When this happens, the board members know I'm going to have them on the phone next week and I'm going to ask them what's been accomplished. Now they have gotten clear about what they want, what they have to do, and how to get there. That's board progress."

I wondered how Gary coached leaders who had to work with an ineffective board. "Pray about it," he responded. "Learn about and work with the communication and behavioral styles of the people on the board. Become a harvester of vision, not just a generator of ideas. As a leader, you collect the little pieces of vision each person on the board might have, put it together and articulate it in such a way that everybody can get a hold of it and get ownership of it. You're bringing a board together around that vision. Then the leader holds the board members accountable. That applies to churches as well as businesses. As a model of authentic accountability, the leader has earned the right to request they be accountable."

How does it work the other way? How does an active board deal with an ineffective pastor or other leader? "You have to start with one person — a godly, wise person — on that board who has the ear of the leader or pastor. They have to do some personal work together. It's not a once-a-month thing; it's going to take commitment, it's going to take time. I can think of a church where that happened, where the board members were wise enough to make a way for that pastor to work with a coach like myself. In that case, there were good results for the pastor and the church. In other cases, coaching may allow the pastor to see that he is not where he really wants to be or effectively can be.

"It's the issue of change and transition. Change is what we may be required to do physically; transition takes place in our heads and our hearts. So you tell your pastor or company leader, 'We want things changed here. You're not doing the job.' But if you haven't gotten to his head and his heart, to help him, to assist him to make that transition, then you're just in for frustration. Get him a coach. Many pastors might not really know themselves or where they are going."

Within recent years, Gary Wood's coaching business has taken a new direction: helping leaders and others deal with burnout. His work has led to the conclusion that "far too many leaders and professionals experience job burnout. As a society, we may lose twenty to fifty years of experienced leadership, innovation, and contribution when a leader retreats or is removed from the forefront and decides to never again assume important responsibilities, all because of burnout. We assist men and women to beat burnout and enlarge their capacity to continue contributing and moving forward. Our programs are designed to help businesspeople sustain productivity and improve life/work balance.

"Really it's a dual purpose: assisting leaders and professionals to beat burnout and then helping them change tactics so they can continue to move forward with significant causes, projects, and programs that make a difference in the lives of people. Obviously, I have Christian leaders and executives in mind, but I'm happy to assist anyone. Our society critically needs good leaders and professionals. We can't lose them to stress, overload, and burnout."[16] This is an important role for coaches in every part of the business world.

AND WHERE IS GOD?

It is not easy to maintain a Christian witness when you are coaching in the corporate or business world. It *is* easy to be so caught up in the issues of the person you coach that your Christian commitment is forgotten, at least temporarily. But that does not describe the people we have met in this chapter and elsewhere in the book. Christian issues might not appear frequently in conversations with their non-Christian clients, but these coaches are very much aware of God's calling and empowerment. Gary Wood spoke for them all when he said, "We ought never to think that things of eternal weight are not happening. The Christian commitment is *never* pushed aside for corporate expediency."

On his final visit to the port of Miletus, Paul reflected on his ministry. He knew that suffering was ahead, and he warned the group of Christians who had come from Ephesus that they would be attacked by false teachers, descending like vicious wolves on the little flock of Christ followers. Paul himself had experienced a lot of difficulty, but he had no regrets. "I declare today that I have been faithful," he said. "My life is worth nothing to me unless I use it for finishing the work assigned to me by the Lord Jesus."[17]

God does not assign us all to work in churches or Christian ministries. He sends most of us into the secular world to do our work as well as we can, even though that work may not appear to be uniquely Christian. You might not be able to pray with the people you coach, but you can pray for them. You might not feel adequate to meet all the coaching issues you encounter, but you can ask for God's guidance and know that ultimately your sufficiency is in Christ. You might not be able to talk openly about your values, beliefs, or evangelistic concerns, but you can let your light so shine among others that they may see your values and good works so that sooner or later, everyone will acknowledge that this is from your heavenly Father.[18] There are numerous examples of people who faithfully have lived like Christ wants them to live so that others, even others who oppose Christianity, have noticed and come to Christ.

If you really believe that coaching is what God wants you to do, never forget that you are coaching because God has given you the privilege of using this tool to impact lives in the corporate world or wherever else you have been called to serve.

CHAPTER 18

CHURCHES, SPIRITUALITY, AND COACHING

I'M NOT SURE when I first heard the words *emergent church*, but my interest was captured immediately. As a child, I was taken to a traditional church that probably could be described as fundamentalist, although nobody ever used that term. I enthusiastically attended the youth group during my high school years, then kept my beliefs and Christian values all through college and into my first job teaching at a small Christian college. I don't remember a time in my life when I seriously doubted those foundational beliefs, but over the years I became increasingly disillusioned with the church. I attended most Sundays, still do, but slowly I began to see the church as a social club, filled with many wonderful people who weren't making much of an impact on their communities or on the world, despite their talk and deeply held beliefs about making disciples. I realize that this analysis is unfair and comes from one man's limited perspective, but still I struggle with the seeming irrelevance of many congregations.

I was a seminary professor when I first heard about postmodernism, constructivism, and the increasing influence of Eastern philosophies. Clearly, there have been major cultural shifts in worldviews, values, and moral standards, but many traditional churches seem oblivious of the changes. The music may have changed a little, but many congregations have continued to do church in the same old ways, wondering why the younger people are leaving or why few new people are coming in. The megachurches rose in the midst of this environment and many continue to have a significant influence for good, but religion has faded in popularity and few of us are surprised when we read books about people, including a lot of churchgoers, who like Jesus and are interested in spirituality but don't like religion or the church.[1]

I was enthusiastic several years ago when I discovered a fledgling movement of diverse, mostly young Christian leaders and Christ followers who were connecting with the younger generation, doing church in unconventional ways but staying firm in their commitment to the biblical basics of the faith. I got to know some of these leaders, started reading their books, and admired what they were doing: reaching out to spiritual searchers in their own communities and circles of influence. I thought of Paul in Acts 17, who was very traditional in his approach when he taught in the synagogues of the Thessalonians and Bereans but very contemporary when he spoke to the Greeks in Athens. Paul was aware of his culture even though his core beliefs never wavered.

Most of the newer churches had their roots in biblical and theological orthodoxy.[2] Many have stayed there as they work to connect with a postmodern society shaped by the media and embracing values similar to those that Paul found in ancient Greece. Sadly, a number of these groups have cut free from their roots and drifted into beliefs and behaviors that don't look very Christian, at least to outsiders. Some of the writings and trends among this group have led Christians like me to shift away from using terms like *emergent* or *emerging*. Even so, I feel a kinship with those who are sensitive to their culture, committed to understanding and connecting to the contemporary world in which we live, and intent on serving Jesus and being his light in the world. I admire their dedication and pioneering attitudes even though their methods may differ from what I might prefer or from what I would consider biblical.

For several years, I have taught a graduate course on coaching and the church. Usually we begin by looking at different types of churches, including those outside our various experiences. We agree that every part of the country, every organization, every working place, every family, and every church has its own culture. Consider a Pentecostal, formal Presbyterian, African-American, traditional Catholic, Southern Baptist, giant megachurch, or house church that meets around a kitchen table. In addition to differences in theology and worship styles, each has a unique personality that sometimes reflects the personality of the pastor. Each has unstated but generally accepted standards for the way people dress, the terms they use, the ways in which they relate to one another, the expectations about "how we do things around here." All of this refers to church culture. These church cultures do not reside so much in the buildings, programs, denominational affiliations, or printed proclamations as in what the people and the church leaders say and embody in their actions.[3]

All of this has great relevance for coaches. Bringing coaching to a church is somewhat like bringing Christianity to a distant culture or bringing Jesus to twentysomethings in a bar. You won't get very far if you ignore the values, leaders, accepted behaviors, beliefs, and ways of thinking of the people with whom you want to connect. The same is true when coaches bring their coaching skills to business settings, academic institutions, or community organizations. Cultural insensitivity on the part of the coach may explain why some groups, including professional groups, reject coaching and miss the benefits coaching could bring.

BRINGING COACHING TO CHURCH

Occasionally I get calls from pastors who want help in developing a coaching program in their churches. Some of these callers have wanted me to teach church leaders how to coach, teach coaching to small groups, or do a seminar on coaching for the whole congregation. Sometimes pastors have asked about coaching for themselves. One or two have wanted to introduce strength-based coaching into their congregations to help people serve in line with their God-given strengths.[4] These callers have all been sincerely interested in maximizing the impact of their ministries. They have wondered if coaching might be useful, but in almost every situation it has become apparent to them and to me that they aren't really sure what they want to accomplish through the introduction of coaching into their churches.

Table 18-1 shows some ways in which coaching might be applied in ministry situations. A number of pioneers are leading the way in this initiative.[5] For example, Fran LaMattina was one of the first to take coaching into a local church.

Table 18-1

COACHING AND MINISTRY: SELECTED APPLICATIONS
▪ Coaching pastors
▪ Coaching individual leaders or church members
▪ Coaching small groups and their leaders
▪ Coaching church boards
▪ Coaching in parachurch ministries
▪ Coaching in Christian organizations
▪ Coaching for leadership development
▪ Coaching and missions
▪ Training church members to coach
▪ Coaching congregations through change
▪ Coaching congregations through pastoral transitions

- Coaching for specific issues
- Coaching and vision casting
- Coaching and strategic planning
- Coaching and church conflict
- Coaching and spiritual direction

Fran's journey to Christian coaching began in the business world, where she encountered a wise and caring mentor who bluntly described her as a workaholic. He told her, "If you don't learn to delegate, you're going to burn out. You've got to stop using people as pawns and start investing your life in them." So Fran began to change, and before long she became a successful business coach who later joined the staff at a large church in Atlanta.[6] I asked what it was like shifting from the corporate world to a church.

"It was a big change," Fran stated. "For twenty-five years, I had worked with just men, and then God started raising me up to have influence in the lives of women. My church asked if I would join the staff on a part-time basis to set up the women's community group ministry while I was developing my private coaching practice. From the beginning, I tried to model a lifestyle that said, 'I'm investing my life in other women.' I met with them on a regular basis to talk about their personal spiritual growth and to coach them to become more effective with investing their lives in other women. We modeled our community group support structure into a coaching-mentoring process for our leaders."

I reminded Fran about the first time we met, when she presented me with a book titled *Visioneering*, written by her pastor, Andy Stanley.[7] At the time, Fran did not think Andy was familiar with the principles of coaching, even though that's what his whole life had been about. Probably Fran would not take any credit for this, but I suspect she had an influence on what has become Pastor Stanley's enthusiastic embrace of coaching. In a book for next-generation leaders, he wrote, "You will never maximize your potential in any area without coaching. It is impossible. . . . To be the best next-generation leader you can be, you must enlist the help of others. Self-evaluation is helpful, but evaluation from someone else is essential. You need a leadership coach. A good coach will evaluate your performance against your potential. A coach will know what you are capable of and will push you to your limit. . . . I can go further and faster with someone coaching me than I can on my own."[8] These are words I often put on the screen when I speak to pastors about coaching and leadership.

I asked Fran if she thought everybody could benefit from coaching, especially in church settings. She responded that "people can't be coached unless they want to be coached. One of the coaches in our coach training said that he believes only 20 percent of the people in the world are coachable. I believe that's true, and I believe that you're really only coachable if you surrender yourself to the Holy Spirit and let him change your life, because coaching involves personal life change, and we don't do that very readily. Most people say they want it, but few are willing to focus their resources on attaining it.

"Let me tell you about a nurse practitioner who worked in the emergency room of a children's hospital. She was a godly single woman investing her life in kids, but she had lots of debt. Because I have a financial background, I was coaching her in the area of finances. One day I said, 'Melinda, what would you do if you had a million dollars?' She said, 'Oh, that's easy. I would set up a retreat at the beach for families of children with cancer.' Then she said, 'Fran, do you know what happens with families of children with cancer? They get divorced, they go bankrupt, their families fall apart, the kids get disconnected.' I could see what a passion this woman had, so I said, 'Melinda, that sounds like more than a dream; that sounds like a vision God has given you. I really would encourage you to pray about that and see if that's what God wants you to do with your life.' This woman took that seriously. She prayed about it, and God led her to do three things: get out of debt, get financially able to move on and do whatever God wanted her to do, and fix her relations with her family, which were not exemplary. Over the course of a year and a half, this woman came to me to work on various aspects of her relationships and worked through some very tough things about how to resolve these. I talked to her about how to get out of debt, and she opened herself up to that. Today she is the executive director of Lighthouse Family Retreats, involved with children who have cancer and their families. I was her board chair for the early years, and she continues to use the resources God has given her."

COACHING BEYOND LOCAL CHURCH MINISTRIES

Tony Stoltzfus is a quiet but effective leader who is bringing Christian coaches together for doing ministry even as he develops coaching materials for pastors, churches, and coaches. His website is a rich source of material for pastors and Christian coaches, and his books have been used widely in coach training programs.[9] Unlike many in the coaching field, Tony is not motivated by a desire for fame or making a lot of money. His life is a reflection of what he states to be his commitment to building leadership character.

"My passion is helping leaders see and engage God's purposes in every situation," Tony wrote in his page on a website that focuses on coaching for pastors.[10] "Too many pastors plateau, get burned or get frustrated, and leave the ministry when those same circumstances, seen in terms of God's purposes, could propel them into an exponentially greater sphere of influence. When doing more of the same things isn't enough, when what you want is to be transformed as a person so your ministry can be transformed," that's when pastors meet with coaches like Tony and they "meet God together."

I am challenged whenever I talk with Tony Stoltzfus. He is concerned about the influence of people who try to coach when they don't have any training. He wonders if we have a fad mentality that sees coaching as a new program for the church. Many want the appearance of quick results that you get by creating a big meeting, even though one-on-one relationships most often produce transformation, not new programs. "Coaches sometimes have unrealistic expectations about bringing this into the church world, as if our training alone makes us fit to lead. We don't understand that character is the fundamental qualification for ministry, not skills training or the ability to lead a seminar.

"Character comes from life; skills and methodologies come from training. Methodologies transform people only to the degree that they are a channel for transformed life. Coaching is a methodology and not an end in itself. We need a much better understanding of what coaching can contribute to the ministry of the church and to the effectiveness of church leaders."

In one of his newsletters, Tony suggests ways for bringing coaching into the church. "First it helps to have a good working definition of coaching. One line I often use is, 'Coaching is a discipline of helping people grow without telling them what to do.' It also helps to contrast coaching with other disciplines, such as mentoring." In addition, there is value in connecting coaching with things people already do, such as parenting. Then there is this final tip: "Never try to describe coaching without demonstrating it. Most people have never seen coaching before. When they see coaching in action, they are much more likely to get what it is. So don't just tell—show."

Tony described his work with a denominational group in Canada. The leaders wanted to provide basic coaching skills to their pastoral staff, so Tony built a training program that uses the telephone plus interactive in-person workshops. The goal is to develop a core group of coaches from among the pastors in the denomination. This group, in turn, will be equipped to train others how to coach. It is not assumed that all of these pastors will become coaches. Some have strengths, gifts, and callings that equip them for ministries other than coaching. But one goal is to teach people in this denomination to learn how to use "coaching encounters rather than long-term relationships." This means teaching some of the core skills of coaching—listening, asking good questions, giving feedback — so these can be used informally, as part of everyday conversations. In this way, coaching can be a useful tool to help advance other ministries.

Tony's approach is similar to work I did with a large parachurch organization that wanted leadership training. After selecting a small group of leaders with clear potential, we found professional coaches who agreed to give one-on-one coaching to each of the selected participants in the program. As they experienced several months of coaching, these people also took training in the form of formal seminars and telephone follow-up. The goal was to teach these men and women to be able to lead using the methods of coaching. A similar program is underway in Asia, where a mission organization wants to teach their leaders both how to lead others through coaching and then how to teach coaching skills to others. The program is ongoing. My role has been to coach each of the participants so they can experience coaching. Then we did a weeklong seminar with follow-up. Eventually, we will select several people from the original class and teach them how to train others.

Here are other ways in which coaching can have an impact within the Christian community, apart from the private for-pay work of coaching practitioners:

- Coaching small-group leaders has been a focus of Tony's ministry since he began to realize how many churches were describing their small-group leaders as coaches. Often these group leaders are labeled "coaches" even though they have no training in coaching skills, no understanding of what coaching really is, and no awareness that coaching is not the same as teaching, advice giving, or directing the group members. In front of me as I write, I have two church-produced coaching handbooks that are beautifully designed but show no evidence of knowing what coaching involves. One states that the coach's role is to develop leadership teams, provide care, support the ministry, and conduct meetings. These are worthwhile goals, but this is not coaching. Tony has been leading training seminars and developing materials for teaching small-group leaders to use established coaching skills, clarify their goals, and move toward greater group effectiveness.
- Peer coaching is another Tony Stoltzfus initiative that is spreading to a number of churches.[11] This involves meetings of two or three friends who are taught coaching principles that can be used to build accountable, authentic peer relationships to help each other grow. It parallels the lay counseling that was popular in churches several years

ago and that still exists in groups like Stephens Ministries.[12]

- Coaching Mission International is one of several groups seeking to make coaching relevant to missions. CMI seeks to "coach missions leaders to greater effectiveness, stronger personal lives, and the fulfillment of their destinies through strategic partnerships with missions organizations around the world." Currently, CMI works with missionaries in Asia and Africa, but they are hoping to expand. Their goal is to "gather excellent, professionally trained coaches with cross-cultural experience and put them to work coaching top missionary leaders who oversee field staff and others," according to the director, Tina Stoltzfus Horst. CMI is working to train national leaders to use coaching skills and also to "train and re-deploy retiring and returning missionaries as missions coaches, thus leveraging the cultural understandings, language abilities, and relationships they already have." Overall, this is a creative initiative designed to impact missions through coaching.[13]

- Coaching as mission is a way to expand Christian coaching into a unique form of ministry. It builds on the model provided by Business As Mission (BAM), a worldwide movement committed to helping men and women in business demonstrate competent business practices combined with making disciples and carrying the gospel to hard-to-reach communities.[14] In a similar way, some coaches are developing Coaching As Mission (CAM). This encourages professionally trained, competent Christian coaches to provide services ethically, honestly, and according to good business practices, even as they view their coaching as a ministry. To paraphrase the BAM mission, spiritually committed coaches demonstrate competent coaching practices combined with making disciples and carrying the gospel to hard-to-reach communities. CAM acknowledges the values and beliefs of clients but looks for opportunities to respectfully share the gospel or raise biblical principles. The CAM model also teaches people with limited coaching experience to become competent coaches who work in communities at home and abroad and who join with professional coaches to develop coaching where it does not currently exist. CAM involves providing at least some services without cost. It is a model that affirms coaching as a Christian calling.

SPIRITUAL COACHING

I was speaking at a seminar in Korea one afternoon when I reached a low point. It was shortly after lunch. I had not had time to recover from jet lag, the schedule had been heavy, the room was warm, and I noticed that some people in the audience were nodding (in sleep, not in agreement with what I was saying). Even my translator seemed to be having trouble with his concentration. Clearly, it was time for a break, which I introduced by saying that everybody seemed tired, including me, and that we all needed time to stretch and get rejuvenated. No sooner had the meeting dismissed than an enthusiastic man rushed to the platform and handed me a little bottle of ginseng. He told me that this would restore my energy quickly and urged me to consume its contents instead of the coffee I was about to drink.

The label on the bottle was in Korean and I wasn't about to follow the stranger's advice and take a swig of something when I didn't know what it was. My translator didn't have the same hesitation. He knew that this liquid, made from the root of a ginseng plant, would cause no harm and might even give me greater energy. I don't remember if the drink made me feel livelier when I resumed my talk, but I do know that I came home from the trip with several little bottles of ginseng juice and packets of ginseng tea given to me by other participants during the course of the seminar.

Wouldn't it be interesting if we could get spiritual rejuvenation by drinking some magic or herbal potion? Of course, it doesn't work that way. The Holy Spirit rejuvenates, strengthens, and guides in the lives of Christians, but despite the enthusiastic proclamations of some magnetic speakers, most lasting spiritual growth and renewal is a slow process. It comes as we faithfully and consistently devote ourselves to spiritual disciplines such as prayer, solitude, worship, meditation on Scripture, fasting, service, and reflection. And most often, spiritual renewal seems to come as we meet with others who can hold us accountable, pray for and with us, and give what Christians for centuries have known as spiritual direction.

Spiritual direction involves one person's helping another with his or her relationship with God. This does not involve giving advice, preaching, teaching, counseling, or dispensing formulas, like the bottle of ginseng. Spiritual direction has been defined as "a prayer process in which a person seeking help in cultivating a deeper personal relationship with God meets with another for prayer and conversation that is focused on increasing awareness of God in the midst of life experiences and facilitating surrender to God's will."[15] The spiritual director guides another person to develop and cultivate a closer personal relationship with God and live in accordance with that relationship.[16] The process involves coming alongside, talking about life and spiritual disciplines, praying and discussing the Bible, listening for God's direction, and giving encouragement. The Christian director does not claim to be a spiritual giant, but he or she seeks to walk with God personally and takes joy in humbly walking with others on their spiritual journeys.

Spiritual coaching often uses principles that are similar to spiritual direction, but the goals might be different and the process uses coaching. I went back to Christopher McCluskey (who has been mentioned in earlier chapters) and asked for a definition of spiritual coaching.[17]

"Spiritual coaching is about helping a person explore, develop, and then live out a more intimate relationship with God. Most Christians have recognized their need for a Savior. They've prayed the sinner's prayer, been baptized, joined a church, ascribed to the 'moral code' of the faith, become active in the life of the body, and participated in Bible studies. They may even have been discipled one-on-one. Yet many complain of a lack of connectedness or intimacy with the Father. They don't seem able to hear his voice or sense his leading. They are not clear about their spiritual gifts and calling. They struggle to see evidence that he is at work in their lives. They wrestle with issues of faith; it's hard to have strong faith in someone you don't feel you know deeply. Scripture might describe them as 'having a form of religion but denying its power'; they don't yet have the spiritual peace, joy, contentment, and fulfillment of the abundant life in an experiential way. But it's not for a lack of sincere effort.

"I believe this problem often is attributable to a lack of familiarity and comfort with intimacy in general. Our fast-paced, disconnected, technologically wired culture is not terribly conducive to intimacy of any kind. Many people complain of not knowing who they really are, what they really think and feel; in other words, they do not know themselves intimately. With so many commitments and so much to distract us, it takes a concerted effort to make time for true reflection and introspection. But this is crucial if we are to intimately know ourselves.

"Not only do we not know ourselves but we often don't know each other intimately. This is due in part to the disappearance of small communities, the rise of dual-income families, a high divorce rate, and families flung all over the globe. We are so relationally disconnected that we can easily be in contact with hundreds of people a day and not make intimate connection with any of them.

"If we're not deeply connected with ourselves and are not experiencing a rich daily intimacy with others (especially spouses and children), it shouldn't be surprising that we don't feel intimate with someone we can't see, touch, or hear! God is there and we are able to experience intimacy with him, but if we don't know how to experience intimacy on the physical plane of this life, it's hard to imagine experiencing it on the spiritual plane.

"It is absolutely critical to spend time alone with God, just as it is critical for married couples to have time alone together. I recommend that all of my clients schedule times of private spiritual retreat as well as private daily devotions. But persons who try to find an intimate relationship with the Father apart from intimacy with others are in danger of developing only an intellectual relationship. We were designed for loving relationship, with God and with each other. When God said, 'It is not good for man to be alone,' he wasn't saying that he wasn't enough for us. He was saying that a large part of how we will experience relationship with him is through relationship with each other. First John 4:12 says, 'No one has ever seen God; but if we love one another, God lives in us and his love is made complete in us' (NIV). We experience the incredible intimacy of God in and through us as we open ourselves up to loving, intimate relationships with others."

Can you give us some examples of spiritual coaching? I asked.

"Sure," Christopher replied. He remembered receiving a phone call from a man who had heard a radio program on Christian coaching. The caller said he was seventy-two years of age but was afraid that he was going to die before he had really started to live. As they began spiritual coaching, Christopher found this man to be "one of the most devout Christians I have ever known. I had no doubt about his salvation, yet he had experienced only rare pockets of intimacy with the Father.

"For this man, developing intimate relationships with others had proven to be very difficult through the years, so one of the primary things we did at that point was to connect at a deeply honest and intimate level. It was amazing to watch the Father reveal himself. This brother just came alive. There was no formula for what we were doing other than to say we were connecting, and the connecting was with a purpose. As he opened himself up to me, God's love became more complete. This was the Holy Spirit working in him, through me.

"I had another client, a Jewish business owner who was not a Christian. He wanted spiritual coaching, but I was amazed when he said, 'I've worked with a spiritual coach who was pretty New Agey and I think I would prefer a Christian.' Here's a man who didn't hold our spiritual faith, but he was hungry for God, exploring, open. He said, 'The main thing I want to do is have a deeper walk with God.' This man did not want to discuss doctrinal issues at that point; he was simply looking for a relationship that would bring him closer to God. And as he connected with me — a fellow human being, but one in whom Christ lives — God was drawing this man to himself. I knew that the doctrinal discussions would come as the relationship deepened. At the beginning, he simply wanted to experience more of God and his love through the probing nature of coaching."

Christopher says that in spiritual coaching especially, he finds the typical coaching conversation to be less like a dialogue between coach and client and more like what he calls a "facilitated monologue. The coach helps the client draw out and hear the things God might be speaking directly to his or her heart. The coach seeks to be as 'invisible' as possible, posing questions and leaving lots of room for exploration and listening but rarely interjecting much at all. Homework assignments seem to present themselves as if the journaling or praying or fasting or Scripture searching or spending time with God in silence and solitude are absolutely begging to be done. The clients hear these inner calls as they really listen to the words coming out of their mouths in response to the very few questions the coach poses."

To conclude, I asked Christopher about the coach's own spirituality and about how one becomes a spiritual coach. He answered that "you can't take someone on a journey you are not also on yourself. If you are doing real spiritual coaching, it's a constant prod to be looking at where you are spiritually, to be always stretching and growing, perhaps with a spiritual coach of your own.

"Anyone who wants to do spiritual coaching must first take a long, hard look at his or her own spiritual walk, making sure he is living in integrity within the dictates of the Christian faith and with his most deeply held spiritual values, gifts, and calling. Dr. John Ortberg has a powerful question he poses to the church at large. It's particularly appropriate for anyone considering becoming a spiritual coach. He asks, 'Is the life you are inviting others to live the life that you yourself are living?' Be certain you are very familiar with your Shepherd and his green pastures.

"Another key is to remember that the role of a coach is rarely to teach or advise. That is more the work of discipleship. The coaching relationship is much more about what is caught than what is taught. Allow the Holy Spirit, at work in the client, to direct the sessions rather than you bringing an agenda."

Perhaps that's a guideline for coaches who want to work with churches. Keep aware of the Holy Spirit's leading and look for opportunities to serve in those settings that are providing unique opportunities for Christian coaches.

SOUL FRIENDS

Almost nothing gives me greater fulfillment and satisfaction than walking on close friendship journeys with the mostly young leaders God has led into my life. Most of us meet regularly, on the phone, or through our computers if we cannot meet face-to-face in some restaurant or coffee shop. We talk about life, careers, families, personal struggles, and sometimes the road to greater intimacy with God. I take joy in sticking with these people, and they, in turn, seem willing to stick with me. I don't think these kinds of soul relationships are very common; few seem to be deep. For me, they don't involve payment for professional coaching, but they do overflow with mutual encouragement, intimate sharing, prayer, vision casting, and a deep Christian love.

Sometimes our conversations discuss parts of the coaching circle: where we are; where we want to go; our strengths, values, passions, life visions, plans and obstacles that impede our progress. We don't discuss these in any order. They come up spontaneously but frequently. We don't see giant leaps of growth. We walk together on the road and sometimes just hang out with each other. But looking back at the footprints in the sand, we see where God has walked alongside us and led. None of this is formal coaching, even though we use a lot of coaching methods to encourage, motivate, and sometimes rejoice or celebrate with each other. Sometimes we coach each other, even though the "c" word is never used. In many ways, these brotherly walks show coaching applied to real life. Rarely does a day pass when I don't pause to think about this and give thanks.

PART 7

THE PRACTICE OF CHRISTIAN COACHING

CHAPTER 19

THE PROFESSION AND BUSINESS OF COACHING

The Dream Giver is Bruce Wilkinson's captivating tale of a "nobody person" named Ordinary, who leaves the Land of Familiar to pursue a Big Dream that was given to him by the divine Dream Giver.[1] It was not easy for Ordinary to leave his Comfort Zone and get past the Border Bullies and fierce Giants in the Land that were blocking the way. Part of the journey involved getting through the Wasteland before reaching the Land of Promise. I rarely read novels, so I picked up this book with reluctance and only because I knew it was an allegory about coaching. I soon concluded that this also is a story that describes the journey of many coaching clients and perhaps most of their coaches. After telling the story, Wilkinson invites readers to let him be their Dream Coach who uses the pages of his book to help other Dreamers move forward in their journeys. Table 19-1 summarizes the process.

Table 19-1

THE DREAM GIVER'S JOURNEY[2]
The epic story of Israel's journey from Egypt to the Promised Land ... reveals a pattern that is repeated throughout the Bible whenever God's people reach for their Dream and attempt great things for him. In almost every instance, they: ▪ Become aware of a personal Dream or calling and then decide to pursue it ▪ Face fear as they leave a place of comfort ▪ Encounter opposition from those around them

- Endure a season of difficulty that tests their faith
- Learn the importance of surrender and consecration to God
- Fight the Giants that stand between them and the fulfillment of their Dream
- Reach their full potential as they achieve their Dream and bring honor to God

The good news for every Dreamer is that each stage or obstacle along the journey is intended not to block our dream but to help us break through to the fulfillment God promises.

Sometimes I recommend Wilkinson's book to my coaching clients. The story paints a picture of what could be on the road for people who dare to believe that God has a plan for their lives and that he guides in the journey. The guidance comes in many ways, sometimes through coaching.

For fifteen years, I've been involved in the coaching movement, watching it develop and allowing it to impact me. Along the way, I've had practical questions about coaching that I now know are common. At times we all may wonder, *Should I get coaching for myself? How does anybody find a coach? Should I become a coach? Where would I get training? Is it important to be certified? If I got into this field, where would I find people to coach? Is coaching a fad, or is it likely to last? Is this something I could do in my church? How could I become a professional coach who charges for my coaching services? Could I make a living as a coach? Is there any real evidence that coaching works?* In the remaining chapters in this book, I seek to answer questions such as these. I'll also point to ways for you to find information online and elsewhere so you can keep abreast of a coaching field that is constantly evolving and growing.[3]

When we first learn about coaching and begin to understand how it works, many of us might want to get involved, even to the point of becoming professional coaches who help others reach their dreams. Maybe that's not for you. Your goal may be to use coaching in your church or at work or home. Perhaps you have concluded that the next step in your coaching journey is to find a coach and experience coaching for yourself. This might be a way to discover and follow your own Big Dream. Maybe this is a time to ask if you should become a coach yourself.

Look into your past and look around your present and you will begin to see the coaches who help you make life healthy and

> whole.... They are just people at the right place at the right
> time with a passion to guide others through the ambiguities
> of living.
>
> —THOMAS BANDY, author of *Coaching Change*

You may be one of those people who has been coaching for years, long before you found this book or ever heard about coaching. Helping others through coaching comes naturally to you, just like it seems natural for other people to come seeking your guidance. Alternatively, you may not have had these experiences but you sense that you have something to give to others who could benefit from spending time or journeying with you. Whatever your situation, ask God to bring people to you for coaching. Seek him for wisdom and commit your coaching to his guidance and blessing. Find at least one other person to whom you can be accountable in your coaching work. Determine to apply the principles of this and other coaching books. Seriously consider more training if you can get it. Periodically check the website that accompanies this book (www.christiancoachingbook.com) to get updates on training opportunities and information about new resources. And watch God work through you to coach others and to change lives. Perhaps a next step is to find a coach for yourself who could walk with you as you pursue your own Big Dream.

BECOMING A COACH

A few years ago, I attended a training seminar led by Thomas Leonard, who even then was known as the father of coaching. At the end of the training, members of the audience were invited to stand and summarize what they had learned. One young lady identified herself as a recent college graduate and described her frustrations in finding a career choice. Then she told us that her search had ended. As a result of the seminar, she had decided to become a professional coach. She talked about how this new career direction would enable her to help people and earn a significant income at the same time.

I've often wondered what happened after the seminar was over and she went home. Sometimes beginning coaches get the idea that building a coaching practice is relatively easy and a painless way to a six-figure income. The reality is very different. Many coaches struggle to find jobs or paying clients. Those who succeed in private practice often do so because they have superior marketing skills and no hesitations about promoting themselves and their businesses. Most are able to demonstrate competence, proven effectiveness, and self-confidence in their coaching abilities. These are major challenges for beginners. In corporations, where coaching brings the highest fees, there is a demand for experienced and competent coaches, but not for young college graduates with enthusiasm but little training and no business expertise.

None of this is meant to be discouraging, although it may have that effect. Instead, the previous paragraph is meant to show that becoming a paid professional coach is difficult. But that does not mean it's impossible. Financial and vocational success as a coach is attainable, especially for coaches who are determined to succeed despite the obstacles. And none of this should hide the fact that many effective coaches never try to build private practices. Instead, they look for jobs in churches, organizations, colleges, or smaller companies where coaching services might be desired.

If you decide to be more involved in coaching, how do you proceed? If possible, try to find a trained coach who can tell you more about coaching and can coach you through your deliberations and steps to becoming a coach. The Christian Coaches Network website is one place to start in finding a competent Christian coach,[4] but many coaching schools and trainers also offer coaching services and so do some counseling practices. As a coaching instructor, I urge my students to be coached for a period of time before or while they are getting coach training. This coaching becomes a powerful learning experience that shows potential coaches how the process works. Remember that many coaches do their work by phone, so they need not live in your neighborhood. Appendix K gives further guidelines for finding a coach.

Then consider the various options for coach training. Sometimes counselors, consultants, teachers, pastors, and other caregivers assume that their education and experience automatically equip them to coach effectively. As a result, they assume that coach training isn't necessary. If they do take more formal coach training, however, many begin to appreciate the uniqueness of coaching. They find that coaching classes and supervision can equip emerging coaches, even those who work in related professions. If the training is good, the trained coaches are better able to excel in this field and be more valuable to the people who are coached.[5]

Some seminaries and university graduate schools offer courses in coaching, and their number is likely to increase. More popular are the independent coach training programs. Rey Carr is a coach trainer in Canada who tracks coaching trends and has compiled a description of coach training schools. At the time when this book was written, there were more than three hundred separate training schools in the United States and Canada with more overseas.[6] They offer almost one hundred coach certification credentials, "some with the same name but with differing requirements that can range from extensive study and practice to just a couple of phone calls." Carr comments that "the general public as well as coaches and those interested in becoming coaches can easily be confused and bewildered."[7]

Even though the quality of coach training differs from school to school, none of this should distract from the fact that some excellent training programs do exist. Without giving evaluations, Rey Carr gives a brief description of many coach training schools. The International Coach Federation describes a smaller number of coaching schools, all of which meet ICF training standards. Training in these schools can be expensive, and often the emphasis is far from being Christian. Nevertheless, the training in these programs contributes to ICF certification, which is rigorous (perhaps unrealistically so) and widely recognized as a standard of quality. Go to the ICF website, click on "Credentialing," and you will learn how to become an ICF certified coach.[8] All of this training and credentialing takes time, but these efforts will make you a better coach and prepare you for the day when standards like these may become the basis for anyone who is licensed to coach.

We should note that at present there is considerable debate among coaches about the value or need for credentials, including certification. It sometimes is noted that the best-known and most successful coaches don't have the standard credentials but do have a demonstrated ability to get results. Perhaps you have noticed that many coaches list initials after their names that begin with a C (for certified), end with a C (for coach), and have a specialization in between. Some observers wonder if all of these credentials really mean anything. As more and more people enter the coaching field, however, including many who have few or poor-quality credentials, there is likely to be more of a push for standardized training and credentialing procedures.[9] Until that happens, any individual or school that wants to give credentials can do so.

CREDIBILITY IN COACHING

Leadership coach Steve Ogne has written about his experience doing autopsies on dozens of failed coaching relationships.[10] He found that in most cases, coaches blame the failure on their clients, describing them as being unresponsive and uncoachable. A closer look shows that the problem more often lies with the coach. It is difficult for a coach to maintain credibility and effectiveness if he or she is personally insecure, spiritually or emotionally immature, insensitive to others, or unable to instill confidence.

One of my friends is a successful coach whose career began when he was still in his twenties. It's different now, but in the beginning my friend didn't have any gray hair and he must have looked very young to the business leaders he wanted to coach. His first challenge with almost every new client was to demonstrate his competence and self-confidence. These clients relaxed and began to make progress when they recognized that their coach was wiser, more perceptive, and more effective than his youthful appearance might have suggested.

> Your life is not your own; it belongs to God. To "be yourself" is to be and do what God wants you to be and do, knowing that God created you for a mission and knows you and your mission better than you do.
>
> — LEONARD SWEET, professor, author of *Postmodern Pilgrims*

Every coach needs to ask and answer this question: What gives me the right or the credibility to coach others? Part of the answer lies in the coach's personality. Table 2-1 listed some of the traits that characterize effective coaches.[11] These traits don't need to be announced or flaunted in any way. They tend to appear naturally and without coaches giving them much thought. When a client has a positive perception of the coach, trust often follows and the coaching succeeds.

But there is more to credibility than being a nice person who is well regarded. Like my friend with the youthful looks, coaches must earn the right to speak into the lives of their coaching clients. This credibility comes from at least six sources. Probably you can think of others.

First, credibility comes from the coach's *reputation*. When we face surgery, most of us want a surgeon who is known to be among the best in the field. The same is true of coaches. Second, the coach's *position* can be of importance. Large companies sometimes employ internal coaches who are assigned to work with managers and other company employees. Those coaches have credibility because they represent the company and sometimes have the power to recommend whether or not the employee-client will be promoted or retained by the company. Third, credibility relates to the coach's *expertise*. At the beginning of his career, my youthful-looking friend did not have an established reputation or position in any company, but he earned the right to coach because he clearly demonstrated his competence. Before long, his former clients became his advocates who told others of their coach's capabilities. Sometimes people who teach coaching or write about it are assumed to have expertise, and this position gives them credibility with potential clients. *Training and credentials* may also give credibility. These show that the coach has gone through a formal process for developing coaching skills. As we have noted, coaches debate the extent to which these give credibility. In some situations, it helps for a coach to be certified, but many clients seem less interested in credentials than about the coach's demonstrated ability to produce results.

The next indicator of credibility may be more important than any of the others. This is the mutually respectful, trusting *relationship* between coach and client. If I look for a coach, I want somebody who is sensitive, somebody I can trust. I want somebody who is a committed Christian, genuine and caring. For many clients, that could be more important than the coach's training, reputation, or any of the other indicators of credibility.

Experience also helps. This includes but goes beyond experience in coaching. It includes experience in areas that are important to clients. One of my former students specializes in coaching battered women. She is very effective in her craft, not only because she is a good coach but also because she came out of a battered relationship herself. She has credibility with her clients because she has experienced what her clients face.

NICHES IN COACHING

If we asked about her work, the coach who works with battered women would say that this specialty is her niche. She could and probably does coach other people, but she's a specialist. Her prime focus is with one group of coaching clients. Specialization like this is common in the coaching field; general practitioner coaches are rare, especially among coaches who are more established. We saw this in chapters 14 through 18, where we met coaches who have built credibility and expertise around specific topic areas. When you have a niche, like those shown in table 19-2, you can work in areas in which you have special competence, interest, and personal experience. Your specialty might be where you feel most comfortable, where you can focus on getting specialized training, and where you build expertise rather than trying to spread your coaching impact too broadly.

Table 19-2

SAMPLE COACHING NICHES
■ Business coaching

- Career coaching
- Church coaching
- Corporate coaching
- Executive coaching
- Leadership coaching
- Life coaching
- Marriage coaching
- Parent coaching
- Relationship coaching
- Transitional coaching
- Coaching boards
- Coaching managers
- Coaching new coaches
- Coaching small-group leaders
- Coaching writers

How does a coach find a niche? Start by thinking about people who might be ideal clients for you, given your interests and experience. Ask yourself these questions: *Whose life intrigues me? Who are the people I like to be with? Who would I like to work with? Who has come to me for advice, guidance, or coaching? Specifically, what attracts or intrigues me about the lives and work of these people?* What is similar about them all? Your answers might be a clue to the niche areas and the people with whom you could work most effectively.

When I asked myself these questions, a niche began to evolve quickly. I like to work independently, largely outside any confining corporate, academic, or church structure. I connect best with young professionals and emerging leaders, including international people, who want to discuss their life directions, careers, spirituality, or overcommitted lifestyles. Notice the theme in this: guiding Christian leaders and potential leaders to find greater life fulfillment, balance, and impact. The more I coach, the more this niche gets refined.

In pondering your niche, you might also ask where you have had experience and where there seems to be a need. This has been called "coaching to the gap." Charisa had built a successful career selling real estate, but when she decided to move to something less demanding, she hired a coach. To her surprise, she decided to become a coach herself and now is taking courses to become equipped for this new career. When she took part in a coaching class, Charisa described the needs of other realtors who, like her, could benefit from coaching services. Building on her experience and drawing on her many contacts with people in the real estate field, she plans to open a private practice coaching realtors. She will be coaching to the gap, working to meet a need that she sees and that few others are seeking to fill.

ETHICS IN COACHING

As part of her training, it is likely that Charisa will take a course in coaching ethics. Sometimes these courses are not the most interesting, but in-depth considerations of ethics protect both clients and coaches and can prevent problems from developing later. Coaching is not regulated by government agencies, so each coach can do what he or she considers right without risking any legal or professional consequences unless there is a violation of existing laws. But consider these examples of behavior that is not legally wrong but that most coaches would consider to be unethical:

- A coach makes statements about his or her training, credentials, or qualifications that are untrue and misleading.
- A researcher publishes reports of coaching effectiveness that are biased and not based on solid scientific procedures.
- In a public lecture (or a discussion with a friend over coffee), a coach shares personal information about a coaching client.
- A coach shares inaccurate or unsubstantiated information with a client, presenting this information as factual.
- A coach exploits a coaching relationship for his or her personal, financial, or other advantage.
- A coach uses methods that are of questionable validity, based on the coach's bias or opinion and not on research or established coaching procedures.

These might seem like obvious issues that clearly are wrong. But when there are no objective guidelines for coaching ethics, a few coaches can mislead many people, present a false and misleading image of coaching, exploit innocent clients, and have potential to do serious damage to clients' careers, lives, dreams, and relationships.

The good news is that ethical codes and standards for coaches do exist. Most of them are similar to the others, and the majority of coaches appear to follow them consistently. Any coach who has credentials with the International Coach Federation can lose his or her credentials if the ICF Pledge of Ethics is breached. On a broader scale, active work is underway to align the ethical codes from the world's major coaching organizations. The goal is to create one globally accepted standard. This is unlikely to have any Christian foundations, but codes of ethics like that of the Christian Coaches Network seek to align, as much as they can, with the codes of recognized coaching organizations. An amended version of the CCN code of ethics appears as table 19-3.

Table 19-3

CHRISTIAN COACHES NETWORK CODE OF ETHICS[12]
As a Christian coach: 1. I hold myself accountable to the highest level of integrity, honoring Jesus Christ individually and corporately, in all my associations with clients and colleagues. 2. I will maintain complete confidentiality with my clients, within the confines of the law. 3. I will be clear with my clients about the nature of the coaching relationship, including structure, fees, refunds, expectations, and guarantees. 4. I will never give a client's name to anyone, for any purpose, without express permission. 5. I will give credit where credit is due for materials supplied by other sources, respecting copyrights, trademarks, and intellectual property. 6. I will judiciously avoid conflicts of interest. If any should arise, I shall, without delay, inform concerned parties of my position. 7. I will represent myself honestly and clearly to my clients and coach only within my areas of expertise. 8. I will actively pursue well-being, wholeness, and continual learning in my own life. 9. I will refer a client to another coach if I am not within my area of expertise or comfort so the client gets the best possible coaching. 10. I will honor my Christian values in my professional conduct, placing neither blame nor blemish on the name of Christ or the coaching profession. The Christian Coaches Network supports and stands in agreement with the Code of Ethics set forth by the International Coach Federation, which outlines standards for professional coaching.

THE BUSINESS AND MINISTRY OF COACHING

Patrick is a thirty-seven-year-old counselor with a doctorate in psychology and a growing private practice. He spent several years and a lot of money to get his training, and by all indications he is competent in what he does. He attributes much of his success to the excellent training he received from a top-quality, fully accredited school of psychology. But Patrick's training lacked two major components: He never had a course on leadership and now finds himself with leadership responsibilities in a community counseling agency, and Patrick never had a course in business. As a young professional, he thrives when he does therapy and sees his counselees often get better. But Patrick struggles to run his counseling business. He lacks the expertise and experience to keep abreast of all that needs to be done, and he's had difficulty finding someone who can help.

Patrick does not really exist as a single person. I can think of eight or ten counselors and coaches who will read the previous paragraph and think that I am describing them. In reality, I have described all of them. They represent caregivers, coaches included, who are skilled in their crafts but lack competence and the confidence to run their businesses. Unlike the school where "Patrick" got his training, many coach training programs now require a course in marketing and business, even for coaches who have no desire to set up a private practice.

> Building a thriving coaching business is a challenge. Despite promises of a lucrative business, coaches report that the coaching business functions similar to any small start-up, with slow growth and slow earnings in the first few years. The most successful coaches are good marketers.
>
> — LYNN GRODZWKI and WENDY ALLEN,
> coauthors of *The Business and Practice of Coaching*

Judy Santos is a coach who also knows about running a successful coaching business. She suggests that in addition to possessing the qualities of an effective coach, builders of successful coaching businesses need:

- Basic knowledge and understanding of business
- The ability to create a realistic business plan

- Sufficient cash reserves for start-up to sustain the business through financial ups and downs, especially at the beginning
- An ability to tend to bookkeeping, taxes, and administrative functions relating to business
- An ability to work alone and manage time well
- The skill, knowledge, and discipline to market the business effectively, including the development and utilization of a solid marketing plan
- Reasonable comfort with the Internet and basic computer programs
- Competence in coaching skills
- Credibility that comes from recognized coach-specific training, from certification or from other sources
- Determination to keep going when obstacles get in the way of progress[13]

I resisted when I was required to take a course in marketing as a part of my coach training. To my surprise, the course alerted me to principles that all coaches can benefit from knowing, even if they never expect or get paid for their coaching. Many of these guidelines apply to small-group leaders or pastors coaching people in their churches as well as to executive coaches wanting to sell their services to corporations.

The first marketing principle is to recognize that people will not flock to you for coaching just because you are trained and available. Many people don't know what coaching is, so they need to be educated. Some coaches do this through what is known as an elevator speech. This is a brief description of what you do that can be stated in the time between the closing of an elevator door and its opening on the next floor. Try this for yourself by filling in the blanks in the following sentence: "I work with _____ to _____." The first blank describes who you work with; the second says what you do. Here are examples: "I work with people who are stuck in their careers to help them find new direction." "I work with small-group leaders in my church to help them lead more effectively." "I work with people who are going through transitions to help them find new direction." Notice that the words *coach* or *coaching* are not used in the elevator speeches. These are short statements that open the door to further communication. Most often they reflect the niche that you have selected.

As an alternative, you may want to follow Paul's example in 1 Timothy 2:7. He wrote, "I have been chosen as a preacher and apostle to teach the Gentiles this message about faith and truth." Try completing this sentence to get greater clarity on what you are called to offer: "I have been chosen as a _____ to _____." Share this with somebody who knows you well to see if they agree or would suggest an alternative.

Second, be aware of your insecurities. Many people take coaching courses but then never coach anybody because they don't know how to market themselves, are too insecure to do coaching, or are held back by those inner mental gremlins that say, "It can't be done, at least by you." Others among us resist marketing on the assumption that this involves manipulation or arm twisting. Instead, think of marketing as a form of teaching or educating people about coaching. If you are among the majority to whom marketing or self-promotion does not come naturally, think of this as raising awareness rather than raising business. Many coaches offer a free coaching session so others can see what coaching is and how it is done. There is no better way to arouse interest and share the coaching message.

Third, develop marketing and business skills. Find some experienced person who can help. Take a marketing course or look at books that suggest ways for marketing your coaching services.[14] Before you move too far into this, develop answers to the following questions, even if you are not building a private for-pay coaching practice:

- Who is my target audience? Who are the people I most want to serve?
- What do these people want or need that I can provide?
- What is my product? What do I have to offer? (This ties to your niche.)
- What indicates that I am equipped to offer these coaching services?
- How might people find out about me?
- How could I persuade them to give coaching a try?
- What are the ways I can get started?

Try to put yourself in the place of a potential client, pastor, business leader, or head of an organization who might be able to use coaching. What is the best and most respectable way to reach that person? What would that person want to know about you and about what you provide? What is the best way to get that information across?

You can take coaching courses, practice your coaching skills, read coaching books, listen to tapes about coaching, and tell your friends about coaching. You can work to build your credibility as a coach, but if you can't find anybody who wants coaching, then all of this preparation may be in vain. Success in coaching almost always involves at least some marketing.

BULLIES, BUDDIES, AND BUSTERS

If you have read to this point in the book, you probably have given some thought to where you might fit into what chapter 1 called the "coaching revolution." Some will put down the book and move on to other things. Perhaps others will have been stimulated to think about their passions, values, strengths, goals, and God-given visions for their lives. Maybe you are among those who will continue to pursue an interest in coaching so that you will become a better coach than you are at present. It could be that you have been encouraged to think about whether God really has a Big Dream plan for your life.

> The key to discovering all you are meant to do and
> be is to wake up to the Big Dream God has given you
> and set out on the journey to achieve it.
>
> — BRUCE WILKINSON, author of *The Dream Giver*

Wherever you are in the journey, Bruce Wilkinson's *Dream Giver* allegory suggests that along the way, you are likely to meet some people who can help or hinder your progress.[15] First are the Bullies. They oppose you by coming with four messages. The *alarmists* tell you about the risks and say that it isn't safe to move forward. The *traditionalists* cling to old routines and say that what you want to do is "not the way we do it." The *defeatists* claim that your goals will never be met. What you dream for can't happen and won't because what you propose is impossible. The *antagonists* try to use intimidation and authority to stop your progress. What or who are the bullies that hinder your pursuit of a dream, maybe the pursuit of a dream to be a coach?

Buddies are different. They care about you. Often they affirm and support you even if they don't take a lot of overt action to help you. Then come the Busters.[16] They believe in what you are seeking to do. They are cheerleaders, but they are more. They help in any way they can. They believe in you. They help you make things happen. They believe that progress and success are possible even when you doubt your own potential and abilities.

As you think about God's dream for your life, maybe including your growth as a coach, expect to encounter some bullies. Ask God to give you some buddies to walk with you on the journey. And pray for at least one or two busters who will help you keep moving. Maybe this book will be a buddy on your coaching journey. Maybe someday you will be a buddy or a buster for people who want to get from where they are to where God wants them to be.

CHAPTER 20

CROSSING CULTURES
IN COACHING

PROBABLY THE BEST coach training I ever had was an intensive three-day workshop in Belgium, sponsored by the Center for Creative Leadership (CCL).[1] Our class consisted of twelve participants. All were businesspeople except me, the one psychologist. None of us had been born in the United States, and only two of us lived outside of Europe. We were a congenial, culturally diverse group who had come to learn how coaching could be applied in our various work settings.

CCL training and coaching builds around a process that has three major tasks: assessment, challenge, and support. All three are needed for results in coaching and they may appear at any time or in any order. In many coaching relationships, one or two of these may be more prominent than the others.

The purpose of *assessment* is to get the clearest possible picture of the person being coached, including some measure of his or her performance and knowledge about where the person lives and works. In doing this assessment, the coach asks questions, listens, observes, clarifies issues, and tries to build a trusting relationship. *Challenge* also involves asking tough questions but includes summarizing what the client has communicated, dealing with resistance, confronting assumptions, and clarifying goals. The challenges come in many forms, but they have one thing in common: They create disequilibrium, an imbalance between current skills and demands that call on people to move out of their comfort zones.[2] When coaches challenge, they nudge people to seek new options and overcome obstacles that are holding them back. *Support* is giving encouragement, feedback, accountability, and sometimes the coach's presence as the client makes choices and goes through change. Support includes helping clients find resources, learn new skills, and celebrate victories when goals are reached. All of this is done within the confines of a trusting and committed *relationship* where one person influences another toward improved performance and positive outcomes. The goal is to get *results*, including personal and professional development in the client, and changes (improvements) in his or her performance, behavior, attitudes, and leadership.

The previous paragraph has five words in italics: assessment, challenge, support, relationship, and results. Each of these words is a core concept in the CCL model, and each can mean something different from one culture to another.[3] Here are examples:

- **Assessment.** In the minds of many westerners, assessment means a rational, objective, and measurable evaluation of behavior and performance. Westerners like using assessment tools similar to those found in the appendixes of this book. Most of these are developed in one country, but few translate easily or apply equally to people in other societies. In many places, western-style assessment tools are not used or valued. In these countries, the assessment of a person may be made subjectively, based on his or her education, or tied to the effectiveness of one's group or team. Cross-cultural coaching can be complicated when the coach and the client have different views of what assessment involves.

- **Challenge.** In Canada, Australia, New Zealand, the United Kingdom, and the United States, challenging another person often means to stretch their goals, push them to overcome obstacles, create action plans for getting things done, and press for improvements in performance. This mostly refers to moving individuals out of their comfort zones and into new actions. In contrast, many people from Asian countries value group harmony over individual achievement. In these settings, coaching clients might resist challenges that urge individuals to take personal responsibility for making change happen.

- **Support.** My business-oriented classmates in our CCL training tended to confront clients as ways to get things done, taking the role of a boss giving top-down directions. They criticized me for being too psychological, too therapeutic, too inclined to lean forward in my chair giving gentle encouragement. Because of our different backgrounds and experiences, we viewed support differently. The way I was inclined to give support was not perceived as supportive or valuable by my European colleagues, who had different backgrounds and cultural perspectives. One CCL article gives the helpful suggestion that if we want to give effective support, "coaches must inquire about and explore what would be most meaningful and valuable" to the person being coached.[4]

- **Relationship.** Maybe you will agree that a good relationship involves effective communication, trust, honesty, mutual respect, and even a willingness to be open and vulnerable. These qualities are valued in many western countries. Relationships build quickly there, although many are not very deep or long-lasting. Western countries are places where telephone coaching is effective and easily accepted.

  In other cultures, relationship building takes more time and arises from ongoing face-to-face interaction. For people with this perspective, telephone coaching might seem more superficial and be less effective than in the United States. One of my closest friends is French. He was born in Paris and has lived there for most of his life. He jokes that his countrymen are like the French baguettes that have a hard crust on the outside but are soft inside. "It takes a while to get past the hard exterior, but once you are inside, you find that the French people are very warm, accepting, and friends for life." I agree.

  Even partnerships have different meanings cross-culturally. In some countries, the partnership between coach and client is a relationship between two equals. Elsewhere, a coaching partnership is viewed as a hierarchical relationship in which the person being coached is guided by an expert who is more like a mentor or master teacher—directive, authoritative, dispensing wisdom.

- **Results.** Probably every culture values results, but we often define results differently. As we have seen, in some Asian cultures results are tied less to individual performance and more to the ways in which team members work together to benefit the group as a whole.

WHY CULTURE MATTERS

None of this may seem important if you coach in your own church or community and have no plans to take your coaching overseas, not even on a short-term mission trip. Many years ago, I took a course in cross-cultural counseling, and I still remember the instructor's main message: All counseling is cross-cultural, even in your own community. I believe the same is true of all coaching. Although you might never step away from your own neighborhood, your coaching is shaped by culture.

Culture might be viewed as a collection of the beliefs, customs, values, and ways of thinking that are common within a group of people. A more formal definition describes culture as a common history, physical environment, and place of living, language, and religion that shapes the members of a society so that they develop and share common assumptions, values, beliefs, and worldviews.[5] There are significant differences within any culture, but it is generally agreed that most countries or geographical regions have their own ways of thinking and viewing the world. For example, American perspectives and ways of doing things often differ from those of Western Europe, the Middle East, Asian countries, or Latin America. Even Canadians and residents of the United States often think differently, despite the fact that they are neighbors and share a very long international border. When families or individuals immigrate, they bring their cultural perspectives with them and this sometimes causes conflict.

Within your neighborhood, there may be a variety of subcultural groups, each built around different religious denominations, businesses, professions, age groups, or people with similar ethnic or socioeconomic backgrounds. Every church has a culture and so does every family. If you coach a person who is different from you in terms of age, education, past experience, gender, occupation, or family background, you are involved in cross-cultural coaching.

Just as fish are unaware of the water in which they swim, most of us don't think much about the cultures where we live and work until we meet somebody who brings cultural views and expectations that are different. Culturally sensitive people, including coaches, take time to ponder their own cultural perspectives—their values, beliefs, attitudes, and group memberships. Think especially about the groups of which you are a member. For example, I am white, married, older, male, Christian, a psychologist. Being a member of these groups gives me perspectives and group affiliations that my clients might not share. Coaches may raise these issues if they sense that the differences between client and coach might be creating barriers to progress or if it appears that cultural and group membership differences may be hindering a client's relationships with other people.

Table 20-1

CULTURAL DIFFERENCES THAT IMPACT COACHING

Each of the following is a continuum. Individuals and cultures can be at either extreme or more likely at some place in between.

1. Individual/Autonomous — Group/Collectivistic

Individualism characterizes societies in which people are expected to look after and assert themselves. Uniqueness, individual initiative, mastery, and self-development are valued. Collectivist societies emphasize group and family loyalty, harmony between people, and group cohesion. Sometimes there is disapproval of individual actions that advance oneself or one's career over group expectations and solidarity.

2. Egalitarian — Hierarchical

In egalitarian cultures, everyone is considered equal. Titles, academic degrees, status, and positions of authority are accepted but minimized. First-name communication is common. In coaching, it is usually assumed that each client will make decisions and take actions based on his or her choices. In hierarchical societies, there is a greater value placed on a person's status, position, title, role, and power. Here the coach often is viewed as an authority with power, wisdom, and the ability to give advice.

3. Traditional — Nontraditional

Every culture has pride in its past history and established traditions, but there are differences in the tenacity with which people cling to the past. More traditional societies are oriented toward the past and the present. They place importance on preserving traditions, maintaining the status quo, fulfilling social obligations, "saving face," and behaving "in a proper manner." In contrast, some groups are less traditional or bound to the past. In these cultures, there is greater openness to change, a willingness to try new things, and a focus on the future. Within one's own culture, there may be differences between people who are older and more set in their traditional ways, unlike those who are less traditional, more "hang loose," and younger.

4. Expressive — Reserved

To a large extent, personality determines how one expresses emotions or attitudes, but culture has an influence as well. In expressive cultures, it is more acceptable to openly show emotions such as sorrow, excitement, joy, and rage. Feelings may be no less intense in reserved cultures, but it is more acceptable to keep one's emotions and attitudes hidden.

Table 20-1 summarizes some of the cultural differences that can have an impact on coaching. Coaching tends to be individualistic with emphasis on personal vision casting, goal setting, self-mastery, and personal initiative for change. This is common in the West, especially in the United States. But in collectivist cultures, many of which are in Asia, there is less emphasis on self-assertiveness and individual development and a greater focus on group harmony, loyalty, and sacrifice on behalf of the community. Here the client's goal may be to strengthen the group and bring greater team cohesion. When a coach fails to understand these differences, the coaching process can be hindered.

Another example might relate to the teaching of coaching. Student learning styles can differ from one culture to another. In the West, we try to engage students in discussion, encourage practice coaching, and have everyone participate in role plays and mutual evaluations. Seminar leaders and participants see each other as equals who are learning together in a process stimulated by the leader. In other cultures, the teacher is seen as having a more prominent role in dispensing knowledge, while the students take notes and become collectors of that knowledge. Students in these settings will be less inclined to engage in dialogue or role-play. They would prefer to listen and write than risk the potential embarrassment of asking a question that might appear foolish or irrelevant. "Just give us the information about coaching," I was told by an older seminar promoter in an Asian country. "Don't expect us to participate in discussions or to ask questions unless we can write the questions on paper and submit them anonymously."[6]

All of this would suggest that the underpinnings of one's culture will greatly influence approaches to both coaching and coach training.[7] It is difficult for people in some cultures to accept the idea that the client comes up with the solution or that the coach is not an advice giver.

How, then, do coaches work across cultures? At least four core guidelines will facilitate the process, even if you are working cross-culturally with people in your own community.

1. Self-awareness. Coaches must be aware of their own assumptions, values, worldviews, and perspectives on how things should be done. Coaches who are trained in the West might assume that good coaching always focuses on individual development, initiative, and problem solving. Clients might not only disagree but also resist the coach's beliefs, refuse to cooperate, or express confusion. It is difficult to coach clients of a different culture if the coach does not recognize his or her own cultural perspectives.

It is not by accident that coaching has proliferated to such
a degree in the United States. The American culture leans
heavily toward a mastery orientation which is . . . individualistic,
egalitarian, performance driven, comfortable with change,
and action oriented. . . . Coaches should not assume that this
carries around the globe.

— LYNNE DELAY and MAXINE DALTON, Center for Creative Leadership

When I was involved in a yearlong program to train executive coaches in China, we began by inviting the participants to experience several personal coaching sessions with the instructor before the training began. Later, when we met for several days of face-to-face training, everybody knew each other and by this time they all knew me. Perhaps because we were so comfortable with each other, one of the participants (who was not from China) felt free to challenge some of my assumptions about coaching. The group quickly came together in support of this challenge. These are gracious people. I know them well and respect each of them highly. But later I wondered if the group was testing me, raising questions about some viewpoints that I held, maybe pressing to see if I could work in partnership with people from a culture that held different assumptions. The discussion on that first afternoon was tense at times (at least for me), but it brought us together and let us explore basic cultural assumptions for discussion and mutual understanding. That self-awareness for the group, including me, was an important part of our training time together.

2. Cultural awareness. Coaches should never underestimate the importance of sensitivity to other cultures. If you travel to some other part of the world to coach or to teach coaching, learn as much as you can about the country, the culture, and the work setting before you go. Search the Internet, find somebody who knows the country where you will work, ask about cultural issues when you get there. Be an eager, humble learner. Your desire to learn about another culture expresses respect and a willingness to honor customs and traditions that may differ from yours.

Even if you work at home with people from different cultures, try to learn about the other person's cultural background and country of origin. If you do this, you are likely to discover that your cross-cultural interaction will be smoother and your coaching more effective.

Coaches who have cross-cultural experience tend
to have an easier time understanding and
accepting differing cultural paradigms.

— TINA STOLTZFUS HORST and PAUL HILLHOUSE,
Coaching Mission International

I once talked with an editor who was sent to a country overseas to help set up a Christian magazine for college students. The trip was sponsored by an organization that provided funds to get the publication started. The goal was to train local editors and leaders who would produce the new magazine, learn to make it self-supporting, and carry on with its production after my friend and his wife returned home.

It soon became clear that there was a problem with this scenario. The local staff assumed that because the editor was skilled in his work, he should be the one to keep the magazine going. Since there clearly was money from overseas to start the magazine, the people in the host country assumed that more money would appear to keep it going. The editor and his sponsoring organization had one set of assumptions; the people in the community had assumptions that were different. As a result, the venture collapsed, the magazine ceased publication, and the editor and his wife returned home. Could some of this have been prevented if everybody concerned had understood these different cultural perspectives before the project began?

3. A learning perspective. There are cultural differences in terms of adult learning. In some countries, continuous adult learning is affirmed and widely accepted. Elsewhere, the assumption prevails that learning is complete when a diploma or degree is given. In these cultures, diplomas often are presented after a seminar and hung proudly in offices to show what one has learned.

Whatever your perspective, be open to learning all you can about cultural perspectives, developments in coaching, and yourself. One of the best ways to learn is to ask questions. Start with your clients. They can be great teachers. Ask, "What does success look like in your country?" "What would be an appropriate way to make progress in your country?" "In your community, what can you do to build friendships?" "In the culture where you work, how could you express your frustration in an appropriate way?" Questions like these move the coaching process forward with an emphasis on the client, but they also enable the coach to get a better awareness of the culture in which your client lives or works.

Coaches must be vigilant in maintaining a learning posture as they coach cross-culturally. Learning to embrace the client's understanding of time, responsibility, identity, and how to handle conflict is essential to effectiveness.

—TINA STOLTZFUS HORST and PAUL HILLHOUSE,
Coaching Mission International

Be sensitive to signs of misunderstanding. These include withdrawal, overreaction, resistance, or confusion in either the client or the coach. When you don't understand what is going on, express your curiosity and ask for clarification.[8]

4. A servant mentality. Try to remember that you are a guest in the client's cultural world, especially if you are in a country other than your own. Strive to be:

- Sensitive
- Humble
- Authentic so people can see what you are really like
- Respectful, even when you disagree
- Flexible
- Open to new ideas
- Able to laugh, since humor calms a multitude of tensions

Much of this involves building and maintaining trust. When a coach and client seek to understand each other and respect cultural differences, coaching can move smoothly. If you sense a misunderstanding or tension, be appropriately proactive in raising the issue so different understandings can be clarified.

AN IN-COUNTRY EXAMPLE:
COACHING NEXT-GENERATION LEADERS

About ten years ago, I was invited to a conference for younger Christian leaders, all committed believers, shaped by the postmodern, media-driven, technologically sophisticated influences of their culture. When I arrived, I discovered that I was thirty years older than the conference leader, who, in turn, was at least ten years older than the conference participants. He and I had met a few months earlier and I was invited because he thought I would be open to learning from this youthful group. I accepted his challenge enthusiastically. For the next several days, I listened, interacted, and hung out. I knew about postmodernism, deconstructionism, and other trends popular at the time, but I was not prepared for the eye-opening and brain-stretching experience that I encountered. It was my introduction to what became known as the emergent church and to the perspectives of younger people comfortable in a culture different from mine and light-years away from the thinking of most people my age.[9]

At that stage in my life, I was becoming well entrenched in coaching. I was knowledgeable enough to question whether coaching could connect with younger people. With its modernistic assumptions and its roots in corporate business culture, could coaching be effective with a generation represented by those conference participants with their tattoos, body piercings, and postmodern perspectives? Over the years, I have concluded that coaching is very appropriate for the postmodern mentality but needs to be adapted. This is a cross-cultural issue that arises for any coach who wants to work with younger or postmodern clients[10] who live in the same geographical community.

The starting place for any coach is to know your audience. Effective speakers know their audiences before they get up to speak. The best missionaries and cross-cultural businesspeople become familiar with their target cultures before any significant work is begun. In similar ways, coaches who want to cross from one generational culture to another must get to know and be able to appreciate the people with whom they want to work.

Perhaps nobody does this better than Earl Creps. He's a professor, author, conference speaker, and church planter. He's also a specialist in hanging out with younger, emerging leaders. He gets to know them in coffee shops, learns about their interests and music, listens to their ideas, and tries to understand their technology (even though most of us who are over forty will never be able to keep up). Earl Creps is a mentor to many who are starved for authentic relationships with older models, but he also believes in reverse mentoring, in which younger leaders mentor those who are older and willing to learn.[11] Political analysts have proposed many theories about why Barak Obama won the presidential election, but most agree on one of the answers: Obama learned to connect with the technologically sophisticated, hope-seeking younger voters, who were such a force in the campaign.

In coaching next-generation people, there can be value in knowing some core characteristics of this group. But remember that cultures change. Because of this, the paragraphs that follow may be outdated in some ways before this book hits the market. Also, every cultural group is composed of individuals who do not fit the norm. This means that effective coaches, teachers, market-ers, and ministry leaders must adapt their methods to meet unique individual needs and emerging cultural trends. Even so, there are general characteristics that coaches are likely to discover in their cross-cultural coaching with next-generation, postmodern leaders.[12] With this group:

Values and experiences are more important than vision casting and reaching goals. The coaching circle that forms the basis of this book builds on the modernistic, results-oriented perspective that characterizes many organizations, academic institutions, and churches. This is a goal-driven perspective, widely accepted in business and in corporations where contem-porary coaching has been developed. But this view tends to be dismissed in a postmodern world where many younger people have watched their driven parents push to be successful, sometimes compromise their values, and miss life in the process.

While modern leaders are primarily motivated by vision and the desire to achieve it, young, postmodern leaders often see vision and vision casting as manipulative and presumptive. They are much more attracted to authentic values that are both articulated and practiced by the leader.

— STEVE OGNE, coauthor of *TransforMissional Coaching*

Steve Ogne understands the postmodern mind-set. He writes that "vision is still important to young leaders even though they resist the concept and the word. People still want to know where they are going," but how is this raised with postmodern coaching clients? Ogne sometimes asks a question like this: "If you live out your values for the next five years and God blesses it, what is likely to happen?" To overcome the contemporary resistance to planning, Ogne invites them to dream by telling stories about a possible future. He writes that "coaches can help postmodern leaders dream and plan by helping them see their plan or vision as a story being lived out."[13] This is a clear exam-ple of adapting more traditional coaching to impact less-traditional clients.

Images and stories are more valued than words and facts. This can be a challenge for pastors and other church leaders who build their ministries on the Word of God but know the importance of telling stories and using props, images, and video clips in sermons. Jesus told parables, rich in imag-ery, even as he presented factual truth. Coaches who connect with younger clients often use imagery, metaphors, and stories. These coaches know that stories and visual images tend to be remembered better than facts, so they listen for imagery that the clients use and bring this into conversation. For example, if somebody talks about a bridge to the future, the coach uses the bridge imagery in subsequent discussions.

Building community may be more important than building individual success. In the conference that I described at the beginning of this section, the participants did not appear to have much interest in seminars, speeches, or notebooks. But they were interested in being together, in listening to each other's stories, in building community.

William Tenny-Brittian was a graduate student when he described an approach that he called "tribal coaching." This is a process in which younger leaders are coached in the midst of a peer community rather than as individuals. There are several benefits. Tribal coaching encourages community and the building of relationships. It stimulates group learning and peer coaching based on the participants' experiences, not solely on the interventions of the coach; it is consistent with the team approach that characterizes ministry among next-generation leaders; and it taps into the belief that accountability is best found in a context of community rather than one-way accountability to a coach.[14] Similar to team or group coaching, this approach is most effective when the group is small (perhaps four to seven participants), has common needs or interests, and commits to meeting at least biweekly for several months.

Active participation and ownership are preferred over passive submission to authority and professional expertise. This is a generation that wants to be involved in planning their educational experiences, participating in multisensory worship experiences, and shaping their treatment if they go for counseling. Here is one area where coaching does not need a lot of adaptation. Coaches assume that the client sets the agenda and that each person maps out action plans in response to the coach's questions and promptings. Advice, preplanned programs, and directive top-down leadership are all shunned by the postmodern mentality.

Spirituality is valued, religion is not. Unlike older Christians, many in the younger generations do not come from religious backgrounds. They lack familiarity with basic Christian doctrine and have little awareness of biblical morals and principles. But these people want to connect with the transcendent. Many are attracted to mystical and liturgical forms of worship that may give stability and an anchor in the past, unlike their seeker-sensitive parents, who often rejected these forms of worship as outdated and irrelevant. Next-generation leaders and their peers often admire Jesus and want to know more about him, but they don't much care for churches and religion, especially religion steeped in denominations.[15] Postmodern people also value relationships with those who appear to have a faith that is genuine and a belief system that works. The Christian coach can be a powerful mentor for many who lack authentic role models.

This list could continue. In addition to what's been mentioned already, many postmodern people are deeply interested in social and ecological issues. Most have grown up immersed in technology, music, and other media. They are deeply attached—some would say addicted—to interactive communication devices that simulate their brains, let them connect continually with "friends" around the world, compete for their attention (even in coaching sessions, certainly in church), and even change the way they think. Each of these characteristics of next-generational leaders could impact the ways in which coaches and their clients work.

Coaching a postmodern leader is an endeavor like that of
a missionary heading for the Congo: First you must learn
the language, the beliefs, the understandings, and the
customs. Only then are you able to engage in conversation,
and even then there may be a learning curve that seems
insurmountable. . . . It is true that old dogs can learn new tricks,
but only when the old dog is willing to put aside their old dog
habits and are willing to suspend their old dog worldviews.

— WILLIAM TERRY-BRITTIAN, next-generation coaching leader

Culture has a huge influence on how coaching has developed, how it is done, and how it is adapted to different groups, including those who are postmodern in their thinking. The most effective coaches are likely to be those who have an awareness of cross-cultural issues and are willing to work with them.

BUILDING A COACHING CULTURE

In this chapter, we have focused on crossing cultures, but many coaches also have interest in building coaching cultures (sometimes called coaching climates) in businesses, organizations, or churches. Dr. Michael Lillibridge is an executive coach and professional speaker who was trained as a clinical psychologist. Several years ago, he developed an assessment tool known as the PeopleMap,[16] and today he works with large companies whose leaders want all of their managers and eventually all employees to relate to one another and lead using coaching principles. In one of these companies, for example, the CEO and senior leaders have each grown through coaching, so they see the value of coach training for their employees. In this way, they are building a company culture that is supportive of coaching and sensitive to coaching issues.

> A coaching culture is one in which a variety of leaders
> and managers in many functions throughout the
> organization apply coaching skills and attitudes daily,
> and they use these skills not only to develop people but
> also to manage people. In order to achieve this desired
> state, more individuals within the organization need to
> be equipped with an understanding of what is meant by
> coaching and the ability to employ basic coaching skills.
>
> — SHARON TING,
> coeditor of *Handbook of Coaching: A Guide for the Leader Coach*

The Ken Blanchard Companies are committed to becoming coaching cultures where "people have the skills, and are given permission, to have timely, relevant conversations about growth, development, performance, tasks, and goals. It's a feedback culture, where there are few surprises." It is a coach-sensitive culture where people are seen as capable, development is as important as deadlines, mistakes are regarded as opportunities for learning, and feedback is given with a "focus-forward" orientation.[17]

How are coaching cultures built? Most often they develop when top leaders in a company, association, or church have been impacted by coaching and are enthusiastic about bringing coaching into their organizations. I once worked with a company that held a coaching seminar that was required for some of the employees but not attended by any company leaders. After the invited speaker left, everybody went back to work and very little changed. Then several months later there was another seminar, in which the trainer learned about the company before the workshop and tried to adapt his comments to the company culture. All of the top company leaders were present as participants in the seminar, and at the end it was announced that coach training would become an important part of how the company would develop in the future. A full-time coach development leader was hired and, as anticipated, the interest in coaching and its impact both grew quickly.

Before the seminar was held, the company leaders had developed a follow-up program that was in place, ready to begin on the Monday after the training workshop ended. Following the seminar, each participant was expected to coach at least one person on his or her work team. Two of these coaching sessions were observed by a master coach who provided each participant with support, feedback, and opportunity for evaluation.

Sometimes outside coaches are brought in to facilitate the development of a coaching climate. Alternatively or in addition, selected company employees may be trained as coaches and given coaching responsibilities as a part of their duties. Often coaching is integrated into leadership development or other training programs. If the momentum is not allowed to fade and if there is evidence that coaching increases productivity and effectiveness, coaching eventually becomes a way of operation and leadership within the organization. It's a slow process, but eventually the coaching mentality permeates the whole environment.

What applies to companies in the development of coaching climates can apply as well to churches and parachurch organizations. Of course, Jesus called us to make disciples, not to build coaching cultures. We exist to praise God—to love, honor, and serve him—but coaching might be one of the tools he has allowed us to discover and use to be more effective in honoring him and ministering to others. Coaching can be used to his glory provided we remember that coaching, including coaching across cultures, is a tool to accomplish greater divine purposes.

CHAPTER 21

THE CHALLENGES OF COACHING

I'M NOT SURE where I first met Dan. For a while we attended the same church and we still see each other on occasion, mostly when we meet in a store or exchange a few greetings as we pass on the street. Sometimes we'll stop and talk about coaching and Dan's efforts to build a private practice as a coach. It's not been easy.

When he first encountered coaching, he was hooked immediately. He took a couple of coaching courses, heard about professional coaches who were earning significant incomes in their work, and discovered that he had potential to become a good coach. "I love coaching," Dan has told me more than once. "I'm passionate about it." Perhaps without much investigation, Dan quit his job and decided to open a coaching practice. He started a coaching newsletter, learned ways to market his services, and concluded that he had found his niche in life. But like thousands of others, Dan has not been able to find paying clients. Occasionally, he takes another course or attends a coaching conference, but Dan is a coach who can't find people who want his coaching, especially if they are expected to pay.

There are many others who have similar stories. They've developed competence in coaching and believe in its potential to change lives. These people are big supporters of coaching, and their enthusiasm is reinforced whenever they get together with other coaches. Buoyed by their belief in the possibilities of coaching, most coaches appear to have high levels of energy and enthusiasm. These aren't the only requirements for effective coaching, but without energy and enthusiasm, nobody is likely to get far in this field. But even optimists and enthusiasts begin to realize that the coaching field faces challenges that must be addressed. In time, most of the challenging issues are likely to be resolved, but today they bring needed caution to the runaway enthusiasm that still characterizes much of the coaching movement.

It's not much fun to face obstacles. I'd prefer to delete this chapter from the book and you may have the urge to skip it. Some of what appears in the following paragraphs might be disturbing. If we face those challenges head-on, however, we can avoid being blinded by them, find ways to overcome them, and move forward to become better, more effective coaches. In many ways, this is the fourth part of our coaching circle, applied to ourselves as coaches. This is looking at the obstacles and getting past them.

THE CHALLENGE OF COMPETENCE:
WHO IS QUALIFIED TO COACH?

In most places, anybody can claim to be a coach and start a coaching business whether or not that person has any training, coaching experience, or proof of competence. If self-proclaimed or minimally trained coaches are persuasive, enthusiastic, and effective as self-promoters, they might attract and even help clients, but these "coaches" also have the potential to misunderstand, mislead, and even cause harm.

As an example, consider the damage that could come when inadequately trained coaches have no understanding of emotional illnesses or the principles of counseling. Several years ago, a powerful article in *Harvard Business Review* warned of the "very real dangers" that come when executive coaches fail to spot evidence of psychological dysfunction in clients and sometimes coach in ways that make the emotional problems worse.[1] In Australia, researcher Anthony M. Grant found that between 25 and 52 percent of life coaching clients may have significant mental health problems, yet this issue is rarely discussed in coaching circles. Grant concludes that "many coaching clients are seeing coaching as a socially acceptable form of therapy." He argues that "the coaching industry has a clear duty . . . to insure that coach training covers the essentials of mental health so coaches can recognize and refer appropriately."[2] Despite cautions like this, even high-quality training programs never mention the symptoms or impact of mental illness as these relate to coaching. As a result, well-intentioned coaches miss unhealthy attitudes, behavior, and influences that need intervention from trained mental health professionals.

In response, many coaches correctly note that they are not therapists. But they also are not fully competent or responsible if they are not skilled enough to spot issues that can interfere with coaching and that should be treated by a trained counselor rather than a coach. It is easy to understand why psychologists and other counseling professionals often have reservations about the coaching industry, wondering if many coaches are inadvertently contributing to mental health problems or practicing therapy without training or licensing credentials.

An additional concern is the negative impact that incompetent or poorly trained coaches have on the coaching field in general. When people without expertise claim to be coaches and charge money for their services, how does that influence the integrity and image of the coaching industry? How does this incompetence reflect on the work of those who are well trained and genuinely qualified to coach in their areas of expertise? Even more disturbing is the tendency of some professional counselors to move into coaching because they want to be free of the ethical and legal restraints of the established mental health professions. The whole field of coaching is harmed as a result of these practices.

In the midst of these concerns, enthusiasm for coaching is growing, despite the reality that some people in the field lack competence, high standards, or common sense. The good news is that various groups in the coaching industry are actively addressing the challenges about competency. Already these issues are being resolved and will become less of a problem as ethical standards are developed further and applied, training programs for coaches become more standardized and affordable, and people looking for coaches learn clearer guidelines for finding competent coaching assistance.[3]

THE CHALLENGE OF CREDENTIALS: IS CERTIFICATION NECESSARY?

When I decided to become certified as a coach, I was confronted with several questions that others surely face as well: *How do I select a good training program from all of the schools that are available? How do I distinguish between a certification program that has high standards and widespread respect as opposed to programs that give little more than a certificate or set of meaningless initials to put after my name if I pay a fee? Do I even need certification? Will certification help me be more effective as a coach? Does certification really indicate that the certified person has special expertise and effectiveness?* Questions like these are at the core of an ongoing debate about the value and quality of coach training and credentialing.

Coach training courses can be very useful and probably all certification programs provide at least some valuable learning. Many give credentials that indicate proven competence. But training and certification are only as good as the groups that train and certify. And while certified coaches often cite and take pride in their credentials, there is evidence that certification doesn't matter much to most clients or to organizations that hire coaches.[4] These potential clients are more concerned about the coach's competence and proven ability to deliver results.

In the midst of debate about coach training, credentials, and certification, there are increasing efforts to improve quality and bring standardization to the diversified, coach-training industry. As more new coaches want to enter the field, it is probable that training and coach certification programs will continue to proliferate. This could lead to a greater need for objective and respected indicators of each coach's competence.

There is danger, however, that the accreditation of coach training programs or the certification of coaches could strangle rather than liberate credential seekers. Some academic accrediting programs force training institutions and individuals into the value-shaped molds of the people who give the credentials. This in turn can squelch creativity or stifle perspectives that differ from perspectives of the accrediting organizations. It is possible to set credentialing standards so low that they are meaningless, but they also can be set so high and made so expensive that new people are prevented from entering the coaching guild. These may be minor issues at present, but they could become major. You may prefer to steer clear of further training or credentialing issues, but sooner or later they are likely to influence what you can do as a coach or coach trainer.

THE CHALLENGE OF CREDIBILITY: HOW DO WE KNOW THAT COACHING REALLY WORKS?

In their competition for students, coach training schools sometimes make flamboyant claims for the effectiveness of coaching and coach training.[5] But do we really have solid evidence that coaching is effective? Stories of coaching success abound, but even beginning researchers know that testimonies from satisfied customers are highly subjective and not necessarily accurate indicators of success. Corporations that hire and pay for coaches, and some individual clients as well, want to see more convincing evidence that coaching actually works and has the credibility that its enthusiastic supporters proclaim. This demand for proof to back up our claims can be a challenge, but it can become a great boost for the coaching field, especially when we can show convincingly that our work really is effective.

We need to be sure that the coaching industry does not fall
into the trap of making wide and unsubstantiated claims
about its effectiveness. Coaching is not a panacea. There is no
research to show, and no reason to believe, that coaching will
create the life of your wildest dreams.

— ANTHONY M. GRANT, director of Coaching Psychology Unit,
University of Sydney

A variety of methods have been used to evaluate coaching. These include:

- **Subjective reports.** The simplest but probably most biased approach is to ask individual coaches or clients to express their opinions or give testimonies about the coaching they have experienced. Apparently, this is the most common method used in organizations.[6]
- **Questionnaires and surveys.** These also are subjective and open to bias or inaccuracy, especially if the questions are poorly phrased or the respondents don't tell the truth. Even so, this is more systematic than individual personal stories. Some coaches or companies give a coach-satisfaction questionnaire to clients one month into a coaching assignment and at three-month intervals until the coaching is completed. This allows individual coaching to be evaluated and gives broader data about overall coaching effectiveness as surveys are combined and results are summarized.
- **The 360 feedback.** Common in corporate settings, 360 instruments are questionnaires about job performance, interpersonal skills, leadership abilities, attitudes, or almost any other trait or behavior an individual might demonstrate at work. In a company or organization, the 360 questionnaires may be completed by an individual's subordinates, superiors, supervisors, peers, customers, or anyone else who surrounds the person like the 360 degrees of a circle. Most often the person being evaluated also completes a self-questionnaire. To encourage honesty, the feedback is given anonymously. The result is a picture of how individuals are perceived by the people who observe and work with them most closely. As used in coaching, the 360 evaluation is done at the beginning and at the end to determine if coaching has made any difference. Sometimes, in addition, other psychological tests are used in the same before and after way.

- **Return on investment (ROI).** This is the least common method of evaluation, in part because it may be the most difficult. Especially in demanding financial times, companies want evidence that the cost of coaching leads to increased financial and other benefits. This is the desire for evidence to show what returns come back in exchange for the investments (ROI) that have been made in coaching. If there are no measurable or demonstrated benefits, often the coaching is terminated.
- **Evidence-based research.** At some time, every coach and the entire coaching industry is likely to be asked for a persuasive answer to this question: "What is the clear evidence that the specific methods used in coaching are effective and really able to produce the changes they claim to bring?"

  The search for evidence-based methods has become a big issue in the mental health professions, in which insurance companies and others who pay for services want evidence for the effectiveness of each method or intervention. In counseling, "evidence-based practice" refers to the work of psychologists or others who only use methods that have been shown to be effective, based on objective empirical research, the informed observations of competent practitioners, and the reported preferences and experiences of counselees. Coaches are joining these counseling colleagues in recognizing the importance of research to determine what works. Some early conclusions are reported in a handbook on evidence-based coaching. According to the author-editors, "relevant coaching methodologies that incorporate both rigor and the lived experience of practitioners and clients will result in a comprehensive, flexible, and strong model of coaching."[7] The book is scholarly and not always interesting to read. But for those with a more serious interest in coaching, this is a good resource to separate solid coaching principles from what the authors describe as coaching "developed from the 'pop-psychology' personal development genre."[8]

To remain robust in the future, coaching may need empirical and other evidence to show that proven results match the enthusiasm of coaching advocates. At present, coaching has a weak research and credibility base, but this is changing. The quality of research is beginning to improve and the data-based evidence for coaching's effectiveness is growing.

THE CHALLENGE OF PROFESSIONALISM: IS COACHING A PROFESSION?

There are those who see no need to debate this issue. For them, coaching is a profession like any other. A contrasting view maintains that coaching is not a true profession even though it might reach that status eventually. Unlike established professions, coaching is an unlicensed and largely unregulated field. There are no accepted criteria for being a coach — anyone can claim and use that title — and no generally accepted accreditation standards for coach training schools. At present, the coaching industry has little credibility or presence in academic circles, has a very limited scholarly research base, and has no ability to enforce standards of training, practice, and ethics despite the admirable ethical codes and efforts of several coaching organizations. Coaches from around the world are coming together to raise standards for training and practice so that coaching can continue to emerge into an increasingly respectable and useful field.[9] But until standards are enforced and policed, declarations and codes of ethics are no more than useful but generally ineffective guidelines.[10]

Partly as a result of the increased academic interest in coaching, we have seen the bar raised substantially in the coaching industry. Both coaching clients and people looking for coach training are demanding that coaching have a solid evidence-based approach. But coaching is still a long way from being a real profession. There are still not barriers to entry. Anyone can call themselves a coach. More disturbingly, anyone can set themselves up as a trainer of coaches — even those with no qualifications or training at all. Many coach-training schools do a very good job. However, these are issues and difficult questions that have not, as yet, been addressed.

— ANTHONY M. GRANT, coaching researcher, University of Sydney

THE CHALLENGE OF VALUES:
TO WHAT EXTENT IS COACHING CONSISTENT
WITH BIBLICAL TRUTH?

There is no such thing as value-free coaching. Everybody has values and so does every profession. Read books on coaching or take coaching courses and you will see values that reflect the backgrounds and beliefs of those who write or teach. Perhaps you will notice that these values are rarely acknowledged or mentioned explicitly, no doubt because most of us take our values for granted and rarely think about them. But it does not take long for the sensitive Christian to notice the secular assumptions that form the basis of most contemporary coaching. For example, consider the great push in some coaches to get clients, build prominence, gain credibility, and make a lot of money, especially in the corporate world, where payment for coaching services is high. The engines of consumerism and materialism never drove Jesus or his followers, but they drive a lot of our society. Do they drive too much professional coaching, including Christian coaching?

Earlier chapters have noted the extent to which coaching is built on humanistic psychology and a widespread belief that reality is based on our subjective experiences. In addition, "coaching has many direct and indirect links to eastern thinking . . . especially Zen Buddhism" that has "avoided outward trappings of worship and instead embraced self-awareness."[11] Maybe the most rock-bottom assumption of coaching is that all the answers to all of our needs and problems are found within. According to one insightful analysis, "coaching rose from the self-development movement and is commercialized and packaged like many self-development courses. 'You deserve to live your dream—now!' has been a powerful message coming from many channels. . . . The coach is for you, for no one else, to work with you on your life, your goals become who you want to be."[12] This permeates much of the coaching movement.

Without being aware of these foundational coaching assumptions, many Christian coaches might embrace the core coaching values without thinking. Hopefully, it is more common for Christian coaches to base their work on a different foundation, one built on what we believe to be the Word of God as revealed in the Bible. We assume that all of us, coaches and clients, are valuable people, created in God's image, marred by our fall into sin but able to be redeemed because Christ died for our sins. We value coaching as a flawed but useful tool that God can use as one of his ways to bring change, but we do not believe that all answers are within, nor do we assume that coaching is about the client's goals exclusively, with no awareness of biblical values or

God's will. The Scriptures give us guidelines for living, wisdom from God himself, and a pathway to abundant life on earth and eternal life after death through our belief in Jesus Christ, God's Son.[13]

Many of us also would challenge the widely held belief that coaching can be completely nondirective. We let clients set their own agendas and we seek to help them set their own life courses, but we know that complete nondirective coaching is a myth, just as nondirective counseling has been shown to be impossible. Even coaches who believe in the nondirective approach sometimes ask clients for permission to share guidelines, challenges, support, and even suggestions that come from the coach's external observations and experiences.

While my way of being with a coaching client may be Rogerian and client-centered, my coaching worldview and treatment plan is Christ-centered. The Scriptures are replete with admonitions to make plans, set goals, and strive toward the finish line. Paul encouraged us to think on admirable, true, and right things and to put these things into practice (Phil. 4). As well, Peter admonished us to add goodness, knowledge, perseverance, etc., to our faith in increasing measure (2 Peter 1). These are scriptures which motivate us forward . . . "forgetting what is behind" and to strain toward the goal (Phil. 3). I believe that God purposefully imbued humankind with a spark of creativity and optimism which, through the power of the Holy Spirit, encourages us forward.

—THOMAS GRAY,
coaching and counseling practitioner, Jerusalem

CONCERNS ABOUT EXPECTATIONS: WHAT IS THE COST OF BECOMING A COACH?

Christopher McCluskey took a big risk when he shut down his counseling practice, moved to a different part of the country, and began to build a coaching business. The McCluskey family chose to live on a farm in an isolated part of the country, far from any city where coaching clients might be found. It was clear from the beginning that finding clients and doing coaching would mostly need to be done by telephone. All of this involved a heavy financial and emotional cost. It's a cost that few coaches anticipate on their way to success.[14] It's a cost that was not considered by Dan, whose story started this chapter.

Some people are able to get coaching jobs within companies, churches, or organizations, but these positions are difficult to find, especially for people without experience. Others move into coaching part-time, working their regular jobs and coaching in the evenings or weekends often without pay. Like any business, building a coaching practice will take more time. To be successful, independent practitioners need to know about marketing, business plans, taxation, legal incorporation, and the other elements of running an independent business. In addition, potential clients will need to be educated on the nature and benefits of coaching. Even more challenging might be the difficulty of convincing potential clients to pay.[15]

Regardless of where it is done, coaching can be challenging and rewarding, but it's not always easy and sometimes it is not even positive. If you are a coach, you won't connect with all of your clients and not all of them will connect at a high level of rapport with you. Whenever this happens, it is best to discuss tensions openly. Sometimes there are personality or value differences that are too big to overcome. At other times, the person being coached may be resisting or sabotaging the coaching process so that progress is impeded. In some cases the problem may be with the coach. If you sense a lack of progress, consider whether or not you are out of your comfort zone or area of proficiency. Might you be trying to move the coaching in directions that may be important to you but not to the client, trying to impress the person you are coaching, preoccupied with other things so you don't really listen, not showing respect, being judgmental or patronizing, sexually attracted to the client, or acting like a parent? Coaches are not hired to set another person's agenda or direct another person's life, and you will get resistance if you try. Maybe we all slide into one or more of these weaknesses at times, but an honest discussion of the relationship, sometimes with your own coach or accountability partner, can alert you to attitudes and mannerisms that you might not have seen. Sometimes the best way to handle a less-than-ideal coaching experience is to graciously end the relationship and encourage the client to let somebody else take over.

WHERE DO WE GO FROM HERE?

When he read the preceding paragraphs, one reviewer wrote that this chapter was "difficult to get through—kind of scary." It puts a cloud over the sunny portrayals of coaching that appear in earlier chapters. Even so, my reviewer friend concluded that "from a professional standpoint, all the points are important and necessary and in need of saying." Encountering challenges like these and overcoming the present obstacles enable all of us to become better coaches. Behind these clouds there is blue sky and a bright future for Christian coaching. That's where we will go in our concluding chapter. Please keep reading.

CHAPTER 22

THE FUTURE
OF COACHING

A FEW WEEKS before this book was completed, a group of sixty-three people from sixteen countries gathered in Ireland for an in-depth conference on coaching. They represented a larger group of 250 coaching practitioners, consumers of coaching, educators, corporate leaders, and representatives of coaching organizations. For more than a year, these people had spent roughly 10,000 hours connecting internationally, talking about coaching, focusing on its strengths and its needs, setting an agenda for the future. There were many differences among this diverse group, but they had a common belief in the "power of coaching to unlock the potential of people, organizations, and society." They shared a desire to cooperate in nurturing the growth and maturity of their emerging profession. For five days, the working group in Ireland pulled together the conclusions from around the world and produced what they termed *The Dublin Declaration on Coaching*.[1] Quickly this document emerged as a concise statement on the status of the "global community of coaches," including recommendations for improving the quality and impact of coaching.

The Dublin Declaration is academic, scholarly, and not always easy to read. Unless you have a special interest in coaching, you may not want to study its contents. You can coach effectively without knowing what the coaching experts expect for the future. We all know that apart from God, nobody can predict how coaching or anything else will develop in the next few years. But as summarized in table 22-1, the Dublin document points to significant issues that are likely to shape the way coaches do their work in the next decade or two.

Table 22-1

THE DUBLIN DECLARATION ON COACHING

The Dublin Declaration on Coaching is a two-page statement with nine appendixes. Each gives a current status, list of issues and concerns, and "stakes in the ground" recommendation for future development and improvement. The nine appendixes are as follows:

- **Professional Status of Coaching.** Coaching draws on multiple disciplines and cultures. How does coaching establish itself as a standardized and recognized profession?
- **Knowledge Base of Coaching.** There is no body of knowledge that specifically defines coaching as in fields like medicine, pharmacology, or psychology. Coaches need an agreed-upon knowledge base.
- **Research in Coaching.** "Research is the life blood of practice," but there are different definitions of research. How can we stimulate more effective, universally recognized research to demonstrate the effectiveness of coaching?
- **Core Competencies in Coaching.** What are the core skills for coaching? Is coaching different in different cultures, countries, and contexts. Can there be universally accepted coaching competencies?
- **Ethics in Coaching.** There are various ethical codes for coaches. There is need for a universal ethics code accompanied by practical guidelines for ethical practice and decision making.
- **Education and Development of Coaching.** Currently, there is great diversity in the quality, formats, and nature of training and credentialing. How can these be standardized internationally? What kinds of education and training are most effective?
- **Mapping the Field of Coaching.** Coaching draws from many disciplines, especially psychology, and has many definitions. How do we clarify what coaching really involves and how it differs from related fields and professions?
- **Selection of Coaches and Evaluating of Coaching.** There are no generally accepted selection criteria, operational standards, practice guidelines, or criteria for evaluating coaching effectiveness. How can these be developed carefully and how soon?
- **Society and Coaching.** Coaching occurs in various contexts, including pay-for-services settings, nonprofit situations, organizations, and society. How can coaches make their skills available to people of all walks of life?

Several years ago, a popular book enthusiastically chronicled the emergence and potential of coaching.[2] The authors wrote about managers who recognize that in a changing workplace, they need to coach—not dictate to—the people they manage. To get results from their teams, supervisors must give up the old command-and-control approach and embrace a coaching model that empowers people to unlock their full potential. There can be numerous payoffs for bringing coaching into the workplace, according to the book's authors. The benefits of coaching include increased productivity, efficiency, reliability, and profitability. Employees are able to reach their full potential when they get individualized attention from coaches and coach managers. In turn, this enables workers to build better careers, happier lives, and stronger relationships.

This may be overly optimistic, but it reflects the widespread enthusiasm about coaching that we have mentioned earlier. One successful coach trainer recently wrote about her passion for coaching and her love of "how it taps the core of human potential and takes people to places they'd never dreamed possible." Other writers have argued that coaching was a method used by Jesus,[3] an approach to ministry and people helping that has potential for use throughout the Christian community. "Jesus did more than coach," write Linda Miller and Chad Hall. "He mentored. He taught. He healed. He atoned for our sins. After all, the world needed a Savior, not a coach. But while Jesus and coaching are not synonymous, we can fix our eyes upon strong similarities between the two."[4] And we can look forward to ways in which Christian coaching can have growing impact in the coming years.

> After spending a lifetime studying the character of Jesus, and the better part of my career working with leaders, I have come to this conclusion. There is no better role model for coaching that gets lasting results than Jesus of Nazareth.
>
> —LAURIE BETH JONES, author of *Jesus, Life Coach*

INNOVATIONS AND FUTURE TRENDS

In times of radical change, it gets progressively harder to anticipate the future. About all we know for sure is that God is still in control and that we will have more and faster change. What I write in these pages may be old by the time you read these words, but even broad speculations could help us shape the future direction of Christian coaching. Undoubtedly, you will have others to add.

Christian coaching will become better known and better accepted. A few years ago, coaching was identified only with athletics. This is not true any more. Almost everybody knows about voice coaches and fitness coaches at health clubs. The media, education, and the arts know about coaching and so do many people in business. Executive coaching has grown in influence although only a few years ago it was likened to "the Wild West of yesteryear, [where] the frontier is chaotic, largely unexplored, and fraught with risk, yet immensely promising."[5] In the past decade, life coaching has extended its influence even though the promise of lucrative private practices for life coaches has proven to be more fantasy than reality. Christian coaching is growing as well, but church leaders sometimes are reluctant to jump onto what may seem like another fad, this one imported from the corporate world without much apparent relevance to ministry. In all of these areas, coaching principles are likely to be accepted more broadly as their relevance becomes more apparent and coaching settles in as a proven way to help people who want guidance but see no need for counseling.

Better training and more resources are coming. We have seen that the number of formal training programs has exploded during the past few years. Some universities and colleges have begun to see the value of degree programs and practicum experiences in coaching, although acceptance of coaching in academia is likely to be slow as long as coaching has a limited research basis and little credibility as an academic discipline. More common are coaching courses in business schools and training programs for counselors. Most often coaching is taught in unaccredited independent training programs that vary significantly in rigor and quality. As the competition for students gets greater, however, hopefully the better programs will thrive while the others fade away. Books, journals, and short-term training resources are appearing with more frequency, but once again the quality varies.

Developing technology will be to the coach's advantage. Technology has emerged as a prime facilitator of coaching, especially life coaching. Consider the following ideas and then add your own to the list:

- The widespread use of webcam communication through the Internet enables coaching and coach training to be done face-to-face and free of cost around the world. This includes one-on-one interaction but also permits coaching and training with more than two people involved.
- Distance learning, using technology, enables trainees to take

academic courses in coaching, interact with other students, hold small-group discussions within the same class, supervise practice coaching experiences, and view PowerPoint slides, video clips, and demonstrations.

- Through various wireless devices, it is possible to exchange documents, provide ongoing accountability, and facilitate easy communication across the street or across the world.

Increasingly organizations are interested in teaching their leaders to be better coaches on the job, a *leader-as-coach* concept. We see a rise in the number of training programs with this aim in mind. Organizations are seeking to engender a more robust coaching culture by equipping their leaders as coaches with coaching skills.

— BRIAN O. UNDERHILL, coauthor of *Executive Coaching for Results*

Increasingly, coaching will be the foundation for leadership. In earlier chapters, we have seen that the very essence of leadership is changing and so is the church.[6] Effective organizations and churches do not want outsiders, including denominations, telling them what to do. Already the most effective businesses and ministries are built around teams of people empowered and turned loose to change their organizations and the world creatively. We are seeing congregations change from tradition-bound institutions into teams. In some places, pastors are changing from dry didactic teachers into mentor-coaches who motivate, encourage, point people to biblical truth, and are empowered by the Holy Spirit to stimulate others to grow. In the world where we live, "everybody on the team is a leader, and everybody on the team is a follower, and the coach helps each player discern when to be one or the other."[7] When it is summarized in a few sentences, this may sound like a radical paradigm change in leadership, but it appears to be penetrating the business world and other organizations. This could revolutionize the way we do ministry. And it has coaching at its core, increasingly emerging as the new model for leadership.

Coaching is expanding from a relationship between two people to team, group, and peer approaches. One trend in coaching is working with a team of people simultaneously, including small groups, boards, and even whole companies or congregations. Peer coaching also involves more than two people but focuses on equipping team members, class participants, or church members to coach one another. This is like the lay counseling that has been effective for many years in congregations. In a similar way, leadership training programs teach managers and others to use coaching in their day-to-day leadership and work with others.

The discipline of coaching is moving beyond professionalism and into mainstream relationships. Much of the discussion in this and the previous chapter has concerned professional coaching in which a trained and certified coach offers coaching services in return for payment. This might be your present or hoped-for place in the coaching field. But what if you have no intention of becoming a professional coach, getting coach training, or charging for your services? What if you see coaching as a way to serve others, to express your spiritual gifts, to contribute to your church and serve Christ? What if your goal is to use coaching methods in your work and life but without any intention of calling yourself a coach? Is there a place for you in the coaching revolution?

I believe that the answer is yes, despite the challenges we reviewed in the preceding chapter. Consider the fields of counseling, psychology, and other mental health professions. Each has emerged as a specialty with high standards for training, rigorous guidelines for credentialing, and — in many countries — legal restrictions on who is licensed to practice in exchange for a fee. This does not limit anyone from informally counseling friends, nor does this restrict pastors from counseling their parishioners or teachers from counseling students. The professional and legal restrictions do not apply as long as the people who counsel do not identify themselves as professionals or charge a fee. The same is likely to be true of coaching should it become more professionalized and licensed.

Many, perhaps most, readers of this book will use coaching principles in their work, life, or ministries without calling themselves coaches or charging fees. You may have been coaching for years, long before you read this book or heard about an emerging coaching profession. Maybe your whole lifestyle has involved coaching others. This comes naturally to you, just as it seems natural for people to come into your life seeking your guidance. But you are unlikely to turn these experiences into a coaching business.

Wherever you are, ask God to bring people to you for coaching. Seek him for wisdom and commit your coaching to his guidance and blessing. Find at least one other person to whom you can be accountable, especially so you don't make the mistake of inadvertently pushing your personal concerns or agendas onto others. Resolve to apply the principles of this book. Commit to more training or reading if you can get it. Periodically check the website that accompanies this book (www.christiancoachingbook.com) to get updates on training opportunities and information about new resources. And watch God work through you to coach others and change lives.

SELF-CARE AND SELF-COACHING

Working with people can be draining even if you work with positive, well-functioning individuals who want coaching to improve their lives. Probably burnout is less common in coaches than in counselors, but all people helpers can wear themselves out when they work intensively with others. The antidotes to burnout are difficult to apply, but they are well known:

- Learn to set and maintain boundaries.
- Get control of your phone, e-mail, text messages, and wireless devices.
- Make time for rest, relaxation, and exercise.
- Avoid working until bedtime. Especially avoid staring at screens because they can suppress the production of sleep-inducing melatonin in the brain.
- Keep consistent contact with people who are supportive, fun to be with, and not involved in your work.
- De-clutter your schedule, removing energy drainers that can suck creativity and productivity from your life.
- Take time to stimulate your brain through reading, listening to or playing music, or other desired activities.
- Frequently take time to reflect, journal, and realign your life direction.
- Connect with a coach who can keep you accountable.
- Above all, make time for God, prayer, Bible study, and worship, both private and corporate.

What about self-coaching? Should that be added to the list? Can coaches or anybody else coach themselves?

"I've done it," said Marjorie Wall Hofer when she was interviewed for this book, "but it's not as successful as having a coach. Coaching yourself is dependent on knowing the techniques and tools that make coaching such an effective method for changing behavior and achieving results. Most people do not know these. I've coached myself regarding parenting issues around work issues. The way I've done it is by setting goals, identifying the blocks and problems associated with them, and creating new and different approaches. With all that said, the biggest changes I've experienced have come from working with a coach. Self-coaching is never as effective as having a coach. Coaches give you the information you've been missing or a different perspective of the situation or a new game to play to win at the old game. Coaches hit you with the right question at the best time to help you make the necessary shift. And a coach holds you accountable."

This skepticism about self-coaching was shared by most of the coaches I consulted. You can ask yourself questions, reflect on the answers, and take tests to increase self-knowledge, but it is impossible to keep an objective perspective with yourself, ask pointed questions, see yourself as others see you, and hold yourself accountable without letting yourself off the hook. You might be able to climb a mountain by yourself, but it is better if someone more experienced climbs with you, giving encouragement, pointing out the dangers you might not notice, reminding you to pace yourself, genuinely believing in you, and urging you on when you feel like quitting.

Fading motivation—the slowing down that eventually brings you to a standstill—probably is the biggest hurdle in any self-help activity. It is hard to keep motivated when you diet alone, go on a solo exercise program, launch out on keeping New Year's resolutions, or take a video or Internet course "in the privacy of your own home." It's even tougher to improve your leadership skills on your own or begin spiritual discipline without someone to encourage and hold you accountable. Follow-up and permanent change after seminars is most likely when coaches help participants remember their action plans, keep applying the seminar learning, and get past motivation lags or other obstacles. A sensitive coach can be the person who comes alongside in these situations and helps you climb.

Even so, some principles of coaching do work when applied to oneself. For self-coaching to be of greatest effectiveness, you must be highly motivated and take action to apply the choices and changes you want to implement. It is best if you have another person to hold you accountable, give encouragement, discuss your progress, challenge your thinking, and bring an outsider's perspective. Recognize too that ultimate transformation is from God. Progress in self-coaching is most effective when it is guided by the Holy Spirit.

To begin, write down one, two, or at most three issues in your life that you would like to see change. Be specific. For example, do not write, "Be a lot happier." That is too vague. Ask what specific change might make you happier. For example, "Have time to read and listen to music at least twice a week for one hour each time," "Get all the stuff cleaned out of the garage,"

"Get a promotion at work." These are all specific and measurable.

Then go through the circle model summarized in chapter 7. Use this as a guideline for your self-coaching. Ask God to guide your reflections. Review parts three, four, and five of this book. Complete the questionnaires and forms in the appendixes. Write down your responses, including your vision, goals, plans for making progress, and specific action steps with completion dates. Recognize again that all of this is likely to be better when you enlist the assistance of a friend to walk through the process with you, give encouragement, and hold you accountable.

You might feel skeptical about the value of coaching yourself, but not all coaches share this attitude. Consider Cheryl Richardson, undoubtedly the most popular advocate of self-coaching. Richardson is a Master Certified Coach who was the first president of the International Coach Federation and voted one of the top ten coaches in America by readers of *Professional Coach* magazine. After several years of success in coaching leaders, she put her coaching principles into a popular book that soared to the top of the *New York Times'* best-seller list and launched a series of talk-show appearances that have made both Cheryl Richardson and coaching increasingly well known.[8]

Richardson and her readers clearly believe that coaching principles can be applied to oneself but don't work unless people take action based on what they read or plan for their lives. She writes that "taking action is the only way to create positive, long-lasting change in your life."[9] To make this lasting change, the most powerful motivating force is a partner or group of like-minded friends who also are interested in changing their lives for the better. Early in her writing career, Richardson concluded that people who buy books on self-coaching often read the chapters but never apply the principles. This isn't because they aren't motivated; it's because other things crowd out the best intentions and without someone holding us accountable, our self-improvement plans go by the wayside.

From a Christian perspective, there is a greater issue to consider in self-coaching, even when motivation is maintained and when people who coach themselves have coaching partners. Human beings are sinful, imperfect people, unable to bring about self-transformation. We can work to change ourselves and others can help us, but it is only God who changes lives. That's why the most effective coaching occurs when the coach and client seek the guidance and transforming power of the Holy Spirit in changing life directions. The books by Cheryl Richardson and others undoubtedly have been helpful to many people, but these authors leave out the biblical perspective, assume we all have the inner power to remake ourselves, and forget God in the process.

The Bible is filled with suggestions for self-improvement. Some sections of the Bible might even seem like coaching guides. In one of his letters, for example, the apostle Peter tells his readers to "make every effort" to add certain qualities to their lives: goodness, knowledge, self-control, perseverance, godliness, brotherly kindness, and love. People who work on building these characteristics are promised that they will be kept from being ineffective and unproductive.[10]

But these instructions for character building are not given as self-transforming actions we can take on our own. Peter also writes that God's divine power has given us everything we need for life and godliness through our knowledge of him.[11] Apparently, God expects us to both work on self-improvement and accept the transformation that comes from Jesus Christ through the Holy Spirit. Coaching, including self-coaching, will have limited success in changing lives permanently if it leaves out God. The coaching that is most effective is coaching done by a person with coach training who seeks the power and guidance of the Spirit of God. That's Christian coaching.

POSSIBILITIES AND PENGUINS

For many years, first as a student and later as a practitioner, professor, and writer, I have watched Christian counseling evolve. It has grown from an infant profession, at first strongly resisted by some articulate and critical church leaders, and evolved into a large and well-developed area of helping, used by God to bring healing and spiritual renewal probably to millions.

Along with its growth, however, Christian counseling has gone in some unhealthy directions. Students and professors talk about integrating our Christian beliefs into everything we do as counselors, but often there is more talk than action. We want to please God and be guided by the Holy Spirit, but too many among us are more focused on pleasing our professional organizations and being guided by the personal motives of building counseling practices and being successful. We want to use our knowledge to help underdeveloped people, but our training mostly focuses on helping people like ourselves. Even with a growing awareness of populations in need and a growing sensitivity to people at risk, there still is relatively minor emphasis on social or ethnic differences and the need for cultural adaptation of our counseling. These trends in the field do not apply to everyone, not even to a majority, but they show how a Christian helping profession can turn subtly away from biblical values and not look to God when helping people. In Christian coaching, we must not make similar mistakes.

The future of the Christian coaching movement is bright, with new coaches entering the field, new leadership emerging, new methods, new training, and new utilization of up-to-date technology. I am most excited about the potential of Christian coaching to impact ordinary people in our church pews, frustrated people in our neighborhoods and communities, and hope-deprived people in countries around the world. Our current methods of coaching will have to be adapted to make them relevant. They will have to be acculturated and redesigned for international use. The coaching area still is being shaped by older people, often dedicated people with years of experience. I see it emerging as a field that increasingly will captivate the young, who can mold and adapt it into a tool that can reach a postmodern generation and be used by God to have a great impact.

Get out there and coach!

— THOMAS G. BANDY, author of *Coaching Change*

I don't know if this is fact or fiction, but I once read about penguins wanting to jump into water but never knowing if there might be predators lurking beneath the surface. To find out if the water is safe, one of the birds jumps in — a first penguin. It's a risky venture. Sometimes the results are disastrous, at least for the first penguin, but at other times the first penguin becomes a leader. He or she jumps in and everyone else follows and swims together.[12]

I hope this book has informed you about coaching and even stimulated your enthusiasm. Maybe you go away encouraged about becoming a coach. Perhaps you have been influenced by the challenges facing the coaching field, motivated to make things better. Most exciting for me would be if some readers, young in age or young at heart, have caught a glimpse of the potential of coaching to impact the world. Maybe your mind is forming big visions for the future of coaching, goals to reach, plans for action. Maybe God will use you to take risks and become a leader in the Christian coaching field, unlikely as that may seem when you first read this sentence. Maybe my concluding six words about coaching will apply to you:

Jump in.

Be a first penguin!

APPENDIXES

GRAPH OF LIFE

HOW SATISFIED ARE you with different parts of your life? Circle a number from 1 to 10 next to each of the following areas of life. If you give an item a 1, you are completely dissatisfied with that part of your life. A 10 means you are completely satisfied and couldn't be happier with this part of life.

Your overall satisfaction will change from day to day, but try to give an overall assessment of **where you are at present**. Skip any items that do not apply to you.

Dissatisfied	**Satisfied**	
1 2 3 4 5 6 7 8 9 10		Physical Health
1 2 3 4 5 6 7 8 9 10		Mental/Emotional Health
1 2 3 4 5 6 7 8 9 10		Career/Employment Satisfaction
1 2 3 4 5 6 7 8 9 10		Financial Stability
1 2 3 4 5 6 7 8 9 10		Marriage/Romantic Relationships
1 2 3 4 5 6 7 8 9 10		Home Life (Immediate Family)
1 2 3 4 5 6 7 8 9 10		Extended Family (Relatives, In-Laws)
1 2 3 4 5 6 7 8 9 10		Friends/Social Life
1 2 3 4 5 6 7 8 9 10		Recreation/Relaxation
1 2 3 4 5 6 7 8 9 10		Lifestyle (Degree of Busyness)
1 2 3 4 5 6 7 8 9 10		Personal Life Fulfillment
1 2 3 4 5 6 7 8 9 10		Personal Spiritual Life
1 2 3 4 5 6 7 8 9 10		Church/Religious Life
1 2 3 4 5 6 7 8 9 10		Current Ministry
1 2 3 4 5 6 7 8 9 10		Physical Comfort (Housing, Location, Cars, and so on)
1 2 3 4 5 6 7 8 9 10		Other _____

Please join the circles together to make a graph.

When this is completed, please complete the form again, only this time put a square around the number that indicates **where you would like to be** if things were ideal.

Once again, join the squares. What areas have the largest gaps between where you are at present and where you would like to be? These may be areas in which coaching can be beneficial.

EVALUATING COACHING POTENTIAL

This evaluation form is designed to assist the potential coach in deciding the potential success of a proposed coaching relationship.

Potential Client's name: _____

Following an introductory interview, assign a number to each statement based on the following:

> **3** — *This definitely or very probably is true of this person*
> **2** — *This appears to be true of this person*
> **1** — *This might be true of this person*
> **0** — *This is not true or very likely not true of this person*

____ Wants to change and grow

____ Has taken efforts to change or grow within the past year

____ Is willing to consider new assumptions, values, and behaviors

____ Is not involved in counseling at present

____ Gives no evidence of personal problems that could interfere with the coaching process

____ Is willing, if it seems wise, to get more training, do reading, and engage in other activities that could bring change and growth

____ Is willing to restructure one's life if necessary

____ Understands that coaching is not mentoring, advice giving, or counseling

____ Is capable of thinking about the future

____ Has goals that are not yet being reached

____ Is willing to work with a coach in a collaborative relationship

____ Is open to learning from others

____ Appears willing and able to persist in moving toward goals

____ Is willing to be accountable to another person

____ Is open for God's leading in the coaching process

____ Appears to be "in sync" and have good chemistry with the coach

____ _____

____ _____

Feel free to add additional statements. There are no right or wrong answers.

The higher the score, the better the potential for a successful coaching relationship.

COACHING FACTS

What is coaching?

The first time it was ever used, the word *coach* described a horse-drawn vehicle—a stagecoach that would get people from where they were to where they wanted to be. A modern bus does the same thing, and often these vehicles are called coaches. Most often today, coaches are people who help athletes and teams move from one place to another that is better and where they want to be. Even Tiger Woods has a coach to help improve his game of golf.

But coaches also help musicians, public speakers, and actors, who rely on coaching to improve their skills, overcome obstacles, remain focused, and get to where they want to be. Coaching is very popular in business and corporate settings around the world where "executive coaches" help managers and other business leaders deal with change, develop new management styles, make wise decisions, become more effective, cope with their hyperactive lifestyles, and deal with stress. Executive coaches work with people in business to help them move from where they are to levels where they are more competent, fulfilled, and self-confident than they would have been otherwise.

In summary, coaches guide people from where they are toward the greater competence and fulfillment they desire. *Christian* coaching is the art and practice of working with a person or group in the process of moving from where they are to where God wants them to be.

Why would anybody want a coach?

Coaching helps people who want to:

- Get unstuck
- Build their confidence
- Expand their vision for the future

- Fulfill their dreams
- Unlock their potential
- Increase their skills
- Move through transitions
- Take practical steps toward their goals

How does coaching differ from counseling?

Unlike counseling or therapy, coaching is less threatening, less about problem solving, more about helping people reach their potential.

- Coaching is not for people who need therapy to overcome painful influences from the past; coaches help people build vision and move toward the future.
- Coaching is not about looking back; it's about looking ahead.
- Coaching is not about healing; it's about growing.
- Coaching focuses less on overcoming weaknesses and more on building skills and strengths.
- Usually coaching is less formal than the counselor/counselee relationship; more often it is a partnership between two equals, one of whom has experiences, perspectives, skills, or knowledge that can be useful to the other.

What do coaches do to help others?

- **Coaches stimulate better skills.** Good coaching helps people anticipate what they could become, overcome self-defeating habits or insecurities, manage relationships, develop new competencies, and build effective ways to keep improving.
- **Coaches stimulate vision.** Many individuals and churches have no clear vision. They keep doing what they have done for years, without much change and with little expectation that things will ever be different. Coaches work with individuals and organizations (including churches) as they think beyond the present, more clearly envision the future, and plan how to get there.
- **Coaches help people grow through life transitions.** Whenever we encounter major changes in our lives—such as a new job, a promotion, a move, the death of a loved one, the launch of a new career, or retirement—we face uncertainty and the need to readjust. Experienced coaches better enable people to reassess their life goals, find new career options, change lifestyles, get training, reevaluate

their finances, or find information so they can make wise decisions.

- **Coaches guide Christians in their spiritual journeys.** Many believers understand the basics of the faith and aren't looking to be discipled. But they need focused time with somebody who has been on the spiritual road longer, who models Christlikeness, can point out the barriers to growth, and can guide the journey.
- **Coaches speak the truth in love.** Good coaches know that sometimes the best way to help is by refusing to ignore harmful behavior patterns. Instead, coaches nudge people to deal with attitudes and behavior that should be faced and changed.

What happens in coaching?

Coaching is a relationship that most often is client centered and goal directed. Every coaching situation is unique, but usually coaches will begin by *exploring the issues* that the person wants to change. In what areas does he or she want to grow? Sometimes the person wants to be a better leader, better self-manager, or someone with a clearer perspective about where to go in the future. Christians in coaching may seek to determine where God appears to be leading them to go.

There is also the need for better *awareness of where the person is at present.* What are his or her strengths, weaknesses, abilities, interests, passions, spiritual gifts, values, worldviews, and hopes? Often the coach will use assessment tools to enable people to learn more about themselves.

Then comes *vision*. Coaches might assist people, organizations, or churches in formulating life-vision or life-mission statements. Coaches might ask, for example, "Considering your gifts, abilities, driving passions, and unique God-given personality, what is your life mission?" It takes time to answer a question like that, but without a clear vision, people, churches, organizations, and even governments tend to drift with no direction.

At some time, coaches will help people set *goals* and plan ways to reach these goals.

When *obstacles* get in the way, coaches challenge, encourage, and give accountability so the person can get past the obstacles and experience success. A coach can help you remove the blinders, allowing you to see what you may not recognize and give support as you move forward. A Christian coach is there for you, prayerfully listening to your concerns and asking questions that will give you clarity on your situation, get you past your own blocks, realize your God-given potential, and challenge you to be your best.

Copyright © Gary R. Collins, 2009, used with permission

COACHING AGREEMENT

Coaching is an ongoing relationship between a coach and a person who desires coaching. We agree that:

1. Coaching is not therapy, counseling, advice-giving, mental health care, or treatment for substance abuse. The coach is not functioning as a licensed mental health professional and coaching is not intended as a replacement for counseling, psychiatric interventions, treatment for mental illness, recovery from past abuse, professional medical advice, financial assistance, legal counsel, or other professional services.

2. Coaching is for people who are basically well adjusted, emotionally healthy, functioning effectively, and wanting to make changes in their lives.

3. Coaching is designed to address issues the person being coached would like to consider. These could include (but are not limited to) career development, relationship enhancement, spiritual growth, lifestyle management, life balance, decision making, movement through transitions, or the achievement of short-term or long-term goals.

4. Coaching will be an ongoing relationship that might take a number of months, although either party can terminate at any time. Some or all of the coaching might be through telephone contact.

5. Coaching can involve brainstorming, values clarification, the completion of written assignments, education, goal setting, identifying plans of action, accountability, making requests, agreements to change behavior, examining lifestyles, and questioning.

6. Coaching is most effective when both parties are honest and straightforward in their communication.

7. Coaching is a confidential relationship and the coach agrees to keep all information strictly confidential, except in those situations in which such confidentiality would violate the law or could jeopardize the safety of the client or others.

8. Coaching is done with the assumption that each person in the relationship is guided by his or her values and beliefs. The Christian coach is a committed follower of Jesus Christ and seeks to live in accordance with this commitment. The Christian coach is honest in making this revelation, but he or she respects the different values and beliefs of others. The Christian coach does not seek to impose his or her values on another, proselytize, condemn, or refuse coaching services to people who do not share similar values and beliefs.

9. For purposes of this agreement, [insert name of client] and [insert name of coach] agree to meet on a regular basis for a minimum of four coaching sessions, beginning [insert starting date]. The fee will be $ _____ per session, payable following each session or at the end of each month. Each meeting will last at least forty-five minutes, but sessions could go longer at no extra cost. There will be no predetermined length of commitment or set frequency of meeting times. These will be determined as the relationship progresses. Efforts will be made to accommodate each other's schedules. This agreement may be extended by mutual agreement or terminated by either party at any time.

10. Each of the parties whose signatures appear below agrees to inform the other of the need to cancel an appointment. Except in unusual circumstances, this cancellation will be given no less than twenty-four hours prior to the scheduled appointment time.

11. Each of the people whose signature appears below agrees that this agreement represents our mutual understanding of the coaching relationship.

Signature _____   Signature _____

Date _____   Date _____

"GETTING TO KNOW YOU" PERSONAL INFORMATION FORM

CHRISTIAN COACHING IS more effective and efficient if you can give the coach some information about yourself at the beginning. **This is confidential information and you are free to pass on any of the questions.** The more you complete, however, the better your coach will know you and be able to provide the best coaching experience. You can complete this online and return it to [insert coach's e-mail address].

Name:

Name you like to be called:

Address:

Home phone:

Work phone:

Cell phone:

(Please put an X next to the best number (above) to call you.)

E-mail address:

Fax:

Occupation:

Employer name:

Date of birth:

Marital status:

Spouse:

Names and ages of children:

Please take as much space as you need to answer as many of the following questions as you wish to answer:

Please write a brief life story, giving whatever background you wish.

Why do you want coaching? What specific issues would you like to work on?

Have you ever been coached before? If so, describe your experience with coaching.

Are you now or have you ever been in counseling or therapy? If yes, please explain.

Describe your spirituality. What is your relationship with God? In what ways do you sense God might be challenging you, nudging you, or trying to get your attention?

What are the major things happening in your life right now?

How would you like your life to be different one year from now?

What is getting in the way of these changes or goals?

List three things you're procrastinating on in your life right now.

If we worked together, in what ways might you undermine or sabotage me as your coach? How would I help you stop doing this?

What are your insecurities about being coached?

Please include any other comments you wish to add.

IDENTIFYING VALUES

VALUES ARE FOUNDATIONAL beliefs that anchor our lives, the things that matter to us the most, the nonnegotiable characteristics that best describe who we are. Look over the following list and circle the words and phrases that best illustrate your values. If you have values not on the list, add your values in the spaces provided. Try to circle between twelve and fifteen words. These are the values that best describe you, even though there may be others that apply as well. (The words and phrases below are listed alphabetically rather than in order of importance.)

Accomplishment	Determination	Genuineness
Affirmation	Diligence	Good taste
Ambition	Efficiency	Growth
Authenticity	Elegance	Hard work
Beauty	Encouragement	Honesty
Being a model	Enlightenment	Humility
Being in control	Excellence	Humor
Career	Excitement	Impacting people
Caution	Experiencing pleasure	Independence
Collaboration	Faithfulness	Influence
Communicating	Family	Inspiring others
Community	Forgiveness	Integrity
Compassion	Forward looking	Joy
Competence	Freedom	Lack of pretense
Competition	Frugality	Love
Consistency with	Fulfillment	Love of learning
biblical teaching	Fun	Loyalty
Creativity	Gentleness	Making money

Marriage
Mentoring
Nurturing
Obedience
Orderliness
Patience
Peace
Perfection
Performance
Persistence
Personal Power
Physical vitality
Productivity
Purity
Quality
Recognition
Relaxation

Respect for life
Respect for people
Respect for the
 environment
Risk taking
Security
Self-esteem
Self-expression
Sensitivity
Servanthood
Service
Sexual fulfillment
Silence
Sincerity
Solitude
Spiritual growth
Stability

Success
Temperance
Tolerance
Tongue control
Tranquility
Trust
Truth
Winning
Worship

_____
_____
_____
_____
_____
_____
_____
_____

WHAT ARE YOUR SPIRITUAL GIFTS?

IN ROMANS 12:6-8, 1 Corinthians 12:8-30, Ephesians 4:11-12, and 1 Peter 4:11, the Bible talks of spiritual gifts given by God to individual believers in accordance with his will. The purpose of these gifts is not to help us build our careers and find success. The gifts are given for one purpose: "so that [the church] may be built up" (Ephesians 4:12, NIV).

Christians are most fulfilled when they are serving through the use of their spiritual gifts. When we understand our spiritual gifts, we are better able to understand ourselves and how God has uniquely empowered us.

How do we determine our spiritual gifts? There are at least two ways: the inventory approach and the checklist approach. You may want to do both to see if they are consistent.

Before beginning this evaluation, pray that the Holy Spirit will guide you and make you aware of your God-given gifts.

A. The inventory approach. Take one of the more standardized spiritual gift inventories that are available in most Christian bookstores.

The following are two examples:

- Bruce L Bugbee. *Discover Your Spiritual Gifts the Network Way.* Grand Rapids, MI: Zondervan, 2005.
- Peter Wagner. *Discover Your Spiritual Gifts.* Ventura CA: Regal Books, 2005.

B. The checklist approach. Make three copies of the following list of spiritual gifts. Look over the list and put a check by the words that seem to describe you.

Spiritual Gifts

____ Administration   ____ Apostleship

____ Craftsmanship   ____ Creative Communication

____ Discernment   ____ Encouragement

____ Evangelism   ____ Faith

____ Giving   ____ Helps

____ Hospitality   ____ Intercession

____ Knowledge   ____ Leadership

____ Mercy   ____ Prophecy

____ Shepherding   ____ Teaching

____ Wisdom   ____ Healing *

____ Interpretation *   ____ Miracles *

____ Tongues *   ____ Counseling **

____ Celibacy **   ____ Serving **

____ Music **

* *These gifts are not included in some lists because they are more easily identified.*

** *These gifts are not listed in Scripture but are identified by some Christians as spiritual gifts.*

Next, go back over the items you have checked and give each a number: 1 for those that are very strong in your life and descriptive of you, 2 for those that are somewhat strong and descriptive of you, and 3 for those that are the least descriptive of the items you checked.

Then ask three people who know you well to do the same on the photocopied lists.

Write down the items that were ranked number 1 on the lists. Probably these are your spiritual gifts.

CLARIFYING YOUR MISSION STATEMENT[1]

1. Pray about your calling and mission. Ask God to reveal his purpose to you. Journal about your reflections. What have you concluded?

2. List several examples of times in your life when you knew you were on purpose, sensing that this was what you were called to do. For each of these, write why the experience was so special. Eric Liddle felt God's pleasure when he was running. In which, if any, of these experiences did you sense God's pleasure in what you were experiencing or doing? What do these reflections tell you about yourself and your life mission?

3. Look at the themes you listed for question 2. What is similar about the experiences? How does this help you form a mission statement?

4. Repeat questions 2 and 3, only start with examples of times when you did something that was highly successful and acclaimed or was something that you sensed was genuinely blessed by God.

5. Complete this statement: I _____ to _____. In the first blank write what you do best based on your strengths, passions, gifts, and values. In the second blank, write why you do this. Here are some examples:
   - I teach to help disabled kids.
   - I mentor inner-city kids to give them hope and life skills.
   - I do research to help doctors treat cancer.
   - I work around the church and neighborhood to serve Christ, help others, and bring improvements.

6. List the basics of your worldview, key values, passions, strengths, personality traits, and spiritual gifts. Summarize this in two brief sentences. What does this say about your mission in life?

7. Ask the people who know you best what they see as your mission in life. Pool the answers. The people who surround you may be the best sources of information about what they see God doing in your life and how he is using you.

WRITING A TEN-YEAR LETTER

BUSINESSMAN TOM CHAPPELL proposed this exercise in his book *Managing Upside Down*.[1] It can be a very productive exercise that can clarify where you want to go and help you develop a mission statement.

Write a letter to a close friend. Date it ten years from today.[2] Assume that everything has gone according to your dreams and wishes. Give a summary of the prior ten years going back to today. Be specific. Include promotions, achievements, accomplishments, areas of growth, and spiritual changes. Keep in mind your gifts, values, passion, and vision as you write.

To help you write a straightforward letter, you may want to write the letter before you continue reading.

When you are finished writing, read this letter to another person, preferably the person to whom you wrote. Discuss:

- Your friend's reaction
- How you felt about sharing what you have written
- What seemed most important to you, judging from the letter
- What you like best about what you wrote
- What things disappointed you
- What the letter said about your relationship with God
- How the exercise helped clarify your future direction
- What you can do to make the letter's contents come true in reality
- What the letter says about your purpose for living

ENERGY DRAINERS

In the spaces provided, list the energy drainers in your life. Use additional paper if necessary.

Energy-Draining People

___ 1.

___ 2.

___ 3.

___ 4.

___ 5.

Energy-Draining Emotions

___ 1.

___ 2.

___ 3.

___ 4.

___ 5.

Energy Drainers at Work

___ 1.

___ 2.

___ 3.

___ 4.

___ 5.

Energy Drainers at Home

___ 1.

___ 2.

___ 3.

___ 4.

___ 5.

Other Energy Drainers

___ 1.

___ 2.

___ 3.

___ 4.

___ 5.

When you have completed your lists, go back and put one of the following letters in the space at the left of each number: **O** by the items you can overlook, and **A** by the items that need some action. In the space below, list some actions you can take to reduce the energy drainers marked with an A.

FINDING
A COACH

COACHES DIFFER IN their training and in the quality of the services they offer. The best way to select a coach is to get a recommendation from somebody you respect. If you have a potential coach in mind, try to interview a former client of that coach to determine if the coach has the qualifications you are looking for. The Christian Coaches Network (www.christiancoaches. com) also will give you the names of their members who might be able to help. Because most coaches have a website, go to these to determine if any potential coach is a person you want to work with.

As you look for a coach:

- Think about the level of coach training and experience you want your coach to have. You will discover that of coaches who advertise their services, some are trained and some are untrained. They differ significantly in the quality of their training and in their level of experience or expertise.
- Give some thought to the issues you want to work on in coaching. Is the coach you are considering best able to help with these issues?
- Try to get some indication of the coach's values, worldview, and Christian commitment. To what extent are these important to you?

Most coaches have designated times or days available for phone interviews. For this reason, it is best to either call or send an e-mail message to request time for an interview. This is a mutual get-acquainted discussion that usually lasts around thirty minutes and is free. Unless you feel at ease with the first contact, plan to interview more than one prospective coach. In these conversations:

- Think about whether you feel comfortable talking with the potential coach. Usually it is best if both the coach and the client sense that they could build a good working relationship, so try to find a coach with whom you will be able to work well.
- Listen for passion, authenticity, style, manner, ego, worldview, humor, and attitudes.
- Be aware of the questions the coach asks you and how they are asked. This likely is how questions will be asked if you hire the person as a coach.
- Determine how much training or experience this coach has. Does he or she have skills that would be helpful to your issues? Ask why the person entered the coaching field and the types of situations he or she has coached. Be cautious when the potential coach is evasive about answering these questions or when the coach claims to have the ability to help anybody regardless of need.
- Ask what is included in the fee, if a time commitment is required (like at least three months of coaching), and what options are available. Coaching fees normally are payable monthly, often in advance, for a specified number of months. How can you terminate the coaching?
- If you interview more than one coach, let them all know of your final decision. This is a matter or courtesy.

These are questions that you might ask a potential coach. Keep in mind that if you become a coach, other people may ask these questions of you. They are designed to enable the potential coach and client to establish a compatible and trusting relationship.[1]

NOTES

Chapter 1: What Is Coaching?

1. Betty Friedan, *The Fountain of Age* (New York: Simon & Schuster, 1993), 13.
2. This is the conclusion of David Logan and John King, *The Coaching Revolution: How Visionary Managers Are Using Coaching to Empower People and Unlock Their Full Potential* (Holbrook, MA: Adams Media Corporation, 2001).
3. Don Shula and Ken Blanchard, *Everyone's a Coach* (Grand Rapids, MI: Zondervan, 1995), 12.
4. Betsy Morris, "So You're a Player. Do You Need a Coach?" *Fortune* 141, no. 4 (February 2000): 144–145.
5. This quotation is taken from the website of the International Coach Federation. Web addresses change with some frequency, but at the time of this writing, the ICF website is www.coachfederation.org. This site gives information about coach training programs and certification. The web address for Coachville is www.coachville.com. Also see Association for Coaching (www .associationforcoaching.org), European Mentoring and Coaching Council (www.emccouncil.org), and Christian Coaches Network (www .christiancoaches.com).
6. From research by Rey Carr, reported on the Peer Resources website, 2007, www.peer.ca/coach.html.
7. David Logan and John King, *The Coaching Revolution: How Visionary Managers Are Using Coaching to Empower People and Unlock Their Full Potential* (Holbrook, MA: Adams Media Corporation, 2001).
8. Dr. Martin Seligman is widely regarded as the father of positive psychology. See Martin E. P. Seligman and Mihaly Csikszentmihalyi, "Positive Psychology: An Introduction," *American Psychologist* 55 (January 2000): 5–14. *American Psychologist* is the official journal of the American Psychological Association. It is of significance that the journal's first issue of the new millennium was devoted entirely to positive psychology.
9. Ted W. Engstrom with Norman B. Rohrer, *The Fine Art of Mentoring: Passing On to Others What God Has Given to You* (Brentwood, TN: Wolgemuth & Hyatt, 1989), 4. For a discussion of Engstrom's later views of mentoring,

published shortly before his death, see Ted W. Engstrom and Ron Jenson, *The Making of a Mentor* (Waynesboro, GA: Authentic Media [in partnership with World Vision], 2005).

10. Morris, 146. Of course, many companies also hire coaches to work within their organizations rather than hiring outside coaches. A recent *Harvard Business Review* article agrees that mentoring has declined in popularity in the business world, "the chief casualty of hypercompetitiveness and rapid growth," and goes on to argue that mentoring is needed now, perhaps more than ever. The same could be said of coaching. See Thomas J. DeLong, John J. Gabarro, and Robert J. Lees, "Why Mentoring Matters in a Hypercompetitive World," *Harvard Business Review* 86 (January 2008): 115–121.

11. What name does one give to the person being coached? Up to this point in the book, I have used the terms *protégé*, *person being coached*, and *client*, among others. In the first edition of this book, I acknowledged that most coaches use the term *client* in referring to the people who are coached but that this term seemed best suited for professional coaches who charge for their services. I rejected the word *coachee* because this seemed to be cutesy and rarely used in the coaching literature. Instead, I used the words *person being coached* and abbreviated this PBC. It has since become clear to me that *client* is the preferred word used almost universally, even for people who receive coaching in informal sessions and in settings where there is no exchange of money. I will use the term *client* in this broader sense throughout this edition of the book.

12. Institute for Life Coach Training, www.lifecoaching.com.

13. Logan and King. An Internet search will reveal that there are perhaps thousands of coaching newsletters and online resources that give information about the coaching revolution. It should be noted that not all of the writers are supportive of the International Coach Federation or view it in a positive light. For a good ongoing source of information about coaching, coaching trends, newsletters, and coach training programs, see www.peer.ca/coach.html.

14. For a brief description of McCluskey's work as a Christian coach and his journey from being a therapist to becoming a coach, see Christopher McCluskey, "Caring from a Distance: Technology, Coaching, and Life Management," *Christian Counseling Today* 8, no. 1 (2000): 20–22, or view his website at www.christian-living.com.

15. Laurie Beth Jones, *Jesus, Life Coach: Learn from the Best* (Nashville: Thomas Nelson, 2004).

16. See John 3:16; 10:10.

17. The Blackabys describe this as "the spiritual leader's task." Henry and Richard Blackaby, *Spiritual Leadership: Moving People on to God's Agenda* (Nashville: Broadman, Holman, 2001), 20–21.

18. Rick Warren, *The Purpose-Driven Church: Growth Without Compromising Your Message and Mission* (Grand Rapids, MI: Zondervan, 1995), 13–14.

19. See Acts 17:10-11.

20. See Ephesians 1:7-8; 2:9; John 3:16; 10:10; 1 John 1:7-9.

21. James Flaherty, *Coaching: Evoking Excellence in Others*, 2nd ed. (Oxford: Butterworth-Heinemann, 2005).

Chapter 2: What Makes a Good Coach?

1. I am deeply grateful to my friend Dr. Jon Ebert for sharing this story about his father, Dr. Larry Ebert, and for giving me permission to share it here.

2. For a challenging and readable discussion of trust, see Stephen M. R. Covey, *The Speed of Trust: The One Thing That Changes Everything* (New York: Free Press, 2006).

3. Tony Stoltzfus, *Leadership Coaching: The Disciplines, Skills, and Heart of a Coach* (Longwood, FL: Xulon, 2005), 52.

4. Marshall Goldsmith, "Changing Leadership Behavior," in Howard Morgan, Phil Harkins, and Marshall Goldsmith, eds., *Profiles in Coaching* (Burlington, MA: Linkage Press, 2003), 45.

5. Without stating that counselors make the best coaches, some writers argue that training in counseling gives advantages to those who want to be coaches. See, for example, Jeffrey E. Auerback, *Personal and Executive Coaching: The Complete Guide for Mental Health Professionals* (Ventura, CA: Executive College Press, 2001); and Patrick Williams and Deborah C. Davis, *Therapist as Life Coach: An Introduction for Therapists and Other Helping Professionals*, rev. ed. (New York: Norton, 2007).

6. Steven Berglass, "The Very Real Dangers of Executive Coaching," *Harvard Business Review* 80, no. 6 (June 2002): 86–93.

7. A later chapter will discuss how people change. According to research summarized by Alan Deutschman in *Change or Die: The Three Keys to Change at Work and in Life* (New York: Regan/HarperCollins, 2007), lasting change does not come by force or from fear that comes from an outside authority. Change most often comes from being in relationships and communities that inspire hope.

8. John Whitmore, *Coaching for Performance*, 3rd ed. (London: Nicholas Brealey Publishing, 2002), 15.

9. This is the title of a book by Dan Kimball, *They Like Jesus but Not the Church: Insights from Emerging Generations* (Grand Rapids, MI: Zondervan, 2007). See also Bruce Bickel and Stan Jantz, *I'm Fine with God: It's Christians I Can't Stand* (Eugene, OR: Harvest House, 2008).

10. Carol Wilson, *Best Practice in Performance Coaching: A Handbook for Leaders, Coaches, HR Professionals, and Organizations* (London: Kogan Page, 2007).

11. Andy Stanley, *Making Vision Stick* (Grand Rapids, MI: Zondervan, 2007), 16.

Chapter 3: Coaching: It's All About Change

1. Alan Deutschman, *Change or Die: The Three Keys to Change at Work and in Life* (New York: HarperCollins, 2007).

2. Alan Deutschman, "Making Change," *Fast Company* 94 (May 2005): 54.

3. Deutschman, "Making Change," 62. See also Roderick Gilkey and Clint Kilts, "Cognitive Fitness: New Research in Neuroscience Shows How to Stay Sharp by Exercising Your Brain," *Harvard Business Review* 85, no. 11 (November 2007): 53–66.

4. James O'Toole, *Leading Change: Overcoming the Ideology of Comfort and the Tyranny of Custom* (San Francisco: Jossey-Bass, 1995), 73–74, 137.

5. Adapted from Robert B. Reich, "How to Detect Change Resisters: It's in Their

Talk," *Fast Company*, no. 39 (October 2000): 150.

6. Deutschman, *Change or Die*, 15.

7. Deutschman, *Change or Die*, 15.

8. For an in-depth discussion of change, including self-change and seven (not four) "levers" that bring about change, see Howard Gardner, *Changing Minds: The Art and Science of Changing Our Own and Other People's Minds* (Boston: Harvard Business School Press, 2004).

9. *Merriam-Webster Online Dictionary*, s.v. "metamorphosis," www.merriam-webster.com/dictionary/metamorphosis.

10. Romans 12:2.

11. See, for example, Joseph Umidi, *Transformational Coaching* (Fairfax, VA: Xulon, 2005); Cherrie Carter-Scott and Lynn U. Stewart, *Transformational Life Coaching* ((Deerfield Beach, FL: HCI, 2007); and Thomas G. Crane and Lerissa Nancy Patrick, *The Heart of Coaching: Using Transformational Coaching to Create a High-Performance Coaching Culture*, 3rd ed. (San Diego: FTA Press, 2007).

12. James O. Prochaska, John C. Norcross, and Carlo DeClemente, *Changing for Good: A Revolutionary Six-Stage Program for Overcoming Bad Habits and Moving Your Life Forward* (New York: HarperCollins, 1994).

13. David Rock and Jeffrey Schwartz, "The Neuroscience of Leadership" (May 30, 2006): 3, www.strategy-business.com. See also David Rock, "The Neuroscience of Coaching: New Discoveries Explain How and Why Coaching Works," recorded audio presentation, International Coach Federation Twelfth Annual Conference, October 31, 2007. Recording available from www.coachfederation.org.

14. Rock and Schwartz, 5

15. Rock and Schwartz, 4.

16. Jeffrey A. Kottler, *Making Change Last* (Philadelphia: Brunner-Routledge, 2001).

17. Kottler, 107.

18. Dan Heath and Chip Heath, "Make Goals Not Resolutions," *Fast Company* 122 (February 2008): 59.

19. Entire paragraph adapted from Heath and Heath.

20. The following principles for relapse prevention are taken from M. D. Spiegler and D. Guevremont, *Contemporary Behavior Therapy*, 4th ed. (Belmont, CA: Wadsworth, 2003).

21. The following conclusions are adapted from Kottler, chapter 7.

22. Ephesians 3:16.

23. See Philippians 3:3; 4:13.

24. For a significant psychological and in-depth discussion of change in nations, groups, and individuals, see Gardner, *Changing Minds*. See also Bill O'Hanlon, *Change 101: A Practical Guide to Creating Change in Life of Therapy* (New York: Norton, 2006).

25. See Acts 10:9-17.

26. See Acts 10:15.

27. See Acts 10:34-45.

28. See Acts 11:18.

Chapter 4: Coaching: It's a Lot About Leadership

1. See 1 Samuel 16:8-13.
2. See Jonah 1:3.
3. This is the theme of a book by Mark Sanborn, *You Don't Need a Title to Be a Leader* (New York: Doubleday, 2006).
4. In addition to "learning more about coaching," these are the top reasons why people seek coaching within the Ken Blanchard organization. See Madeleine Homan and Linda J. Miller, *Coaching in Organizations: Best Practices from the Ken Blanchard Companies* (New York: Wiley, 2008), 139.
5. Warren Bennis, *Leading People Is Like Herding Cats: Warren Bennis on Leadership* (Provo, UT: Executive Excellence Publishing, 1997), 64.
6. Don Shula and Ken Blanchard, *Everyone's a Coach* (Grand Rapids, MI: Zondervan, 1995), 51.
7. Robert B. Kaiser, Robert Hogan, and S. Bartholomew Craig, "Leadership and the Fate of Organizations," *American Psychologist* 63 (February–March 2008): 96–110.
8. Steve Ogne and Tim Roehl, *TransforMissional Coaching: Empowering Leaders in a Changing Ministry World* (Nashville: Broadman, Holman, 2008), 29–30.
9. See Madeleine Homan and Linda J. Miller, *Coaching in Organizations: Best Practices from the Ken Blanchard Companies* (New York: Wiley, 2008), 141, where leadership coaching and executive coaching are used interchangeably.
10. Daniel White, *Coaching Leaders: Guiding People Who Guide Others* (San Francisco: Jossey-Bass, 2005); and Brian Underhill, Kimcee McAnally, and John J. Koriah, *Executive Coaching for Results: The Definitive Guide to Developing Organizational Leaders* (San Francisco: Barrett-Koehler, 2007).
11. I'm assuming that most buffalo leaders are male. They have not yet learned what human males are finally discovering: Competent leadership is not limited to one gender.
12. The contrast between buffalo and goose leaders is described in James A. Belasco and Ralph C. Stayer, *Flight of the Buffalo: Soaring to Excellence: Learning to Let Employees Lead* (New York: Time Warner, 1993).
13. Warren G. Bennis and Robert J. Thomas, *Geeks and Geezers: How Era, Values, and Defining Moments Shape Leaders* (Boston: Harvard Business School Press, 2002), 98.
14. Daniel Goleman, *Emotional Intelligence: Why It Can Matter More Than IQ*, 10th anniversary ed. (New York: Bantam, 2006); Daniel Goleman, Richard Boyatzis, and Annie McKee, *Primal Leadership: Realizing the Power of Emotional Intelligence* (Boston: Harvard Business School Publishing, 2002).
15. Daniel Goleman, *Social Intelligence: The New Science of Human Relationships* (New York: Bantam, 2006).
16. Daniel Goleman and Richard Boyatzis, "Social Intelligence and the Biology of Leadership," *Harvard Business Review* 86, no. 9 (September 2008): 74–81.
17. Goleman and Boyatzis, 80.
18. Tim Stafford, "The Business of the Kingdom," *Christianity Today* 33, no. 13 (November 15, 1999): 45.
19. Stafford, 50.

20. Pete Hammett, "The Paradox of Gifted Leadership: Developing the Generation of Leaders," *Industrial and Commercial Training* 40, no. 1 (2008): 3–9.

Chapter 5: The Coaching Relationship

1. The magazine *Christian Counseling Today* was a quarterly publication of the American Association of Christian Counselors.
2. Laura Whitworth, Karen Kimsey-House, Henry Kimsey-House, and Phillip Sandahl, *Co-Active Coaching: New Skills for Coaching People Toward Success in Work and Life*, 2nd ed. (Mountain View, CA: Davies-Black Publishing, 2007).
3. Whitworth, Kimsey-House, Kimsey-House, Sandahl, xix.
4. Whitworth, Kimsey-House, Kimsey-House, Sandahl, 5.
5. Steven J. Stowell and Matt M. Starcevich, *The Coach: Creating Partnerships for a Competitive Edge* (Sandy, UT: Center for Management and Organizational Effectiveness, 1998), 46.
6. See Luke 24:13-33.
7. See Romans 11:33; James 1:17.
8. See Matthew 7:24-25.
9. See Colossians 1:16-17.
10. See Philippians 1:6.
11. Gary J. Oliver, Monta Hasz, and Matthew Richburg, *Promoting Change Through Brief Therapy in Christian Counseling* (Wheaton, IL: Tyndale, 1997), 105.
12. This list and the questionnaire in appendix B are adapted from Frederic M. Hudson, "Who Can Be a Client?" *The Handbook of Coaching* (San Francisco: Jossey-Bass, 1999), 25.
13. See John 4:4-12; 8:3-11.
14. As I write this book, there is nothing legal that would prevent you from coaching in exchange for fees. But professional standards, coaching credentials, and payment criteria are being discussed in many places, and it seems only a matter of time until payment for coaching services will be regulated in the same way counseling services currently are controlled legally in many countries.
15. For sample items that might go into a welcome packet, see Patrick Williams and Deborah C. Davis, *Therapist as Life Coach*, rev. ed. (New York: Norton, 2007), 213–228.
16. James Collins, "Built to Flip," *Fast Company*, no. 30 (January–February 2000): 140.
17. See Hebrews 12:1-3.

Chapter 6: The Coaching Skills: Listening, Questioning, Responding

1. I cringed at this remark but was able to restrain myself from responding negatively. I remembered that these were coaching students who were beginners. The coaching session described in the text came at the end of the week when the students were almost ready to return to their homes. As we evaluated the training, it was clear the participants needed specific training in listening, questioning, and responding. A few weeks later, they all took trains, buses, and airplanes back to the place of our training for an intensive one-day seminar that

focused solely on coaching skills. After this, the group members made great strides building on what they had learned in the training. I learned the hard way that we cannot assume that trainees (or readers of this book) will have the expertise to listen and respond appropriately. These skills are the focus of the present chapter.

2. At this point, I have drawn on Laura Whitworth, Karen Kimsey-House, Henry Kimsey-House, and Phillip Sandahl, *Co-Active Coaching*, 2nd ed. (Mountain View, CA: Davies-Black Publishing, 2007). These author-coaches distinguish between Level I listening, which involves listening for facts that apply mostly to the listener, and Level II listening, in which the listener's awareness is totally on the client. These two types of listening parallel the *informal* listening and *active* listening discussed in the text. *Co-Active Coaching* also identifies Level III listening, which the authors call global listening and parallels what others refer to as *intuitive* listening.

3. Patrick Williams and Deborah C. Davis. *Therapist as Life Coach*, rev. ed. (New York: Norton, 2007), 5.

4. For an excellent and practical guide to asking powerful questions, see Tony Stoltzfus, *Coaching Questions: A Coach's Guide to Powerful Asking Skills* (Virginia Beach, VA: Pegasus Creative Arts, 2008), www.Coach22.com. The author is a respected Christian coach and coach trainer whose book includes several hundred samples of powerful questions arranged into categories.

5. Dr. DeShazer's wife and cofounder of Solution Focused Brief Therapy has combined this with coaching in Insoo Kim Berg and Peter Szabó, *Brief Coaching for Lasting Solutions* (New York: Norton, 2005).

6. Laura Whitworth, Karen Kimsey-House, Henry Kimsey-House, and Phillip Sandahl, *Co-Active Coaching*, 2nd ed. (Mountain View, CA: Davies-Black Publishing, 2007), 97.

Chapter 7: Coaching Models and Issues

1. A variety of useful coaching models exist. There can be value in looking at different models, evaluating each, and determining which may be the best model for you and for the clients with whom you work. Despite this diversity, the detailed summarizing and evaluating of different coaching models is beyond the scope of this book. Instead, one model is presented in detail but with the assumption that there are other models that can be useful and that readers might want to investigate and follow in their coaching.

2. For a consideration of alternative coaching models, see www .christiancoachingbook.com.

3. Readers of the first edition of this book will recognize that the present model is a change from what appeared before. I have combined the six segments of the first model into four. "Issues" and "awareness" from the earlier model are combined into "awareness" in this book. The two previous categories of "strategy" and "action" also have been combined into one.

4. Laura Whitworth, Karen Kimsey-House, Henry Kimsey-House, and Phillip Sandahl, *Co-Active Coaching*, 2nd ed. (Mountain View, CA: Davies-Black Publishing, 2007), 166.

Chapter 8: Getting In Touch with the Present

1. I learned this life-changing fact from an advertisement in the *Harvard Business Review.* "Goldfish can't even see the past, much less the future . . . but you can," stated the advertisement. To my surprise, I discovered an entire website dealing with this crucial issue. Go to www.sas.com/goldfish and you will discover that goldfish can be taught basic conditioning; therefore, they must have some longer memory. This, of course, has no relevance to Christian coaching!
2. Lou Tice with Joyce Quick, *Personal Coaching for Results: How to Mentor and Inspire Others to Amazing Growth* (Nashville: Thomas Nelson, 1997), 80.
3. See Jonah 1:1-3.
4. Many of the appendixes in the back of this book can be downloaded from www.garyrcollins.com or www.christiancoachingbook.com and used in your coaching.
5. See Mark 5:24-34.
6. Adapted from Keith Yamashita and Sandra Spataro, *Unstuck: A Tool for Yourself, Your Team, and Your World* (New York: Portfolio, 2004), 30–46.
7. For a more in-depth discussion of getting unstuck, see Timothy Butler, *Getting Unstuck: How Dead Ends Become New Paths* (Boston: Harvard Business School Press, 2007.)
8. Graham Jones, "How the Best of the Best Get Better and Better," *Harvard Business Review* 86 (June 2008): 123–127.
9. Unless otherwise indicated, the perspectives on worldviews in these paragraphs are adapted from my earlier book *The Biblical Basis of Christian Counseling* (Colorado Springs, CO: NavPress, 1993), 12–24.
10. One exception is the discussion of "mental models" by Daniel White, *Coaching Leaders: Guiding People Who Guide Others* (San Francisco: Jossey-Bass, 2006). It appears that when White discusses mental models, he is discussing what we have called "worldviews."
11. See 2 Corinthians 5:17.
12. See Galatians 5:22-23.
13. Bill Parcells with Jeff Coplon, *Finding a Way to Win: The Principles of Leadership, Teamwork, and Motivation* (New York: Doubleday, 1995).
14. Noel M. Tichy, *The Leadership Engine: How Winning Companies Build Leaders at Every Level* (New York: HarperCollins, 1997).
15. For a detailed description of how this creative exercise has been used to clarify values, see Hyrum W. Smith, *The 10 Natural Laws of Successful Time and Life Management: Proven Strategies for Increased Productivity and Inner Peace* (New York: Warner Books, 1994), 48–55.
16. Adapted from Laura Whitworth, Karen Kimsey-House, Henry Kimsey-House, and Phillip Sandahl, *Co-Active Coaching*, 2nd ed. (Mountain View, CA: Davies-Black, 2007).

Chapter 9: Getting In Touch with the Person

1. Anthony M. Grant, "Personal Life Coaching for Coaches-in-Training Enhances Goal Attainment, Insight, and Learning," *Coaching: An International Journal of Theory, Research, and Practice* 1 (March 2008): 54.

2. Richard Chang, *The Passion Plan: A Step-by-Step Guide to Discovering, Developing, and Living Your Passion* (San Francisco: Jossey-Bass, 2000), 16.

3. Selfish ambition is mentioned in Galatians 5:20; Philippians 1:17; 2:3; James 3:14,16.

4. See 1 Corinthians 9:16.

5. I am grateful to my friend Tony Stoltzfus for some of the ideas about calling that appear in this paragraph.

6. I am indebted to Susan Britton Whitcomb, whose class on career management coaching reminded me that passion is not something that we expect to drive us without letup and without expenditure of any energy.

7. Following the Paris Olympics, Eric Liddle did go to China as a missionary. Following the Japanese invasion, he was incarcerated but was able to have a ministry to the other prisoners. He died of a brain tumor at age forty-three, only six months before the liberation of China in 1945.

8. See Ephesians 2:8,13.

9. See Ephesians 2:10.

10. See Ephesians 5:10; 1 Corinthians 10:31.

11. Nehemiah's prayer is summarized in Nehemiah 1:5-11. We see a short prayer in 2:4.

12. See Nehemiah 2:4-8.

13. In a remarkable way, God provided the needed tuition money when Mike came home after that initial information-gathering trip. At the time of this writing, Mike is a PhD student who continues to follow his passion, working on behalf of mistreated and misused children around the world.

14. See Nehemiah 4:8-9.

15. Some of the world's most influential leaders and movement makers are people who have passion but don't have titles or positions of authority. See Mark Sanborn, *You Don't Need a Title to Be a Leader* (New York: Doubleday, 2006).

16. Richard J. Leider, *The Power of Purpose: Creating Meaning in Your Life and Work* (San Francisco: Berrett-Koehler, 1997), 103.

17. Howard Gardner, *Multiple Intelligences: New Horizons in Theory and Practice* (New York: Basic Books, 2006); and Daniel Goleman, *Social Intelligence: The New Science of Human Relationships* (New York: Bantam, 2006).

18. Daniel Goleman and Richard Boyatzis, "Social Intelligence and the Biology of Leadership," *Harvard Business Review* 86 (September 2008): 74–81.

19. Goleman and Boyatzis, "Biology of Leadership," 80.

20. Goleman and Boyatzis, "Biology of Leadership," 78.

21. Albert L. Winseman, Donald O. Clifton, and Curt Liesveld, *Living Your Strengths* (New York: Gallup, 2004), x.

22. See, for example, Curt Coffman and Gabriel Gonzalez-Molina, *Follow This Path* (New York: Warner Books, 2002); Marcus Buckingham and Donald O. Clifton, *Now, Discover Your Strengths* (New York: Free Press, 2001); and Marcus Buckingham, *Go Put Your Strengths to Work* (New York: Free Press, 2007).

23. The following two books include one online strength-finder assessment with the price of the book: John Trent, Rodney Cox, and Eric Tooker, *Leading*

from Your Strengths (Nashville: Broadman, Holman, 2004); and Tom Rath, *Strengths Finder 2.0* (New York: Gallup Press, 2007). For a free online assessment, check www.authentichappines.com.

24. See 1 Corinthians 12:31.
25. See 1 Corinthians 12:2; Ephesians 4:11-12.
26. Henry and Mel Blackaby, *What's So Spiritual About Your Gifts?* (Sisters, OR: Multnomah, 2004).
27. See Judges 6–7.

Chapter 10: Clarifying the Vision

1. Burt Nanus, *Visionary Leadership* (San Francisco: Jossey-Bass, 1995), 3.
2. Neil H. Snyder, James J. Dowd Jr., and Dianne Morse Houghton, *Vision, Values and Courage: Leadership for Quality Management* (New York: Free Press, 1994), 75.
3. See Matthew 28:19.
4. See Psalm 138:8; 139:13-16.
5. Rick Warren, *The Purpose-Driven Church: Growth Without Compromising Your Message and Mission* (Grand Rapids, MI: Zondervan, 1995), 98.
6. Andy Stanley, *Visioneering: God's Blueprint for Developing and Maintaining Personal Vision* (Grand Rapids, MI: Zondervan, 2005), 26.
7. These include Andy Stanley, *Visioneering*; Andy Stanley, *Making Vision Stick* (Grand Rapids, MI: Zondervan, 2007); George Barna, *The Power of Vision* (Ventura, CA: Regal, 2003); and Burt Nanus, *Visionary Leadership* (San Francisco: Jossey-Bass, 1995).
8. See Acts 8:9-11,18-23.
9. George Barna, *Turning Vision into Action* (Ventura, CA: Regal, 1996), 36.
10. Andy Stanley, *Making Vision Stick* (Grand Rapids, MI: Zondervan, 2007), 18. Stanley's five principles for making vision stick are: state the vision simply, cast the vision convincingly, repeat the vision regularly, celebrate the vision systematically, and embrace the vision personally. Stanley's conclusions have helped shape some of the paragraphs in this section of the chapter.
11. For example, see Nehemiah 4.
12. Rick Warren, e-mail message received October 22, 2008.

Chapter 11: Moving with a Mission

1. Warren Bennis and Patricia Ward Biederman, *Organizing Genius: The Secrets of Creative Collaboration* (Reading, MA: Addison-Wesley, 1997), 64.
2. Rick Warren, *The Purpose-Driven Church: Growth Without Compromising Your Message and Mission* (Grand Rapids, MI: Zondervan, 1995).
3. Warren, 87.
4. See Matthew 22:37-40.
5. See Matthew 28:19-20.
6. Warren, 1–3.
7. Warren, 124.
8. Nikos Mourkogiannis, *Purpose: The Starting Point of Great Companies* (New York: Palgrave Macmillan, 2006).

9. Rodd Wagner and James K. Harter, *12: The Elements of Great Managing* (New York: Gallup, 2006). The conclusions of this book are based on a Gallup survey of ten million workplace interviews worldwide. The eighth element is having a connection with the mission of the company.

10. Laurie Beth Jones, *The Path: Creating Your Mission Statement for Work and for Life* (New York: Hyperion, 1998).

11. Jones, 3–4.

12. Richard J. Leider, *The Power of Purpose: Creating Meaning in Your Life and Work* (San Francisco: Berrett-Koehler, 1997), 34.

13. Rick Warren, *The Purpose-Driven Life: 7 Steps for Discovering and Fulfilling Your Life Mission* (Grand Rapids, MI: Zondervan, 2000).

14. Genesis 12:1.

15. The conversation is recorded in John 21:15-19. Verse 17 states that Peter was hurt by the repeated question about his love for Jesus.

16. John Whitmore, *Coaching for Performance*, 3rd ed. (London: Nicholas Brealey, 2002), 148–150. See also Richard Leider, *Power of Purpose*.

Chapter 12: Coaching for Action: Goal Setting and Strategies

1. See Proverbs 16:9; 20:24.

2. See Proverbs 15:22; 20:18; 21:5.

3. A year or so after he did the life plan with me, my coach offered a small workshop and taught six of us how to do life plan coaching for others. Daniel Harkavy is a Christian business coach who describes life planning as "the coaching leader's most powerful tool." Rather than the two-day intensive time with a coach, Harkavy suggests a day alone for writing a life plan. See Daniel Harkavy, *Becoming a Coaching Leader* (Nashville: Thomas Nelson, 2007), 57–73.

4. For a detailed discussion drawn from the business world, see Larry Bossidy and Ram Charan, *Execution: The Discipline of Getting Things Done* (New York: Crown Business, 2002).

5. Larry Bossidy and Ram Charan, *Execution: The Discipline of Getting Things Done* (New York: Crown Business, 2002), 14.

6. See Joshua 3:4.

7. Joshua 3:5.

8. See Joshua 3:3-4.

9. See Joshua 3:9-17.

10. See Proverbs 3:5-6.

11. See Psalm 32:8.

12. See Matthew 28:20.

13. See John 14:26; 16:7.

14. See Exodus 3:10; 16:18.

15. James C. Collins and Jerry I. Porras, *Build to Last: Successful Habits of Visionary Companies* (New York: HarperCollins, 1994), 91–114.

16. John Whitmore, *Coaching for Performance*, 3rd ed. (London: Nicholas Brealey, 2002), 83.

17. Bossidy and Charan, 214.

18. See Luke 10:1-23. Mark 6:7-13,30-31 records a similar situation, in which Jesus sent out the twelve disciples and met with them for rest and possibly reflection and feedback after they returned.
19. In writing this paragraph, I have been grateful to Russ Hopkins, formerly with ETFS Travel and Health Care Solutions in Sherbrook, Quebec. The last sentence in the paragraph is his.
20. See Matthew 28:18.
21. Encouraging clients to act *as if* has emerged as a standard coaching technique.
22. See John 14:1,15,26-27; 16:33.

Chapter 13: Coaching Through Obstacles

1. Ferdinand F. Fournies, *Why Employees Don't Do What They're Supposed to Do and What to Do About It,* rev. ed. (New York: McGraw-Hill, 2007); and *Coaching for Improved Work Performance*, rev. ed. (New York: McGraw-Hill, 2000).
2. This was suggested "playfully" by Laura Whitwoth, Karen Kimsey-House, Henry Kimsey-House, and Phillip Sandahl in *Co-Active Coaching*, 2nd ed. (Mountain View, CA: Davies-Black, 2007), 147.
3. Diane Menendez has been a full-time professional coach since 1988. In addition to teaching courses at the Institute for Life Coach Training (ILCT), she coaches executive clients in reaching their goals and creating lives that are richer and more satisfying. With Pat Williams, she is coauthor of *Becoming a Professional Life Coach: Lessons from the Institute for Life Coach Training* (New York: Norton, 2007).
4. W. Timothy Gallwey, *The Inner Game of Tennis* (New York: Random House, 1975).
5. W. Timothy Gallwey, *The Inner Game of Work: Focus, Learning, Pleasure, and Mobility in the Workplace* (New York: Random House, 2000).
6. The neurophysiology of coaching is a highly significant topic likely to influence what coaches do within the next few years. I try to keep abreast of some of this literature, but it changes quickly as more research data emerges on the neurophysiological bases of behavior. As a start, there is value in listening to an address by David Rock at the 2007 conference of the International Coach Federation. Titled "The Neuroscience of Coaching: New Discoveries Explain How and Why Coaching Works," a tape of the talk is available from www.audiotapes.com.
7. The concept was developed most clearly in a book by Richard D. Carson, *Taming Your Gremlin* (New York: Harper & Row, 1983).
8. See Philippians 4:13.
9. See 2 Corinthians 12:10.
10. See 2 Peter 1:3.
11. See Proverbs 3:5-6.
12. Jessica Gould, "Get Real: Feel Like an Imposter? You're Not Alone," *Monitor on Psychology*, no. 39 (July–August 2008): 76–78.
13. This is one of the most common mistakes in coaching, according to David B. Ellis, *Life Coaching: A Manual for Helping Professionals* (Banceyfelin, Carmarthen, Wales: Crown House, 207), 116.

Chapter 14: Transitions and Life Coaching

1. Dave Ellis, *Life Coaching: A Manual for Professionals* (Bethel, CT: Crown House, 2006), chapter 1.
2. For information about the Christian Coaches Network, go to www .christiancoachesnetwork.com. You can reach Ms. Santos at coach@ judysantos.com.
3. Adapted with permission from Judy Santos, C.C.N. Communiqué: A Monthly Publication of the Christian Coaches Network, August 2000.
4. Some of this research is summarized by Nadya A. Fouad and John Bynner, "Work Transitions," *American Psychologist* 63 (2008): 241–251.
5. Nadya A. Fouad and John Bynner, "Work Transitions," *American Psychologist* 63 (2008): 248.
6. Fouad and Bynner, 249.
7. Adapted from Frederic M. Hudson, *The Adult Years: Mastering the Art of Self-Renewal*, rev. ed. (San Francisco: Jossey-Bass, 1999), 99–123.
8. Frederic M. Hudson, *The Handbook of Coaching* (San Francisco: Jossey-Bass, 1999), 111.
9. The theory is summarized in Frederic M. Hudson, *The Handbook of Coaching*, 105–115, 201–235. For a more detailed discussion, see Frederic M. Hudson, *The Adult Years*, 99–123.
10. Adapted from Frederic M. Hudson, *The Adult Years*, 53–98.
11. Laura Whitworth, Henry Kimsey-House, and Phillip Sandahl, *Co-Active Coaching* (Palo Alto, CA: Davies-Black, 1998).
12. Whitworth, Kimsey-House, and Sandahl, 127, 128, 141.
13. For information on the Professional Christian Coaching Program at the Institute for Life Coach Training, visit www.christianliving.com. Christopher McCluskey can be contacted at chris@christian-living.com.

Chapter 15: Relationship and Marriage Coaching

1. Ricky Byrdsong with Dave and Neta Jackson, *Coaching Your Kids in the Game of Life* (Minneapolis: Bethany House, 2000), 21.
2. Byrdsong with Jackson and Jackson, 21.
3. More information about marriage coaching and marriage coaching training is available from Jeff and Jill Williams. Contact them at 301-515-1218 or Jeff@ GraceAndTruthRelationship.com for consultation, speaking, training, and direct service.
4. Jeff's definition of marriage coaching has been largely influenced by the concepts and skills presented in Tony Stoltzfus, *Leadership Coaching: The Disciplines, Skills, and Heart of a Coach* (Longwood, FL: Xulon, 2005).

Chapter 16: Career Coaching

1. Nadya A. Fouad and John Bynner, "Work Transitions," *American Psychologist* 63 (2008): 241–251.
2. Nadya and Bynner.
3. Keith Webb, "Career Coaching," in Tony Stoltzfus, *Coaching Questions: A Coach's Guide to Powerful Asking Skills* (Virginia Beach, VA: Pegasus Creative

Arts, 2008), 86, www.Coach22.com.

4. www.careercoachacademy.com.

5. In addition to the training that I took, The Career Coach Academy also offers a Christian training track as part of its training.

6. Susan Britton Witcomb, *The Christian's Career Journey: Finding the Job God Designed for You* (Indianapolis: Jist Publishing, 2008).

7. www.leadershipcoachacademy.com.

8. Colossians 3:23.

9. www.leadersecrets.com.

10. Daniel H. Pink, *Free Agent Nation: How America's New Independent Workers Are Transforming the Way We Live* (New York: Warner Books, 2001), quotation from cover copy.

11. Douglas T. Hall, *Careers In and Out of Organizations* (Thousand Oaks, CA: Sage Publications, 2002).

12. Fouad and Bynner, 244, 247.

Chapter 17: Executive and Business Coaching

1. Sharon B. Merriam and Brendan Leahy, "Learning Transfer: A Review of the Research in Adult Education and Training," *PAACE Journal of Lifelong Learning* 14 (2005): 1–24.

2. Merriam and Leahy, 14–16.

3. Gerald Oliverro, K. Denis Bane, and Richard E. Kopelman, "Executive Coaching as a Transfer of Training Tool: Effects on Productivity in a Public Agency," *Public Personnel Management* 26 (Winter 1997): 461–469.

4. This paragraph is adapted from an excellent article on executive coaching: Douglas F. Hall, Karen L. Otazo, and George P. Hollenbeck, "Behind Closed Doors: What Really Happens in Executive Coaching," *Organizational Dynamics* 27 (1999): 39–52.

5. Richard R. Kilburg, *Executive Coaching: Developing Managerial Wisdom in a World of Chaos* (Washington, DC: American Psychological Association, 2000).

6. Adapted from Mary Beth O'Neill, *Executive Coaching with Backbone and Heart*, 2nd ed. (New York: Wiley, 2007), 5.

7. www.CA-Ministries.com.

8. www.KenBlanchard.com or www.Coaching.com.

9. Madeleine Homan and Linda J. Miller, *Coaching in Organizations: Best Coaching Practices from the Ken Blanchard Companies* (New York: Wiley, 2008).

10. www.InterLinkTC.com. Linda Miller can be reached at Linda.Miller@ CA-Ministries.com.

11. marcel.henderson@googlemail.com.

12. Michael Watkins, *The First 90 Days: Critical Success Strategies for New Leaders at All Levels* (Boston: Harvard Business School Press, 2003).

13. www.billzipp.com. Bill is president of Leadership Link and coauthor, with Stephen G. Fairley, of *The Business Coaching Toolkit: Top Ten Strategies for Solving the Toughest Dilemmas Facing Organizations* (Hoboken, NJ: Wiley, 2008).

14. Bill Zipp, "Small Business Coaching," in Tony Stoltzfus, *Coaching Questions:*

A Coach's Guide to Powerful Asking Skills (Virginia Beach, VA: Pegasus Creative Arts, 2008), 84, www.Coach22.com.

15. For more about Gary and his company, GE Wood and Associates, see www .gewood.com.

16. For more information about Gary's burnout work, see www .leaderandprofessional.com.

17. Acts 20:26,24.

18. See Matthew 5:16.

Chapter 18: Churches, Spirituality, and Coaching

1. Dan Kimball, *They Like Jesus but Not the Church* (Grand Rapids, MI: Zondervan, 2007); David Kinnaman and Gabe Lyons, *UnChristian: What a New Generation Really Thinks About Christianity* (Grand Rapids, MI: Baker, 2007).

2. My perspectives on the changing church were shaped originally by the late Robert E. Webber, *The Younger Evangelicals* (Grand Rapids, MI: Baker, 2002). Some of these themes are discussed briefly and applied to coaching by Steve Ogne and Tim Roehl, *TransforMissional Coaching* (Nashville: Broadman, Holman, 2008), 1–21.

3. Robert Lewis and Wayne Codeiro, *Culture Shift: Transforming Your Church from the Inside Out* (San Francisco: Jossey-Bass, 2005), 19.

4. For further information on strength-based coaching as it applies to the church, see Albert L. Winseman, Donald O. Clifton, and Curt Liesveld, *Living Your Strengths: Discover Your God-given Talents and Inspire Your Community* (New York: Gallup, 2004).

5. In addition to the leaders I mentioned in the text, several writers have developed useful materials that have relevance for coaching and ministry. These include Steve Ogne and Tim Roehl, *TransforMissional Coaching* (Nashville: Broadman, Holman, 2008); Roger Erving and Jerome Daley, who cofounded *Christian Coaching Magazine* (www. christiancoachingmag.com); Jane Creswell, *Christ-Centered Coaching: 7 Benefits for Ministry Leaders* (St. Louis: Lake Hickory Resources, 2006), Linda J. Miller and Chad W. Hall, *Coaching Christian Leaders: A Practical Guide* (St. Louis: Chalice Press, 2007); and Tony Stoltzfus, www.christiancoachingcenter.com.

6. Fran LaMattina can be contacted at Franla@bellsouth.net.

7. Andy Stanley, *Visioneering* (Sisters, OR: Multnomah, 1999).

8. Andy Stanley, *The Next Generation Leader: 5 Essentials for Those Who Will Shape the Future* (Sisters OR: Multnomah, 2006), 88–89.

9. The website is www.Coach22.com. The books include *Leadership Coaching: The Disciplines, Skills, and Heart of a Christian Coach* and *Coaching Questions: A Coach's Guide to Powerful Asking Skills*. Both are self-published and available from the website.

10. www.CoachingPastors.com. For another perspective, see www .coaching4clergy.com.

11. For information on the peer coaching program, see www.Coach22.com/

PeerCoaching.html. See also www.peer.ca.

12. www.stephenministries.org.

13. www.coachingmission.com. Their goal: support coaching for missionaries and leaders.

14. Michael R. Baer, *Business as Mission* (Seattle: YWAM Publishing, 2006).

15. David G. Better, *Sacred Companions: The Gift of Spiritual Friendship and Direction* (Downers Grove, IL: InterVarsity, 2002), 95.

16. William A. Barry and William J. Connolly, *The Practice of Spiritual Direction* (San Francisco: HarperCollins, 1986), 136.

17. www.professionalchristiancoaching.com.

Chapter 19: The Profession and Business of Coaching

1. Bruce Wilkinson with David and Heather Koop, *The Dream Giver* (Sisters, OR: Multnomah, 2003), 70. In this paragraph, I have followed Wilkinson's use of capital letters for terms like Dream Giver and Land of Familiar.

2. Wilkinson, Koop, Koop, 70.

3. Please see www.christiancoachingbook.com.

4. See footnote 2.

5. If you are a trained counselor, for example, general coach training may be less helpful than coach training designed specifically for therapists. See www.executivecoachcollege.com. This website identifies itself as "a leader in coach training for professionals with graduate degrees." Institute for Life Coach Training (www.lifecoachtraining.com) apparently began as a training school for therapists, but in recent years the school appears to focus less on professional counselors and more on anyone who wants coach training, although many of the students are therapists and most appear to be college graduates.

6. This figure is from www.peer.ca, updated to the beginning of 2009.

7. Go to www.peer.ca and find the information on coaching.

8. www.coachfederation.org.

9. This is a conclusion of the *International Dublin Declaration on Coaching*, published in 2008. The best way to get a copy is to do an Internet search for "Dublin Declaration on Coaching." For more detailed information about coaching ethics, see Patrick Williams and Sharon K, Anderson, eds. *Law and Ethics in Coaching: How to Solve and Avoid Difficult Problems in Your Practice* (New York: Wiley, 2006).

10. Steve Ogne and Tim Roehl, *TransforMissional Coaching: Empowering Leaders in a Changing Ministry World* (Nashville: Broadman, Holman, 2008), 261.

11. See chapter 2.

12. Reproduced with permission from the Christian Coaches Network.

13. Adapted from Judy Santos, private communication.

14. For example, see Stephen G. Fairley and Chris E. Stout, *Getting Started in Personal and Executive Coaching: How to Create a Thriving Coaching Practice* (New York: Wiley, 2004); and Lynn Grodzwki and Wendy Allen, *The Business and Practice of Coaching: Finding Your Niche, Making Money, and Attracting Ideal Clients* (New York: Norton, 2005).

15. Wilkinson, Koop, Koop, 102–106.

16. I am not sure why Wilkinson chose to call these people "Busters." The term may have come from the now abandoned practice of referring to the group that followed Baby Boomers as "Baby Busters." The word *Busters* might be no more than an attempt to find another word to start with a B to follow the Bullies and Buddies. As described in the book, *Builders* might have been better. These are people who give consistent support. They are "nearly always experienced Dreamers who have been where you are." They are dream champions like Wilkinson's friend who "saw things I missed . . . believed when I didn't, made things happened that I couldn't. And poured courage from his heart right into mine." Sounds like a supportive coach. See *The Dream Giver*, 105–106.

Chapter 20: Crossing Cultures in Coaching

1. www.ccl.org.
2. Sharon Ting and Doug Riddle, "A Framework for Leadership Development Coaching," in Sharon Ting and Peter Scisco, eds., *The CCL Handbook of Coaching: A Guide for the Leader Coach* (San Francisco: Jossey-Bass, 2006), 46.
3. The following discussion of the cross-cultural implications of the CCL model is adapted from Lynn DeLay and Maxine Dalton, "Coaching Across Cultures," in Sharon Ting and Peter Scisco, eds., *The CCL Handbook of Coaching*, 122–148.
4. Lynn DeLay and Maxine Dalton, "Coaching Across Cultures," in Sharon Ting and Peter Scisco, eds., *The CCL Handbook of Coaching*, 141.
5. DeLay and Dalton, 125.
6. It should be noted that this is the perspective of many older teachers, pastors, and professors. In contrast, many younger people are more willing to engage in interaction, especially when this is encouraged by their instructors.
7. At present there are few in-depth books about coaching across cultures. See Phillipe Rosinski, *Coaching Across Cultures: New Tools for Leveraging National, Corporate, and Professional Differences* (Boston: Nicholas Brealey, 2003).
8. Tina Stoltzfus and Paul Hillhouse, "Cross-Cultural Coaching," in Tony Stoltzfus, *Coaching Questions* (Virginia Beach, VA: Pegasus Creative Arts, 2008), 96–97, www.Coach22.com.
9. The best way to learn is to spend time with people who describe themselves as postmodern, connected, emergent, or missional. I have tried to be a student of the developing emergent, emerging, and missional churches with their diversity of theologies and sometimes "less-than-holy systems of morality and ethics." I might not agree with everybody in this broad movement, but I applaud those who are trying to reach their own generations in ways that may differ from what their grandparents or Baby Boomer parents might think of as more traditional.
10. It is important to recognize that not all younger people are impacted by post-modernism, and not all people with a postmodern perspective are young.
11. Earl Creps, *Reverse Mentoring: How Young Leaders Can Transform the Church and Why We Should Let Them* (San Francisco: Jossey-Bass, 2008). See also Earl Creps, *Off-Road Disciplines: Spiritual Adventures of Missional Leaders* (San Francisco: Jossey-Bass, 2006).

12. The following paragraphs are based on my interactions with members of this generation. My best teachers have been interaction with participants in seminars that I have taught on these topics, my growing (but still limited) understanding of ministries that seek to reach contemporary people who are shaped by postmodernism, and a lot of reading. Portions of this section of the book are adapted from Steve Ogne and Tim Roehl, whose book *TransforMissional Coaching: Empowering Leaders in a Changing Ministry World* (Nashville: Broadman, Holman, 2008) is the only Christian coaching book I have discovered that directly addresses coaching and postmodern leaders. See Chapter 11, "Young and Restless: The Challenge of Empowering Postmodern Leaders."

13. Steve Ogne and Tim Roehl, *TransforMissional Coaching: Empowering Leaders in a Changing Ministry World* (Nashville: Broadman, Holman, 2008), 219, 220.

14. The tribal coaching approach is described by Ogne and Roehl, *TransforMissional Coaching*, 224–225, and adapted from William Tenny-Brittian, "Coaching the Postmodern Leader" (paper submitted to Northwest Graduate School, 2003).

15. Dan Kimball, *They Like Jesus but Not the Church* (Grand Rapids MI: Zondervan, 2007).

16. For information about the PeopleMap of the work of Dr. Lillibridge, see www .peoplemap.org or write to peoplemap@aol.org.

17. Madeleine Homan and Linda J. Miller, *Coaching in Organizations: Best Coaching Practices from The Ken Blanchard Companies* (New York: Wiley, 2008), 16–17.

Chapter 21: The Challenges of Coaching

1. Steven Berglas, "The Very Real Dangers of Executive Coaching," *Harvard Business Review* 80 (June 2002): 87–92.

2. Anthony M. Grant, "Reflections on Coaching Psychology," in Joseph O'Connor and Andrea Lages, *How Coaching Works* (London: A & C Black, 2007), 213.

3. The Christian Counseling Network, the International Coach Federation, and similar organizations around the world are devoted to the improvement of coaching standards and to stimulating better coaching.

4. Brian O. Underhill, Kimcee McAnally, and John J. Koriah, *Executive Coaching for Results* (San Francisco: Berrett-Koehler, 2007), 114–115.

5. This conclusion is based on a research study done in Australia and reported by Anthony Grant, "Reflections."

6. "Approximately 65 percent of organizations told us that they gauge leader satisfaction [with coaching] by informally checking with the leader." This is reported in a chapter titled "Measuring Impact" in Underhill, McAnally, and Koriah, *Executive Coaching*, 96.

7. Diane R. Stober and Anthony M. Grant, eds., *Evidence Based Coaching Handbook: Putting Best Practices to Work for Your Clients* (New York: Wiley, 2006), 6.

8. Stober and Grant, 5.

9. This will be discussed in more detail in the next chapter as we consider the *Dublin Declaration on Coaching*.

10. For a short article on professionalism in coaching from a Christian perspective, see Christopher McCluskey, "Professional Christian Coaching: How Christian? How Professional?" *Journal of Christian Coaching* 1 (Summer 2008): 18–21.

11. Joseph O'Connor and Andrea Lages, *How Coaching Works* (London: A & C Black, 2007), 43.

12. O'Connor and Lages, 43.

13. See John 10:10; 3:16.

14. Christopher McCluskey, "A Christian Therapist-Turned-Coach Discusses His Journey and the Field of Life Coaching," *Journal of Psychology & Christianity* 27 (Fall 2008): 266–269.

15. The methodology was not very rigorous and by now the research results might be dated, but for a sobering picture of the difficulty of starting a coaching business, see the introduction of Stephen G. Fairley and Chris E. Stout, *Getting Started in Personal and Executive Coaching* (New York: Wiley, 2004).

Chapter 22: The Future of Coaching

1. *The Dublin Declaration on Coaching Including Appendices* is a thirty-page document, available free online. The final report is version 1.4, dated September 1, 2008. To access and download the document, do an Internet search for "Dublin Declaration on Coaching."

2. David Logan and John King, *The Coaching Revolution: How Visionary Managers Are Using Coaching to Empower People and Unlock Their Full Potential* (Holbrook, MA: Adams Media Corporation, 2001). This book was mentioned earlier, in chapter 1.

3. See, for example, Laurie Beth Jones, *Jesus, Life Coach: Learn from the Best* (Nashville: Thomas Nelson, 2004).

4. Linda J. Miller and Chad W. Hall, *Coaching Christian Leaders: A Practical Guide* (St. Louis: Chalice Press, 2007), 123.

5. Stratford Sherman and Alyssa Freas, "The Wild West of Executive Coaching," *Harvard Business Review* 82 (November 2004): 1.

6. At the beginning of the millennium, this argument was made persuasively by Thomas G. Bandy, *Coaching Change: Breaking Down Resistance, Building Up Hope* (Nashville: Abingdon, 2000), 10.

7. Thomas G. Bandy, *Coaching Change: Breaking Down Resistance, Building Up Hope* (Nashville: Abingdon, 2000), 51. See also, Jim Herrington, Mike Bonem, and James H. Furr, *Leading Congregational Change: A Practical Guide for the Transformational Journey* (San Francisco: Jossey-Bass, 2000).

8. Cheryl Richardson's most recent self-coaching book is *The Art of Self-Care: Transform Your Life One Month at a Time* (Carlsbad, CA: Hay House, 2009). See also Joseph J. Luciani, *The Power of Self-Coaching: The Five Essential Steps to Creating the Life You Want* (New York: Wiley, 2004); Terri Levine, *Coaching Is for Everyone: Learn How to Be Your Own Coach at Any Age* (Garden City, NY: Morgan James Publishing, 2008); and Talane Miedaner, *Coach Yourself to Success: 101 Tips from a Personal Coach for Reaching Your Goals at Work and in Life* (Lincolnwood, IL: Contemporary Books, 2000).

9. Cheryl Richardson, *Life Makeovers* (New York: Broadway Books, 2000), 6.
10. See 2 Peter 1:5-8.
11. See 2 Peter 1:3.
12. Randy Pausch, *The Last Lecture* (New York: Hyperion, 2008), 148–149.

Appendix H: Clarifying Your Mission Statement

1. Some of these exercises are adapted from the books by Pat Williams and Diane Menendez and by Laura Whitworth, Karen Kimsey-House, Henry Kimsey-House, and Phillip Sandahl.

Appendix I: Writing a Ten-Year Letter

1. Tom Chappell, *Managing Upside Down: The Seven Intentions of Values-Centered Leadership* (New York: William Morrow, 1999), 118–119.
2. If you would prefer, write a three- or five-year letter instead of a ten-year letter.

Appendix K: Finding a Coach

1. I am grateful to Judy Santos of the Christian Coaches Network for her input into this appendix.

INDEX

AUTHOR

GARY R. COLLINS is a licensed clinical psychologist with a PhD in clinical psychology from Purdue University. A native of Canada, Gary Collins served on the faculty of Bethel College in Minnesota and for twenty years taught psychology and counseling at Trinity Evangelical Divinity School in Deerfield, Illinois. Gary has led seminars and accepted invitations to speak in more than fifty countries. He was the cofounder and first president of the American Association of Christian Counselors, founding editor of *Christian Counseling Today* magazine, and general editor of the forty-two-volume Resources for Christian Counseling book series published by Word Publishers. He has written about 200 articles and more than fifty books, including his classic textbook, *Christian Counseling: A Comprehensive Guide*.

Gary Collins is a certified life coach and a graduate of the Institute for Life Coach Training. He maintains a small coaching practice and frequently travels overseas and within North America to speak on coaching, leadership, trends in Christian counseling, and related issues. He is committed to equipping and empowering next-generation and emergent leaders through coaching and one-on-one mentoring. Gary continues to write and teach, and serves both as Distinguished Visiting Professor in the School of Psychology and Counseling at Regent University in Virginia and Distinguished Professor of Leadership and Coaching at Richmont Graduate University (formerly Psychological Studies Institute) in Atlanta and Chattanooga. He and his wife, Julie, live in a Chicago suburb.

KEEP UP WITH EMERGING COACHING TRENDS

This book is just a start.

www.christiancoachingbook.com

- View Gary's video introductions to the different sections of this book.

- Interact with and subscribe to Gary's blog.

- Read Gary's weekly newsletter dealing with coaching and related issues.

- Download coaching forms to use personally or with your coaching clients.

- Download selected chapters or other parts of this book.

- Read updated articles on coaching by Gary and others.

- See and hear examples of coaching.

- Learn how to get coach training from Gary and his associates.

- Connect online with other coaches and readers of this book.

- Experience periodic audio or video classes and webinars led by Gary and others.

- Learn about new coaching products and resources as they become available.

It's all at www.christiancoachingbook.com.

More leadership titles from NavPress!

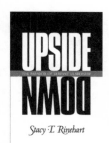

Upside Down
Stacy T. Rinehart
978-1-57683-079-6

Servant leadership—the kind of leadership Jesus practiced—is something that sets believers apart. The choice of whether to follow the leadership path to power, authority, and control or the road to humility and putting others first is an important one. Learn how to be the kind of leader Jesus was. Includes discussion questions.

The Making of a Leader
Dr. J. Robert Clinton
978-0-89109-192-9

By studying the lives of hundreds of historical, biblical, and contemporary leaders, author Robert Clinton has determined six stages of leadership development to help you determine where you are in the process. Each chapter concludes with a personal-application section.

The Heart of Mentoring
David A. Stoddard with Robert J. Tamasy
978-1-60006-831-7

Spend your time and energy truly making a difference in someone's life. Mentoring is a relational process that involves life-to-life exchanges to help others discover and pursue their passions. With ten proven principles for developing people and advice for older generations mentoring younger generations, *The Heart of Mentoring* is a must for all those who wish to disciple others.

To order copies, call NavPress at 1-800-366-7788
or log on to www.navpress.com.